Also by Marina Warner

JOAN OF ARC

MARINA WARNER

JOAN OF ARC

The Image of Female Heroism

ALFRED A. KNOPF NEW YORK 1981

Grateful acknowledgment is made to the following for permission to reprint previously published material:

Burns and Oates Ltd./Search Press: Excerpt from St. John of the Cross, "The Ascent of Mount Carmel," trans., E. Allison Peers, *The Works of St. John of the Cross*, Vol. I, 1943. Used by permission of the publishers, Burns and Oates Ltd.

A. J. Kennedy and K. Varty: Excerpts from *The Ditie de Jehanne d'Arc* by Christine de Pisan, edited by A. J. Kennedy and K. Varty, published by The Society for the Study of Medieval Languages and Literature, Oxford, 1977.

Librarie Hachette and Eyre Methuen Ltd.: Excerpts from *The Retrial of Joan of Arc: The Evidence at the Trial for Her Rehabilitation*, ed. Regine Pernoud, translated by J. M. Cohen. Published in Great Britain by Eyre Methuen Ltd. French rights owned by Librarie Hachette. Used by permission.

Routledge & Kegan Paul Ltd: Excerpts from *The Trial of Joan of Arc*, translated by W. B. Barrett, London, 1931. Used by permission of the publishers, Routledge & Kegan Paul Ltd.

LIBRARY OF CONGRESS CATALOGING IN PUBLICATION DATA
Warner, Marina, [date]
Joan of Arc: the image of female heroism.
Includes bibliographical references and index.
1. Joan, of Arc, Saint, 1412–1431.
2. Christian saints—France—Biography.
DC103.W27 1981   944'.026'0924 [B]   80-2720
ISBN 0-394-41145-5   AACR2

For Thierry

That which we now call the world is the result of a host of errors and fantasies which have gradually arisen in the course of the total evolution of organic nature, have become entwined with one another and are inherited by us as the accumulated treasure of the entire past—as a treasure: for the value of our humanity depends on it. Rigorous science is in fact able to detach us from this ideational world only to a slight extent . . . but it can gradually and step by step illuminate the history of how this world as idea arose. . . .

NIETZSCHE

Contents

Illustrations

BLACK AND WHITE PLATES—FOLLOWING PAGE 228

Acknowledgements

Without the resources of the fascinating specialist library of the Centre Jeanne d'Arc in Orleans and the patient attention of its staff, I could not have researched this book. My deepest thanks go to the Centre's founder, inspiration and director, Mlle. Régine Pernoud, and to her indefatigable band of *documentalistes*, Bernadette Bouteille, Josceline Fleury, Marie-Véronique Clin and Chantal Touvet. At the Warburg Institute, London, Dr. Elizabeth McGrath was especially helpful; at the London Library, Mr. Douglas Matthews was as always consideration itself. The many people who helped me with their encouragement and their advice deserve far more gratitude than these brief acknowledgements can possibly convey. Professor John Hale gave me that most precious of presents—confidence that the enterprise was worth it—and then did me the great kindness of reading the manuscript and making invaluable and trenchant comment, eliminating many lapses through his knowledge and sense of style. Dr. Roy Foster helped me throughout the research and the writing with his enriching curiosity and enthusiasm and also with continual bibliographical guidance and textual observations. Dr. Malcolm Vale illuminated the political context of the period with his unmistakeable clarity and provocativeness and took valuable time to read the text and offer useful comments. Dr. Janet Nelson helped me enormously by her rigorous reading of the manuscript. Her observations have helped me to avoid many an error.

Throughout the period I was working, I was the lucky receiver of innumerable kindnesses: Mrs. Rhoda Sutherland, who at Oxford first set alight my fascination with medieval France, helped with reading lists with great insight; Mrs. Joan Crow also led me toward important materials. Yvonne Lanhers, John Roberts, Peter Burke, Jonathan Sumption, Roger Highfield, David Mitchell, Antony West, Fr. F.-M. Lethel, Deborah Fraioli and Michael Jones all helped me at different stages with references and advice. Nigel Nicolson, by so generously lending me books from the library of his mother, Vita Sackville-West, gave me an extraordinary and potent link with her strong and admirable tradition. The book would never have been written without those helpers who travelled with me and my son Conrad to France at different times, Kathy Bone and Iris St. Martin, nor without the treasured friendship and hospitality of John Graham, Irene Andreae and Stephen Bishop-Kovacevich. To them, my very special thanks. Without the breadth of Dom Sylvester Houédard's quest for knowledge, I would have failed to ask many necessary questions. Christiane Besse gave me wonderful rare books about Joan of Arc; Kevin Brownlow organised to show me rare films. To both of them, much gratitude. My thanks also to Carine Slade, who typed the manuscript at an early stage; and especially to Maria Ellis, who typed the final stage. In London and New York, this book benefited from scrupulous editors' attention. Gila Falkus of Weidenfeld and Carol Brown Janeway of Knopf are a little like musicians giving master classes; their reactions to my performance shaped my own estimation of it and provoked new inspiration and excitement on which to build revisions.

France at the Time of
Joan of Arc's Campaigns,
1429-1430

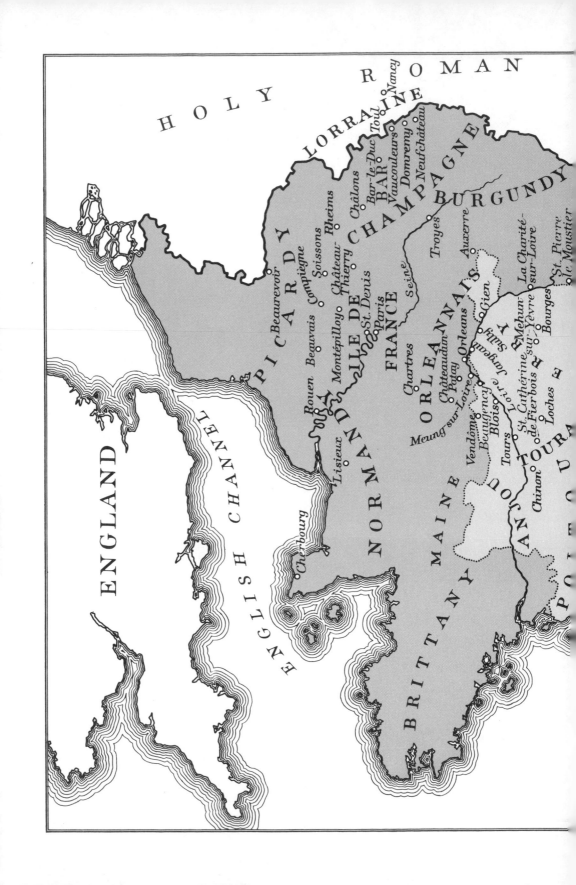

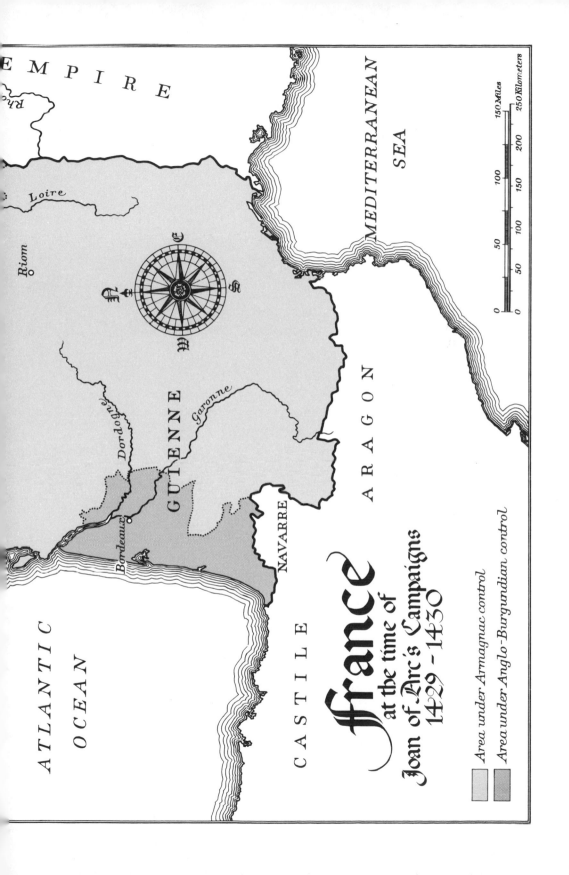

EMPIRE

ATLANTIC
OCEAN

Loire

Riom
○

Dordogne

Bordeaux ○

GUIENNE

Garonne

NAVARRE

CASTILE

ARAGON

MEDITERRANEAN
SEA

France
at the time of
Joan of Arc's Campaigns
1429 – 1430

Area under Armagnac control

Area under Anglo-Burgundian control

150 Miles

250 Kilometers

Chronology

1380	Charles VI, king of France, accedes.
1399	Henry IV accedes. Richard II of England murdered.
1403	Charles, future king of France, born.
1404	John the Fearless becomes duke of Burgundy.
1407	Louis, duke of Orleans, murdered.

DOMREMY

1412? 13?	*Joan of Arc born.*
1413	Henry V becomes king of England.
1415	English victory at Agincourt.
1416	Anglo-Burgundian alliance.
1418	John the Fearless becomes master of Paris. English take Rouen.
1419	John the Fearless murdered. Philip the Good becomes duke of Burgundy.
1420	By the treaty of Troyes, Charles is disinherited and Henry V's heir named heir to the throne of France.
1421	Henry, future Henry VI of England, born.
1422	Henry V dies. Charles VI dies. John, duke of Bedford, becomes regent of France. Charles VII proclaimed king of France at Mehun-sur-Yèvre.

		Henry VI proclaimed king of France in London and Paris.
C. 1425		Joan first hears voices.
1428	C. JUNE	Joan and family flee to Neufchâteau.
	OCT.	Siege of Orleans begins.

VAUCOULEURS

1429	C. JAN.–FEB.	*Joan leaves Domremy for Vaucouleurs.* French defeated at Rouvray in Battle of the Herrings.

CHINON

	LATE FEB. / EARLY MAR.	*Joan arrives at Chinon.*

POITIERS

	C. MAR.–APR.	Interrogated at Poitiers by Parlement in exile.
	24 APR.	Leaves Tours, with military equipment, for Blois.
	28 APR.	March on Orleans begins.

ORLEANS

	29 APR.	*Joan enters Orleans.*
	4 MAY	*Fall of bastion Fort St. Loup.*
	7 MAY	*Fall of bastion Les Tourelles, Orleans.*
	8 MAY	*English retreat from Orleans. Siege raised.*

THE SUMMER OF VICTORIES

	9 MAY	Joan and Dunois meet Charles at Loches.

14 MAY	Joan with Charles at Tours.
11–12 JUNE	Jargeau falls to French.
15 JUNE	Meung-sur-Loire falls to French.
17 JUNE	Beaugency falls to French.
18 JUNE	Victory of French at Patay. Joan rejoins Charles at Sully. Army assembled at Gien.

MARCH TOWARD RHEIMS

29 JUNE	Charles begins march toward Rheims.
30 JUNE	Auxerre changes allegiance and recognises Charles.
5–12 JULY	Troyes changes allegiance and recognises Charles.
14 JULY	Châlons recognises Charles.

RHEIMS

16–21 JULY	Joan and Charles at Rheims.
17 JULY	*Charles VII crowned king of France.*
21 JULY	Charles performs ceremony of the king's evil.
23 JULY	Arrives at Soissons.
29 JULY	Arrives at Château-Thierry.
2 AUG.	Charles begins to withdraw back to Loire, reaches Provins.
6 AUG.	Charles at Coloummiers and Château-Thierry.
10 AUG.	Charles at La Ferté-Milon.
11 AUG.	Charles at Crépy.
14–16 AUG.	Skirmishes at Senlis; battle at Montépilloy. Joan does not take part.

| 18–22 AUG. | Compiègne, Senlis and Beauvais recognise Charles. Cauchon, bishop of Beauvais, leaves his see. |
| 29 AUG. | Edict of Compiègne, declaring Franco-Burgundian truce till Christmas, signed. |

PARIS

8 SEPT.	*Joan assaults Paris; fails.*
13 SEPT.	Charles leaves headquarters at St. Denis to withdraw to Gien.
END SEPT.	Army disbanded at Gien.

THE DIFFICULT WINTER

25 OCT.? / 2 NOV.?	Joan attacks St. Pierre le Moustier.
9 NOV.	Joan at Moulins.
24 NOV.	Joan lays siege to La Charité-sur-Loire.
19 DEC.	Joan revisits Orleans.
29 DEC.	Joan and her family ennobled.

1430

| 3–28 MAR. | Joan at Sully. |
| APR. | Joan fights at Lagny. |

COMPIÈGNE

22 MAY	John of Luxembourg lays siege to Compiègne.
23 MAY	*Joan captured at Compiègne;* news reaches Paris, 25 May.
26 MAY	University of Paris urges her condemnation; Joan taken to Arras.

	14 JULY	*Cauchon, bishop of Beauvais, begins proceedings to bring her to trial.* Joan held at Beaulieu and Beaurevoir.
	25 OCT.	Siege of Compiègne raised.
	NOV.	Joan handed over to Cauchon.

R O U E N

1431	DEC. / JAN.	*Joan arrives at Rouen castle.*
	9 JAN.	Court of judges and assessors assembles.
	21 FEB. / 3 MAR.	*Public sessions of Joan's trial.*
	10–17 MAR.	*Sessions in prison cell.*
	27 MAR.	Charges read to her.
	18 APR.	Joan "charitably" admonished.
	19 MAY	University of Paris condemns Joan; letter read to her.
	23 MAY	Final admonitions.
	24 MAY	*Joan led to cemetery of St. Ouen; abjures.*
	27 MAY	Withdraws recantation.
	28 MAY	Condemned as heretic; handed over to secular arm for burning.
	30 MAY	*Joan at the stake.*
	16 DEC.	Henry VI crowned king of France in Paris.
1435	21 SEPT.	Treaty of Arras between Charles VII and duke of Burgundy.
1436		Paris returns to Charles. Claude des Armoises claims to be Joan.

1437	Charles VII enters Paris.
1448	The French regain Rouen.
1450	English struggle in Normandy ends. First inquiry, by Bouillé, into Joan's sentence.
1452	Second inquiry, by Cardinal d'Estouteville, into Joan's trial and sentence.
1455–56	The *procès en nullité:* the 1431 verdict on Joan rescinded.
1869	*Case of Joan's canonisation placed before Vatican.*
1903	Joan declared Venerable.
1909	Joan beatified.
1920	*Joan made saint.*

JOAN OF ARC

PROLOGUE

A story lives in relation to its tellers and its receivers; it continues because people want to hear it again, and it changes according to their tastes and needs. Joan of Arc is the centre of a story so famous that it transcends the media or the forms that have transmitted it: she is a heroine of history. Unlike a fictional character, she does not belong to the mind of a writer or the imagination of a painter. She has objective reality; and in her solid and material existence, she bears the mark Carlyle considered the primary stuff of heroes, "sincerity, a deep, great, genuine sincerity." She had a calling, which she phrased with great clarity and simplicity: to throw the English out of France and bring her Dauphin to his throne. She pursued it with great bravery; she was loyal to her innermost convictions, in the face of terrible ordeals. These composing parts of her greatness have invited generation upon generation of enthusiasts to identify with her and to adopt her as the palladium of their cause.

It is usual, when telling of Joan of Arc, to attribute the extraordinary and compelling quality of the story of which she is the heroine to the specialness of her personality. Her individuality created the reality of

3

the story she dominates. But this is only one way of understanding a story and of writing history: to give an account of the deeds of the great. To reserve all understanding of a story to its protagonists and their characteristics is limiting. With Joan of Arc, we are faced with a phenomenon so exceptional that it is essential to examine the context on which her personality scored its deep mark in order to understand her at all.

The story, in its most familiar, chapbook-like form, tells of the glory of a national heroine. According to this perspective, Joan of Arc's presence and activity changed the course of the Hundred Years' War between England and France, the war which had begun in 1337 when Edward III claimed the throne of France through his mother. The two great dynastic powers of medieval Europe, Lancastrian England and Valois France, were still struggling for supremacy in France in 1429 when a peasant, a girl, a seventeen-year-old—that triple cluster of exceptional attributes—appeared from her home village on the borders of the duchy of Lorraine, introduced herself to the Dauphin Charles of France as his God-given saviour and reversed his fortunes.

Before Joan's appearance, Charles was a vacillating, uncrowned pretender to a throne he had almost forfeited through defeat in battle and at the negotiating table. Henry V, renewing his grandfather Edward's ambitions, won the great victory of Agincourt in 1415 and then, by the treaty of Troyes of 1420, appointed his heir, Henry VI, the future king of France and England. This claimant to the double crown was the son of Charles's own sister, and so he united Henry V's august blood and the Valois lineage. The duke of Burgundy, Charles's uncle, who with his large and rich possessions held the balance of power in France, had allied himself to the English cause. In 1429, Paris was in Anglo-Burgundian hands; the Parlement, loyal to Charles, was in exile in Poitiers; the English occupied territories north of the Loire and were laying siege to Orleans, the gateway to domination of southern France.

But with Joan's inspiration, this version relates, Charles was transformed, his troops rallied and their cause began to prosper. In the major battle for the relief of Orleans in May 1429, the English were turned back. With their hegemony over half of France having been fatally weakened, the ground was clear for Charles's triumphant coronation in July and for the eventual destruction of English hopes to establish a Lancastrian monarchy in France. Joan of Arc's charismatic presence at the battle of Orleans effected this astonishing victory; her encouragement brought Charles to his anointing; she was the saviour—appointed and guided by divine messengers, her voices—who created the modern nation-state of France.

After glory, the tragic fall: the familiar story leaves the panoply of the medieval battlefield and cathedral and palace for the mean dimensions of the prison cell. Captured by her enemies during a skirmish at Compiègne in May 1430, only nine months after her apotheosis at Charles's side in the cathedral at Rheims during his coronation, she is sold to the English by her Burgundian captors, turned over to the Inquisition, treacherously tried at Rouen and burned as a heretic in May 1431.

This is the triumphant tale. Substantial though it appears to be, it leaves entirely vague some crucial questions: Why was Joan accepted by Charles and the Valois party? What was her contribution to the military campaign? Why, after achievements so signal, was she allowed to be sold and executed when ransoms were the custom? Yet these three points are only the bare beginning of the mysteries.

The prime source, of remarkable and intense interest, is the record of Joan's trial, conducted between 9 January and 30 May 1431, when she was burnt. Joan was tried before a large tribunal, composed principally of ecclesiastics and lawyers—sometimes numbering more than seventy men—on suspicion of heresy allied with witchcraft. As was the custom in inquisitorial trials, she was not formally charged until after the cross-examinations had taken place, and by then it had emerged incontrovertibly that she was adamant on two counts: the truthfulness and heavenly origin of the voices who counselled her and her loyalty to her male costume. On these two matters, she would not submit to the authority of the court. As it represented the Church Militant, Christ on earth, she was found guilty of insubordination and heterodoxy and was condemned to the stake.

The trial survives in different manuscript versions (15): one copy is most probably the actual transcript established at the time for the presiding judge, Pierre Cauchon, bishop of Beauvais. In this document, Joan's turn of phrase brings her voice leaping from the page with dramatic, painful authenticity. Half a millennium later, her sincerity is unadulterated; her conviction rings like a bell. It is this quite extraordinary quality of directness in the trial document itself that has, since the 1840s and its first publication, made Joan of Arc an unforgettable source of inspiration. As the trial sought to prove her falsehood and, indeed, succeeded in doing so to the satisfaction of some of the most learned men of the time, this is highly paradoxical.

By contrast, the second major source of knowledge about Joan, composed in her defence by her partisans, does not have the brilliancy of her self-portrait in the trial. In the trial, she stands for unflinching loyalty to a heroic inner conviction; in the documents of the rehabilitation hearings, held at different times between 1450 and 1456, there is often a leaden tone of self-servingness and prudence among witnesses who were anyway recalling events of twenty-five years before.

Nevertheless, few medieval figures are as well documented as Joan of Arc. Yet until the dissemination of these extraordinary records of her career, her chroniclers and panegyrists did not for the most part consult these manuscript sources, but drew on different material and in particular on existing narrative conventions to bring Joan of Arc before their audiences. It is this unfolding of the character of Joan in history that I wanted to trace. It is in some ways terrible to look upon such epic events with a cold eye; it is pitiless to appraise other men's tears without feeling sympathetic tears oneself. But it is also part of the sincerity admired in someone like Joan to own that heroes and heroines are often the vessels of our most self-flattering illusions, that sometimes the ideals they embody are questionable, however brave and loyal and true they themselves were in pursuit of their aims.

I wanted to learn about Joan not just because her story is so grand, so odd, so stirring. I wanted to learn about her because she has an almost unique standing: she is a universal figure who is female, but is neither a queen, nor a courtesan, nor a beauty, nor a mother, nor an artist of one kind or another, nor—until the extremely recent date of 1920 when she was canonised—a saint. She eludes the categories in which women have normally achieved a higher status that gives them immortality, and yet she gained it. She is one of the few historical personalities who, like Henry VIII, Florence Nightingale, Robin Hood, and Davy Crockett, is immediately known to every child. In England, she is one of the very few foreigners who is a household familiar— with the exception of another great enemy, Napoleon. She is *literally* a cypher. Just as a feather in the cap, green doublet and hose and a merry gallantry signify the figure of Robin Hood, so Joan is instantly present in the mind's eye: a boyish stance, cropped hair, medievalised clothes, armour, an air of spiritual exaltation mixed with physical courage.

But such rapid strokes of the pen that now bring her breathing and alive into the schoolroom were made differently by the historians of her own time and differently again by the men and women of the Renaissance and differently again by the painters and writers of the nineteenth century. In the transformation of her body, and in the different emphases of different times, we have a diviner's cup, which reflects on the surface of the water the image that the petitioner wishes to see, its limits and extensions drawn, as in all magic operations of this kind, according to the known quantities shared between diviner and petitioner. Thus, basic themes, suggested by the recorded historical events of her life, must recur: her departure from her native village of Domremy in Lorraine; her arrival at the court of the uncrowned king of France, Charles VII; her extraordinary successes in battle, first at the relief of Orleans in May and then at Patay in July; the march in triumph with Charles toward Rheims; his anointing and crowning in the cathedral there as the legitimate king of France; her capture and long imprisonment, first by the Burgundians and then by the English, with whom they were allied; her cruel and prolonged interrogation by the Inquisition; her death at the stake in May 1431. Just over a year of freedom, with a few months' glory, after her emergence into public life; a year of lingering in different gaolers' different gaols; five centuries of questions, interpretations, ideas and conflicting passions. Although her story contains these same elements in almost all its tellers' versions, the variations in emphasis and in interpretation are multiple and rich; and even in negative, through what is omitted, what is not discussed, they reveal the preoccupations of a shared culture. Joan of Arc was an individual in history and real time, but she is also the protagonist of a famous story in the timeless dimension of myth, and the way that story has come to be told tells yet another story, one about our concept of the heroic, the good and the pure.

To find out the reasons why she lodged in the minds of people who heard her story, so that it came to be told again and again until it passed into the collectivity of our culture, is a wonderful and gripping problem. By decoding the context in which she flourished—both of her own lifetime, when she was accepted by her own people, and of her posthumous fame, when she was described and reinvented by wave upon wave of new generations who adopted her—I want to make her real again.

It appears to devalue Joan of Arc to write that it was not blind political enmity of the English that caused her death, but the fears of her own countrymen about heresy and its subversiveness. It appears to belittle her to claim that she alone was not responsible for her luminousness, but those who saw it were equally responsible; that it was not her character, but the combination of her character and a thousand other circumstances, that has created the brave, noble, poignant, bracing figurehead of freedom and truth we think of as Joan of Arc. It is demythologising, perhaps. We want our heroism cut from the air, pristine and timeless, free from all contingencies, rather than shifting in the soil of circumstance. Idealism that informs faith in a heroine like Joan of Arc finds it hard to tolerate any reservations about her absolute goodness and her complete responsibility for that goodness. But by serving this yearning for unqualified nobility, we run the risk of thinning history's rich diversity, of attenuating the model that the past presents to us for our future learning, of turning to simple formulae that will fail us, since they apply to the organised "real" of fables and not to the inchoate flux of reality. To restore Joan to her background moves heroism back onto the plane of daily life. But no iconoclasm, however severe, could quite make Joan and her story mundane. If an archaeologist discovers the provenance of an exquisite fragment of carved stone and replaces it on the temple from which it was long lost, the splendour of the stone is not diminished, only changed.

In Part One of this book, The Life and Death of Jeanne la Pucelle, I have tried to restore her to her own context, to create a foreground of the religious beliefs and political struggles that made her activities acceptable and intelligible. So the starting points of this narrative are not her birthday and her birthplace, but instead the physical nature of her virginal body, because that is the starting point of her impact on her contemporaries. Then, like the cutout figure of Joan of Arc in a children's game of the early 1900s, she appears again, dressed in the various costumes that she herself chose to wear—the dress of a man, the splendour of a knight—and in the guises that her contemporaries thought she had assumed—the role of female prophet, of insubordinate heretic, of dangerous witch.

The second part, The Afterlife of Joan of Arc, follows the thread of posthumous tributes to the heroine, both visual and verbal, and the successive transformations her figure undergoes as different pressure groups make her their own, like the unsettled aristocracy of sixteenth- and seventeenth-century France or the ardent xenophobic and anti-Semitic activists at the end of the nineteenth century. Throughout this section I hope to have developed the underlying theme that when a story is told, it is told according to the perceptions of its hearers or its readers: the teller unconsciously provides points of reference to make the material intelligible. In the case of Joan of Arc, this shared information altered her story considerably, and circumstances of her life that I have outlined in Part One vanish almost completely. The narrators of the seventeenth century, for instance, did not elaborate on the numbers of female visionaries and prophets of Joan's day. Such a calling no longer played a part in the collective sympathies of the groups to whom the story of Joan's life was addressed. Instead other common points of reference were marshalled: the lore of Amazons, for instance, had become a motif of dazzling and compulsive popularity in Renaissance Europe, and so Joan was assimilated to it, to give her a context in which she appeared natural and explicable, though still unusual.

By showing that a historical figure like Joan merges and to a certain extent disappears under the influence of other more prevalent and more charming images at different times, this book is intended as a plea. Joan was presented as an Amazon, or a knight of old, or a personification of virtue, because the history of individual women and of women's roles has been so thin. In the writing of female biography, it is easy to revert unconsciously to known stereotypes. Joan of Arc is a preeminent heroine because she belongs to the sphere of action, while so many feminine figures or models are assigned and confined to the sphere of contemplation. She is anomalous in our culture, a woman renowned for doing something on her own, not by birthright. She has extended the taxonomy of female types; she makes evident the dimension of women's dynamism. It is urgent that this taxonomy be expanded further and that the multifarious duties that women have historically undertaken be recognised, researched and named. Like Eskimos, who enjoy a lexicon of many different words for snow, we must develop a richer vocabulary for female activity than we use at present, with our restrictions of wife, mother, mistress, muse. Joan of Arc, in all her brightness, illuminates the operation of our present classification system, its rigidity on the one hand, its potential on the other.

Although the forms in which a story is conveyed change, the questions remain eternally. The human face is no longer painted in the finely invisible brush strokes of the Renaissance portrait, nor is the human adventure recounted in the form of the classical epic. But the same questions are being asked: What did so and so look like? What happened then, and how? In the case of Joan of Arc, I am not trying to tell her story as Anatole France or Vita Sackville-West did in their enduringly readable biographies. I am trying to see how Joan fitted into an intellectual and emotional tradition of thought concerning women. So the reader alert for the flourish of medieval trumpets on the bloody battlefield will be disappointed. I have tried to tell the story of how the story came to be told, to find out why Joan of Arc was believed, how that belief was expressed, what its expression affirmed and what causes it has served.

Joan is the dancer; we have watched her down the centuries. Her body has swayed to the music of different players, we have seen her brightening glance. Now is the time to turn from her face and her foot-work, hear the music which commands the steps, analyse its measure. For, as Yeats has written, "How can we know the dancer from the dance?"

THE LIFE AND DEATH OF
JEANNE LA PUCELLE

MAID OF FRANCE

What human words can make you realise such a life as this, a life on the borderline between human and celestial nature? That nature should be free of human weakness is more than can be expected from mankind, but these women fell short of the angelic and unmaterial only in so far as they appeared in bodily form, were contained in a human frame, and were dependent on the organs of sense.

SAINT GREGORY OF NYSSA,
De Vita Sanctae Macrinae[1]

W hen the body of Joan of Arc was burned and her ashes gathered up and scattered into the first reaches of the Seine estuary at Rouen on 30 May 1431, its lineaments were blotted from the collective memory. The very body of Joan of Arc was freed from the bonds tied by information and was released to inhabit that wider universe where the imagination is mistress of knowledge. She passed from the condition of the knowable to the condition of the all-imaginable; since then, her destroyed body in the pyre and her scattered handful of dust have acted as powerful stimulants to that creative faculty of the human mind that finds in historical figures the reflection and confirmation of its best and worst desires and fears.

There is no record of what Joan of Arc looked like. The colour of her eyes, the colour of her hair, her height, her weight, her smile, none of it is described until later. The face of the heroine is blank; her physical presence unknown. From the days when she was alive, all we know of her body is that she was about nineteen in 1431, as she told her examiners at the trial;[2] that she had a light, feminine voice;[3] and that on the day of her death at Rouen, she was shown to the crowd to be a woman, because many feared she was a demon or a phantom. The Bourgeois de Paris, an anonymous Parisian who kept an invaluable record of life under the Anglo-Burgundian regime, wrote:

> She was soon dead and her clothes all burned. Then the fire was raked back, and her naked body shown to all the people and all the secrets that could or should belong to a woman, to take away any doubts from people's minds. When they had stared long enough at her dead body bound to the stake, the executioner got a big fire going again round her poor carcass, which was soon burned, both flesh and bone reduced to ashes.[4]

The only picture of Joan that survives from her lifetime is a doodle in the margin of the records kept by Clément de Fauquemberghe, clerk to the Parlement of Paris, beside his entry reporting the defeat of the English at Orleans. It is a stiff, unskilled, rather remote sketch of a young girl holding a pennon in her right hand, with her left on the hilt of a sword. Her hair is long, wavy and swept off her forehead and temples to flow over her bared nape down her back. Her dress is scooped above her bust, which the artist has rendered generously. The initials JHS, the medieval monogram for the Holy Name of Jesus, can be seen on the first fold of the banner. She is drawn in profile, with a stern, small mouth and a roman nose (16). But the Parisian recorder had not seen Joan.

We know that Joan was painted from life and that medals were struck with her image to celebrate her victories. Her interrogators at the trial attempted to prove that she had allowed herself to become the object of a cult and encouraged her image to be used to propagate it.[5] No contemporary image done from life survives today, though three carved and helmeted stone heads, now in Orleans, Loudun and Boston, have all been thought at one time to be portraits of Joan of Arc. None is authenticated any longer.[6]

The epoch was concerned with inner significance and its expression in emblematic forms, as in the language of chivalric blazonry. But it was also the great prelude to Renaissance portraiture. As J. H. Huizinga has pointed out, Jan van Eyck, court painter to the duke of Burgundy, Philip the Good, was in Arras in the autumn of 1430, at the same time as Joan, and could have painted her with that same intensity of characterisation that has made the face of the merchant Arnolfini one of the most famous faces in Europe. If we knew her with the particularity and the insight that Jan van Eyck would have brought to the task, prejudice, wishful thinking and prior assumptions would not have played so freely with her figure.[7] As it is, Joan was already, in her lifetime, slipping away into a world of emblems, of personified abstractions. Previous modes of thought tugged on her individual person so powerfully that she could not withstand it; she, the figure of valour and strength, gave way before the assault of combined forces raised through the centuries to deal with the definition of femaleness. When we feel we are approaching what was peculiar to the girl called Joan of Arc, we are very often in a tanglewood of preconception and convention.

The only certain aspect of her physical being that emerges from the trial and the rehabilitation is that Joan of Arc was a virgin. She told her questioners in 1431 that since she first heard her voices at the age of thirteen, she had vowed not to marry, and she had resolved to remain a maid as long as her voices were pleased.[8] She volunteered this information: chastity was the touchstone of female virtue; it was widely believed that the devil could not have commerce with a virgin. She angrily refuted the accusation that she had ever been about to marry and told her judges clearly that the ecclesiastical court in Toul had rightly vindicated her of a charge of breach of promise brought against her. So the examiners at Rouen did not press the subject, but preferred to insinuate that Joan had led a disorderly life, following soldiers like any barrack-room trull.[9]

In the rehabilitation hearings, the issue of Joan's virginity gains much greater definition. Yet most of the witnesses were not specifically asked about it. Only in Lorraine, where Charles's investigators summoned the villagers of Domremy to prompt their memories of events forty-odd years before, did they ask an open question about Joan's conduct as a young girl. The trial lawyers had alleged that Joan had lived like a camp follower with soldiers in an inn at Neufchâteau. The Domremy witnesses were asked if her mother and father had been with her throughout this period.[10] Otherwise, the prepared questionnaires issued to the witnesses were principally concerned with establishing the illegal conduct of the Rouen trial,[11] for the main aim of Joan's rehabilitation was to prove that its condemnation of her as a heretic was invalid, not on her account, but on Charles's, in order to clear him of taint by association.[12] Yet, time and time again, the testimony digresses from this major purpose to tell of Joan's specific virtue of chastity.

The image of Joan's body drawn in the rehabilitation documents is one of an intact, unassailable, unspotted container that, strong through its exceptional purity, was broken only by the exceptional evil applied to it. But, though broken, it was broken only on the material plane, since pollution's victory takes place in this world and has no wings for the next.[13] A pattern familiar from Christian hagiography can be discerned, a pattern that provides the dynamics of the martyrs' stories, of Saints Cecilia, Lucy, Agnes and, naturally, the saints who were Joan's voices, Margaret and Catherine.[14] A vessel filled with pure essences is smashed. In the impact, there is the tragedy; in the shed blood, the sacrifice; in the immolation, the consummation. It is a hagiographical design that echoes the mystery of the Redemption as enacted in the Mass. As this ceremony had been central to European civilisation and had constituted the only universally attended drama for several centuries by the time Joan's case was reopened in 1456, its view of the holy naturally influenced the witnesses.[15] What they chose to express was conventionally admirable, and what they left out was left out because it belonged to no familiar category or pattern.

According to her posthumous acquittal of 1456, Joan of Arc was examined on different occasions by both sides to ascertain if she was a virgin. Each of the struggling parties needed to make sure of this, her physical intactness. A Dominican, Séguin de Séguin, whose evidence is circumstantial and lively, testified that he had been present soon after Joan arrived at court in 1429. She satisfied the churchmen who cross-questioned her and was then "handed over to the Queen of Sicily, the mother of our sovereign lady the queen [thus the mother-in-law of the Dauphin], and to certain ladies with her, by whom the Maid was seen, visited and privately looked at and examined; and after examination made by the matrons, the lady stated to the King that she and the other ladies found most surely that this was indeed a true Maid."[16] In prison at Rouen just over a year later, the duchess of Bedford, wife of the regent ruling in English-occupied France on behalf of the child king Henry VI, visited Joan to examine her or at least ordered some of her attendant women to do so. Afterwards, she gave orders that Joan was not to be abused. One witness claimed Joan, taunted by her gaolers, had herself asked to be put to the test.[17] Even Jean Beaupère, one of the most obdurate of her judges, who persisted in his low opinion of Joan and in 1450 gave the most hostile testimony heard before the first rehabilitation tribunal, declared that Joan had never given him the impression she had been violated.[18] He affirmed this to defend himself and his party from charges of ill-treating her in gaol; but his words admit her innocence. Thomas de Courcelles, also an ardent prosecutor in 1431, deposed in the course of his vague and disdainful evidence that although he was not sure whether her virginity had been put to the test or not, Cauchon, the leading judge, himself had told him she was a virgin. Besides, he admitted, the trial would certainly have used any unchastity against her.[19]

Numerous stories were told to emphasise Joan's maidenhead, so numerous that the insistence must indicate a deeper need than biographical accuracy. Jean d'Aulon, who had been Joan's squire, avowed:

> Although she was a young girl, beautiful and shapely, and when helping to arm her or otherwise I have often seen her breasts, and although sometimes when I was dressing her wounds I have seen her legs quite bare, and I have gone close to her many times—and I was strong, young and vigorous in those days—never, despite any sight or contact I had with the Maid, was my body moved to any carnal desire for her, nor were any of her soldiers or squires moved in this way.[20]

Jean de Novelompont, who with Bertrand de Poulengy accompanied Joan on the first momentous journey from her native country to Chinon to find the Dauphin, emphasises the same quality: "On the way both Bertrand and I slept each night with her. The Maid slept beside us without taking off her doublet and breeches; and as for me, I was in such awe of her that I would not have dared go near her; and I tell you on my oath that I never had any desire of carnal feelings for her."[21] Another witness said that a tailor, ordered by the English to make a woman's dress for Joan, had tried to caress her breasts. She slapped him.[22] Haimond de Macy, a French knight who saw Joan in the tower of Beaurevoir when she was a prisoner, showed similar preoccupations: "I tried several times playfully to touch her breasts. I tried to slip my hand in, but Joan would not let me. She pushed me off with all her might."[23]

Even witnesses who could not recall such anecdotes volunteered their opinion as to Joan's virginity and often on the slenderest conjecture. Marguerite de la Touroulde, the widow of the king's receiver general in Bourges, with whom Joan had once stayed, described accompanying her to the public baths, which were still the custom in France at that time: "I saw her several times in the bath and in the hot-room, and so far as I could see, I believe she was a virgin."[24] Another knight, Gobert Thibault, who had known Joan less well but seen her on frequent occasions, corroborated Novelompont, using almost the same words:

> In the field she was always with the soldiers, and I have heard many of Joan's intimates say that they never had any desire for her. That is to say they sometimes had a carnal urge but never dared to give way to it; and they believed that it was impossible to desire her. And often if they were talking among themselves about the sins of the flesh, and using words that might have aroused lecherous thoughts, when they saw her and drew near to her, they could not speak like this any more. Suddenly their sexual feelings were checked. I have questioned several of those who often slept at night close to Joan, and they answered me as I have said, adding that they never felt sensual desire when they saw her.[25]

Joan's beauty, which D'Aulon mentions, adds to the virtuousness of her resistance and becomes a commonplace of the saint's life later. In the seventeenth century, René de Cériziers, a Jesuit at the court of Louis XIII, saw Joan as the prototype not of a heroine or virago, but of "wronged innocence," and he embroidered prettily on the theme of her resolute chastity at Domremy: "There was a certain look in her eye that inclined the hearts of many young men toward her. As soon as anyone saw her, he would pursue her and seek her out." One suitor became ardent and continued to insist, even though Joan made it quite plain she would have none of it: "The courtesies and attentions of this young man began to be importunate to Joan. . . . There is a kind of coolness that is most suitable in young women when they are sought in marriage; but this coolness is blameworthy if it is used for a purpose, and if one knows that they are cool only because they want to fan the flames in the hearts of their swains. Our young innocent girl was incapable of such stratagems."[26] But in the end, as the suitor inveigled the consent of her parents, Joan was forced to leave home to avoid him. Thus Cériziers managed to give Joan a laudable motive for a step that he, as an upholder of filial obedience, would otherwise have found difficult to approve.

Cériziers, in the tradition of the rehabilitation witnesses, also forestalled insinuations about her life among soldiers, declaring that a great miraculous power was hers: "whenever anyone looked upon her with impurity or thought dirty thoughts about her, he was immediately struck impotent *forever*."[27] This accretion to Joan's legend echoes an earlier story, also told by her supporters. A soldier seeing her in Chinon scoffed at her: "By God, is that the Maid? If I could have her for one night, I'd not return her in the same condition." Joan retorted: "In the name of God, you deny him and you so near your death!" An hour later, the man fell and was drowned in the Vienne.[28]

A story like this belongs to the long medieval tradition of moral exempla used by preachers to press their audience into submission. In the thirteenth century, a Dominican, Jacques de Vitry, collected together dozens of similar cautionary tales about unchaste sinners in a handbook used extensively later.[29] Rooted to the spot, dumb, paralysed, blind or otherwise stricken, they are for the most part forced to repent, usually by the purifying magic of the virgin mother of God. In Joan's case, the magic of her inviolate body, reflecting that of the Virgin Mary's, exercised as wonderfully the minds of her contemporaries.

Jean d'Aulon, her squire, thought that Joan never menstruated: "I've heard it said by many women, who saw the Maid undressed many times and knew her secrets, that she never suffered from the secret illness of women and that no one could ever notice or learn anything of it from her clothes or in any other way."[30] This inference, circumstantial as it is, becomes an accepted aspect of Joan's power and uniqueness. The *Alamanach de Gotha* of 1822, a sober summary of her history, refers to Joan's amenorrhea: "Finally, there is the added, remarkable peculiarity, which makes manifest the plans God entertained for her. Womanly in modesty, but exempt, by a particular design, from the weaknesses of her sex, she was also not subjected to those periodic and inconvenient dues, which, even more than law and custom, prevent women in general fulfilling the functions that men have taken over."[31] Jules Michelet picked up the inference and expanded it in his stirring account of Joan's career which, published in 1844, had an incalculable influence on subsequent thinking about Joan: "She had, body and soul, the divine gift of remaining childlike. She grew up, she became strong and beautiful, but she never ever knew the physical miseries of womankind."[32]

On the one hand, Joan is all woman, seductive, even beautiful, with the full complement of sexual characteristics; on the other, she annuls the usual consequences of those characteristics, remaining in the virginal state of prepubescence.

D'Aulon's remarks are not necessarily untrue: the portrait we have of Joan need not be false. The examinations of her hymen, the attempted seductions, the absence of menses could have taken place in the dimension of fact. But the evidence should be put in context. The outcome of such tests for virginity depends more on the expectation of the ministers than on the state of the subjects. The medieval ordeal by fire or water, applied by the Church to discover a criminal or a witch, precipitated the crowd's response to the victim so that the dominating common wish was crystallised and expressed in the result. In the case of women who, in the sixteenth and seventeenth centuries, were ducked in village ponds to find out whether or not they were witches, the decisive role of the onlookers is clear. The rule was that if the water rejected the woman, if the pure element spewed her forth, then she was a witch. If she remained under, then she was innocent of a league with the devil. It is a physical law that a body will float, even if clothed. Sodden cloth will keep the victim down a little while, as will the impact of her fall. But after a time she will reappear near the surface. That interval is the crucial factor to determine, and it is the crowd that decides whether in the time that has passed—naturally a variable period—their victim has been accepted by the water and there-fore needs rescuing. Even ordeals by fire exhibit the same dependence on the onlookers' sympathies. For the question was not whether the fire burned the victim's hand, but how quickly the weal healed. Again, the measure is sympathy, and the sufferer of the ordeal is dependent on the unconscious leanings of the crowd and of the officials applying the test, not on the behaviour of the elements. Yet this human consensus was automatically identified with the will of God. The ordeal was one way, a cruel way, of making a joint decision in ambiguous circumstances.[33]

Joan's tests for virginity are similar, though she, if she requested one herself, as the witness Jean Fabri related, believed in their absolute value as the expression of God's will.[34] It is possible to tell if a hymen has not been penetrated; but it is not easy now, and it was certainly more difficult at the beginning of the fifteenth century, when the physiology of the sexual organs was hardly understood. Besides, if it really were the king's mother-in-law and the duchess of Bedford who examined Joan, their opinion is worthless, since they were not medically trained. Not that doctoring was so well developed in this specialty that it would make a difference if they had been qualified. Medicine was used to support preconceptions, not to remove them. In the sixteenth century, the physician Johannes Wier (d. 1588), campaigning against witch-hunting, suggested that nuns who confessed to having intercourse with incubi at night should have their hymens examined, in order to show how deluded they were; his pragmatism was so alien that he was not understood.[35]

Joan almost certainly was a virgin, in the sense that she had never made love. Whether her hymen was broken is another matter—after all that riding and wielding of lance and sword it seems likely that it would have been—but the eminent noblewomen who visited her found what they expected to find. There is not one jot of science in the enumerated statements of Joan's virginity. The great weight of arguments in favour can hardly be gainsaid, but they are psychological and cultural, not medical.

Jean d'Aulon's deposition, the only one to survive in the original French, is vivid and touchingly affectionate and shows a certain care for detail in the recapturing of events that had occurred twenty-five years before. He probably spoke the truth when he said Joan did not menstruate. The relationship between the behaviour of hormones, the ovarian cycle and mental disposition is close. With the disorder known as anorexia, for instance, the hypothalamus in the brain ceases to function. It normally controls the endocrine system, which in turn regulates menstruation. The origins of anorexia are not physical, but mental; its symptoms have grave consequences for the body, including the disappearance of the menses. There is evidence that women under stress can stop menstruating. Female troops, patients in mental hospitals and victims of civil strife sometimes suffer from amenorrhea.[36]

Joan of Arc ate abstemiously. Several witnesses commented during her vindication how even after battle she only soaked some bread in a little wine. The lawyer Jean de la Fontaine, cross-examining her about her visions during her trial, asked her if she had been fasting. It was Lent, and she had been.[37] When after Easter she was sent a carp by her chief judge, Pierre Cauchon, bishop of Beauvais, she became ill. Carp is a notoriously rich and greasy fish and, if she was a fastidious eater, might well have upset her stomach. Witnesses at the rehabilitation said she thought she had been poisoned.[38] Fear of food, nausea, horror of outside impurities entering the stronghold of the personal body—all are characteristics of anorexics, who, if they eat rich food, vomit it later.

If indeed Joan never underwent menarche, her contemporaries would hardly have understood the phenomenon as we do now. For them, her condition was magically holy. To be a woman, yet unmarked by woman's menstrual flow, was to remain in a primordial state, the prelapsarian state of Eve, before sexual knowledge corrupted her. But amenorrhea was not only a sign of innocence. One medieval medical commentary explicitly linked it with outstanding strength: "Such a failing of the menses happens on account of the power and quality of strength, which digests well and converts the nourishment from the limbs until no superfluities remain, as it so happens amongst strong, mannish women who are called viragoes."[39]

In their stress on the pure, strong body of Joan of Arc, the witnesses of the vindication were in concord with the image Joan purposefully claimed as her own. When d'Aulon implied Joan's innocence of adult womanhood, he was in complete sympathy with her own projection of herself. For in the evidence of the trial and in Joan's letters that have survived, written at her dictation with her guided, uncertain signature appended in some cases, there is only one name she used, and that is Jehanne la Pucelle. Asked her name at the beginning of her cross-examination, she said that in her own village she had been called Jhanette, but this diminutive had not been used since she had arrived in "France" to fulfill her mission.[40] Later, under pressure, she insisted that her voices had called her "fille de Dieu";[41] later still she gave her father's name as Jacques Dars and her mother's as Isabelle Romée and added that in her own country it was the custom for a girl to take her mother's name.[42] But the name she always used herself was Jehanne la Pucelle.

Pucelle means "virgin," but in a special way, with distinct shades connoting youth, innocence and, paradoxically, nubility. It is the equivalent of the Hebrew *'almah*, used of both the Virgin Mary and the dancing girls in Solomon's harem in the Bible.[43] It denotes a time of passage, not a permanent condition. It is a word that looks forward to a change in state. In Old French, it was the most common word for a young girl; in Middle French, *damoiselle* began taking over. By Joan's day *vierge* was also sometimes added to *pucelle* to clarify the meaning of chastity; this shows the underlying ambiguity of the word. Its etymology is disputed, but both possibilities catch its flavour. It may derive from *pulcra* (beautiful), corrupted into *pulcella*, which in Latin was used humorously and affectionately for young girls, or, even more aptly, from *pulla*, giving *pullicella*, a little animal. The inference of virginity became firmer through the Middle Ages, especially after *despulceler*, meaning "to deflower," was introduced in the twelfth century.[44] But again the choice reveals the word's underlying sense of promise: *vierge* could have as easily been used as the foundation of the new verb, but it fails to imply a transitional state.

Pucelle was often used in gallant contexts. Eustache Deschamps (d.c. 1406), the prolific poet of the generation before Joan, wrote a *virelai* called "Portrait d'une Pucelle." It is a frankly admiring description of his subject's charms, written in the first person, with the enticing refrain:

Aren't I, aren't I, aren't I beautiful?[45]

The Château des Pucelles, carved on many ivory wedding caskets, was a maiden's castle assaulted by knights; the defenders on the battlements were armed only with roses.[46]

The word implied no rank, and it was current at every level in society. This made it an inspired choice in Joan's case. It cancelled out her background, without denying it, and this, as we shall see, was important to her.[47] As well as forming part of the language of the courtly romances, *pucelle* was a country word and survived, for instance, in a local children's game, Le Jeu de la Pucelle, recorded by Rétif de la Bretonne at the end of the eighteenth century. A group of boys chases a girl; once caught, she is paired off with one of them and told she will be "stripped like a rose, shaken like a plum, eaten like a field rat, wilted like the flower of the pasque anemone." Needless to say, the game was banned when the indulgent parish priest was replaced by a reformer.[48]

With an instinct for seizing a central image of power, which Joan possessed to an extraordinarily developed degree, she picked a word for virginity that captured with doubled strength the magic of her state in her culture. It expressed not only the incorruption of her body, but also the dangerous border into maturity or full womanhood that she had not crossed and would not cross. In this sense she was a tease. During the whole course of her brief life Joan of Arc placed herself thus, on borders, and then attempted to dissolve them and to heal the division they delineated. In the very ambiguity of her body, which had to be shown to the crowd to assure them she was a woman, in the name that she chose—which means "virgin" and yet simultaneously captures all the risk of loss—she shows herself to span opposites, to contain irreconcilable oppositions.

Her virginity was magic: it was up to the witnesses of the rehabilitation to lay claim to her, as a talisman of the rightness of the cause she had supported. It was magic because of the long Christian tradition that had held since the second century that the inviolate body of a woman was one of the holiest things possible in creation, holier than the chastity of a man, who anatomically cannot achieve the same physical image of spiritual integrity as a woman. The twelfth-century English homily *Hali Meidenhad* extolls in extreme feminist language the liberation of a virginal life and declares: "This [virginity] is yet the virtue that holds our breakable vessel, that is our feeble flesh, in whole holiness. And as that sweet unguent and dearest beyond all others that is called balm protects the dead body that is rubbed therewith from rotting, so also does virginity a virgin's living flesh, maintaining all her limbs without stain."[49] The virginal ideal also flourished under the influence of the cult of the Virgin Mary, Mother of God, who, in the early fifteenth century, was seen above all as a powerful and merciful intercessor, who could grant humanity forgiveness through the purity she had preserved, even in childbirth.

In Joan's case, there was a specific reason beyond the purely symbolical for the rise of a *pucelle* as palladium of the country: it was expected to happen. Numerous and confused prophecies circulating in France promised the rise of a virgin saviour, and these were as greedily received by the literate and illiterate alike. In 1456, Jean Barbin, a lawyer and advocate at the Parlement, gave hearsay evidence about the inquiry Joan underwent at Poitiers after her first meeting with the Dauphin Charles at Chinon in 1429. Joan's questioners raised the subject of a recent prophecy made by a visionary called Marie d'Avignon, concerning an armed woman who was to save the kingdom. When Marie became afraid that she herself was being called into battle, she was reassured by her vision and told that it was another maiden, who would come after her. The professor of theology who had recalled this prediction, Master Jean Erault, declared to the Poitiers judges that he was certain Joan was the maid in question.[50]

Marie d'Avignon, or Marie Robine, was Joan's predecessor in other ways, for she was a prophetess politically involved in the crisis of the Great Schism that divided the Western Church between two rival popes. Around 1387 she was miraculously cured after a pilgrimage to the tomb of Pierre de Luxembourg in Avignon, at a healing ceremony in which the anti-Pope Clement VII took part. The cure naturally helped to confirm the latter's shaky position and so Marie stayed on, the recipient of numerous benefits, as a recluse in the church near Pierre's tomb. She continued in high esteem through the next reign of anti-Pope Benedict XIII, and she published her visions of peace and doom.[51] Yet in all twelve volumes of these visions, there is no prophecy as related by Jean Erault. He either made a mistake and attributed another current expectation to the wrong seer; or the prophecy might have been made orally and he might have heard it circulating in Paris; or, in order to urge approval of Joan, who had engaged his sympathies, he made it up, using a staple method of the Middle Ages, the invocation of the supernatural.

Quoting prophecies in support of Joan became quite commonplace. When the evidence of the rehabilitation of 1456 was summed up by the Inquisitor Jean Bréhal, he cited many others. Some he left anonymous, and their sources are still not known. Others he gave, with suitable amendments to render them apt, to the wizard Merlin, of the Arthurian cycle. But they were appropriate to Joan because they used the word *puella*, always the Latin rendering of *pucelle*. One echoed Marie Robine's message in different cryptic phrases:

> *The young cocks of France will prepare wars for the throne.*
> *Behold, the wars break out, now the Maid carries forward*
> *her standards.*[52]

Merlin was then believed to have foreseen and foresuffered all, like Tiresias, and his rigmaroles were greatly feared: they defied sense and were therefore possible of infinite interpretation.[53]

Christine de Pisan (d.c. 1430), Joan's contemporary, historian of chivalry and society, poet and feminist, was so moved at the end of her life by the news of the raising of the siege of Orleans that she broke her self-imposed silence and, from the convent at Poissy to which she had retired in despair at the state of her country, wrote a eulogy of the Pucelle.[54] She had heard the news that, at her examination at Poitiers, Joan had been recognised as the saviour prophesied not only by Merlin but by the Sibyl and the Venerable Bede. Through Joan, she wrote, the sun had begun to shine once again on France: "It was found in the history records that she was destined to accomplish her mission; for more than 500 years ago, Merlin, the Sibyl and Bede foresaw her coming, entered her in their writings as someone who would put an end to France's troubles, made prophecies about her, saying that she would carry the banner in the French wars."[55]

Did Joan know, before she was examined at Poitiers, the predic-

tions that an armed maid would be called to lead France in battle, and
did she use them consciously to command belief? At her trial, Joan explained that she had been told yet another, different prophecy, *after*
she arrived at Chinon, not before she conceived of her mission. The
king, prompted possibly by his confessor, Gerard Machet, asked her
if there was an oak wood in her part of the country, because it was
prophesied that a maid would come out of such a wood and work
miracles. Joan added crisply that she put no faith in that.[56] But from
the first, Joan's followers identified this *bois chesnu* with the forest at
Domremy where she sometimes heard her voices.

Also, according to the evidence of the rehabilitation, Joan had
heard a similar prediction before arriving at court and set more store
by it than she admitted at the trial. Two witnesses quoted her. They
knew each other and had therefore probably pooled their memories.
Durand Laxart, her neighbour and cousin by marriage, was the man
who took the crucial initial step of accompanying Joan at the start
of her mission when she left her native village of Domremy to see
the captain, Robert de Baudricourt, of the nearby fortified town of
Vaucouleurs.[57] Laxart told the magistrates of 1456: "I went to fetch
her from her father's, and brought her to my house; she told me she
wished to go into France, to the Dauphin, to have him crowned:
'Was it not said that France would be ruined through a woman, and
afterwards restored by a virgin?' "[58] Catherine Royer, with whom
Joan stayed at Vaucouleurs when she was trying to persuade Robert
de Baudricourt to give her an escort to the king at Chinon, told the
same story, with more particulars. " 'Have you not heard,' she said,
'the prophecy that France was to be ruined by a woman and restored
by a virgin from the Marches of Lorraine?' I remembered having heard
that, and I was flabbergasted."[59] Joan was the maid from Lorraine,
according to her contemporaries' interpretation; Queen Isabella of
Bavaria, who in 1420 had made the treaty with England that dispossessed her son Charles of the French crown, was the woman who had
destroyed her country.[60]

Joan herself never claimed outside corroboration for her chosen
destiny; indeed, her stubbornness and unshakeable commitment to the
interior and personal character of her voices are among the features that
have most inspired the writers who have attempted her likeness. On
the evidence of the trial, she never invoked the prophecies that could
have helped her standing with her judges, and they were careful not
to produce them in the questioning. Merlin, for instance, was an inter-

nationally accepted source and possibly was consulted even more in England than in France.

Durand Laxart and Catherine Royer may have been using the wisdom of hindsight; also, as we shall see in Chapter 4, the support of external verification from apparently disinterested sources, like Merlin, formed an important feature of every party's struggle in the civil strife of France to claim God firmly for its side. But even if current gossip shaped the stories of Laxart and Royer, their testimony concurs with the portrait drawn by the rehabilitation as a whole, and the prophecies they quote only reinforce the obsession that the evidence betrays with the saviour's literal purity, with Joan's virginity. She had to be uncorrupted, whole, firm, dry, a creature above many of nature's laws and, though assailed on all sides, invincible—until the fire.

A secondary theme also returns again and again to support the physical portrait of Joan drawn by her vindicators: the persecutions she underwent are insistently described. By prevailing against torments and lewdness, her spiritual power seems even more preternatural. In 1456, the witnesses who had seen her imprisoned in Rouen all answered vividly the questions put to them about the conditions in which she was held. She was taunted by her English guards, soldiers "of the lowest sort." "Common torturers," said Jean Massieu, the court usher.[61] It was alleged that she was mocked and derided by her gaolers and by visitors; that she was duped by Nicolas Loiselleur, a canon of Rouen, who posed as a friend and counsellor from her native Lorraine;[62] and, above all, that attempts were made to violate her.

Other participants in the earlier trial talked of the chains loading her body, of an iron cage made on purpose too small for her to lie down in it. No one said they had actually seen it used. Surprisingly the threat of torture, recounted in the trial itself, is not repeated by the witnesses of 1456, except that Thomas de Courcelles, one of the three judges who in 1431 had voted that she should be tortured, smoothly denied that he had ever given an opinion about the punishments she should receive.[63]

Carl Théodor Dreyer, in his 1928 masterpiece, *La Passion de Jeanne d'Arc*, organised the phases of this cinematic poem about Joan's imprisonment and death according to the mysteries of Christ's cross. The face of Joan of Arc, the face of the actress Falconetti, unravished, tear-streaked, filled with inner certitude and sacred simplicity, is framed by the leers and snarls and the ugliness of her gaolers in a sequence that explicitly reinterprets fifteenth-century paintings of the mocking of

Christ, such as Bosch's disturbing evocation of the holy simpleton in the picture now in Washington, D.C.[64]

In Joan's case, because she exists in recorded history and not in hagiography alone, the patterns of saints' lives exert an influence, but cannot altogether metamorphose circumstance into myth. Elements of mimesis, of the attempted representation of reality, cling to the witnesses' accounts of her passsion and her death, while at the same time an accretion of semiosis, the search for inner meaning, covers their story and profoundly alters its character.

Virgin martyrs, like Saint Catherine and Saint Margaret and other heroines in the ranks of the saints, could not have the physical life in them destroyed by physical means until it pleased God to allow nature to take its course. But Joan in death was subject to nature; she died in front of a crowd; she was burned for all to see. Yet because she was the living totem of a just cause for her supporters, the miraculous had to be present. After the crescendo of her innocence and her torments, it was not possible to release her into the banality of mortal law, where death claims the body and cannot give it back. She died calling on her lord, "Jesus, Jesus," until the fire choked her. "And almost everyone wept for pity."[65] This might seem grand enough; but reality is not adequate, and the minds of the witnesses of 1456 used the means available to them to describe her victory. The veil of the temple must be rent; darkness must fall in the afternoon.

For Thomas Marie the word *Jesus* was seen written in the flames.[66] The Dominican who attended her at the end, Isambart de la Pierre, told another story. He said that an Englishman who had helped burn Joan was struck with horror after her death. He realised he had burned a saint: "For it seemed to this Englishman that he had seen a white dove flying from the direction of France at the moment when she was giving up the ghost."[67] G. B. Shaw used the incident as the climax of Joan's death in his famous play of 1923, *Saint Joan*.[68] Dreyer also expanded the image in his film: from the tower of Rouen castle, white birds flock toward heaven, signalling widespread distress and disorder in creation as the flames leap to Joan's face. With intense, almost grotesque forcefulness, Dreyer intercuts these birds, the pyre, the flurry of wings and the tongues of fire with the surging spectators and the mailed soldiers with flails and clubs, laying about the crowd like Herod's henchmen.

For Isambart de la Pierre, the dove, symbol of the Holy Spirit, of love, of peace, of sanctity, served to exalt Joan at the moment of her death; and the fact that the dove was seen by an Englishman to come "from France"—that is, from the Ile de France, not from English-held Normandy—makes the point that the English had misinterpreted the will of God, who was now identifiably over the border, with the other side. Isambart's image satisfies, poetically and politically; it does not quite suffice for the logic laid deep in the forms of Christian thought, for the religion that uses the body of the Saviour as its lodestar needs to return to the body at every stage of its journey toward holiness. The pattern of the Word made flesh must repeat on all strata of the Christian bedrock. The spiritual victory over death must have an analogue in the physical world. So when Isambart comes to the end of his story of how Joan died, he produces the master image, the equivalent, in Joan's case, of the Eucharist: "Immediately after the execution, the executioner came up to me. . . . He said and affirmed that, notwithstanding the oil, sulphur and charcoal that he had applied to Joan's entrails and heart, he had not found it possible to burn them or reduce them to ashes."[69]

Jean Massieu confirms Isambart. He told the tribunal: "I heard from Jean Fleury, the bailiff's clerk and scribe, how the executioner had told him that when the body was burnt in the flames and reduced to ashes her heart remained intact and full of blood."[70]

The pure vessel cannot, in the last analysis, be smashed; nothing can prevail against it. The image of Joan's unconsumed heart became a new touchstone, of her integrity, her incorruptibility, her charity, her love for God and God's love for her. The Jesuit Fronton-du-Duc, who wrote a play about her for the Jesuit university at Pont-à-Mousson in Lorraine in 1589, apostrophised her heart in the faggots:

> *As one sometimes sees amid a sheaf of brambles*
> *The blush of a red rose's folded petals.*[71]

When Joan was finally beatified in 1894, the papal decree introducing the cause of her full canonisation described the miracles that attended Joan's death:

> With the name of Jesus ever on her lips, she died the precious death of the just, distinguished, as the story runs, by signs from Heaven. . . . Men then began to repent of the deed, and in the very place of execution to venerate the sanctity of the Maid; so that, to prevent the people from possessing themselves of her relics, her

heart, uninjured by the flames and running with blood, was thrown together with her ashes, into the river.[72]

No witness had claimed personally to have seen Joan's heart. Symbolism had the better of realism.

René Char (b. 1907), the French poet and Resistance fighter who is still writing, published after the war seventy-two copies of a tiny prose poem. It was printed privately on beautiful handmade white-paper squares in large type. He opens with a question about the nature of Joan's holiness, avows that he would have indeed fought beside her, and then, drifting naturally on the incarnational current that makes the body of the holy a dominant question, he describes Joan:

> Waist in a vertical rectangle like a plank of walnut. Long, strong arms. Late romanesque hands. No buttocks. They tightened up as soon as the decision to go to war was made. Her face was the very opposite of thankless. An extraordinary power of emotion. A living mystery made human. No breasts. The chest has overcome them. Two hard ends only. A high, flat stomach. A back like the trunk of an apple tree, smooth, and well defined, wiry, rather than muscly, but hard as the horn of a ram. Her feet! After traipsing in the wake of a well-fed flock, we see them suddenly arise, beat their heels into the flanks of warhorses, kick over the enemy, trace the wandering site of the bivouac, and in the end suffer all the ills suffered by a soul imprisoned in a dungeon and then brought to the stake.
>
> Here is what it gives us in the form of *earth:* "Green earth of Lorraine—Earth clinging to battles and sieges—Holy earth of Rheims—Dead, dread earth of the dungeon—Earth of polluted things —Earth seen *below* under the wood of the pyre—Earth in flames— Earth perhaps all blue in her horrified gaze—Dust."[73]

Char called this illumination *Jeanne qu'on Brûla Verte.* Her body is green wood; at the end it is dust. From that beginning to that end, however detailed and apparently biographical or circumstantial the description of her person by the witnesses of her day and those who came later, the journey's course is prescribed, its rhumbs traced according to the central Christian mystery, the sacrifice of the Lamb, the destruction of the innocent, followed by rebirth and triumph. It is the symbolic body of Joan that matters, that has mattered, to the people who want her for their own. The indelible outline, traced by Christian sacramentalism, makes the colour of her eyes irrelevant; but the indestructibility of her heart is all-important. Even when the author evoking Joan's body stands outside the immediate Christian tradition, does not profess faith or claim that a divine spirit truly possessed her frame, the fundamental pattern of the Christian sacrifice is there. She was virgin, she was tormented, she was destroyed, but her triumph was a triumph of her frail flesh, as well as of her redoubtable spirit.

CHAPTER 2

A DIVIDED REALM

What could be as hard as
Losing your own country,
Beside which the sweetest love a man can enjoy
Is as nothing, unless he be raving mad?
O natural, unfeigned love,
More precious than fine gold . . .

ROBERT BLONDEL,
The Complaint of Good Frenchmen[1]

O f the many puzzles about Joan of Arc, the chief remains: How did she happen? How did a girl, about seventeen years old, from an obscure village, arrive at court and persuade her listeners she was able to accomplish what she claimed, to make everyone feel her power, so that her friends followed gladly and her enemies fell back in alarm? How was it that the duke of Bedford, the English regent in France, a sophisticated, experienced, political animal, that Charles the Dauphin, a suspicious, wily intriguer, and their subjects on both sides became convinced?

The answer can be only partial, and even the partial answer has endless byways and forks. But one broad path is certainly a readiness to be convinced, and this relates to the conditions obtaining in France when Joan arrived at Chinon. The concept of virginity which she embodied--literally—had enormous power in her culture. Juxtaposed to the vivisected and dismembered body of the kingdom, her virginity provided an urgent symbol of integrity. By synecdoche, Joan's intact sexuality stood for the whole of her and, in the ambitions of her supporters, for the whole of France.[2]

Joan was intelligible in her day as a figure of virtue; but no one would have been looking to understand her if there had not been conspicuous vice to countermand. She was noticed and understood and recognised because the conditions of disruption necessary for the emergence of a saviour existed. As sociologist and historian Bryan Wilson has observed about charismatic figures:

> We may suppose that without the impress of external events, the growth of anxieties, and the disruption of normal life, there would be little demand for a man of supposed *extraordinary* supernatural power, and that it would be difficult for such an individual to arise. Once a society has experienced events of this kind, however, the impulse to look for such a man to deal with the new evils appears to grow almost as a normality in itself. . . . the basis of charisma is less the quality of the actual leader who comes to be called charismatic, than the will to believe.[3]

Wilson is drawing conclusions from the circumstances in primitive societies, but his prescription holds for the France of the Hundred Years' War, though it was not in any manner of speaking primitive, but was instead a highly sophisticated organism. Part of the stress experienced by France arose from this very complexity. Division ruled early fifteenth-century France. The kingdom was split through its length and breadth. There were divisions by race—French and English. There were divisions by fealty. The French, English and Burgundians and the great lordships of Brittany, Foix and others each commanded separate loyalties. There were divisions by class, divisions by calling. *Flail* is the word the chroniclers of the time used again and again to describe the misery the divided society caused its members in the first decades of the fifteenth century.[4]

This civil war was a period of remarkable cruelty and remarkable treachery. The English had entered France, it was said at the time, through the hole in the head of John the Fearless (1). John, duke of Burgundy, was the assassin of Louis of Orleans, the uncle of Joan's Dauphin. Louis was John's first cousin, and his rival to the most luxurious court and establishment in France. Louis was ambushed in Paris in 1407 by John's agents as he was returning home from dining with the queen, Isabella of Bavaria, his probable mistress and his brother's wife; his body was thrown in the street (19). The French faction who rallied to his side to avenge him were called Armagnacs, after their leader Bernard d'Armagnac. John's murder took place twelve years later, on the bridge at Montereau during peace talks that the Dauphin, the future Charles VII, had requested in order to settle the quarrel between the French royal house and its greatest vassal, Burgundy. After John and Charles had been speaking on the bridge a few moments, John was assaulted under the very eyes of the Dauphin and by the Dauphin's closest associates. An axe blow through the skull killed him. It was never discovered who had given the order, if an order had indeed been given. Whatever the origin of the second assassination, the death of John the Fearless meant an end to the hopes of reconciliation between France and Burgundy. For a time at least, their enmity was to cleave France in two. The English rushed in through the breach between the Armagnacs and the Burgundians, marshalling the latter to their side in order to pursue their ambitions in France.

The Hundred Years' War perpetrated cruelties throughout society until the quality of ordinary existence was profoundly altered. The word *brigandine*, which had meant a short coat of mail, acquired its connotation of brigandry.[5] *Ecorcheurs*, or flayers, lived off loot and terror. Mostly casual soldiers, disbanded when the fighting of the English or the Burgundians slackened, rejoining when it intensified again, they were a scourge, as their name justly indicates, of the countryside and of the peasants and smallholders who tried in the midst of the civil war to carry on farming. Monks petitioned the pope to change their white habits for camouflaged robes so that soldiers would not pick them off as they worked in the fields; country churches were sacked and pillaged by roving bands of soldiers.[6]

All were caught in a trap: if the war slowed down, the *écorcheurs* became a worse danger, for at least they were employed and sometimes paid when they were fighting; but if the war reached home, it was hard to know which catastrophe was preferable. Around 1461, the devastation twenty years before was recalled by the chronicler Thomas Basin:

> From the Loire to the Seine, and from there to the Somme, nearly all the fields were left for many years, not merely untended but without people capable of cultivating them, except for rare patches of soil, for the peasants had been killed or put to flight. . . . We ourselves have seen the vast plains of Champagne, Beauce, Brie, Gâtinais, Chartres, Berry, Maine, Perche, Vexin, Norman and French, Caux, Senlis, Soissonais, Valois, as far as Laon and beyond, as far as Hainault, absolutely deserted, uncultivated, abandoned, devoid of all inhabitants, overgrown with brushwood and brambles.[7]

Basin was bishop of Lisieux, and he shows himself more acquainted with and horrorstruck by the barrenness of once fertile northern fields. But the picture was similar all over France: marshes that had been reclaimed for land were lost, vineyards were abandoned, population dropped sharply until ghost villages were no longer surprising. In the Ile de France, the population was halved between 1348 and 1444. The Black Death, striking in 1348, had carried off thousands of victims.[8] But it was not the only cause. Intermittent plague, famine, massacres and dire poverty contributed to the ravages of the civil war. In a small district like Montmorency, in the Ile de France, there were nineteen households per kilometre in 1328; by 1470, there were only five. Around 1430, in the country of Quercy, only about four hundred churches out of a thousand remained active. In 1434, the newly appointed abbot of La Sauve Majeure found "the land without a labourer, the parishes without a parishioner, the churches deserted and surrounded by thickets and brambles."[9] The pattern was repeated all over the country. In one century, the number of taxed households fell to half the pre-1350 figure. It was not until 1550 that it reached its former level again.[10]

A state of revolt existed throughout society. The astrologer Simon des Phares reported uprisings of "common folk" in Guienne, Auvergne and Limousin: "earthworms who sucked all the noble blood of France, who killed many gentlefolk in their beds and committed many crimes against humanity," cutting off a priest's fingers, hanging a monk from a tree and shooting him full of arrows. The duke of Berry put down this outbreak—one of many—either by having the peasants strangled or by killing them in so-called battle, though the inequality of *matériel* on each side makes such encounters massacres rather than wars.[11] In Paris in 1413, butchers and bourgeois, led by Simon Caboche, a former *écorcheur*, rose in favour of the Burgundians. Their violence heralded a terrible massacre of Armagnacs by Burgundians entering Paris with Caboche support. As Robert Blondel, a Norman who remained loyal to the Valois cause, lamented in his long poem, *La Complainte des Bons Français*:

> *The hands of infamous butchers*
> *Have killed members of the royal line,*
> *And have thrown them, it is a matter of fact,*
> *In the fields for dogs to ravage.*
> *You will not find men charitable enough*

To have them buried.
Their blood flowed in the streets,
Crimson, spilled in great rage,
Like water when clouds
Explode in the fury of a storm.
O insatiable cruelty
And harsh madness of these butchers![12]

The pro-Burgundian chroniclers do not disagree on the horror.

The nobles, too, felt the strain of civil war and attendant social change. Their hereditary occupations—landowning and war—were both in a state of upheaval. The ancient feudal aristocrat's way of life was becoming obsolete. The decline in population affected the price of a worker's labour to the latter's advantage: real wages had never been so high, according to the opinion of the great historian of the quality of life, Fernand Braudel; moreover, while reduction of manpower increased its value, it diminished the levy of taxes on households, on which noblemen and the church had depended for their power and its expression.[13] In Joan's day, the idleness of so many churches bore witness to the weakening of the ecclesiastical grip on society. Meanwhile, the nobles were hastening their own overthrow by their impotent pursuit of an old warrior way of life. Their bloody factionalism set them one against the other in a travesty of chivalry's aims. It was from this welter of political and social change that the monarchy was to emerge in France stronger than it had been before: a comparatively firm building above the landslip zone where the great feudal lords were struggling for a foothold. The achievement of these uprisings was only the strengthening of the central authority.

Joan's own immediate circle at court inhabited a dark, grim world. Guy de Laval, for instance, was the grandson of the heroic constable of France Bertrand du Guesclin (d. 1380), the pattern of chivalry and the first French champion of the Hundred Years' War. Guy had inherited all his family's battling patriotism. When he came across Joan of Arc at Selles-en-Berri in June 1429, he wrote his grandmother, Bertrand's widow, a charming and enthusiastic letter about the meeting.[14] But for all his courtliness and soldierliness, he belonged too to the world of personal outrage. Guy married a widow, Françoise de Dinan, whose first husband had been left to die in a ditch by his own brother, the duke of Brittany. André de Laval, Guy's brother, was married to Marie de Rais, daughter of Gilles de Rais. Her tomb in Notre Dame de Vitré is still pointed out as the tomb of Bluebeard's daughter.[15]

Gilles himself fought beside Joan at Orleans, at Patay and before Paris. He carried the holy chrism at the coronation of Charles. Joan called out for him when she fell wounded in the assault of Paris. Gilles spent the winter of 1429–30 plotting with Georges de la Trémoille, Charles's current favourite advisor. A man of subtle financial mind who has come down to us as a notorious fat cat, lazy, unscrupulous, greedy and faithless, La Trémoille was Gilles de Rais's mentor and counsellor; Joan of Arc stayed in his castle at Sully on the Loire after the spring of 1430, when the attack on Paris had fizzled out and her other winter campaigns, mostly skirmishes in the lower Loire area, had been largely unsuccessful. She was still trying to mount the liberation of northern France, but Gilles meanwhile was actively pursuing his mentor's ambitions. Their plans included the murder of Yolande of Anjou, Charles's mother-in-law and the inspiration of the powerful Angevin faction in the court. But this faction prevailed, and La Trémoille fell: in 1433, Charles's new favourite, Pierre de Brézé, arrested him at the king's orders in the castle of Chinon. He was not the first or the only one of Charles's intimates to be so abused.[16]

La Trémoille's case exemplifies the fissiparous condition of France. Like many of the great landowners, his family had land scattered all over the country and was eager not to forfeit it; Georges and his brother Jean, lord of Jonvelle, therefore remained on the best of terms, although Jean was chamberlain and counsellor of Philip the Good, duke of Burgundy, while Georges, of course, was counsellor of Charles VII. Georges retained the family possessions in Armagnac territory, Jean in land held by the Burgundians. When Charles and Joan travelled through Burgundian territory to Charles's coronation at Rheims in July 1429, they passed through La Trémoille land. There, Georges de la Trémoille did homage as their vassal for the first time.[17] The La Trémoille family stratagem was successful. Their method was popular, but it often failed when private factionalism imitated the factionalism of the greater world.

The duke of Alençon—Joan's "*beau duc*," with whom she fought at Orleans and Jargeau—turned traitor on Charles VII and was arrested less than a month after he gave evidence at Joan's rehabilitation trial. D'Alençon came from a proud line of French champions: his father had died at Agincourt, his great-great-grandfather at Crécy. He himself had been captured at the battle of Verneuil in 1424 at the age of twenty-one; his subsequent ransom had beggared him. When Joan first met him, he had just been released from five years' captivity in English hands.

Yet in 1456, he was condemned to death by Charles because he was plotting with the English. The sentence was commuted to life imprisonment. Because D'Alençon had supported the Dauphin Louis against his father, he was released when Louis came to the throne.[18]

Dunois, bastard of Orleans, who was also Joan's companion at arms and leader of the army at the relief of Orleans, arrested D'Alençon in person for treachery in 1456. In 1440, he had been on his side, with the Dauphin against the king, in the nobles' uprising called the Praguerie. While D'Alençon had not been forgiven for his participation, Dunois had won himself back to favour at court and to a key position in Charles's private working council[19] (20).

Wavering in loyalty to others, Dunois was faithful to Joan. In 1429, when he first heard of her, in the neighbourhood of Orleans, he was interested and sympathetic; in 1456, he was convinced "that her deeds were of God."[20]

Arthur de Richemont, brother of the duke of Brittany, returned to support Charles's claims in France and arrived with much needed troops in the Loire valley in June 1429, just before the decisive battle of Patay. According to Richemont's panegyrist and chronicler, Guillaume Gruel, Joan of Arc fell at his feet to embrace them and welcome him back.[21] But other chroniclers tell a different story: Richemont prostrated himself to beg Joan to intercede on his behalf with Charles and win him back to favour at court.[22] If Joan tried, she did not succeed. Richemont and his reinforcements took part in the relief of the keep at Beaugency, but were banned from the more important battle a few days later in the fields at Patay.

Richemont's career was even more turbulent than D'Alençon's, his shifts of allegiance more frequent and more abrupt. Unlike D'Alençon or Dunois, Richemont came from a province—the dukedom of Brittany—that had always guarded its autonomy of action. A scarred survivor of Agincourt, Richemont played a key role in the successes of Charles's reign. But he and La Trémoille were rivals, and in March 1432, after Richemont had backed the plots to depose La Trémoille, he was allowed to return.[23] In the opinion of the Bourgeois de Paris, Richemont "cared nothing for King, Prince or people, nor what towns or castles the English might take, as long as he had money."[24] But his evident self-interest did not jeopardise his standing. It was Richemont as constable of France who represented Charles when the Valois formally reentered Paris in 1436, the capital from which they had been expelled twelve years before.

All such changed relations were ratified and encoded in new vows and oaths of allegiance. "One could not be entirely informal in one's treachery," the historian P. S. Lewis has commented.[25] But the decay of the chivalrous code meant life was prodigal—and informal—with its cruelties. Two of the heroes who rode with Joan of Arc on her great campaign—La Hire (the sobriquet of Etienne de Vignolles) and Poton de Xaintrailles—had the manners of bandits, not of parfit gentle knights.[26] They were *écorcheurs* when it suited them. Shifts into periodic service and out of it were inspired by considerations of their own advantage. La Hire and a group of companions, while working for Charles VII in 1434, called on a castle held for the duke of Burgundy by the lord D'Auffémont. According to the laws of hospitality, D'Auffémont received them with ceremony. La Hire, over the cups of wine, clapped him in irons and threw him in a dungeon, holding him there until a ransom of 14,000 *écus* of gold (4,000 more than the price for which Joan changed hands), a horse and a quantity of wine had been made over to him.[27] Poton de Xaintrailles, byword for bravery, who in 1449 had borne the sword Joyeuse behind the king when he made his solemn entry into the regained city of Rouen, spent a lifetime marauding on either side of the narrow path between brigandry and soldiering. Michelet wrote, in a fine fury against the barbarousness of the times: "It was even better then, in point of safety, to be an enemy than a relative. In those days, it seems, fathers were no longer fathers, nor brothers brothers."[28]

These tensions were recapitulated throughout France: Domremy accurately reproduces the overall image. From an early age Joan was well acquainted with the grief and ambiguity of warring loyalties.

Domremy is still a very small village, and in order to interpret Joan's career its ground has been worked over by scholars with more persistence than any terrain except perhaps the putative sites of Troy. Domremy stands on the border between Lorraine and Champagne. A branch of the Meuse meandering through meadows in the shallow, wide valley still divides the village; but the course of this stream changed, it is thought, at some vague point between Joan's time and the nineteenth century, when "Johannine" studies began in earnest, and we no longer know on which side the D'Arc household stood. This is of some importance, because this tiny village acknowledged two masters: households on the south bank were serfs of the local lord, of Bourlémont, whose castle stood close by. He was a vassal of the duke of Bar, which was a fief of the Holy Roman Empire to the east. When René d'Anjou, duke of Bar, inherited the dukedom of Lorraine in 1431, the year of Joan's death, these separate geographical provinces became a political entity.

The houses on the north bank belonged to freedmen and depended on the local fortified town of Vaucouleurs for their administration. They formed part of the Barrois Mouvant, the part of the Barrois that had been made over to the French crown in 1335, in an exchange between King Philip VI and Jean de Joinville, the local nobleman and landowner of the same family as the chronicler. Vaucouleurs stood in the bailiwick of Chaumont.[29] When Joan was charged, she was described as coming from "Domremy on the Meuse, in the diocese of Toul, in the bailiwick of Chaumont-en-Bassigny, in the provostry of Monteclaire and Andelot."[30] As a direct possession of the crown, Chaumont enjoyed certain privileges: exports to the Empire from the surrounding district had to pass through Vaucouleurs and pay a tariff. This royal connexion, without feudal intermediary, was most unusual, and it gave Vaucouleurs and its governor, Robert de Baudricourt, a special standing.[31]

Domremy's position was further complicated by its ecclesiastical organisation. Although it seems clear that the village—at least the northern part—formed part of a royal French domain, the church belonged to the parish of the next-door village of Greux, which was administered by the diocese of Toul. Toul is one of the three cathedral cities of Lorraine, and its prince bishop was a feudal lord who did battle frequently to guard his temporal power. When Joan was summoned for breach of promise, the case was heard in Toul.[32]

The quarrel about Joan's origins raged in the nineteenth and early twentieth century, Champagne claiming vehemently that she belonged exclusively there, Lorraine replying in kind.[33] Neither side can reduce her case to a simple conclusion, because Joan's single example illustrates the multiple allegiances owed by people when different systems of authority overlap during a time of struggle. Domremy lay in a part of France that saw more strife than anywhere except the Seine basin and Paris itself. The Meuse had originally formed a natural border between Champagne and Lorraine, between France and the Empire. But the frontier had been pushed east by negotiation and battle, and it was drawn with the kind of imprecision that leads to atrocities. Joan's childhood was spent in an atmosphere of bloody fights, and the war against the Anglo-Burgundians was by no means the only source of the trouble.[34]. In 1412, the year it is thought she was born, the duke of Lorraine was condemned by the Parlement of Paris for trying to seize Neufchâteau, a town upstream on the Meuse from Domremy.[35] When fighting over this died down, the prolonged war between England and France continued to provide a convenient pretext for the adventures of professional soldiers. La Hire was active in Champagne on behalf of the crown, against the locals who sympathised with Burgundy. Throughout the early 1420s, he reduced villages to loyalty and penury. On the other side, Robert de Saarbruck, a military man of equal personal ambition, was active devastating the Barrois all around Domremy. The village was forced to pay him taxes in October 1423, when Joan was about eleven. Her father had just been appointed dean of Domremy, with responsibilities to protect the community, organise the watch, check weights and measures, supervise the distribution of bread and collect the taxes. Joan therefore saw Saarbruck's irregular levy at first hand.[36]

The count of Salm, who was governor general of the Barrois, was naturally incensed by the pillage and the plunder of these adventurers on his land. In 1423, he laid siege to Sermaize, a neighbouring small town that La Hire had seized as an advance post. It is a battle we would never have heard anything about, one of the scores of horrors that are forgotten unless they happen in such regular series that they are seen to form part of a full-scale war. But this siege killed Collot Turlot, and he was the first husband of Mengette, a cousin of Joan of Arc and a childhood friend, who gave evidence at the rehabilitation in 1456.[37] Two years later, someone in Domremy stole livestock belonging to the peasants of Greux and Domremy. A local bandit, a sympathiser of the Burgundians, was suspected and murdered. Barthélemy de Clefmont, a local man, was pardoned for the deed thirty years later. Such a crime, committed against a criminal in just reprisal but outside the normal channels of justice, would have bewildered and terrified a child, with a child's desire for order and clarity in moral choice and conduct. The scholar Siméon Luce has suggested that this horror in particular might have precipitated Joan's first vision of an angel.[38]

As the Anglo-Burgundian cause prospered in the territory around Domremy, the village's sufferings increased. This was not because it remained steadfast on the French side, but because agricultural workers, whatever their loyalties, took the brunt of fighting's side effects. In July 1428—Joan was now about sixteen—the governor of Champagne, Antoine de Vergy, a supporter of Burgundy, attacked Vaucouleurs with a small army. The attempt failed, but not before Domremy and surrounding villages had been put to the torch. The church of St. Rémy, beside which stands the house attributed to Joan's family, was burned.[39] The village was evacuated: Joan went to live in Neufchâteau, on the visit to La Rousse's hostelry that gave rise to close questioning at the trial and detailed defence of her moral conduct at the rehabilitation. She herself said she stayed there "for fear of the Burgundians" for a fortnight; at her vindication this was shortened to "four or five days."[40] When the charge was read to her, Joan expanded on her childhood memories of similar upheavals, adding that she did not watch animals, except when there were threats of roaming soldiers. Then she helped herd them for safety on to the island in the bed of the Meuse, the one on which stood the Bourlémont castle that had been leased by the villagers of Domremy for their use.[41]

Division of this kind is a malignancy, taking up its dwelling without prejudice, anywhere. All bodies are hospitable to it. The sufferings of Domremy were not intermittent; they lingered on at home, even after a particular freebooter had been despatched or a mercenary captain crossed the furthest field. Suspicion, hostility, instability remained.

At the trial, Joan described how the children of Domremy fought the children of Maxey, which is an almost identical village a little way upstream, for Maxey sided with Burgundy, while Domremy remained faithful to the Dauphin's cause. She remembered they came back sometimes "wounded and blooded."[42] According to the evidence at the rehabilitation, Joan spied Burgundian supporters in her own village and avoided confiding in them. A witness, Gérardin of Epinal, says she was still fearful later, during her mission: "I saw her afterwards at Châlons with four people from our village, and she said that she was afraid of nothing except treason."[43]

Insecurity was the watchword for Joan's childhood, but it was not individual insecurity. She shared it with everyone around her. But she tolerated collective insecurity less well. She had a natural inclination for clear-cut situations, with identifiable centres of authority: the king's supreme position and her magnetic attraction for it bear witness to this taste. She liked unity, organisation, rallied groups. She could not abandon the military way of life, after her failure to take Paris in September 1429, and beat a retreat into private life, because, unlike the court and its intrigues, it seemed to conjure away divisiveness. There is nothing like a pitched battle to stir rousing feelings of togetherness.

This fundamental streak in Joan's character clarifies another aspect of her in a curious but important way. Joan loved bells. Usually the raptures Joan experienced at a "carillon" are linked by way of explanation to her visions. But they reveal less about her voices than about her concept of a united realm. On 24 February, she told her accusers that she had heard her voices when church bells were rung, in the morning, at vespers and again when the evening angelus was tolled, as well as numerous other times.[44] In a disputed tailpiece of the trial documents, containing evidence given on the day of her burning, Joan is reported to have maintained stoutly to Maître Pierre Maurice, and to the two friars who heard her confession and gave her communion, that she truly heard her voices, especially when bells were being rung for compline and for matins.[45] The vindication witnesses reiterate her love of pealing bells: two childhood friends say she knelt in the fields when she heard them, and the beadle of Domremy, Perrin Drappier, told the tribunal that Joan had "scolded" him for forgetting to ring for compline. She bribed him with a present—either some wool or some cakes (the word *lune* could mean either)—if only he would not forget in future.[46] Dunois added to this: Joan in the days of her glory would have the church bells rung for her for half an hour on end, while she prayed in the church.[47]

It is possible that these stories were repeated at the rehabilitation as a veiled explanation of Joan's voices, which were otherwise not discussed. By being attributed to the peals of bells, they acquired a semblance of reassuring normality: it is more understandable to mistake the pealing of God's church for heavenly voices than to hear them in solitude, without aid.[48]

But bells also had a specific function in medieval village life: they rallied the community as a whole, they called out to it as a unity, and they paid no heed to difference of degree or allegiance, to private quarrels or public status. They were democratic in their equality of appeal, but authoritative in their central position in the village church. Topographically as well as metaphorically, this was frequently the case. Communal feasts were celebrated by the ringing of bells: saints' days and private rites of passage that needed public witness to mark their happening; baptisms and funerals. When dangers struck, the whole village was told by the bells. They were rung in times of flood, war, raids by soldiers. Even the angelus performed a service for the community that had no religious purpose. In the days without watches, when clocks were rare, the angelus told the time. This communal aspect of church bells was so pronounced that when a peasants' revolt in the Angoûmois was crushed by the king, the bells were broken up and the bell ringers castrated.[49] The same symbolism, that of a society working through a central system for its freedoms, underlies the founding of the Liberty Bell by the leaders of the American Revolution. A bell peals for cohesiveness, not chaos; for harmony, not division. Joan, from the battered and broken village of Domremy, itself a mirror of *"la grande pitié en France,"* as she called it, loved their reassuring sound.[50] They were enormously precious to her, just as they are to the lover in the later French folk song, *Auprès de ma Blonde*, who, when he is asked what he would give to see his *amie* again, sings out:

> *I would give Versailles,*
> *Paris and Saint-Denis,*
> *The towers of Notre-Dame,*
> *The belfry of my land!*[51]

Joan saw split loyalties everywhere, from Domremy to Rouen. At the end of her brief career, when she was handed over by her captor, the bastard of Wandomme, to his overlord, John of Luxembourg, she did not find herself in altogether hostile company. The two great ladies of the castle of Beaurevoir, where she was taken and imprisoned from July to December 1430, were sympathisers with the French cause. At her trial, Joan avowed passionately that if she had been able to change her male dress, if it had pleased God that she do so, she would have accepted female clothing from "those ladies" more than from any others in France, except Charles's own wife.[52] One of these two ladies was Jeanne of Luxembourg, John's aunt, from whom he had inherited his land and his fortune. Her brother, John's father, had supported the Burgundians, as the son continued to do; but Jeanne the dowager was Charles VII's godmother, and her sympathies lay with him.[53] John's wife, Jeanne de Béthune, was the other lady to whom Joan in captivity gave her open affection. Her first husband had been killed at Agincourt: she, too, sympathised with the French cause against the English.[54] But John of Luxembourg's possessions lay close to Burgundian territory, and he desired his suzerain's friendship. He did not, therefore, want to anger Burgundy, who was allied with England, by handing Joan back to the French; but he did not immediately answer the letters demanding the surrender of Joan into his hands. Joan told her judges at Rouen that Jeanne of Luxembourg had pleaded with her nephew not to yield her up.[55] But her intercessor died on 13 November. Joan hurled herself from the tower of Beaurevoir when she realised she would be sold to the English; but she survived and was sold, within a month. At that time, it suited John of Luxembourg's fortunes better to keep the English sweet.

There was no simple solution to the demands of conflicting loyalties such as reigned in the house of Luxembourg. Each side had its arguments, and many of these were strong and sound. Among Joan's judges were the most formidable and, indeed, refined proponents of the Anglo-Burgundian policies that she had dedicated her life to fighting, for the French who opposed Joan's chosen party did not see themselves as traitors, but rather as patriots, patriots with the correct remedy for the *"pitié en France."* The University of Paris, the powerhouse of French political analysis, saw the consequences of the treaty of Troyes as healing. It was from the university that the initiative against Joan first came. The dismembered country would be united, not under the king of England ruling from London, but under the same individual acting as king of France, ruling through the Parlement in Paris. This constituted a fundamental difference of approach from that of the Lancastrian English, and it created sore disputes between them and their supporters over questions of authority. When, for instance, Bedford, as regent of France, tried to create a separate fountainhead of English authority in Rouen and to make it capital of a separate English duchy of Normandy, the lawyers of the university fought him vigorously, demanding that cases be brought to Paris before the Parlement and angrily refuting the sovereignty of decisions made in Rouen. The intention of the treaty, according to their interpretation, was to reunite English conquests to the French crown, not to continue the fracture of the kingdom. The English were to govern in France through the existing structure of the administration; they were not going to be permitted to supplant it nor to set up a parallel, rival authority which would undermine it. The "double crown" worn by Henry VI was meant to guarantee the French kingdom, not to continue its destruction.[56]

The French argument for collaboration with the Lancastrian cause was persuasive. Although the nature of individual performance could not discredit an institution—a bad priest could not impugn the sanctity of the church he served—individuals could lose their right to their status within it. Persuading themselves of the degeneracy and dissipation of the Valois dynasty, the English felt morally fortified to invade and occupy France, and they were able to rally their French supporters. Edward III had exclaimed after the battle of La Rochelle in 1372: "God help us and Saint George! There has never been so wicked a king in France as the present one."[57] The shifts of opinion of the Bourgeois de Paris illustrates how this principle of personal responsibility can cut both ways: he first railed against the Armagnacs, whom he blamed for the loss of Normandy to the English. They were weak, and they were cruel, no better than Saracens. But after thirteen years of Burgundian rule, he exploded against the very leaders whom he once had so warmly endorsed: "And this whole devilish war was continued and prolonged by three bishops: the Chancellor, a very cruel man, who was Bishop of Thérouanne; the then Bishop of Lisieux, formerly of Beauvais; and the Bishop of Paris. There is no doubt that it was through their madness that many people were pitilessly killed, secretly and openly by drowning and by other means, not counting those who died in battle."[58] Two of these bishops were among Joan's judges: Thérouanne was Louis of Luxembourg, the brother of John, who handed Joan over to the English, and a witness at her execution;[59] Beauvais was Pierre Cauchon, chief mover of her trial and condemnation.[60]

On the other hand, Cauchon, probably in his fifties in 1431, was one of the leading intelligences on the English side in France. An ambitious, skilful, clever and determined man, he had, from an early age, made his fortune using God to rule Caesar. He had adopted the Anglo-Burgundian cause against the Valois or Armagnac party claims, and his turbulent career reflects accurately the shifts in the bitter struggle both of the papal schism and the civil war. His adventurism and the frequent fluctuations of his fortunes are also essential to an understanding of the motives driving the people who wanted to prove Joan false. The rationale of their lives' work depended on such props. Joan's claims gave Charles VII the divine seal of legitimacy, and Henry VI's servants could not allow that to pass.

As a student at the University of Paris, Cauchon rallied during the Great Schism against the Avignon pope, who enjoyed the support of the French throne, and gave his allegiance to the pope in Rome, who was also favoured by the English and the Burgundians. He was then given the task of presenting the university's case against the Avignon papacy in the debate at the Parlement. Afterward, he was sent with other scholars to see Benedict XIII in Avignon to persuade him to abdicate. During the Caboche uprisings, Cauchon supported the Burgundian rebels; when the Armagnacs returned briefly in 1414, Cauchon fled the capital. Philip the Good, the new duke of Burgundy, sent him to the Council of Constance as his ambassador. He returned to Paris four years later, during the terrible Burgundian massacres, to reap the rewards of his loyalty with new posts, as *vidame* of Rheims and *maître des requêtes du roi*. He pleaded for, and successfully obtained, the provostship of Lille the following year. He became inseparable from the Anglo-Burgundian cause as put forward by the University of Paris, and he shared the deepest sympathy with Pope Martin V's plans to create peace in the Church, both spiritual and political, a policy which John the Fearless, Cauchon's staunchest patron, supported.

Cauchon was a successful pluralist in the manner of the times, adding benefice to benefice for his personal wealth and aggrandisement. He was chaplain of St. Etienne of Toulouse, archdeacon of Chartres, and chaplain of the duke of Burgundy's chapel at Dijon. His income was more than two thousand *livres* a year. In 1420, after swearing to the terms of the treaty of Troyes as representative of the University of Paris, he gained the bishopric of Beauvais by gift of his patron, Philip the Good.

His ties with the English were close: as a member of Bedford's council from 1423 on, he earned a handsome stipend, and his niece Guillemette, the daughter of his sister Joan, married King Henry VI's French secretary, Jean de Rinel, who later penned the letter granting full amnesty to all who had taken part in the trial of Joan of Arc.[61] Cauchon himself came from a bourgeois family of Rheims, recently ennobled, and he had both the self-made man's characteristic impatience with the decadent aristocracy represented by the Valois court and a natural affinity with the fundamental hard-headedness of the court of Burgundy, for all its splendour and pageantry.

It was Cauchon who pursued Joan, who wrested her from the hands of Burgundian vassal John of Luxembourg for a king's ransom, though he reminded John that "certainly the capture of this woman in no way resembles the capture of a king, or princes, or other persons of high rank." Cauchon himself was paid well—756 *livres* (just under a tenth of Joan's ransom)—for the pains he took to gather evidence for Joan's prosecution.[62]

His determination to try her sprang from the alliance of politics and faith at the foundation of his character: to justify the cause for which he laboured, he must extirpate all the other side's claims to justice and certainly all their claims to divine right. Joan must be proved to lie and Charles's crown to be usurped.

Certain historians have attributed personal animosity to Cauchon, because during Joan's victorious rampage in the summer of 1429, his see of Beauvais fell into French hands, and he was forced to take flight. This is unlikely, since bishops in the Middle Ages rarely felt attached to their dioceses. Cauchon did need to feel, however, that the decline in the English fortunes was not blessed from above. In this, he resembled many other Frenchmen on his side. Of the 131 assessors who attended Joan's trial at one session or another, only 8 were English-born, and 6 of these were irregular visitors. Only 3 Englishmen may have heard the evidence on more than three occasions.[63] Joan's enemies were men like Cauchon, advocates of the English cause, members of the pro-Burgundian University of Paris, churchmen in dioceses occupied by the English. She had managed to convince Charles of his kingship, and so she fed their doubts and they turned dangerous. Jean Beaupère, who joined Cauchon as Joan's most hostile interrogators, was Cauchon's colleague and his creature. Both were Normans, and Beaupère became a canon of Beauvais when Cauchon was appointed to the see; in 1412 and 1413, he was a rector of the University of Paris, from which he held a degree in theology. The year before Joan arrived in Rouen, Beaupère was made a canon of the cathedral there by Henry VI; in April the following year, he began to draw payment for his role in Joan's trial.[64] He later went with Cauchon and other representatives of Burgundy to the Council of Basle and again, like Cauchon, inevitably drifted along by his Burgundian sympathies into working for the English. Beaupère is the only one of Joan's assessors whose hostility to her did not change. In 1450, he curtly maintained: "I held, and still hold, the opinion that they [Joan's apparitions] rose more from natural causes and human intent than from anything supernatural."[65]

Joan was not contending with a gang of depraved and ignorant individuals, as her hagiographers have sometimes suggested. She was trapped in a situation of extreme delicacy and complexity, which gave major reasons for struggle to all sides.

What is extraordinary to our eyes now is that when historians and witnesses of the time describe the horrors that beset France—the free-lance exploits of La Hire or Xaintrailles, the depredations of famine and war, the trickiness of the great nobles and the tidal pull of self-interest on the actions of powerful men—they come to a halt to lament individual misdemeanour, to reproach particular persons with wickedness. The social framework in which such people live and behave remains unimpugned; indeed, the more righteous anger is heaped upon individuals, the more innocent seem the institutions within which they functioned.[66] Chivalry was a social code that emphasised the independent hero's undertakings; it contained the seeds of its own disintegration. The champion of single combat is not always happy to return to the ranks, let alone to put off his fine armour and gay plumage and find another job. Feudal loyalties create dangerous strains in a nation. But such obvious analyses are quite alien to the fifteenth-century mind. It is only now that we can write, as Georges Bataille has done, for instance, of the way the institutional framework obliged the hero of chivalry to behave the way he did:

> He who wishes to escape a servile life in principle cannot work. He has to play. He has to amuse himself freely, like a child: freed from his homework, a child plays by himself. But an adult cannot amuse himself like a child unless he has privileges. Those who do not have privileges are reduced to work. On the other hand, the privileged adult has to make war. In the same way as a man without privileges is reduced to work, so a man of privilege has to make war. . . . In the days of Gilles de Rais, war was always the nobles' game. It might lay low whole populations, but it remained a game that raises up men of privilege.[67]

To judge that the feuding nobles and the civil skirmishes between rival authorities were endemic to the dynastic pluralism of medieval society as it crumbled and the nobility lost its traditional hegemony, to see the collapse of chivalry's positive values as part of its closed-circuit system, is to see with modern eyes. Their contemporaries, men like the duke of Burgundy and his English allies, were godless because they disobeyed the code that had been handed down by God; they were seen to flout such institutions as knighthood and the Church, not to obey the inner law of their structure. Thus when Robert Blondel in his *Complainte* of 1420 analyses the reasons for the piteous state of France, he blames the dukes of Burgundy with particular vehemence for turning traitorous vassals to their rightful lord, the king of France, at that date Charles VI, and to his rightful heir, Charles, Joan's Dauphin.[68] The personal character of their private morality does not worry

Blondel; he never mentions the numerous bastards (over forty!) of Philip the Good, John the Fearless's son and successor. What grieves, what hurts, is Philip's sin against society as it is structured: Philip's blasphemous contravention of feudal law. But, he adds, it is not surprising that Burgundy should have made an alliance with England. Both are guilty of the most heinous of crimes, a crime that inspires holy horror when it is contemplated in the mists of distant history and yet is committed even now, within man's memory: Henry V, king of England and conqueror of France at Agincourt, inherited the crown from Henry Bolinbroke, who murdered Richard II for it. As Shakespeare's play *Henry IV* makes clear, the illegitimacy of a claim based on regicide was a live issue, even in Elizabeth's day.[69] Similarly, Blondel points out, John the Fearless murdered the king's brother Louis, duke of Orleans. For this reason, Blondel knows that justice in the quarrel lies with the Armagnacs. Henry is a usurper:

> The English kingdom you hold, does it come to you by right?
> No, no.[70]

It did not matter one jot to Blondel, nor to many of the jurists who occupied the power conduits of medieval life, that Charles VI became raving mad, that Henry was a brilliant soldier and a great king. They were aware of the differences of their nature, but these could not bear upon the legitimacy of their claim. Though individuals could be blamed for the failures and the disasters abounding, they were not important enough intrinsically to sway opinion about the correct way—the moral way, that is—that something should be done. Individuals could forfeit their privileges, by angering God through their sins against His ordained structure of human society. But institutions were above the reach of the individual, either to illumine them or to sully them. They were constant. The disposition of societies and government was made by God and handed down to man to be carried out according to His will. If His commandments appeared to be modified by circumstance, as often happened, this was not acknowledged as change. Innovation was the greatest peril. In periods of prosperity and success, the world had supposedly come closer to conforming more perfectly to the absolute model laid down for it in heaven. This world view corresponds to the Catholic theologian's view of Revelation: newly proclaimed dogmas are not novelties; they are rediscoveries of ancient but hitherto obscured truths. Thus nothing is allowed to appear to have moved into a new stage; the danger of breaking the connexion with an ideal, immoveable fixedness is averted; time present is seen as a return to time past, a golden age. It is an essentially conservative view.

In the civil war in France in Joan's lifetime, there is a constant paradox at work: the most fervent and rousing pleas for national unity and liberation on the part of the oppressed French, cries which one would normally associate with revolutionary sentiment, are also treatises of reaction, blaming the present state of the country on its members' failure to acquit themselves properly of the obligations to their role in its ancient structure. In Alain Chartier's *Quadrilogue Invectif* (An Invective for Four Speakers), written in 1442, a widely diffused and magnificently stylish jeremiad, the organisation of society is never blamed at all for France's griefs.[71] But each of the three estates—the people, the army, the church—appears in turn, personified, to rail at the others for their shortcomings in the presence of Mother France. The People blames the soldiers:

> What do I call war? It isn't war that is waged in this realm; it's private robbery, unbridled theft, public violence under the guise of arms and deadly rapine, which a lack of justice and good governance is allowing to take place. A call to arms is made, standards are raised against the enemy, but the exploits take place against me, at my expense, and destroy my poor substance and my miserable living.[72]

The Knight defends the nobility, saying that they no longer grow rich from the land, that they risk dying in battle and that the people's fickleness in turning from one master to another has aggravated France's sufferings.[73] The Clergy laments the degeneracy of chivalry and the ambition of nobles, but feels certain that God will spare France more of His wrath: "If a horse, by dint of beating and whipping, and an ox, by dint of spurring hard, drag their waggons from the wrong, collapsed pathway, so I believe that the flail of divine justice . . . should move us to take courage to pull ourselves out of this misfortune."[74] There is no doubt in Alain Chartier's mind that France is undergoing "the just vengeance that God takes on our wickedness."[75]

Chartier was also convinced that right was on the side of the Valois line and that God could not possibly allow its enemies to triumph, in spite of Valois misdeeds. Although individual conduct can incur a divine penalty, it cannot overturn the decreed order. Thus no one in the fifteenth century ever maintains that, after the deaths of Henry V and

Charles VI, the rival heirs to the French throne—the baby Henry VI (18) and the Dauphin Charles (17)—should be assessed as individuals. The picture of Charles losing ground because he was a despised and pusillanimous weakling who could rally no one to his side is a clumsy reading of the fifteenth century. It is neither accurate about Charles's personal ability nor revealing about the issues then alive. No one was much bothered about Charles's character. The issue was his legitimacy. Consulting the past, all sides wanted to discover the right and abide by it. The treaty of Troyes of 1420 had granted the French crown to Henry V's heir. Was it legal and binding or not? Joan of Arc had a conviction about the claims of the institutions she saw herself as destined to promote: the Valois monarchy personified by Charles and the nobility who remained loyal to him. It was her extraordinary arrival at the French court in Chinon in 1429 that helped decide the question.

CHAPTER 3

THE KING AND HIS CROWN

We are amaz'd; and thus long have we stood
To watch the fearful bendng of thy knee,
Because we thought ourself thy lawful king:
And if we be, how dare thy joints forget
To pay their awful duty to our presence?
If we be not, show us the hand of God
That hath dismiss'd us from our stewardship;
For well we know, no hand of blood or bone
Can gripe the sacred handle of our sceptre,
Unless he do profane, steal, or usurp.

WILLIAM SHAKESPEARE,
Richard II[1]

Henry V had won the French crown for his heir by conquest, at the battle of Agincourt in 1415. He then negotiated with the defeated French king, Charles VI, to obtain his daughter Katherine in marriage and thus seal the pact, securing, by the treaty of Troyes of 1420, that their son would inherit the double crown at Henry's death and become king of France and of England. Henry saw Agincourt as the God-given reward and proof of his just claim to France, just as his grandfather Edward III had done after his great victories of Crécy and Poitiers. There ran through medieval philosophy about the just war a strain comparable to the Chinese belief in the mandate of heaven. God gives the victory to the most deserving. After Poitiers, the English poet John Lydgate wrote:

An hevenli signe be influent purueiance
Sent from above to shewe Edward's riht.[2]

Fate obeys moral law; God sees that the just prevail; unreasoning, chaotic fortune does not command the outcome of events.

But an ambiguity existed, and it was troublesome: past sins, like regicide, could alter individuals' position in God's design. This anxiety was compounded in the Hundred Years' War during the stalemate that ensued after the deaths of both Henry V and Charles VI in 1422, when Henry VI, then one year old, and Charles VII, then nineteen, were proclaimed kings of France. The French lost dramatically the battle of Verneuil in 1424, but their defeat did not substantially improve the English position. In 1428, the English began to lay siege to Orleans, but no clear outcome ensued. The Bourgeois de Paris's jaundiced view of the long-drawn-out and inconclusive struggle in France echoes a growing hesitation among the English about the cause they had once felt to be just. There were no longer incontrovertible signs from on high as to whose should be the victory. Though Charles's position has usually been derided by historians, and the Valois cause seen as parlous, this is not really the case: both the Anglo-Burgundians and the French were stuck in their respective territories. Treaties and alliances between the great lords on one side and the other were made and remade; small armies met and fought battles that altered frontiers of allegiance to some small degree; for some short time, towns on the various lords' borders changed hands. But the basic situation was a deadlock: Charles held sway south of the Loire, Henry north of it.[3]

It was sometime in February 1429—the exact date is debated—at this stage of the protracted, frustrating, baffling and appallingly painful war that Joan of Arc appeared at Chinon. A voice from God, she said, told her to raise the siege of Orleans, help Charles recover his kingdom and drive the English out of France.[4] As the familiar story goes, her appearance dissolved Charles's doubts, filled him with strong purpose and brought a radiance to his features. At a time when none of the instruments would agree, when the barometer of God's will was impossible to decipher, she appeared with a reading for which she had divine authority itself. News of her firmness had spread: she had already been summoned by the sick duke of Lorraine to help him recover, but she had insisted to him that her mission only concerned Charles. She always portrayed herself—literally—as providential. She was the medium through which the mandate of heaven could be known, and she represented a challenge that had to be met.

She did not remember the date, she said at her trial, but it was during Lent, and around noon, that she arrived at Chinon and put up at a hostel in the town. After dinner, she went to see "her king"; and when she entered the room, her voices led her to recognise him. She told him

she wanted to wage war against the English. Her account is laconic
and sober; the only touch of high colour comes when Joan says that
Charles, before he met her, had seen many visions and had "beautiful
revelations."

Joan's judges and assessors were not content with her brief narrative
of the momentous meeting; in prison, in closed session nearly three
weeks later, the cross-examination about Chinon reopened, with Cauchon himself prosecuting. Jean Le Maistre, the inquisitor's deputy in
Normandy who had hitherto showed some reluctance to attend the interrogations, was helping.[5] Together, they forced Joan to elaborate about
Chinon. She did so, at length.[6] It is not surprising that the question of
the sign by which Joan convinced Charles to rely on her puzzled her
judges so profoundly. How had she rallied him; how had she persuaded
him of the justice of his struggle? Could the sign she gave him hold for
his enemies, too? Could it be proved to have come from God? Was she
a divine messenger, and had the cause that her judges followed lost the
mandate of heaven?

We will never know what happened at Chinon. It is one of the
abiding mysteries of history, not because the external circumstances
could not be more fully described by some newly unearthed source, not
because further ingenious solutions might be proposed. It is the irrational
element in it that will always defy analysis. The encounter belongs on
that level of human psychology where circumstances take on the impress
of beliefs. It belongs not in the empirical world of phenomena, but in
that of unknowable noumena. Not supernatural, but natural, because
in nature, but a nature that has as yet no Linnaeus or Darwin to render
it intelligible.

Joan's own account changed under examination. In the public
sessions, she was evasive, pleading that she had sworn not to tell and
would not. By 10 March, the first session held in prison and the sixth
encounter with her cross-examiners, she is weakening; and when Cauchon and Le Maistre return to the question, she begins to answer them,
more and more fully, and more and more confusingly. At first she says
merely that the sign was "beautiful, honourable and good, and the richest
there could be." She tells them others had seen it, too—the duke of
Bourbon, D'Alençon and La Trémoille. It would last for a thousand
years or more. Her questioners want to know if she is speaking of a
material crown. She evades them. Her voices had told her, "Go boldly!
For when you stand before the king, he will have a sign [that will make

him] receive you and believe in you." She was grateful, she admits revealingly, that the sign had been recognised by others, because that had softened the opposition of the clergy in her own party.[7] When the questioning continues, she says that an angel from God had given the sign to the king and that when she returned from the chapel where she had retired to pray, she found that over three hundred people present had seen it, too.[8] Two days later, however, she begs them not to press her further on the point. But when they persist, her circumstantial evidence changes. She declares firmly: "The sign was that an angel assured her king by bringing him the crown and saying he should possess whole and entire the kingdom of France, by help of God and labours of Joan; and he was to put her to work and give her soldiers, or he would not soon be crowned and consecrated." When they urge her to tell how the angel had brought a crown, Joan answers hesitantly: "as it seemed to her," the crown was given to the archbishop of Rheims by the angel, and he gave it to the king. They ask her to describe it. She tries, but is unsure of herself.[9]

Throughout these exchanges, it is impossible to tell whether Joan speaks metaphorically or not. Of the angel, she says that "he stepped on the ground" and "entered the room by the door," yet the others, who saw the crown, did not see him. He came to Joan in her lodgings, accompanied her to Chinon and left her praying in the chapel, at which she wept.[10] Regarding the crown, her statements are even more enigmatic: it was kept in the king's treasury, yet it was, like the crown in the New Testament, beyond earthly price, imperishable.[11]

In the coda to the trial, the evidence taken down after the sentence, Joan is reported to have admitted that there was no angel but herself at Chinon.[12] The notaries did not sign the parchment leaves of this evidence given to Pierre Maurice and the two friars (pages in which she also spoke of the bells, as we saw earlier). Joan's partisans have therefore rejected it as an unscrupulous forgery by Cauchon to discredit her. He could not get the honest notaries Boisguillaume and Guillaume Manchon to ratify it with their signatures as they did every other page of the trial document.[13] But even an avowal that the angel was Joan herself does not discredit her. Under stress at her trial, she tried to render into objective reality a situation in which the divine will was expressed on earth at a particular moment in time. An angelic messenger—be it a spirit materialised into a body visible only to her, or herself in her other, inspired aspect as God's medium—was present at Chinon in her experience and, as she insisted, in the experience of hundreds of others. But the importance of a messenger who exists for one space of time and then vanishes lies not in the individual but in the substance of the message. This is what makes the messenger heard, understood and remembered. Joan, or the angel, embodied that message. The message, according to Joan, was the crown given to the king.

Biographers of Joan have not been satisfied with this simple formula, nor have her illustrators or her shrines. The "sign" she gave has been consistently interpreted without much regard for her own words and with recourse to other sources and other circumstances in her story. The recognition scene at Chinon has been depicted, in paint and in words, as a secular equivalent of the Annunciation to Mary, with Joan as Gabriel announcing to Charles that he is himself France's Messiah (21).

The leading contender for the message Joan gave is that she banished all Charles's fears about his legitimate birthright to the crown of France by assuring him that she was certain, through divine aid, that he was his father's true son. The sign she gave him was her knowledge that one night, in the castle of Loches, he had risen from his bed and, in the privacy of his chamber, prayed on his knees that if he were not the true son of Charles VI, he might be allowed to leave France, seek refuge in Scotland or in Spain and give up the kingdom to the English to survive in peace. Joan could have known of this secret prayer only in a vision, by prophetic power, and so her assurance that Charles's anxiety was groundless inspired his confidence in her and gave him the conviction he needed to press his claim and renew the battle.

The story first appears in the memoirs of Pierre Sala, *Hardiesses des Grands Rois et Empereurs*, written in 1516. Sala had it, he says, from the lord of Boisy, one of the *mignons* of Louis XI, Charles VII's son, who himself told the story one night while they lay in bed together. The closet origin perhaps strengthens the anecdote's authenticity for some.[14] Even if the story had a firmer basis, it still depends on the widespread belief that Charles feared he was illegitimate because he was born after his father went mad, when his mother, Isabella of Bavaria, was having an affair with his uncle, Louis of Orleans. Isabella herself, referring to him as "the so-called Dauphin" in the treaty of Troyes, had patently insinuated that Charles was not the king's son.

The problem with this story is that Charles's legitimacy was never in doubt until it became convenient for Henry V to assert it, and then the only sources are Henry's supporters. Charles enjoyed the luxurious and learned upbringing of a royal prince, even before his three elder brothers died and he became heir apparent.[15] Nor did bastardy carry a pariah's stigma. One need only look at the contemporary career of Dunois, bastard of Orleans, who in Joan's day was the leader of the Orleans family interests and by no means debarred from its honour nor outcast from high-ranking society on account of his mother's unblessed union with his father, the duke. Besides, Charles's putative father was Louis of Orleans, the king's brother. His chief rival to the crown of France would therefore have been the latter's son, the reigning duke of Orleans, Charles, his senior in age, though his claim might have been weaker—the Salic law notwithstanding—by the fact that his mother was not the queen. Moreover, biological bastardy would in no way give the right to Henry VI of England, since his claim came through the female line. It would therefore be a nonsense to pray that he should abandon France to the English if he were illegitimate. There would still be a Valois claim in defiance of the treaty of Troyes. Nor was it firmly held that a king could disinherit his own son, as Charles VI had done. The law (institutions again) must stand higher than personal decisions (the individual).

When in January 1420 the lawyers of Charles VI, Isabella of Bavaria and Henry VI disowned the Dauphin Charles and banished him from France, they said it was the penalty for the "evil deed he has done to the duke John of Burgundy"— the murder at Montereau of John the Fearless. In 1435, when, admittedly, the Burgundians were desirous of changing their relationship with England, the legal aspects of the case for Charles's disinheritance were reviewed at their request by lawyers at the University of Bologna. These replied that the son and true heir in a kingdom where primogeniture was the law could not be overturned by his father; that Charles VI was of unsound mind at the time; that a single man—Charles VI—could not be both accuser and judge; and that, particularly, he "could not deprive his son of the right to succeed him in the kingdom merely on the death of that great prince [John the Fearless]."[16] Crime was not sufficient grounds for the loss of a birthright. An Armagnac supporter, the constitutionalist Jean de Terre-Rouge, had made this argument around 1418, saying that the royal dignities were not a matter of private ownership. They belonged to the body politic, and an individual king could not dispose of them arbitrarily.[17]

Bastardy is a profound anxiety, widespread in a patriarchal kinship system, and Charles's case has stirred many historians. The theory developed that Joan had confirmed his conviction of legitimacy in a practical way, not only by occult knowledge of his secret prayers. In 1805, Pierre Caze, a subprefect of Bergerac, wrote a tragedy, *La Mort de Jeanne d'Arc*. Fourteen years later, he elaborated the thesis advanced in his drama in a lengthy two volumes, *La Vérité sur Jeanne d'Arc, ou éclaircissement de son origine*. With one blow, Caze solved two knotty problems: how Joan gained access to court and why Charles believed her. *She* was the illegitimate child, he declared, of Charles VI's wife, Isabella of Bavaria, and of Louis of Orleans, his brother, and as an infant was confided to the care of the D'Arc family at Domremy to be fostered until the time came for a strategic appearance as a heaven-sent deliverer. Political chicanery then produced her to put the fear of God into the English; simultaneously, as Charles's sister, she had inside family information to prove his legitimate birth.[18]

This theory has spawned a vast progeny, and Caze's proliferating circumstantial detail is still being added to in volume after volume asserting the royal descent of Joan of Arc.[19] In order for the theory to command credence, it must be accepted that Joan lied throughout her trial. Not one circumstantial detail of her life as described by her—her age, her parents, her home—can be believed.[20] Given that, almost any theory is possible. But another fundamental question remains: Why should the sister who had been buried in the country since infancy be able to prove her half-brother's legitimacy? Why should one bastard disprove another?

The tensions created by the needle of God's mandate as it quivered toward the rightful king were severe. It was a sensitive, finely primed pointer, influenced by individual action and wobbling accordingly, now withdrawing, now returning, now withdrawing again. Shakespeare's trilogy about Henry VI, dramatising events in later fifteenth-century England, mirrors the conditions in France in 1420. Rival claims to legitimate succession on account of untainted moral worth create intolerable strains. The houses of York and Lancaster thrash out their superior entitlement on the grounds of superior virtue, more deserving of God's favour. Defeated in battle by his cousin, the duke of York, Henry VI agrees, just as Charles VI had done when defeated by Henry

V, to disinherit his own son on the grounds that his right to the throne is besmirched by his grandfather Bolinbroke's murder of Richard II. Regicide, not his mother's obvious infidelities, makes him a bastard. He cries out: to be a king "in mind," is that not enough? Yet he accepts the ending of his line with fatalism.[21]

If Joan confirmed Charles in his legitimacy by some extraordinary knowledge, it was not the purity of his blood that she stressed.[22] However anguishing Isabella's life and his father's insanity may have been to Charles personally, they would not have stained him so deeply that he need relinquish his crown.

Another, more widely known version of Joan's confirming "sign" is the miracle that, in the crowd of courtiers surrounding Charles at Chinon, she picked him out even though she had never laid eyes on him before. The cycles of her life in stained glass in the cathedral of Orleans and in fresco in the church at Domremy, the immensely popular illustrated children's book of her life by Boutet de Monvel, the bas reliefs on her statue at Orleans and innumerable other renderings of her life, both written and painted, choose this episode as one of the moments of truth, the trope encapsulating the marvellous nature of her mission. She herself told her judges when they asked that she recognised Charles because her voices had guided her.[23] But she did not emphasise it as a special miracle. Simon Charles, master of the Court of Requests in 1429, was present at the meeting. When he gave evidence to the rehabilitation inquiry, he had risen to be president of the Chamber of Accounts, an important post. His statement is the only source of the famous story. It reads: "When the King learned that she was approaching, he withdrew behind the others; Joan, however, recognised him perfectly, made him a bow, and spoke to him for some minutes. And after hearing her, the King appeared to be joyous."[24] These sentences alone contain the thread that has been used to embroider with sustained fancy the story that Charles disguised himself to test Joan's clairvoyance. In Shaw's Saint Joan, Charles even changes costume with Gilles de Rais and places him on his throne instead.[25]

The point of the traditional, expanded recognition scene is twofold: it underlines both Joan's divinatory faculties and Charles's ineffaceable aura of kingship. Obviously to a prophet gifted by God with higher powers, his holy calling could not be camouflaged.

The Brevarium Historiale is a chronicle of world history from the creation until the beginning of 1429, compiled by an anonymous clerk who had an intense loyalty to the Valois claim and was working at the papal court in Rome. He was so excited by the appearance of Joan of Arc at Chinon that he added a postscript about her. In it, he compares Joan to heroines of the Bible and antiquity, to Deborah, Esther and Penthesilea. Then he tells an extraordinary story, which is not supported by any other writers and has not often been told again. Joan asks Charles to make his kingdom over to her. Much astonished, he nevertheless complies, and a ceremony of conveyancing takes place, in which a charter granting Joan the realm is solemnly read aloud. She then says, pointing to Charles: "Behold the poorest knight in his kingdom." In turn, she solemnly remits the precious gift to God. But after a few moments, Charles is reinvested by her with his sacred realm, and a new document is drawn up, at Joan's request, recording the proceedings.[26] The import of the clerk's story forms a counterpart to Joan's: the gift of the crown to Charles by God. The concept embedded in both is that kings are made in heaven, not by treaty. The differing stories are all struggling to express the same idea, the idea that Joan also groped for when she said that the sign was a crown brought by an angel: God (manifest in supernatural events, be they apparitions, miraculous visions, secret prayers or prodigious recognitions) was for Charles (Charles was legitimate; the realm of France was rightfully his; the crown was on his head). The mandate of heaven had returned. No wonder he was joyous.

Joan, in her ambiguous use of the term *crown*, was not showing careless thinking, but was following the tradition of medieval theology, in which the crown was both invisible and visible at once. She was using it with its full symbolic weight, deriving in part from the richness of this ambivalence between material and spiritual, to designate the kingdom as it exists in God's gift, distinct from the person of the king and from the country itself on earth.[27]

Joan could have absorbed the idea of the crown through visual symbolism. All French society was permeated with the idea of the God-bestowed kingship present in the enduring crown. Domremy's church was dedicated to Saint Rémy (as the village's name also denotes), the patron saint of Rheims, the coronation city of the kings of France where the holy phial of imperishable chrism was kept. The anointing ceremony was essential to the consecration of the French king, since Carolingian times.[28] The legend of the holy oil's descent from heaven in the beak of a dove in order to consecrate Clovis, first Christian king of the Franks, was very widely disseminated, carrying much further than the borders of France the mystique of the king's person.[29] The sacredness of the crown was also common stock of knowledge. If Joan had seen, for instance, or heard described many of the coins struck by Philip VI or Charles VI, she would have become familiar with the conjunction of ideas she described at Chinon. Philip's famous and beautiful piece, the huge Ange d'Or minted in 1341, shows a crowned angel holding a fleur-de-lys sceptre and a shield also emblazoned with fleurs-de-lys. On the reverse, the crown of France, composed of fleurons in the shape of lilies, stressed the heaven-sent quality of the kingship. Charles VI amplified the idea on a gold *écu*, by giving the crown bearers: an angel on one side, Christ on the other.[30]

There is, of course, no direct evidence that Joan ever did see such valuable gold pieces. One can only surmise that from the prevalence of the notion, she had retained its image. Again, when Henry VI entered Paris in 1431 to be crowned king of France, part of the festivities included a play about the king's court, or *lit de justice*, in which Henry was performed by a boy "with two crowns, both very rich, as anyone could see, hanging above his head." The language comes very close to Joan's description of Charles's crown.[31]

The events at Chinon remain mysterious, as said before. A mass vision could have occurred, as at Fatima in 1917 when a crowd, gathered at the grove where the Virgin appeared to three children, saw the sun dance in the heavens.[32] But no witness later corroborates Chinon. Joan could have whispered something wondrous to Charles. Or she could have used the existing symbolism of legitimate kingship to persuade him that God knew he should be king. There is no evidence, however, that Charles had ever doubted this: he had stuck fast in the territory loyal to him after his disinheritance and maintained around him a tight body of working counsellors. He was restless, impatient, devious and distrustful, but he was not the infirm and pusillanimous fool that history has preferred.

But he was impressed by Joan at Chinon and wanted to hear more of her. The climate in which his belief and others' became possible will be more fully described later. Charles gave her the retinue of a knight: a page (Louis de Coutes), a squire (Jean d'Aulon) and some soldiers.[33] The exact number is not known, for the figure Joan claimed under cross-examination—ten to twelve thousand—is probably larger than the entire French forces. It was either the result of a fault in the transcription or Joan's metaphor for her troops' invincibility. Other remarks of contemporaries suggest that at Orleans the combined French forces were small, under three thousand in toto.[34]

Charles did not put his full trust in Joan after the scene at Chinon in February, in spite of his radiant face. Joan was first sent to Poitiers to be examined for three weeks by a tribunal of the Parlement of Paris in exile. Only then was she allowed to take up her military career in the Loire valley. On 22 March, she issued a challenge to the English; on 24 April, she reached Tours; a week later she set out from Blois to rejoin the troops under Dunois that had been defending Orleans from the English besiegers.

The mandate of heaven, as we have seen, becomes clear when there is a winning side. It is a sextant rather than a compass: it gives a reading when there is a fixed point on which to orient it, when the sun is visible above the horizon. At Chinon, Joan made the bold and amazing statement that she had come from God; it is only *after* her victory at Orleans in May that year, just two months after Chinon, that the chroniclers of the period openly agree with her. It is only then the sign at Chinon becomes convincing. Between Chinon and Orleans, Joan was an unproved medium of the divine will. But after the raising of the siege, a treatise attributed to Jean Gerson, the exiled chancellor of the University of Paris and a leading intellectual force of his time, declared that Joan should be believed to be truly divinely inspired because the goodness of her deeds and the fulfilment of her prophesied mission proved it.[35] God crowns the victor after the battle has been won. Christine de Pisan, writing in euphoria at the news of Orleans, used the argument that the divine purpose was made manifest in Joan's case because her deeds were indeed "beyond nature." Through the very unlikelihood of a young girl's achieving what Joan achieved, the intervention of God was made plain.[36] The archbishop of Embrun, Jacques Gélu, exulted that God in his magnanimity had chosen nothing but "a little flea" (*puce*) to be His instrument and to alight on the dunghill of France.[37]

In 1903, during the inquiry into the case for Joan's canonisation, the same point exactly is made: "In the light of her natural infirmity, the very success in arms of the Venerable provides more than sufficient proof that her mission was from God."[38] It is ironical to find the principle applied by Christine, one of feminism's most outspoken voices:

It is a fact worth remembering that God should nevertheless have wished (and this is the truth!) to bestow such great blessings on France, through a young virgin. And what honour for the

French crown, this proof of divine intervention! For all the blessings which God bestows upon it demonstrates how much He
favours it.[39]

When Joan said after her trial that she had been the angel, she may
have echoed the way she had indeed been perceived, as a heavenly
messenger.

The three weeks that elapsed during the examination at Poitiers, as
well as other incidents, reveal that Joan's position was not secure until
after the successful raising of the siege at Orleans. Before she had shown
herself true to her word that the siege would be raised, Joan did not
occupy a preeminent position in the renewed French efforts to prise the
English from the ring of fortresses they had established around Orleans.
She was not accepted until after this proof. Both in Dunois's evidence—
which is adulatory—and in her squire D'Aulon's—strongly loyal and affectionate, too— at the rehabilitation hearings, stories are told revealing
that Joan's ambitions to participate in the army's council were frustrated.
There is no evidence at all, contrary to the popular story, that she was in
command of the troops at Orleans in any official capacity. That she
roused their loyalty and fighting spirit is irrefutable; but the king had
not given her the command.

On the march from Blois toward Orleans, Joan realised, for instance, that the army was taking the southern or left bank through the
Sologne countryside. Angrily, she rounded on Dunois, saying she had
told him that her voices had expressly commanded the entry into Orleans be made by the Beauce, on the right bank to the north. The
English held a girdle of forts to the west and south of Orleans, so the
more obvious strategy was to proceed through Sologne, as Dunois was
doing, skirt the English redoubts and cross further upstream at Chécy
and Jargeau, making a loop to reach the city by the undefended northeast.

Dunois gave his account in some detail, but not in order to reveal
how Joan's opinion was not respected. Rather he wanted to enhance the
miracle—in his view—worked by Joan's live contact with the supernatural. When they reached the riverbank, they found that the wind blew
strongly against them and therefore the army and supplies and *matériel*
could not be transported across the stream to the right bank, on which
the city of Orleans itself stood. They were stranded and vulnerable to
attack before they could even embark. Joan reproached Dunois with
allowing her counsel to be overruled: "You thought you had deceived

me," she said, "but it is you who have deceived yourselves, for I am bringing you better help that ever you got from any soldier or any city. It is the help of the King of Heaven." Dunois then described: "Immediately, at that very moment, the wind, which had been adverse and had absolutely prevented the ships carrying the provisions for the city of Orleans from putting out, changed and became favourable."[40]

He saw in this the hand of God, and he was won over to belief in the Pucelle, as he always called her. Together with La Hire, Joan then crossed the river and entered Orleans. She was received with jubilation —news of her divine mission having travelled before her.[41] The rest of the troops returned to Blois and crossed the river there, agreeing to advance toward Orleans on the northern bank.

From a military point of view, Dunois's anecdote reveals Joan's complete ignorance of the terrain. If at any point in the march from Blois to Orleans she had seen the river Loire, which is most probable, and if she had known that it flowed westward to the sea, she would have realised that they were following the left bank of the Sologne, since the current would have been flowing past her on her left as she rode eastward.

This lack of elementary geography did not disturb Dunois at all, but the changing of the wind did.[42] And by winning his approval and his faith, Joan gained to her side the leader of the Orleans defences, chief representative of the Orleans house in France, half-brother of the duke of Orleans about whom, she said at her trial, she had more revelations than about anyone else; as part of her mission, she wished to bring him back from his prolonged captivity. Charles, duke of Orleans and son of the murdered Louis, had been in the Tower of London since 1415.[43] That it was a divine intervention, not a piece of astute warcraft that persuaded Dunois, reveals the role La Pucelle played in the battle for Orleans. Joan's prowess was not credited to her military skills until the rehabilitation of 1456, when witnesses like the duke of Alençon praised her placing of artillery pieces.[44] Instead, the miraculousness of her victories is stressed, even by hostile sources. The Bourgeois de Paris comments in wonder at her entry into Orleans: "None of the [English] army made any move to stop her, although they could see [the Armagnacs] going by about one or two bowshots away from them and although they needed food so desperately that one man could well have eaten 3 blancs' worth of bread at one meal."[45] After the relief of the town, Alain Chartier, the poet, identified the victory with God's will in a letter to a foreign prince: "Here is she who seems not to issue from any place on earth, but rather sent by Heaven to sustain with head and shoulders a France fallen to the ground. O astonishing virgin! . . . Thou art the honour of the reign, thou art the light of the lily, thou art the splendour, the glory, not only of Gaul but of all Christians. . . ." Charles himself, writing to the town of La Rochelle, attributed the sudden, brilliant victory to Joan, "the Maid who was always present in person at the doing of all these things. . . ."[46] But neither he nor Chartier describe her military actions as such. Jean d'Aulon, however, in his rehabilitation testimony, expands on her keenness and her bravery. In his account, Joan is constantly leaping to her horse to mount freelance attacks and defend the comings and goings of the relieving forces and their provisions.[47] But again, he tells a story that shows that in spite of her eagerness, her military advice was not sought by the commanders, not even by Dunois himself. Joan demanded that Dunois inform her when Fastolf, bringing up English reinforcements, should be near: "For if he gets through without my knowing it, I swear to you that I will have your head cut off." Dunois said he believed her and promised he would send her word.

Joan lay down to rest but, as D'Aulon goes on to relate, "the Maid suddenly sprang out of bed and woke me with the great noise she made. . . . 'In God's name, my Counsel has told me that I must attack the English. But I do not know if I should go to their bastille or against Fastolf, who is to revictual them.' " D'Aulon began arming Joan, but in her impatience she could not wait for him to prepare himself, but seized a horse belonging to a page outside and rode out, making her way past wounded French being brought back into the city, to join the assault on the Fort Saint Loup.[48]

It was her first victory. But it was only by dint of her superior faculties—her hunch, her voices, her instinct, what she called her "counsel"—that she made it to the battle at all.

At least one eminent member of the king's entourage, the bailiff of Orleans, Raoul de Gaucourt, was against Joan's impulsive independence of action. Even though he was in command at the Fort St. Loup, which was saved from defeat by her arrival with troops, he refused to let her have her way two days later, on 4 May, when she insisted that the French continue the fight and not await any longer the reinforcements promised from Blois.[49]

The Loire at Orleans is very, very wide. Standing on the southern bank, with its sweeping vista of the spire-crowned city, one can see how bitter the fighting for the bridge that held access to it must have been. That day, 4 May, there had been severe combat in Orleans. The English had advanced from their stronghold on the southern bridgehead in the former Augustinian convent and the fortress of Les Tourelles, but had been repulsed by the French. There the English rallied and inflicted great losses on the French. They retreated. Joan forced a new assault; again, the English were pushed back along the bridge into the fortress at Les Tourelles.[50]

The war council had had enough fighting; they wanted more troops to bring an assault on the embattled English. Joan defied it and rode out with her own men toward Les Tourelles. Gaucourt, who must have been enraged by this unruliness, intercepted her at the city gate and tried to prevent her leaving. She was carried forward by the crowd, for whom she had already acquired the nimbus of God's messenger; and the English, driven back into the last bridge fortress, out of the Augustinian convent, lost their grip on the river and the southern access to the city they were besieging.[51]

The famous battle for Les Tourelles, a fort occupied by about seven hundred English soldiers, took place on 7 May. The fighting was prolonged and ferocious. Scaling ladders were set against the fortress's high walls, but time and time again the defenders repulsed the attackers. Only toward evening did Joan, wounded in the neck, rally the men to her standard and surge once more against Les Tourelles' formidable walls. The groundworks and the drawbridge had been piled with faggots and smeared with tar; they caught; Glasdale, the English commander, and the English knights with him leaped from the defences of Les Tourelles to escape the flames. Their armour weighed them down. Joan stood by and watched them go under in the Loire.

It was an important battle: the English who survived retreated the following day, and Joan, at a special Mass in the cathedral of Orleans, gave thanks for the relief of the city. Its story has been told in detail many times since the fifteenth century, but many puzzles remain. How determining was the battle itself? Possibly not very; the main grounds of the English defeat had been prepared by Burgundy, who in February 1429, for complex reasons of statecraft, withdrew the troops that had previously helped the English.[52] Earlier, the English suffered a powerful blow to morale when their renowned leader, the earl of Salisbury, was killed by a stray cannon-shot in October 1428. How important was Joan herself? She was keen; she was brave; she was inspiring. She gave living breath to the saying that she put the fear of God into her enemies. But at the assembly of the three estates at Blois in 1433, only two years after Joan's death, when Jean Jouvenel des Ursins reviewed the successes of Charles VII's reign, he gave thanks for a number of valiant heroes whom God had raised up to fight on the Valois side. He did not mention the heaven-sent Pucelle at all.[53] Perhaps her condemnation for heresy made her too dangerous a champion to remember; perhaps her contribution to the military successes of the régime could be conveniently forgotten. At her trial, Joan insisted that she had never killed anyone.[54] She must therefore have been more of a standard-bearer than a soldier, since the assaults on the various forts regained in the fighting for Orleans made hand-to-hand combat necessary; and hand-to-hand combat is usually mortal.

Interestingly, at her trial, Joan also refused the post of strategist or commander at the battles for Orleans with which she is most associated. She amended her own challenge to the English, written on 22 March and sent on 30 April by herald to the duke of Bedford and to Suffolk, Talbot and Scales, present at Orleans as commanders of the besieging forces. In it, a missive Joan proudly maintained she had dictated herself without help from anyone, Joan ordered the English to retire:

> King of England, and you Duke of Bedford, calling yourself Regent of France, you William Pole, Count of Suffolk, you John Talbot and you Thomas Lord Scales, calling yourself lieutenants of the said Duke of Bedford, do right in the King of Heaven's sight. Surrender to the Maid sent hither, by God the King of Heaven, the keys of all the good towns you have taken and laid waste in France. She comes in God's name to establish the Blood Royal, ready to make peace if you agree to abandon France and repay what you have taken. And you, archers, comrades in arms, gentles and others, who are before the town of Orleans, retire in God's name to your own country. If you do not, expect to hear tidings from the Maid who will shortly come upon you to your very great hurt. And to you, King of England, if you do not thus, I am a chieftain of war and whenever I meet your followers in France, I will drive them out; if they will not obey, I will put them all to death. . . . I am sent here in God's name, the King of Heaven, to drive you body for body out of all France. . . . You will not withhold the Kingdom of France from God, the King of Kings, Blessed Mary's son. The King Charles, the true inheritor

will possess it, for God wills it and has revealed it through the Maid, and he will enter Paris with a good company.[55]

When the letter was read out to Joan two years later by her accusers, she claimed it for her own, except for three phrases. These, she said, had been inserted. Instead of "surrender to the Maid," she had written "surrender to God"; she had not said "body for body"; and, crucially for our purposes here, she had not described herself as *"chef de guerre"* (chieftain of war).[56]

It was only after the raising of the siege and the surge of euphoria surrounding her fulfilled promises that Joan was given command, with D'Alençon, of the attack on Jargeau, a small strategic town downstream.[57] Yet the document recording this may even be spurious. (See Chapter 9.) Jargeau fell on the night of 11 June, the first of three key positions to be taken by the Armagnacs in a week.[58] Meung fell on the fifteenth and Beaugency, where Joan fought hard at the assault on the keep, on the seventeenth.[59] On the eighteenth, the English were routed, with severe loss of life, in the battle of Patay. But Joan was bringing up the rear and did not take part in the fighting.[60] In just over a month since Orleans, the English had indeed been swept from their Loire strongholds, and whether or not Joan played a key part in the military manoeuvres fades into insignificance beside the historical truth that her contemporaries, on both sides, thought that she had.

Joan's interpretation of the divine will did not stop at military successes that altered the de facto balance of power; when she wrote that she wished to restore the Blood Royal and the true inheritor Charles, she sought sacramental confirmation as well. The crown must be both visible and invisible at one and the same time. She transformed passive acceptance of heaven's mandate in the truly active Christian spirit. One of the current proverbs she used was *"Aide-toi, le ciel t'aidera"* (God helps those who help themselves). She produced it as a defence of her desire to escape her prison,[61] God would be on her side in her attempt. Her dynamism reflects exactly the relationship between individual and institution obtaining around her: the sacred character of God's ordained social structure permitted people within it to struggle for change without their seeming to aim at revolution or subversion. It created a climate of moral heroism, in which independent deeds of valor appeared socially useful. The very strength credited to institutions made all kinds of freelance action possible in a way unthinkable today. No modern commander, knowing its style to be unconventional, would have allowed Joan to send her challenge to the English. But Dunois did. "She cited the English," he said, "in a letter written in her mother tongue, in very simple language."[62] Joan's position as an equipped knight in Charles's service at the beginning of the battle for Orleans did not make her very different from the other adventurer captains who, like La Hire or Xaintrailles, suited their own interests when they lent Charles their strength or their cunning.

After the raising of the siege of Orleans, Joan the Pucelle played a different role. She insisted then that the king complete the second part of her God-given mission and march to Rheims to be crowned.[63] As Dunois reported in 1456, "once the king was crowned and anointed the power of his enemies would decline continually until finally they would be powerless to harm either him or his kingdom."[64] Joan believed in the powers of ceremony to change a private into a king. A king was not a king without a crown given him through God's intermediaries on earth: the angel at Chinon, whom she first said gave Charles the sign of his crown, and the archbishop of Rheims, whom she spoke of later, are in this respect interchangeable, both of them reservoirs holding the waters of grace from a higher stream, waiting to open the gates once the right vessel has entered the channel.

The coronation of Charles VII as king of France on 17 July 1429 must be one of the few that have taken place of a legitimate ruler in occupied territory behind enemy lines. Yet no battles were fought to secure the advance, and the retreat was planned beforehand to take place after the ceremony. With the army at his back and Joan at his side, urging him forward to the cathedral of Rheims, where the kings of France were always crowned, Charles penetrated deep into the parts of his country held by the Burgundians. A series of towns switched allegiance at his approach—Auxerre and Châlons yielding up their keys with good grace; Troyes making more of a fuss, forcing a feint assault on the part of the French under Joan's influence and rapidly surrendering at the sight of the siege preparations.[65] It must have given Charles a certain grim pleasure when this town, which had seen the signing away of his birthright, acknowledged him overlord again.

Rheims itself allowed his entry unopposed. This is mysterious, since the English attached equal value to the solemnity of a crowning as the French. Yet neither Burgundy nor Bedford moved to prevent

Charles's anointing. The ritual ceremony was performed; it was a threadbare sackcloth compared to the fabulous scope of earlier coronations. But it sufficed to the purpose. In the chroniclers' accounts, the words "glorious" and "magnificent" do not occur, but "customary" returns again and again.[66] The coronation confirmed Charles's kingship in the customary way, established for centuries. It restored a look of normality to the abnormality of his situation; it provided a relief from craziness, from disorder, from a sense of not knowing where things stood. It did this in spite of the scissors and paste needed to perform the ceremony on this occasion: the twelve *pairs de France*, the great lords most closely related to the throne, were not present in their mustered number as they should have been. The greatest magnate of all, the duke of Burgundy, naturally stayed away, not even answering Joan's letters of invitation, and his role in the ritual had to be taken by D'Alençon, who duly dubbed the king a knight, as the ceremony required. Not a single one of the other five lay lords attended; of the six ecclesiastical lords, three were present.

The archbishop of Rheims (at least he performed) crowned and anointed Charles. The *Sainte Ampoule*, the phial of holy oil, had been kept safe throughout the civil war in its traditional resting place at the abbey church of St. Rémi. Several of Charles's attendant nobles, including Gilles de Rais, were sent to fetch it. According to custom—the propriety of their actions was crucial—they made their solemn professions to the abbot that they would take due care of it and return it to the abbey. They then rode back, with the abbot arrayed in cloth of gold and bearing the *Sainte Ampoule*, down the short slope that separates the austere Romanesque abbey from the more recent cathedral, and passed under its fleuron-crested spires and twin towers to ride up to the altar itself. The anointing with the chrism of the *Sainte Ampoule* conferred the sacral kingship on Charles, mediated the special grace of Christ on his human image, the Christian king, according to the rite established by Charles's Carolingian predecessors.[67] As for the crowning, it could not be carried out with the due regalia since there was a hitch about the crown itself; the cathedral treasure had been removed for safekeeping. But another was produced in time.[68]

When Charles emerged onto the parvis, crowned and anointed, the people hailed him, "Noël, Noël," the traditional cry; the trumpets sounded, and others who attended professed themselves well satisfied. As the coronation took place under conditions of war, neither Charles's wife, Marie of Anjou, nor her mother, Yolande, was present, but a courtier, Pierre de Beauvau, reported back in a letter to them: "A right fair thing it was to see that fair mystery, for it was as solemn and as well adorned with all things thereto pertaining . . . as if it had been ordered a year before."[69]

In the castle of Loches, where Charles and his retinue were staying after the relief of Orleans, Joan had thrown herself at his knees to implore him to forge his way north and be crowned.[70] Here again, at Rheims, Joan expressed her tempestuous heart in a dramatic gesture. Again she knelt down before him and clasped his knees and, weeping hot tears, so Jean Chartier tells us, said: "Gentle king, now the will of God has been accomplished, who wished that I should raise the siege of Orleans and bring you to this city of Rheims to receive your solemn consecration, showing that you are the true king, that you are he to whom the kingdom of France should belong." She touched the hearts of all those present there who saw her, the chronicler writes.[71]

On the third day after the coronation, Charles duly fulfilled another essential duty of the sacred king and made the pilgrimage to the abbey of Saint Marcoul at Corbény near Rheims to touch the relics of the martyr and through his intercession heal the scrofula, or king's evil, of his subjects.[72] Scrofula is a disfiguring, incurable disease of the skin, and the only remedy in medieval times was believed to be the touch of the legitimate, God-appointed and God-pleasing king.

We have no records of Charles's visit: the numbers of sick who came to see him that July are unknown. But although arguments from silence are not adequate, it is very unlikely indeed that anything at all exciting took place, for the chroniclers pass over this occasion in a sentence. No crowds are described, no cure, no miracles. If there had been, they would surely have been used to prove how successful his anointing had been.[73] There can hardly have been six hundred people to draw into their stricken bodies the magic of the king, as there were in the ten days after Charles II's return to England as king.[74] Instead the event functions as further proof that Charles, once anointed, conducted himself as the king of France had always done; and in that attention to tradition, the unifying, God-ordained continuity with the past was established and the man-made breach of the Troyes treaty repaired.

Charles's subsequent movements have puzzled historians. He was determined to withdraw and began his retreat to the Loire, accepting the homage of towns on the way back to Sully. In mid-August, an inconclusive battle was fought at Montépilloy, just north of Paris; and on 28–29 August, he signed the edict of Compiègne with the duke of Burgundy. They agreed to a truce till Christmas. Paris meanwhile would be governed by the duke, and the French retained the right to attack the English, without exciting the Burgundians to counterattack. But at the end of September, Charles disbanded the army altogether.

Joan was angered by every turn of events in these two and a half months before the soldiers on whom she relied vanished from official control. The war was slipping from her grasp. She wrote a letter to the citizens of Rheims saying so. Reading it, one must remember that her frank fury and frustration were meant to be known by everyone, since letters were then used to make a position public. She wrote, in her bold and imperious manner, with the usual syntactical havoc:

> My dear and good friends, the good and loyal French people of the city of Rheims, Joan the Maid sends you her news and begs you and demands that you entertain no doubts about the just quarrel she is pursuing on behalf of the Blood Royal; and I promise you and assure you that I will never abandon you as long as I live and it is true that the King has made a fifteen-day truce with the Duke of Burgundy by which he should render him the city of Paris peacefully at the end of the fortnight. However do not be surprised if I do not enter it as quickly; for a truce made in this way is so little to my liking, that I do not know if I shall keep it; but if I keep it, it will only be to safeguard the honour of the king.[75]

Within a month, Joan appeared before Paris. True to the people of Rheims, she decided to ignore the terms of the truce and attack Burgundian Paris. It was a costly failure. She tried to storm the Porte St. Honoré by filling a ditch with faggots. But she fell back, seriously wounded.[76] But more serious than her hurt was her diminished radiance. She had chosen Our Lady's birthday, 8 September, an important feast of the Church, for the assault.[77]

At Orleans, much had been made of her pious observance that no fighting should take place on Ascension Day. Now, she had violated God's mother with impunity; worse, far worse, she had failed. The trembling needle of the mandate of heaven had quivered and swung away. Her failure to take Paris, part of the plan she claimed to have received from God, started the steep decline of her fortunes in her last seven months of freedom.

Surprisingly, therefore, the coronation had accomplished different things for Joan and for the king. Joan was the prime mover behind its happening at all, yet it did not assuage her desire for struggle, her appetite for continued war. It was paradoxically less of a serene conclusion for Joan, who had urged it, than for the king, who had hung back. He pursued a less bellicose, diplomatically tough policy, capitalising on the authority with which his kingship had invested him in the eyes of Burgundy and the English. With the edict of Compiègne that August, Charles promised all his Parisian supporters that their property lost since the Burgundians' occupation of the city of 1418 would be restored to them in the condition it was in at that date. Though he had to call back these brave words in the treaty of Arras, which he made with Burgundy in 1435, he still promised the restoration of property in its contemporary state.[78] Both diplomatic manoeuvres reveal his fighting form, a politician's equivalent to Joan's assault and battery.

Realist considerations were interwoven with ideological ones: the importance of Charles's anointing and crowning was certainly a factor. As soon as Bedford, the regent, thought the roads safe, he brought the boy king Henry VI down to Paris from the English stronghold of Rouen to be crowned king of France. This rival coronation took place on 16 December 1431 in Notre-Dame. Henry entered the city under a canopy scattered with fleurs-de-lys, "just as is done for Our Lord at Corpus Christi," wrote the Bourgeois de Paris, pressing home the point of the holiness of the king's body.[79] But it was too late; Charles had been king, anointed with the holy chrism of Rheims, for nearly a year and a half already.

After the failure to take Paris in September, faith in Joan deteriorated. As a freelance captain of war, she had trouble raising money, first for the winter campaign in the lower Loire, then for her spring plans in the Burgundian-held territories in the northeast. Fickleness towards idols is not a development of modern life, and her magnetism was growing weaker and weaker as one unresolved minor battle followed upon another. On 24 May, she rode out of the town of Compiègne to mount a surprise attack on a Burgundian force standing before the town. It was evening; she crossed the river in the company of about five hundred troops from the town's defending force. They were caught in a sudden pincer movement of English soldiers from the south and Burgundians from the north and were put to flight, retreating back across the river. In the town, having received back safely most of the force, Commander Guillaume de Flavy ordered the gates to be closed and the drawbridge raised.

Joan of Arc had miscalculated, and no doubt because it was not the first time she had done so, Flavy did not consider jeopardising his stronghold on her behalf. She was trapped on the other side of the causeway with no line of retreat from the enemy encircling the city. An archer called Lyonnel, in the service of the bastard of Wandomme, pulled her from her horse by the long panels of her golden surcoat and took her prisoner. Her squire D'Aulon, her brother Pierre and Poton de Xaintrailles were captured with her. According to the customs of chivalry, Joan la Pucelle, still a tremendous spoil of war, was made over to Wandomme's feudal overlord, John of Luxembourg.[80]

After her capture, the archbishop of Rheims commented icily that she had failed in her mission because she did as she pleased out of a proud heart, without humility.[81] Regnault of Chartres, the archbishop of Rheims, who had been present at the decisive meeting at Chinon and had, according to Joan, seen her sign, and who since had crowned the king she brought to Rheims, had lost faith in her. He abandoned Joan and took up instead another prophet, Guillaume the Shepherd, as a new epiphany of the just Valois cause, a talisman of God's pleasure. Guillaume came from Gévaudan in the Cévennes, a district that produced one of the earliest freelance messiahs, one whose story was told in the sixth century by Gregory of Tours.[82] He bore the stigmata in his hands and side and feet, in imitation of Christ. But the Bourgeois de Paris caustically commented, he was "a bad man . . . who caused people to idolise him . . . blotched with blood, like St. Francis."[83]

The English soon captured him, and in the coronation procession with which they tried to rouse the loyalty and faith of the Parisians to their new king Henry VI, they paraded him as a bound captive, like the prize spoil of a Roman triumph.

When the English displayed the shepherd in fetters, they were demonstrating, as they had done in May that year in Rouen, that these icons of flesh and blood put up by the opposition had no truth in them. In Joan's case, they paid her, as we shall see, the solemn tribute of a major inquisitorial trial. Guillaume, her successor, was used for Henry VI's triumph, then tied up in a sack and thrown into the Seine.[84] No learned body of doctors was needed to prove this prophet false. No painstaking labour of the Inquisition was undertaken to catch Guillaume. He was just one more of the long line of living saints who appeared on one or other side in the quarrels of medieval Christendom, not quite trivial enough to ignore, not quite important enough to make of him great capital. Joan was a far more glorious and challenging representative of the tradition of messiahs.

CHAPTER 4

PROPHET

Et ce grand général qui ramassait les bourgs
Comme on gaule des noix avec un grand épieu
N'était qu'une humble enfant perdue en deux amours
L'amour de son pays parmi l'amour de Dieu.

CHARLES PÉGUY
Eve[1]

isions, by their very nature, cannot usually be verified by someone else, although Joan in her uniqueness thought they could be. But a prophecy can. The outcome proves it, one way or the other; and with its fulfilment or nonfulfilment, the prophet is made or undone. Joan was peculiarly vulnerable to the insatiable demands of her adherents for more assurances, for more prodigies. All spiritual leaders who have built up a following on the basis of their miraculous powers—and not of their moral teaching—are liable to fail in the endurance test and become victims of pious inflation. After Orleans and Rheims, Joan failed to conjure the wonders to which her side had become accustomed. She had said she would take Paris, and this promise, accepted as a divinely inspired prophecy, had been broken. She tried to storm the city, expected support from within to rise to help her, generated by news of her invincible mission. But it had not.[2] Her eclipse was so marked that a rumour of her death began. In November, she tried to take La Charité, held by the freelance adventurer Perrinet Gressart, and failed.[3] In April, she fought unsuccessfully at Lagny; in May, she was trying to relieve Compiègne, in vain.

Her public had grown used to her effortless victories; it seemed that she had lost her touch or, rather, the touch of the Almighty, who had sustained her.

Joan suffered especially from this type of disillusionment among her followers because her prophecies—or, rather, the divinely backed plans she proclaimed—were so firmly planted in this world and because her field of vision was so narrow. Until her trial, as we shall see, she had not even spoken of her visions in detail to anyone except the king. Her predecessors in the prophetic tradition had foretold all manner of gnomic wonders and horrors attendant upon the arrival of the Antichrist. If Joan had followed them, if she had expressed her knowledge of the supernatural in unverifiable imagery and language, if her utterances had lent themselves to wider interpretation, if she had been more otherworldly, she would have been able to command credence for longer. Saint Hildegard of Bingen and Saint Mechtild of Magdeburg, for instance, prophesied in the early middle ages portents of highly ambiguous meaning. But, when it came to temporal matters, they confined themselves to giving advice and did not tell the future. Their visions escaped the test of time, for they were set at the end of the world; Joan's did not.

It would be the height of cynical rationalism to think that this was a conscious decision on the part of the mystics. Instead, it was the stuff of the medieval apocalyptic tradition, from which the mystics derived their emotional intensity and their highly coloured, often erotic, inspirational language. Joan never shows any signs of having learnt anything about this tradition or of coming close to it by accident or instinct. She has often been praised by her biographers for the level-headedness she shows at a time when hysterical raptures, self-inflicted pain, fits of demon-conquering were the hallmark of the visionary. But it has never been pointed out how dearly this cost her, since the supernatural was expected to manifest itself in just such a manner. Her failure to give proof of her contact with God in this way aggravated her failure in the military sphere after she had promised to prevail through His immediate help.

Living saints did not survive through qualities of honesty, courage, charity or any personal virtue other than chastity, to which enormous importance was attached.[4] The edifying lives of Bridget or Catherine were written by their devotees as appendices to the portrait of their holiness and not as its substance. That lay in the marvels of their contact with the supernatural. Joan is a unique case because, apart from her claim that God had given her a mission to accomplish, she never pretended to anything wondrous. But by making that claim to a divine call, she placed herself within the ranks of medieval prophets who were directly linked to God and were hungrily welcomed and heard throughout the Middle Ages; when her own public saw that she was not the kind of thaumaturge they were used to expect, she palled.

To be a prophet, in Joan's day, was to speak with God's tongue unaided by human association, to be in touch with God in such an intimate manner that others could derive and benefit. This type of living saint was a mobile generator, boosting with brilliant flashes the normal radiance that comes through the established church. Public enthusiasm regularly conferred this status on men and women, some in recognition of their express wish, others without it.[5] It is significant that during Joan's few months of public activity—from February 1429 to May 1430—she personally encountered no less than two claimants to such a title; she may even have known a third. As we have seen, Guillaume the Shepherd, whom she did not know, quickly assumed her mascot role on the French side.

The two Joan knew were Brother Richard, a wandering preacher, and Catherine de La Rochelle, a visionary whom Brother Richard favoured. Joan first met Richard at Troyes in July 1429. He was sent out by the town council to verify her goodness, and she mockingly assured him, when he sprinkled her with holy water, that she would not fly away. Under Richard's wing, Catherine de La Rochelle first appeared in Jargeau and then, in November, at the small town of Montfaucon-en-Berry.[6] Joan had been wandering about inconclusively since September when she had failed to take Paris, trying to raise money for more arms and more provisions, in order to mount attacks on Burgundian strongholds in the lower Loire. She had succeeded in liberating St. Pierre le Moustier in October.[7] She was now planning to lay siege to La Charité. But she was short of cash and, on 9 November, wrote to the people of Riom for aid.[8] The arrival of Catherine de La Rochelle, bubbling with airy advice, must have been very unwelcome indeed. Catherine declared that she, too, received her instructions in a regular series of visions. She could hardly have been a clearer rival if she had staked out the ring for a prize fight.

Catherine said that a white lady, dressed in a golden gown, appeared to her and told her to travel through the loyal towns of France.

with heralds and trumpets that the king would give her, to rouse the people to part with all gold, silver or hidden treasure. If they would not, Catherine would discover their secret avarice with her special powers and then use their wealth to pay Joan's soldiers. She had, she implied, equal faculties of divination. To this Joan retorted—so she tells us in her trial—that Catherine should go back to her husband, look after her house and feed her children.[9]

But she was shaken, and she asked her voices about her rival. They told her it was all poppycock: "*C'était tout néant.*"[10] She wrote to Charles saying as much and, when she saw him again, repeated it.[11] She was anxious, it is clear, and her anxiety was compounded, as one reported, when Brother Richard believed Catherine and wanted to use her help, "to put this Catherine to work."

Questioned further about the meeting, Joan told her judges that Catherine de La Rochelle opposed her plan to besiege La Charité because the weather was too cold. Besides, she said she would not join Joan. She wanted to sue for peace with the duke of Burgundy instead. Joan brusquely reiterated, as she continually had to during these times of appeasement, that she thought peace would come only at the point of a lance. But even though she knew beforehand from her voices that Catherine's claims were rubbish, she agreed to try her out.

The night Joan spent with Catherine de La Rochelle in the winter of 1429, trying to discover if there were any truth in her, is one of the most interesting and extraordinary incidents in the whole of Joan's career. When Catherine said that her white lady came to her every night, Joan asked if she could spend one with Catherine in the same bed. She agreed. Joan did so, keeping awake till midnight and seeing nothing; when morning came, Catherine told Joan that the white lady had come and gone while she slept, that Catherine had tried to wake her but could not. Joan asked Catherine if she would be coming again that night, and when Catherine again said yes, Joan repeated the experiment, this time sleeping during the day in order to be able to stay up all night. "But she saw nothing, even though she often asked the said Catherine if this lady was coming or not and Catherine answered: 'Yes, soon.' "[12]

What is fascinating is, first, Joan's trust in Catherine's possible genuineness and, second, Joan's belief that Catherine's vision could be shared and that the visibility of her white lady to others would be a proof of her validity. Such an attitude points back to Joan's own insistence that her sign was seen by many, many others at Chinon, that the crown of which she spoke had even been handled by someone else and not by her, that God's intervention was not exclusive, but mediated through her to reach others. Later in the trial she makes the point again somewhat peevishly: she would not have asked to see Catherine's sign if so many others had not seen her own.[13]

At Chinon, the will to believe in the mystery of the crown Joan expounded was so powerful that it was fed back to reinforce Joan's own belief. Was Joan hoodwinked by the noblemen and grandees of the Church who fervently agreed her sign was visible to them as well? We shall never know. But we do know that for Joan herself the outside testimony to her interior visions developed into a principle she applied to judge the visions of others who, like herself, claimed divine guidance.

Catherine de La Rochelle, worsted in this vigil, was not used as a Valois fund-raiser. Instead, she reappeared later as a hostile witness to Joan. Before the Parisian magistrates in 1430, she made a statement that Joan frequently boasted she had two advisors called the "advisors of the fountain," who still came to her after she was captured, and that she had said she would escape from prison, with the help of the devil.[14]

In May 1431, when the Bourgeois de Paris reported the preaching in Paris of sermons to justify the burning of Joan of Arc, Catherine was back with the Armagnacs, and she was alleged to be one of Brother Richard's heretical followers, along with Joan herself, an unnamed girl, and another, called Pieronne. We know the last only from the Bourgeois de Paris's journal, and he tells us she was burnt for her loyalty to Joan.[15]

Brother Richard himself appeared in Paris in April 1429—during the preparations for the battle of Orleans. Spiritual incendiaries always appear suddenly, and their worldly circumstances are normally known in the most imprecise detail, while their divine revelations are highly circumstantial. Brother Richard began preaching on 16 April for a week, from five in the morning till ten or eleven, five or six hours without halt, at the cemetery of the Holy Innocents, "with his back to the charnel houses," says the Bourgeois, near the grim merriment of the Danse Macabre fresco.[16] Brother Richard was a millenniarist: the Antichrist was imminent. He was anti-Semitic: the Jews were to be given back the Holy Land through the agency of his Antichrist. He was a brilliant rabble-rouser: it was said that five to six thousand people came to hear him daily. Women hurled their finery into his bonfire of vanities; sorcerers, their mandrakes. Enthusiasts assumed tin or lead medallions stamped with the monogram IHS for the Holy Name of Jesus. The English found his popularity dangerous and were—rightly, as it turned out—uncertain of his loyalty. After a week's triumphs, his preaching was banned, and he was driven from Paris.[17]

Richard was probably a follower of San Bernardino of Siena (d. 1444), a fiery, colloquial, irrepressible speaker (we have some of his sermons on record) who was the chief mover of the cult of the Holy Name. Richard was also, as the Bourgeois himself noticed, very close in spirit to the fire-eater Vincent Ferrer, who, after a vision in 1396, wandered for twenty years over Europe from Valencia northward to France and the Low Countries. Though Vincent always spoke in his native dialect, he attracted crowds so huge that in Provence a wall was taken down in the Pré d'Ainay at Lyon to accommodate the audience that gathered there for sixteen days on end.[18] He, too, mixed messages of ascetic salvation, apocalyptic doom and avenging fury against the followers of the Antichrist, the infidel incarnate in the Jews. Pope Calixtus III canonised him in 1455, only thirty-six years after his death, in the same year as he began to review Joan's condemnation.[19]

John Capistrano (d. 1456) struggled for his great friend Bernardino's recognition and urged the swift canonisation of 1450.[20] Again, Capistrano presents the era's mixture of violence toward his own self and toward pagan, Jew, Saracen, Hussite and witch alike. He, too, was a rootless traveller, blazing his vengeance on God's enemies all over Europe, sometimes on commissions for the pope, as inquisitor or legate, sometimes as his own man. Capistrano himself had to wait until 1734 for the solemnisation of the sanctity that most people accorded him in his own lifetime.

Brother Richard emulated Ferrer and Capistrano, not least in the political aspect of his career. The business of salvation was inextricably linked with right thinking, and the coming apocalypse was the retribution for the sins of nations against God, not just for the luxury and idleness of individuals. Where indecision reigns about what constitutes public wrong, there flourishes the preacher who links it firmly with private sin. By translating the political situation into individual guilt, a preacher can make change, even reform, seem within human grasp and not beyond the bounds of control or possibility. Improvements in the microcosm can have macrocosmic effects.[21] The Parisians were naive to be so disillusioned when Brother Richard went over to the other side at Troyes, converted by the progress of Joan through enemy territory to Rheims. They threw away the medals he had given them and went back to "all their vices."[22]

To Bedford, Richard was Joan's mentor in the black arts—"that mendicant friar, a seditious apostate"[23]—and he reproached Charles bitterly for using him in his campaign. Her questioners thought her relations with him close, even unsavoury. They asked if he had held her standard at the crowning. She denied it.[24] After the coronation, Brother Richard vanished into history's dark, and we know nothing more about him.

In November 1429, Joan stayed at Moulins in the Bourbonnais, in the convent that Marie de Bourbon, one of Joan's patrons at court, had endowed for Nicolette Boilet, the visionary Saint Colette (d. 1447). Colette was born near Corbie in northern France in 1381; after the age of twenty-one, she lived as a recluse, though she was not a professed nun. She had made three attempts to take vows, but failed. Her austerities were rewarded with visions telling her that she must reform the order of the Poor Clares. She obeyed, abandoned her seclusion and founded twenty new convents. In northern France and Belgium, a new branch of the Poor Clares, the Coletans, was established.[25]

Because they lived in the same place at the same time, there is a tradition that one of Joan's rings, inscribed "Jesus Maria," was given to her by Colette.[26] But, to our knowledge, Joan herself never spoke of Colette nor met her.

A contrast of voluptuous, ecstatic vision and ascetic, practical enterprise is often found in the living saint. Colette was opulent, extravagant, fantastical in the proliferating detail of her visions about the Holy Family, but her dramatic energies in real life were channelled into stripping the surplus wherever it might be found, imposing absolute poverty and rigorous fasting on her novices. But when the world cannot touch you, the world desires you; and Colette, like many other flesh-and-blood icons whose holiness was symbolised by their rejection of fat and their love of lean, was in demand. The mother of the duke of Burgundy, Margaret of Bavaria, consulted her throughout her life after their meeting in 1406, and later Colette acted as an intermediary in negotiations about the position of the anti-Pope Felix V who, as Amadeus of Savoy, was an old friend and patron. She did not succeed in making him stand down, but because she was proof against political self-interest, she was interesting to use politically. Also, there was always the hope that by employing someone whom God had favoured, His love might be transferred.[27] Colette of Corbie was the successor of Bridget of Sweden (d. 1373) and Catherine of Siena (d. 1380) who, under the inspirations of visions, had also left secluded lives in the previous century to fulfil missions of social reform, travelled far afield to do so and reformed or founded orders.[28] Bridget's book of revelations, translated from Swedish into Latin by her confessor, and Catherine's letters and biography, taken down at dictation and compiled by her confessor and devotee, Raymond of Capua, reveal their minds to be filled with intense, dramatic dreams.[29] Yet their descents into hell, ascents into heaven, their mystic nuptials with Christ, their excruciating sympathy with fellow sinners' torments, their ineffable bliss never weaken their grasp of current affairs or their ability to make their views known and felt and understood.[30] We are in the presence of a phenomenon that has vanished from modern European society: the belief that the sane human mind can be a clear window, on ecstasy and on *res politicae*, at one and the same time.

Paradoxically, the possibility existed because both Bridget and Catherine lived in a time of division. They were involved in different ways in the papel schism; Catherine in particular helped to confirm Gregory XI's decision to return to Rome from Avignon. It is in times of division that individuals are able to exert pressure on long-established institutions, that personal vision is allowed to effect change. People whose bids to be living saints are successful are usually associated, in their own time, with returns to a previous age when things were better or are, at least, thought to have been better. The changes they urge are seen as unifying, strengthening, conservative, because they heal the divisions of the present to recover the pure wholeness of the past. A return to the asceticism of Saint Clare herself, as Colette wanted, parallels the return of Burgundy to his friendship with the French throne; a renewal of the early austerities of the Dominican order, as achieved by Raymond of Capua in the Observant convent he founded under Catherine of Siena's influence, reflects the return of the pope to Rome, which she desired.

As we have seen, Marie d'Avignon was consulted by Charles VI. Keeping a saint at beck and call becomes almost *de rigueur* for the kings of France, especially in the tension caused by the Great Schism. Jeanne-Marie de Maillé, a young, well-born widow who withdrew into seclusion and made prophecies concerning the rightful pope in the customary fashion, was, for instance, frequently and lovingly consulted by the hard-headed Queen Isabella and her husband, Charles VI. Before Joan's advent, Charles summoned on several occasions in 1421–22 the hermit of Ste.-Claude, a famed seer who reassured the recently disinherited Dauphin with two ringing predictions: that Henry V would soon be dead and that he, Charles, would have male issue. On both counts, it turned out as the prophet said.[31]

This son of Charles, Louis XI, inherited his father's faith in living saints. Denis the Carthusian, learned and inspired, was kept at court as a token, as if by his presence the virtue in him could pass to the king.[32] In 1482, during one of his illnesses, Louis summoned another celebrated holy man, the hermit Fra Roberto of Calabria, all the way from his home province to Plessis to heal him by his goodness. Fra Roberto had lived under the same outcrop of rock for twenty years and had not left it since the age of twelve. But his wisdom amazed first the pope, whom he saw during lengthy interviews on his way to France, and then the courtiers.[33] Francis of Paola (d. 1507), whom Louis XI also summoned when he was dying, had a highly successful career as political advisor. He had become a hermit at the age of thirteen or fourteen, inspired by a pilgrimage made with his parents to Rome and Assisi. He soon attracted followers, and his fame reached France.[34]

Joan of Arc undoubtedly benefited by a strong tradition of prophets in public life that continued after her death. Prophets were not exactly numerous: the fact that Louis sent as far afield as Calabria for Fra Roberto shows that they were few and far between.[35] But the expectancy of prophets and the receptivity to them were prevalent and very high. Joan's success, from her first appearance in public life at Vaucouleurs, was helped by this: indeed, as we have seen, she herself was immediately identified with prophecies about a saviour.

Prophecy was also one of the few *carrières ouvertes aux talents:* belonging to no guild, no social class, no particular occupation, one could still take up prophecy. Above all, it was open to men and women, and the latter had been spectacularly conspicuous in the ranks of medieval prophesying mystics, so that sometimes their monopoly of this means of communication and influence distorts the impression of women's general effacement in the period. Women used prophecy because so few other means of expression were available to them. As Keith

Thomas has written about the continuation of the phenomenon in England after the Reformation:

> Indeed the prominence of women among the religious prophets of this period is partly explained by the fact that the best hope of gaining an ear for female utterance was to represent them as the result of divine revelations. Women were forced into such postures because the more conventional vehicles of pulpit and printed sermon were denied them. . . . Before the Civil War recourse to prophecy was the only means by which most women could hope to disseminate their opinion on public events.[36]

Times of schism, civil war, general social upheaval were propitious to the rise of the prophet. Then outsiders could seem healing, because they came without the stain of the contending parties' loyalties upon them. The human being who is part of society and yet has a peripheral relationship to it can often speak out freely as the mouthpiece of a new vision: artisans who have lost their living in times of unemployment, peasants driven from their land, the beggars and the dispossessed are typical material for an inspired leader. Of course, the disruption of the times makes any calling more precarious, and messiahs were vulnerable to suspicion of charlatanism, if not witchcraft.[37] The weak status definition of women on their own in medieval society gave them the equivalent looseness, unattachedness of the displaced and the poor. For once, women were able to turn their perennial condition as the other to their own advantage.

Numbers of distinguished women made themselves heard by means of prophecy, though perhaps we consider them distinguished merely because they were able by this means to make themselves heard. Many may have failed to do so. Among the most famous, Saint Hildegard of Bingen (d. 1178) and Elizabeth of Shönau (d. 1164) both used their spiritual visions to influence political affairs.[38] Saint Bernard, whose temper was not easy and whose prestige was immense, wrote respectfully to Hildegard: "They tell us that you understand the secrets of heaven and grasp that which is above human ken through the help of the Holy Spirit. Therefore we beg and entreat you to remember us before God and also those who are joined to us in spiritual union."[39] Her book, *Sci Vias* (*sciens vias Domini*, knowing the ways of the Lord), opens characteristically with explosive apocalyptic horrors and ends with practical matters; Elizabeth of Schönau, who saw the risen Virgin in her visions and influenced profoundly the development of the doctrine of the Assumption, also wrote tracts of moral advice against the corruption of the times, women's love of luxury and dress.[40]

But it should not be overlooked that both participated in the political fray from the shelter of their convents. They needed social status of some kind to communicate the inviolable privacy of their visions and command an audience: the status of nuns was high or, at least, higher than that of a woman in secular life.

The pattern is often repeated: even when a visionary is married and a mother, like Bridget of Sweden or Margery Kempe (b.c. 1373),[41] she breaks with this life to embark on her visionary career. The role of prophet needs support, not exactly from the church's institutions, but from other traditions of goodness within Christianity: renunciation of the world in a convent, of the flesh in a celibate marriage. Margery Kempe took a vow never to sleep with her husband again; Bridget, widowed in her early thirties, decided never to marry again. In Flanders and Germany, the Beguine movement, composed of laywomen who were grouped together in loosely structured communes but remained in the world, dedicated themselves to an active Christian life. They encountered suspicion and hostility throughout the thirteenth century and were stamped out in the next. Because the Beguines emphasised the personal, inspirational life, they were continually identified with the heresy of the Free Spirit. Its chief crime was, it was thought, a mystical conviction of impeccability or freedom from all sin, such as was suspected in Joan. It is significant that the visionary Beguine needed more support than her own voice or her chosen independent status as a laywoman provided.[42]

Marguerite Porete, also a laywoman, who influenced the Beguines though she never joined a community, was the author of the daring handbook on the seven stages of illumination, *The Mirror of Simple Souls*. She was burned at the stake in 1310 in the Place de Grève by the Inquisition after a long struggle to win approval for her work.[43] Porete is Joan's direct predecessor in another way: her case created the precedent of submitting a summary of evidence from a provincial court to the University of Paris's canonists and theologians for assessment.[44] They found Marguerite's book suspect, and she was condemned. Yet her contemporary, whom she may even have known in Brabant, the Flemish Beguine Bloemardinne (d.c. 1335), was accorded the protection of Marie of Evreux, duchess of Brabant, and was revered as a holy thaumaturge during and after her life. She preached and prayed from a silver chair, in the erotic terms of the *Minnemystik*, or bride-mysticism. Angels were seen to accompany her to communion. She has been identified with Heylwig, from the patrician family of Bloemart, and, if this was the case, her powerful connexions probably saved her from the usual harassment.[45]

Though prophecy was a legitimate vocation for a woman at a time when any career was a rarity, it was a dangerous one. And it was becoming more dangerous. The Church has always found the rightful place of personal divine guidance a problem. The Bible contains numerous instances of it—above all, the speaking with tongues after the descent of the Holy Spirit at Pentecost (Acts 2:4). Whether the Virgin, present at this first Whitsun, became herself filled with the Holy Ghost has been debated. The text is not clear on this point. But the book was egalitarian to an unusual degree on the question of women's powers of prophecy: Miriam sang the prophetic hymn of triumph, beating her tambourine, after the Israelites passed through the Red Sea and the pharaoh's chariots were swallowed up (Exodus 15:20). The prophet Joel explicitly included women in the words of his god, who discriminates against no one: "And it shall come to pass afterward, that I will pour out my spirit upon all flesh; and your sons and your daughters shall prophesy, your old men shall dream dreams, your young men shall see visions: And also upon the servants and upon the handmaids in those days will I pour out my spirit" (Joel 2:28–29).

The mystic sought union with God. But the annihilation of self in the Godhead could dissolve all personal sin as well: hence the frequent charge that mystics heretically believed that they were not in a state of sin, that they could not be, that they did not need the Church to be absolved, for they reached the plenitude of grace in their visions. The problem reached a legal formulation in the Clementine Decrees of the Council of Vienne (1311–13), and they in turn provided a tool by which the inquisitor could crush beguinal movements and any individuals who appeared to hold beliefs that the Church—for the most part incorrectly—attributed to these mystics.[46]

Joan's cross-examiners at Rouen tried to manoeuvre her into admitting the heresy of impeccability. The connexion between visions and antinomianism—the belief that the soul, in perfect communion with the Godhead, is above the moral law—was very widespread in their inquisitorial handbooks and in popular anecdotes about heretics, enshrined in the Clementine Decrees. Joan countered them with skill, saying that she did not think she would receive her visions if she were in a state of sin.[47] But this reply was ambiguous, for it implied that she knew herself to be in a state of grace through her visions, not through the Church and God's sacraments. So Joan did not escape the charge, made commonly in fourteenth- and fifteenth-century Inquisition trials, that like a heretic she believed herself to be in a state of grace, however much she sinned.[48] She herself never made any assertion of that order.

Joan was a very plain speaker, with a very limited vocabulary; she was unequipped to deal in abstractions. Theological questions were beyond her sphere of curiosity; and to our knowledge, she never expanded on metaphysical or moral problems. We have no record of her preaching or even making any long speech; she never uttered a word of millenniarist doom, she never roused any audience to mass repentance for its sins, and she never saw the torments of the damned or any of the other commonplaces of medieval mystical experience. She shows no trace of the wide influence of Joachim of Flora's chiliastic prophecies, which were still echoing in Savonarola's sermons at the end of the century. Her enemy was simply the English, whom she wished to *"bouter hors de France"* (boot out of France), and, after the English, the heathen.[49] She never mentioned the Antichrist, who looms in the visions of illuminati throughout the medieval period. There is not a trace of Minnemystic in her.

So it is a mistake to place Joan in the tradition of mystical prophets so fundamental to political life in the fourteenth century. But her supporters did it, and it is among the chief reasons that they believed in her; her enemies did it, and it inspired them to attack her; history has done it, because to group Joan with other female contemporaries gives an appearance of system, which is one of the aims of history. But in Joan's case, the thrust of her ambition strikes aslant the main direction of prophecy in the Middle Ages. Joan was not a mystic: her visions are always of tasks to be accomplished in this world, not of the world to come. There was a widespread hunger, far exceeding Joan's own, for supernatural wonders. Simple events in her life, easily attributable to reason, were given complicated and irrational origins. The divine current electrifying her made her inexpressibly exciting. No one wanted it to dim. So when she sent for her special sword, and it was found under the ground at the shrine of Saint Catherine of Fierbois, it was a miracle; and her courage at Orleans, the storming and capture of Les Tourelles

after she was wounded was another. It was rumoured that she had persuaded Robert de Baudricourt to arm her because she knew, with clairvoyance, about the defeat of the French in the battle of Rouvray near
Orleans, the so-called Battle of the Herrings, in February and told him
about it *before* the news reached Vaucouleurs.[50] When a dying baby
revived for a few hours after he had been brought to her to cure in
March 1430, it was another prodigy.[51] Her judges were armed with
stories about her identifying an unworthy priest who lived with his
housekeeper and about her finding a lost cup.[52] Joan said she had never
heard of either incident. Even butterflies seen fluttering around her
standard at Château-Thierry were considered prodigious: witchcraft
to the prosecution, a godly marvel to Joan's supporters.[53] Her judges
reproached her angrily for allowing people to venerate her as a living
saint, for encouraging medals with her image to be struck and for
permitting followers to kiss her hands, her feet, her clothes. She was
adored by her own people, who ordered Masses and collects to be said
in her honour; her picture was set up in the churches. Her rings
were touched by the credulous. All this was false idolatry that she
encouraged.[54]

We have corroborating evidence of some of these charges made by
her enemies. A calendar from Grenoble contains three prayers to be
said at a Mass offered for Joan's safety after her capture in 1430. Prayers can of course be offered on behalf of anyone, no matter how
wretched or obvious a sinner, but the description of Joan tallies with
the accusation that she was thought a divine messenger, a saint in contact with the Almighty:

> Almighty and Everlasting God, Who in Thine holy and ineffable
> clemency and in Thine admirable power hast ordained the coming
> of a young girl for the glory and preservation of the realms of
> France and also to repel, confound and destroy the enemies of
> that kingdom, and Who has allowed that when she had devoted
> herself to the holy tasks by Thee commanded, she should be im-
> prisoned by the enemy, grant us, we beseeech Thee, through the
> intercession of the Blessed Mary ever a Virgin and all the Saints,
> that she may be delivered from their power without suffering any
> hurt and that she shall accomplish all that Thou hast prescribed
> by one and the same mission.[55]

When Joan entered Orleans, Jean Luillier, a mercer who gave evidence at the rehabilitation, tells us "she was received with as much joy

and enthusiasm by all, men and women, small and great, as if she had been an angel of God. For they hoped that, by her agency, they would be delivered from their enemies; as afterwards happened."[56] At Lagny, she was called to the church in which a baby, who had not stirred for three days, had been laid before an image of the Virgin. Other young girls of the town were praying there for the baby's life; and when Joan came, he yawned, changed colour and recovered sufficiently to be baptised before dying. He could then be buried in hallowed ground, a privilege not permitted to the stillborn.[57]

Miracles were expected of her: Joan herself registers either her surprise or her displeasure. Her strong words about the baby at Lagny, the he was "black as her tunic" before he changed colour, show that the incident had moved her deeply; she also tells the story more freely and clearly than others at her trial. But when asked about the cult surrounding her, she makes a distinction between the crowds' desires and her own.[58] Simon Beaucroix, one of Joan's companions at arms, said at her vindication: "Joan was very upset and most displeased when some good women came to greet her, and showed her signs of adoration. This annoyed her."[59]

It must have distressed her greatly. Joan had not set out to be a miracle worker; she had claimed she had a political mission in France that God had given to her to fulfil. But the fourfold mission—the raising of the siege of Orleans, the crowning of the king, the liberation of the duke of Orleans and the delivery of France from the English—had nothing to do with prodigies of raising from the dead or finding lost cups. The prophecies she made remain strictly within the narrow political sphere of the war with England, with the exception of her conviction that her voices would deliver her from captivity. She foretold the retreat of the English from the whole of France within seven years[60] (Charles's triumphal entry into Rouen, the English stronghold in Normandy, took place in 1449; but Paris was recovered in 1436, near enough fulfilling Joan's words of 1431); she knew beforehand that she would be wounded, above her breast, at the battle for Orleans;[61] and her voices had revealed to her that she would be taken.[62] Contrasted to the copious spouting of predictions by medieval prophets, Joan is extremely restrained. Even her account of the finding of the sword of Saint Catherine of Fierbois is sober, unadorned by the supernatural ornament given it by her friends (see Chapter 8).

Joan often rejected the role of living saint, refusing to perform in the manner expected, with cures or fortune-telling. Her public career as a seer was inaugurated before she left for Chinon, when a summons came from the sick duke of Lorraine, Charles, and she travelled to Nancy to see him. But her refusal to bother herself with his future shows she spurned the prophetic role. She only wanted his military support.

This type of discrepancy, between Joan's ambition on the one hand and the typecasting of those who showed a friendly interest in her on the other, appears throughout her story. For instance, seers like Catherine of Siena and Bridget of Sweden, as well as lesser preachers whose names are not so well known to us, made it their business to pronounce on the papal schism. Division, as we have seen, was their forcing-ground and their main sustenance. Joan was again identified with this type of prophet, and again the mistake was not of her seeking, was of no interest to her, and placed her in great danger.

Once Joan had become famous, Jean, count of Armagnac, wrote her letters asking her which pope should command his allegiance. On 22 August 1429, Joan despatched an answer to him from Compiègne. In it, she said she was too busy with the war to find out at the moment, but as soon as she reached Paris, he should get in touch with her again and she would let him know. She dictated it in great haste just as she was mounting her horse, she said at her trial, and if she had not let the messenger go, he would have been thrown in the water and not by her: one imagines a camp preparing for attack.[63] She temporised, and it plunged her in terrible trouble: the orthodox Christian world in 1429 recognised without question Pope Martin V in Rome. Yet Joan, who purported to know things directly from God, inadvertently threw doubt on this by her deferred answer to the count of Armagnac.

The count was among those who had given their loyalty to the Avignon line. He had been excommunicated and debarred from his lands and family by Martin V for his disloyalty. If Joan had answered that Martin V was without doubt the true pope, he would probably have felt honourably released from his previous vows of fealty and changed sides, thus regaining his possessions. But Joan failed to give him this comfort and at the same time got herself stuck in the lime of Church politics.[64]

Innocent ignorance combined with lack of interest can be the only grounds of her letter. At the trial, she asks, with a sweetness and simplicity one can still hear, are there really two popes? Then she adds that she feels sure that we ought to obey our lord the pope who is in Rome and that he is the one she believes in. It seems probable she did not even know his name.[65]

But because she was a prophet who should know secret things, she was charged with overweening presumption: not only had she placed the true pope in doubt, but "holding of little weight the authority of the universal Church, preferring her word to the authority of the whole Church, she affirmed that after a certain period of time to come, she would answer him as to whom she should believe, and that she would have discovered it through the counsel of God."[66]

Joan's attachment to the Church Militant, the Church on earth, was indeed light, as her judges often pointed out. But there is no reason for us now, in the light of modern ecclesiology, to see this as disobedience to God. In her own time, Joan's aloof disregard of ecclesiastical institutions was violent and unusual. Her career lies outside the main current of medieval mysticism because her consistent tendency was to prefer secular channels of power to religious ones. She did not, for instance, operate from a basis in orders. Unlike so many of the prophets before her, she was not a nun, nor had she even taken third vows, dedicating herself to God, but remaining in the world. Her vow of virginity was made privately. She appealed to the king not through the Church, but through the lay chain of command, represented by the garrison at Vaucouleurs.

She was pleased, as she told her judges, when the communal vision of her crown sign was seen by the clergy of her party and converted them to her side. She showed unceasing marks of intense private fervour in prayer and sacraments. But she did not use the Church to underpin her mission. Her voices told her to seek out Robert de Baudricourt, the commander of the local royal fortress. From that first decision, the secular savour of her enterprise was given, for she could have gone to Toul, the seat of her diocese's bishop, and used the political power in its ecclesiastical form to help her. She knew Toul; she had been there, in the Church court itself, to defend herself against the breach of promise charge.[67] Toul cathedral towers above the watermeadows of the wide Meuse valley. As Joan walked or rode southward from Domremy, she would have seen it ahead from a great distance, and the sight, so striking today, must have been equally unforgettable then. But she did not remember Toul cathedral when she wanted help. She did not even tell a priest about her mission—a fact that was to prove a great stumbling block in the process of her canonisation in this century, as well as proof

of her irreligiousness in 1431. Unlike the female mystics we have mentioned, Joan had no confessor nor acolyte to hear the secrets of her soul
and interpret them for her, to urge her on and stiffen her resolve. She
was friendless in the religious world. Jean Pasquerel, an Augustinian
friar who joined Joan's retinue at Tours before the battle at Orleans,
became her confessor, according to the rehabilitation. We have heard
nothing about him before this. His disposition of 1456 contains stories
that place Joan firmly in the circle of medieval clairvoyants: when the
man swore at her that she would be a maid no longer after a night with
him, she told him he would be dead soon, and so it turned out; she foretold she herself would be wounded, just above her breast; she gave the
king a secret sign at Chinon. Pasquerel strikes the reader as so self-serving that he has even been suspected of being a plant by the court, who
wished to observe Joan closely from the privacy of the confessional
itself.[68]

Joan does not talk about Pasquerel, nor of any priests except the
curé who gave her communion, the Franciscan friars at Neufchâteau
who sometimes heard her confession, and Regnault of Chartres, archbishop of Rheims, who gave Joan such an earnest and solid belief in
herself that she asked her judges: "Send for him; he will not dare contradict what I have told you."[69] But Rheims had already disowned her
in favour of his new totem, Guillaume the Shepherd.

Joan knew "neither A from B," said one witness of 1456.[70] Her
last letters bear what is probably her own signature, but in May 1431
she made a cross on documents, so that her name on the last writings
made in freedom was probably traced with another's help.[71] She knew
her prayers: her mother taught her the *Pater Noster*, the *Ave Maria*
and the *Credo*.[72] She uses proverbs from time to time, like "God helps
those who help themselves" and the child's saying, "A man can be
hanged for telling the truth."[73] She never uses a biblical tag nor mentions
the name of any character from the New or Old Testament except for
the Virgin, Jesus and the angels Michael and Gabriel. A country girl in
the 1420s, she could hardly be of the people of the Book, but she shows
no knowledge of it at all, not even the occasional reminiscence from
some sermon or homily she may have heard. The lack of apocalyptic
material in her visions may be due to this, for a knowledge of John's
revelations that close the New Testament permeates the mystical tradition. It was not necessary to be literate to absorb it; verbal and visual
means of communication disseminated John's violent dooms very

widely. But the mystics of the Middle Ages' golden era were literate; for the most part, they were well-born, like Catherine of Siena, Heylwig and Jeanne-Marie de Maillé. Joan betrays no knowledge of the Apocalypse whatsoever. Her angels have promised her she will go to paradise;[74] the word *hell*, or *damnation*, does not rise quickly to her lips at her trial. This sobriety did not help Joan, because it circumscribed the range of her prophecies and limited the ambiguity of their meaning. It made her claims extravagant, while their nonfulfilment cast doubts on the heavenly origins she asserted, for which she would accept no other authority than her own conviction. This was the position of a visionary, but a visionary of the kind that had always troubled the Church and given rise to accusations of heresy.

CHAPTER 5

HARLOT OF THE ARMAGNACS

For the lips of a strange woman drop as an honey-comb, and her mouth is smoother than oil; but her end is bitter as wormwood, sharp as a two-edged sword. Her feet go down to death; her steps take hold on hell.

PROVERBS 5 : 3 – 5

The University of Paris was a stronghold of European learning, one of the most distinguished bodies of theologians in Christendom. It was from this noble and learned institution, not from the English occupiers of France, that the call came for Joan of Arc's examination on suspicion of heresy. On 25 May 1430, the very day after her capture, the doctors of the faculty of theology wrote to the duke of Burgundy, in his capacity of overlord to John of Luxembourg, and requested that he order his vassal to hand her over for trial.[1] When the same body of doctors deliberated the charges drafted against her, one year later, they were assessing the evidence of a formal and traditional trial of the Inquisition. They returned the verdict that "having weighed the aim, manner and matter of [Joan's] revelations, the quality of her person, and the place and other circumstances, they are either lies of the imagination, corrupt and pernicious, or the said apparitions and revelations are conjured up and proceed from malign and diabolical spirits, Belial, Satan, Behemoth."[2] Joan was an invoker of evil spirits, an idolator, an apostate; though the explicit word *sorcière*—"witch"—was not used by the doctors, all Joan's heretical crimes included activities and attitudes ascribed to witches.[3] Her side saw her as a holy virgin; her enemies, as a polluted sorceress. For her side, for a time, she confirmed their faith; for the other, she was a heretic who subverted the Church's authority. Their stances were mirror images of each other, for her followers and her executioners belonged to one culture and one place, and they shared the same dread of evil and the same thirst for an antidote.

After John the Fearless, duke of Burgundy, was murdered in 1419, his right hand was cut off as a precautionary measure, to undo the sorceries his enemies believed he practised. Two court favourites of Charles himself—Pierre de Giac (in 1426) and Le Camus de Vernet (in 1427)—were later assassinated at the orders of rivals to the Dauphin's favours; both murders were justified on the ground that the dead men were possessed. Each also lost a hand in death.[4] During the same reign, the terror of *maleficium* and the Faustian powers it promised grew to such enormousness that Gilles de Rais, Joan's intimate and fighting companion, marshal of France and one of the greatest inheritors in France, confessed to the murder of unnumbered children, sacrifices to a devil he believed would visit him if he satisfied him with enough evil. Gilles was tried and hanged as a sorcerer and a mass murderer in 1440, nine years after Joan died, though it is not at all clear that his witch-trial was any more reliable than his contemporaries'.[5] In the same year as her rehabilitation, her other close friend and comrade-in-arms, D'Alençon, was also tried for treason allied with sorcery.[6] On the other side of the Channel, the picture was no different. Eleanora Cobham, duchess of Gloucester and sister-in-law of the regent of England, was denounced for using witchcraft to depose or kill the boy king Henry VI and replace him with her husband. She had consulted necromancers, it was alleged, out of ambition for her family's future. Her associates were hanged and burned; her life was spared, but she was sentenced to walk in penitential dress through London and then exiled to the Isle of Man. Shakespeare dramatises her fall in *Henry VI, Part II*, in which, as in *Macbeth*, the witches' prophetic words all prove to be true.[7]

It was among the richest, the most learned, the most privileged, the highest of England and of France that the terror of heresy and the practice of witchcraft took its firmest hold. When Jean Petit, a renowned doctor of the University of Paris, preached a notorious sermon in 1407 justifying the murder of the duke of Orleans by the duke of Burgundy according to the Church's tradition of permitted tyrannicide, one of the reasons he gave was the necromancy practised by Louis of Orleans. According to Petit, Louis cast spells. An amulet that he wore against his breast contained the crushed bone-dust of a hanged man. His right hand, too, was severed after his death (19). Petit himself was admired for his powers of prophecy and was known to have predicted the great frost of 1407 and the massacre of the rebellious Liégeois in 1408.[8]

Louis certainly kept about him men of learning who worked the borderline between science and magic, astrologers using the astronomical knowledge of the day to make forecasts and their chemical expertise to search for the philosopher's stone. Almost all Louis's contemporaries among the higher nobility who could afford it retained such people in their households. Curiosity about the supernatural led them into dangerous dabblings with ill-understood forces, spelling danger, suspicion and crime—not because witchcraft summons the devil without, if indeed evil does have an independent life, but because it conjures demons within.

Jean Petit preached his famous sermon at the duke of Burgundy's orders, but he was no doubt sincere in the accusation he made against Louis. The charge of witchcraft was beginning to weigh hard, whereas a hundred years before, men of equal standing in the Church had scorned it. The battle to master arcane powers was internecine: one of Louis's astrologers, Master Gencien of Beaugency, had denounced one of the duke of Burgundy's men of science as a heretic and a magician. His quarry was later burned.[9] Nor was the feeling for witchcraft confined to circles outside the faith: the papal court at Avignon was riddled with dread of black magic, ever since Pope John XXII, fascinated and at the same time appalled, had crystallised his fears in one of the fundamental documents that laid down the path of the great witch-hunt of the sixteenth and seventeenth centuries. His constitution of 1326–27, *Super Illius Specula*, permitted the use of the Inquisition against ritual magic alone, not only against heresy allied with magic.[10]

This credulous, suspicious, tormented, guilt-racked society was conjuring its own dreams; where the inquisitor appears, there immediately you find the devil and the witch. The devil's features themselves were gaining sharper definition. In the twelfth century, on the reliefs of Conques and Moissac, for instance, he appeared monstrous and misshapen, a loathsome being, a mere assemblage of grotesque limbs and features, related to humanity only on the most broken of evolutionary chains.[11] By the end of the fourteenth and beginning of the fifteenth century, the devil was sometimes incarnate in ordinary human flesh, as Christ himself was; evil began to take on a cast of countenance as anthropomorphic as Jesus. *Les Très Riches Heures du Duc de Berri,* one of the most richly illuminated and most beautiful of the prayer-books that were painted in dozens for the aristocracy of the time, reflects its opulence, grace and frivolity, but at the same time its profound spiritual fixation. The Limbourg brothers painted this manuscript, around the time of Joan's birth, for Jean, duke of Berry, uncle of John the Fearless and his saddened adversary in the civil war in France.

One of the illuminations shows Lucifer's fall. In it, he is indeed the unrivalled archangel of archangels, streaming down galactic stardust toward hell, his blonde curls, pale naked body, serious sweet youthfulness the inverted image of the crucified, Hanged Man of the Tarot. The rebel angels whom he led flow down after him like sparks of fire[12] (3). Elsewhere in the book, the images of the devil are less surprising: in the image of exorcism, he appears a bat-winged, black hobgoblin, and in the large illumination of hell's lower depths, he lies on a gridiron, a bloated monster, exhaling a blast of fire in which naked souls are hurled upward.[13] The young blonde prince Lucifer, painted for the duke of Berry around 1413, leads us more surely into the most frightened corner of the contemporary mind. One of the greatest medieval terrors was the protean cunning of the devil and one of the greatest tools of discipline for the Church was that she alone had the knowledge, the authority and the guidance to recognise the devil's presence, however brilliant his disguise. He could assume at will a human shape, male or female, to tempt souls; above all, he could appear divinely beautiful, radiant, worthy of the adoration reserved for God alone. The fanged, clawed, cloven-hoofed monster of the early Middle Ages was firmly set to one side of human experience. His habitat was an elsewhere into which a soul could be snatched away; it could coexist not in the real world, but only below it. But the human devil's dwelling place became here, inside each one of us, gnawing at the divisions between himself and us, eroding the border between hell and earth. Once the devil has human shape, all ordinary human sufferings, not only extraordinary disasters, can testify to his presence. The Bourgeois de Paris comments often on unnatural occurrences—a spring running blood, the birth of Siamese twins —and he diagnoses in them supernatural signs and punishments of ambiguous origin.[14] Such strange horrors can more understandably be caused by a malignant fate, but this period is the time when the most

natural of human experiences, mortality itself, seems to fall to the devil's
portion. It seems at times as if he were acting as the agent of God
Himself in anger. *The Dance of Death*, the grisly ring-à-roses of skele-
tons dragging off men and women by the hand to their ultimate fate,
was painted in 1425, the Bourgeois tells us, in fresco on the walls of
the Cimetière des Innocents in Paris.[15]

Death also provides the theme that most inspired the sombre skills
of the Rohan Master. This artist, who painted the early fifteenth-century masterpiece, *The Rohan Book of Hours*, was under the patronage
of Yolande of Anjou, the mother-in-law of Joan's Dauphin. Yolande,
queen of Sicily, lived in the Valois court and wielded a subtle but
powerful influence in every field. Though the Rohan Master's name
is not known to us, his style cannot be mistaken, and he is much darker,
more intense than the lyrical, nature-loving Limbourg brothers. Yolande
had bought *Les Belles Heures du Duc de Berri* from his estate after his
death in 1416, and so the Limbourgs' work was available to the Rohan
Master. But he often surpasses them in originality of composition,
displaying an almost modern ability to disturb and alarm. One extraordinary illuminated page, the illustration for the Mass of the Dead, shows
a body lying in stiff grip of death, pricked with wormholes and beginning to decay.[16] This was the imagery that governed the court Joan
entered in 1429.

Death—like the devil, to whom death is analogous—could not be
held down under lavish rituals and display; he was forcing his way to
consciousness, breaking up through the forms that embellished life. It
is at this time, too, that familiar images showed death the reaper carrying
off lords and ladies out hunting, or appearing in order to end their
pleasures, as in the parable of the Three Living and Three Dead.[17] The
same desiccated corpse, halfway down the path to the skeletal and all
the more macabre for the fragments of flesh that still adhere to its bones,
appeared to Louis of Orleans in a dream before he was murdered. For
death was not the devil himself, but rather the image of the person
about to die, his or her future self. However, death belonged to the
devil's realm, because it had entered the world with the Fall; and that
fall was replicated in each sinner's life, especially at the moment he
or she left it, when the devil tussled with the angels to gain possession
of the departing soul. Only through the extraordinary mercy (and
deliberately blind eye) of the Virgin Mary and other saints could the
ordinary human expect to come out the other side of this battle safe

I

Left: The murder of John the Fearless, duke of Burgundy, who is painted here by Jan van Eyck, severed hopes of reconciliation between the houses of France and Burgundy, allied Burgundy with the English claim to rule in France and so plunged the country into another bitter phase of the Hundred Years' War (CHAPTER 2).

Below: Les Vigiles du Roi Charles VII, a rhyming history of his reign by Martial d'Auvergne, was richly illustrated with miniatures in a manuscript of 1484, but the artist neglected the documentary evidence of Joan's life in favour of a more conventionally feminine martyr with long blonde hair.

2

4

Left: Saint Catherine of Alexandria, one of Joan's voices and one of the most popular saints of Joan's time, was tortured on the wheel that is her emblem. Angels visited her in prison afterwards and anointed her wounds, as shown in this illumination from the Limbourg brothers' *Belles Heures* (CHAPTER 6).

Left: The Fall of the Rebel Angels, painted by the Limbourg brothers for *Les Très Riches Heures du Duc de Berri,* uses only the sumptuous blend of gold leaf and azur d'outremer, made from crushed lapis lazuli, to express a solemn warning that evil can come in sympathetic—even beautiful—human shape (CHAPTER 5).

Right: Saint Margaret of Antioch, another legendary martyr, was Joan's other female voice. She refused marriage with a Roman prefect, seen here riding past, rather than lose her virginity. In this miniature, Jean Fouquet showed Margaret keeping sheep in the same iconography of holy simplicity that was later chosen to depict Joan herself (CHAPTERS 6 AND 12).

5

Saint Michael the archangel was the first
of Joan's voices to tell her of her mission to
save France. The country's patron saint,
he epitomised the spirit of chivalry that
helped to give France's wars a sacred
character and, in his epicene sexlessness,
painted here by Gentile da Fabriano,
expressed the angelic androgyny
that Joan's transvestism strived
to achieve (CHAPTERS 6 AND 7).

6

7

8

Above: The city of Orleans commissioned this painted banner in the early sixteenth century to be carried in the annual procession giving thanks for the raising of the siege in 1429 (CHAPTER 9). Joan kneels beneath Orleans's patron saints, Aignan and Euverte, with the then duke of Orleans opposite her. Her raised hands, her long hair and her armour were influenced by the city's earlier monument to her and, in turn, inspired Rubens's figure, painted around 1620 (*right*).

Above: Claude Deruet, court painter to the dukes of Lorraine at the beginning of the seventeenth century, specialised in fantasias, like this pyrotechnical allegory of the element Fire, and had a special fascination with Amazons. In his circle at Nancy, Joan was identified with the dashing cavaliers whom Deruet portrayed (CHAPTER 10).

Right: After the edition and publication of Joan of Arc's trial in the 1840s, images of the heroine began to include accurate historical detail, as in Ingres's monumental painting of Joan, standing by the altar in Rheims cathedral during Charles's coronation and holding her battle standard in her hand. It had undergone the suffering, she said, so it deserved the glory (CHAPTER 12).

Left: Minerva, goddess of wisdom and peace, survived as another manifestation of the righteous female warrior. Christine de Pisan, the poet and historian who was Joan's contemporary, evoked her as muse in her treatise on the arts of war (CHAPTERS 8 AND 11).

Below: The convention of personifying the Virtues as female stemmed from classical philosophy and held throughout the Western tradition, as in this Botticelli allegorical fresco of a Florentine bride, Giovanna degli Albizzi, receiving the Cardinal Virtues: Temperance, Prudence, Justice and Fortitude. Joan of Arc, as a figure of heroic virtue, belongs to this tradition (CHAPTER 11).

13

14

In World War II, Joan of Arc became the figurehead for both sides in occupied France. A pro-German poster of 1943, *above,* declares that criminals always return to the scene of their crime and shows Rouen burning under Allied bombs beside Joan at the stake (CHAPTER 13), while another image of Joan's martyrdom, *left,* bears the cross of Lorraine, emblem of the Gaullist resistance to the Vichy government (CHAPTER 13).

from Satan's clutches. Death and hell were inseparable, for instance, in the dramatic moral teaching of a much reprinted illustrated work like the *Ars Moriendi*, in preachers' sermons and in both popular and elevated poetry.[18]

The devil could dissolve the ancient boundaries between ontological categories: he could seem sublime; he could assume the appearance of grace. He could adopt the recognisable features of a good, beloved person, sometimes a known saint. He had always possessed this cunning for those most fearful of him. In the monastery of Cluny, which was haunted by devils, he even appeared disguised as the abbot of Grotta-ferrata.[19] In literature, the charms of his female disguises had tempted Saint Antony Abbott and Saint Jerome. Hincmar, archbishop of Rheims in the ninth century, maintained a demon could seduce a woman by appearing to her in the form of the man she loved.[20] To Saint Pachomius, he had even taken on the appearance of Christ himself. One of the major refinements on this theme in early fifteenth-century art was that the devil began to appear more frequently in the form of a beautiful woman. He often assumes that shape and becomes the mirror image of Eve herself during the temptation in the garden. The serpent has a pretty face and a pretty bosom in the Limbourg brothers' illumination of the Fall in the *Très Riches Heures*; in a French manuscript of Augustine's *City of God*, of the same period, the snake is also a woman.[21] In Italy, in Germany, in Holland, exquisite feminine demons with braided hair and jewelled necks and limbs begin to haunt the fifteenth-century temptations of Saint Antony and deathbed scenes.

Thus it was altogether possible for Joan's voices to be demonic, however heavenly their appearance. This was the ambiguity at the heart of the society that tried Joan of Arc, the crevasse that opened at its feet. It was wedded to an ancient dualism, seeing an eternal contest between absolute good and absolute evil taking place perpetually in the world and in the microcosm of each person's soul; but such a cosy surface of absolutism was cracked by a deep relativism in the diagnosis and location of evil. The society was pain-wracked and haunted; it sought to pinpoint the nature and the place of evil, to find the person embodying it, because in an age when the patterns of thought have become anthropomorphic, it must be embodied. This attempt was like trapping mercury, for what seemed evil slipped away from the analyst's finger and thumb with maddening agility. The location most feared for evil's thriving was in the heart of heresy and of heresy's handmaid, witchcraft. Therefore, in a case like Joan's, it is often difficult to disentangle accusations of specific *maleficium* from terror of general heterodoxy. The former is an effect of the latter, but often its most characteristic and revealing mark. Joan's cross-examiners concentrated on charges of minor sorcery because by implicating her in such activities, she would be naturally guilty of the more fundamental crime.

The terror of heterodoxy which gripped the nobility was intensified during Joan's brief lifetime in her immediate surroundings by an extremely dangerous development of the crisis in the Church, brought about by the lengthy and seemingly unresolvable Schism.[22] In Bohemia, the revolutionary thinker Jan Hus, inspired by the writings of the Englishman John Wycliffe, had declared that the Church was a solely spiritual body, with no dominion in secular matters, and that it was composed of those members only who were in a state of grace. This doctrine, which swiftly achieved a large and fervent following, controverted the most fundamental principles of papal and episcopal and clerical authority of the church. With its emphasis on the witness of the individual and its stand against the ecclesiastical hierarchy, Hussitism represents the most egalitarian and libertarian aspects of early Protestantism. Jan Hus himself, tricked into trusting Rome, was summoned to Constance to be examined by the Church council there convened; his safe conduct was not respected, and he was condemned and burned in 1415, fourteen years before the events that brought Joan of Arc to prominence in France. With Hus's death, the Hussite menace only increased, and in 1427, Pope Martin V took the extreme step of ordering the cardinal of Winchester, his legate in England, to raise an English army to fight the Hussites in Bohemia. This force was to be a holy army, a crusade.[23]

Martin V's vigilance communicated the same fear to the great administrators and ecclesiastics of the day: that heterodoxy of thought would lead to social and political upheaval, and that where the authority of the church weakened, there too would civilised values and social order decline. The duke of Bedford, writing to his king in 1428, grieved bitterly at the contemporary state of affairs and expressed his fears of the devil's work: "the malice of him that been about to subvert the Christian and Catholic faith . . . and not only the faith but all political rule and governance, stirring the people to rebellion and disobedience of her lords and governors."[24]

The duke of Bedford took no direct part in Joan of Arc's trial, though he was in keen sympathy with its aims. But there were present other eminent and influential clerics in the Lancastrian party who were as conscious as Bedford of the threat of heresy to the stability of institutions. (Indeed, as if to prove their fears valid, popular discontent and heresy continued to be linked well into the seventeenth century.) William Alnwick, bishop of Norwich, who attended one session of Joan's trial, came fresh from extirpating Wycliffite heresy in his diocese; he had recently sent three relapsed heretics to the stake. Robert Gilbert, who was present when Joan was finally sentenced, had served on an Oxford University commission into the theological errors committed by Wycliffe.[25] A heightened sensitivity to the devil's works animated Joan's cross-examiners, and as the interrogation was prolonged, session after session, through part of February, March, April and part of May 1430, it became clear that this unlettered girl, be she acquainted with the teachings of Wycliffe or Hus or not, shared with them an unshakeable conviction in the primacy of the individual conscience. Joan stated again and again that she knew the truth of her revelations independently of the Church and knew it despite what the Church's authorities might say. In this respect she defied the Church Militant and thus declared herself a heretic. It has been only very recently, in the constitution of Vatican II and the new theology of the laity, that a stand like Joan's has been legitimate.[26]

The heterodoxy Joan's judges saw in her did not taint only her spiritual self. It recreated her physical being in a polluted image that forms an exact opposite to the icon of seamless and virginal integrity presented by her partisans. It inspired a tradition of portraying Joan of Arc as a harlot and a witch which lasted from her day until the eighteenth century in England and in history and literature deriving from England.

Joan of Arc, a historical woman without a historical face, becomes diabolically ugly. Whereas the French comment on the temptations her beauty presented and on her signal chastity, the English, if they credit her with purity at all, maintain she was so ugly that she had no difficulty. Edward Hall and his plagiarist Grafton describe her face as *"foule."*[27] They also see her as lecherous and impure. Her confessor, Jean Pasquerel, testified at her vindication that Joan broke down and wept at the insults hurled at her by the English from the fort of Les Tourelles on the bridge at Orleans before the battle. She had sent a letter to the English commander Glasdale, ordering the English to surrender and

leave; they retorted with barrack-room ribaldry at her effrontery, calling her the harlot of the Armagnacs.[28] The duke of Bedford, regent of
France, wrote to Charles VII in September 1429, after the defeat of
the English at Orleans in May and the coronation at Rheims in August.
His letter, in its haughtiness and ferocity, ranks with the missives of
Chinese emperors: "This is not and will not be tolerated! Consider the
means you have used and still use to delude and abuse the ignorant. You
are aided and abetted most of all by superstitious and depraved individuals, by that disorderly and deformed travesty of a woman, who dresses
like a man, whose life is dissolute . . . rather than by the force and
power of arms."[29] The charge that Joan's life ran at cross-purposes to
nature, that by her male dress she offended a divinely ordained order,
was crucial to her condemnation, as we shall see when we consider her
dress: but Bedford also believed that she was "dissolute."

The French chronicler Monstrelet, whose loyalty to his patrons
and protagonists, the Luxembourg family, rallied him to the cause of
the house of Burgundy, displays anger mingled with contempt when he
talks of Joan. Another Burgundian sympathiser, Jean de Wavrin,
changed Monstrelet's *"ladite Pucelle"* to *"femme monstrueuse."*[30] Monstrelet relates that Joan had been an ostler, helping at an inn with the
horses, riding them, and doing other jobs and acquiring other skills "that
young girls do not usually do."[31] The inference is plain, for the same
slur appears in the trial, when Joan was charged with leaving home
without permission at the age of fifteen to stay with a woman called
La Rousse (the Redhead) at an inn in Neufchâteau "where many
unguarded women stayed and the lodgers were for the most part
soldiers."[32] Nicknames of this sort were applied to independent women
conducting their own affairs and, often as not, making money at it.
In the sixteenth century, La Reine d'Hongrie and La Capitaine des
Vaches were heads of households in Lyons; a woman called La Varenne
was a midwife in Le Mans; another, La Catelle, was a schoolmistress in
Paris: in Orleans, a pedlar was known as La Grosse Marguerite.[33] Joan,
it was alleged, lived profligately with this dubious woman La Rousse,
visited nearby Toul frequently, and spent everything she had. On account of her immorality, the man she was betrothed to refused to marry
her, so she summoned him to court for breach of promise. According
to this story, the fiancé then died—conveniently for the purposes of the
evidence—while the case was pending.[34]

Joan of Arc rebutted the charge vigorously, telling her judges, as

we have seen, that she had pledged her virginity to God. When the
original seventy charges were distilled into twelve, the reference to
La Rousse herself was dropped, but Joan was still accused of living
with men-at-arms and of "never, or rarely, having another woman with
her."[35] The patent tendentiousness, and also the unsureness of the accusations, can be seen in that "never, or rarely." But the charge was
still made.

It was of paramount importance to Joan's accusers that her body
be corrupted and unholy. Her declared love of virginity was used,
later in the same document, only to be twisted into the terrible sin of
presumption, a belief that her saints had promised her paradise if she
remained chaste.[36] According to the witness Michel Lebuin at the
vindication, inquiries were made in Domremy in early 1431 to obtain
information about Joan's mores; Jean Moreau, a merchant living in
Rouen, amplified this statement. In the usual secondhand fashion of so
much of the rehabilitation testimony, he said that he had met a man
at Rouen who had helped with the inquiry and that when the latter had
failed to produce anything damaging, Pierre Cauchon, Joan's leading
judge, called him "a traitor and a sinner." Cauchon then refused to
pay him because he had heard "nothing about Joan that he would not
have liked to hear about his own sister." The same charge of disloyalty
to the English in France was made to Nicolas Bailly, a scrivener and
magistrate, who had taken part in the same commission and found
nothing in Joan's childhood or adolescence that would count against
her.[37] These reminiscences could have been prompted by the eagerness
of the French in 1456 to prove Joan's innocence; on the other hand,
they might also reflect authentic distress on the part of her enemies
that they could not pin any unchastity upon her. Between Bedford's
letter of 1429 and the final condemnation for heresy in 1431, all accusations of dissoluteness disappear. As Courcelles admitted at the rehabilitation, the evidence would have been used against her, if it had existed.

But for the purposes of Joan's treatment, this reality was of no
consequence. The body that for one side was impermeable and unbroken
became vulnerable, broken, permeable, impure to the other. This opposition expresses itself in the imagery used: where the French perceived a
dry, sealed vessel, a womb that had not undergone menarche, the
English found wetness, rottenness, sickliness and blood.

Her eating habits, so praiseworthy for her own side, become
repugnant to her enemies. When she is sick after the gift of carp in

prison, the promoter, Canon Jean d'Estivet, reproaches her bitterly, so the doctor Jean Tiphaine tells us: "It is you, you wanton, who have taken aloes and other things that have made you ill." She had vomited a great deal, he said. Guillaume de la Chambre, another doctor who attended Joan and gave evidence at the vindication, said that she had been bled to lower her fever. The earl of Warwick, governor of Rouen castle, warned them, "Take care with your bleeding. For she is a cunning woman and might kill herself." D'Estivet came in and abused Joan, calling her "a wanton and a whore." Joan began again to run a temperature.[38]

The coexistence of heresy and chastity in one person created intolerable tension: Haimond de Macy, the same knight who tried to caress Joan's breasts, testified at the repeal that he had visited her at Rouen as soon as she arrived. He was accompanying Warwick; the earl of Stafford, then constable of France on the English side; John of Luxembourg, who was handing Joan, his prisoner, over to the English; his brother, the bishop of Thérouanne; as well as Henry Beaufort, cardinal of Winchester, half-uncle to King Henry VI of England and his chancellor in France. It was a gathering of the most eminent and the most powerful men in the English presence in France. According to Haimond, John of Luxembourg offered a ransom for Joan on condition that she would fight the Burgundians no longer. It was, if it took place, a last-minute act of chivalry on the part of her captor. When Joan retorted that nothing would induce her to abandon her struggle against the invaders of France and their friends, it was alleged that Stafford lost his temper, drew his dagger and had to be restrained.[39]

Joan's intransigent conviction of her personal truth destroyed her enemies' equilibrium. The insults, the torments, above all the attempted violations are acts of defiance, not of confidence. Her supporters saw the sufferings of her captivity as a form of Christ-like passion; her enemies inflicted them to neutralise her power. Three witnesses at the later hearings about the trial of 1431 describe how Joan was sexually abused. Significantly, in all three cases, they place the attempt after the recantation Joan made and before she withdrew it. If the English guards did try to rape her, as these witnesses declare, they tried at a time when she had admitted that she was false, in the very brief interval when she had lost faith in herself. To lay hands on her body, they needed her word that its magic powers had run out.[40]

Although these anecdotes are told by the French at the vindication, they reflect how dangerous Joan's physical condition was for the English and their partisans. To exorcise its powers, they tried to reduce it to ordinariness. Ignoring the evidence of her chastity, the English circulated a rumour—at least it is possible that they did, since it appears in English chroniclers soon afterwards—that Joan herself admitted her unchastity. In *The Chronicles of England with the Fruit of the Times*, compiled by Caxton and another in 1480–83, a rumour comes to light that was perhaps put about by the English at the time: "And were all brought to Roen, and there she was put in pryson, and there she was judged by the lawe to be brent. And then she sayd that she was with childe; wherby she was respited a whyle; but in conclusyon, it was founde that she was not with chylde, and then she was brent in Roen."[41] In the last act of *Henry VI, Part I*, Joan makes the same plea, but her claim is again a ruse to obtain reprieve. When she hears Warwick calling for enough faggots to burn a maid, she names two candidates for father-hood: first D'Alençon, then René of Anjou. At last, imprecating and cursing and calling on her familiars like a veritable witch, she collapses and confesses she lied about the child. Whether she lied about the lovers is left unanswered.

This slander on Joan had a brief life in France as well, surprisingly. The historian Girard du Haillan, in what is regarded as the first account of the nation's story published in French in 1570, knows he is being provocative when he casts doubts on her virginity: "Some say that this Joan was the mistress of John, bastard of Orleans, others of the sire of Baudricourt, others of Poton" [Xaintrailles, her fellow soldier]. His contemporary, François de Belleforest, waxed indignant at Haillan's slur: "I am amazed that a Frenchman should yield to the fantasies of foreigners."[42]

Shakespeare expresses the serious ideas at issue, for his portrayal of Joan seizes on the polarity of her image to strong dramatic effect. To the Dauphin, she is holy:

> *No longer on St Denis will we cry,*
> *But Joan la Pucelle shall be France's saint.*

To Bedford, she is profane:

> *Coward of France! how much he wrongs his fame . . .*
> *To join with witches and the help of hell.*[43]

In the accusations of the trial, Joan's impurity was compounded by blasphemy. Article XI of the charges drafted against her declared

that she became "familiar" with Robert de Baudricourt, the captain at
Vaucouleurs, who sent her on her way to Chinon. She boasted to him
that, after her mission was accomplished, she would have three sons, of
whom the first should be pope, the second emperor, the third king.
Robert rejoined he should like to father one of them himself, but Joan
rebuked him, saying her children would be the work of the Holy Spirit.
Joan denied the charge, which had not been even raised during her
interrogation. Interestingly, Robert himself was cited as the source.
This is not impossible, since little in his subsequent career gives the
man much dignity.[44]

In the year of Joan's death, he joined up with another local commander, the Damoiseau de Commercy, and attacked neighbouring Toul.
He was taken prisoner and censured by the Church for violating ecclesiastical land. At this stage, Charles VII refused to extend help even
to the man who had introduced the Maid to court, and Baudricourt,
failing to gather the ransom money, remained in gaol until his death
in 1454. The sentence was lifted, however, so he could be buried in
sacred ground.[45] Baudricourt has become famous in the lives and dramas
about Joan of Arc, usually figuring as a doughty and generous-minded
soldier.[46] The other aspect, that he is one of the only two named
witnesses for the prosecution in Joan's trial (the other being Catherine
de La Rochelle), is not usually noticed: Robert de Baudricourt, the man
who first believed in her at Vaucouleurs enough to give her men-at-
arms, was as easily swayed to forswear her, it seems.

Guilty of lechery and falsehood, Joan also inspired widespread
belief in her maleficence. Dunois gave evidence that the earl of Suffolk,
one of the English commanders, had been shown the prophecy about the
champion who would "come from the *bois chesnu* and trample on the
backs of archers."[47] The graphic goriness and the apparent reference to
Joan's country of origin filled the English with dread. There were
desertions from their camp at the news of Joan's coming, and, after
the raising of the siege, instructions had to be issued to watch the boats
sailing back to England for departing troops.[48]

Again Shakespeare develops the imagery with telling bloodiness.
His Joan is Lady Macbeth's predecessor, conjuring spirits to steel her
strength and unsex her mind. She herself obeys a law of witchcraft,
that holy things are reproduced in mirror image by the unholy. She
promises her spirits a gruesome sacrifice:

> *O hold me not with silence over-long.*
> *Where I was wont to feed you with my blood,*
> *I'll lop a member off and give it you.*[49]

Bloodletting could be used to seal a pact, as a pledge of the witch's faith, because if given to the devil, it was a sign of surrender. Control a witch's blood, and you control her. Her blood was the innermost symbol of her being, the seat of life, the matrix. It was believed, for instance, that to scratch a witch cancelled her power, in the same way as one could avert her black magic with the name Jesus or with holy water. Letting the blood of a witch flow could place her in your power, could break the spell of her wholeness: her flow restored her to the normal world, where the blood of menstruation is a badge of lowliness and weakness.[50] So John Talbot, swearing to avenge the death of the English commander Salisbury, in Shakespeare's *Henry VI, Part I*, is particularly bloodthirsty:

> *Pucelle or puzzel, dolphin or dogfish,*
> *Your hearts I'll stamp out with my horse's heels*
> *And make a quagmire of your mingled brains.*

When he comes into hand-to-hand combat with Joan, he cries:

> *Devil, or Devil's dam, I'll conjure thee:*
> *Blood will I draw on thee, thou art a witch,*
> *And straightway give thy soul to him thou servest.*[51]

Joan's invulnerability to wounds, to bloodletting itself, terrified the English. On 7 May at Orleans, during the storming of the fort on the bridge, Les Tourelles, she was wounded in the breast by an arrow from a crossbow. Her soldiers suggested magic charms. She refused, using instead a poultice of lard and olive oil. As she said with some pride at her trial, in spite of the wound, she did not give up working, and within a fortnight she was healed.[52] When the English defenders saw her rise again, unharmed apparently by the arrow, and continue fighting as eagerly and as tirelessly as before, their courage died. This moment marks the turn of the tide of the battle, according to Dunois:

> Joan was wounded by an arrow which penetrated her flesh between her neck and her shoulder for a depth of six inches. Despite this, she did not retire from the battle and took no remedy against the wound. . . . I was going to break off, and intended the army to retire into the city. Then the Maid came up to me and requested

me to wait a little longer. Thereupon she mounted her horse and herself retired into a vineyard at some distance from the crowd of men; and in that vineyard she remained at prayer for the space of eight minutes. When she came back, she immediately picked up her standard and took up her position on the edge of the ditch. The moment she was there the English trembled with terror.[53]

Imperviousness to pain is always uncanny: in horror stories and films to this day, such powers of insensibility are often given to disciples of the fiend. In Joan's case, the uncanniness was increased by her foreknowledge: her chaplain, giving evidence in 1456, reported that she had told him on the eve of the battle of Les Tourelles, "Tomorrow blood will flow on my body from a wound above my breast."[54] At her trial, when she was asked if she really had known beforehand, she replied, "Indeed I did. . . . I told the king about it." But she denied that she had promised her soldiers that she would assume sacrificially all the wounds of the day in order to spare them.[55]

However, the fact that the judges even articulated such a question reveals their credulity and their absorption with her powers. The English side believed in Joan the Maid more than the French. If they had not, they would not have tried her judicially at such expense: in August 1430, a special tax was levied by the Estates of Normandy to raise 120,000 *livres*, of which 10,000 was set aside for the price of Joan's purchase from Louis of Luxembourg, her captor. If the French had continued to have a similar faith and dread of her, they would have tried harder to get her back, either by ransom or by force. Dunois attempted a skirmish outside Compiègne soon after her capture and seems to have proposed extending the war in Normandy later, perhaps with intent to rescue her. But the chronicler Antonio Morosini, writing to his Italian patrons at the time, is the only contemporary writer to report that Charles VII threatened reprisals against English prisoners in order to soften Joan's treatment. Otherwise the documents yield nothing about Charles's reaction to Joan's loss. There was apparently no attempt, on the part of the French, to raise a ransom for her.[56] This suggests, hard as it may seem, that Charles and his advisors were disillusioned enough to tolerate her condemnation as a heretic.

The Anglo-Burgundian party and their French adherents show by contrast an eager excitement in the pursuit of their quarry. In 1433, the duke of Bedford, writing to the government in London about affairs in France, attributed English losses above all to the unlawful supernatural forces deployed by Joan of Arc, "a disciple and limb of the Fiend, called the Pucelle, that used false enchantment and sorcery."[57] Joan had to be torn, like a rotten branch from the vine, as it was preached according to the text used by Master Guillaume Erard in the cemetery of St. Ouen, Rouen, to Joan when she was first condemned as a heretic.[58] The sentence of dismemberment inverts the sacrifice of her martyrdom, according to the dualist principle that opposing forces borrow from each other with chameleon-like ease. Diagnosis of good or evil thereby becomes all the more difficult. The floundering of these men of the fifteenth century, Joan's judges, has a long tradition behind it: the first Christian to be executed for witchcraft, the learned Spanish ascetic Priscillian (d. 385), justified his fascination with demonology and the hermetic sciences by saying, "we need to know about darkness, that we may desire the Lord's light."[59] The deeper the concern with rooting out evil, the closer up against it one is. The more the English magnified their task, the more afraid of their victim they became and the greater her uncanniness appeared. When Joan was in their power, they attributed to her demonic powers, just as the French themselves had before they decided to trust her. When Joan first appeared at Vaucouleurs, she was exorcised by Jean Fournier, its parish priest, who cried out, "If you are an evil spirit, avaunt! If you are a good spirit, approach!" Joan knelt before him and reproached him, saying how could he act so, when he had heard her confession.[60] Again, when she approached the town of Troyes in July 1429 on her way to Rheims with the Dauphin and his troops, as we have seen, she was met at the city gates by Brother Richard. He had been sent out to meet her because the people of Troyes feared that, as she herself reported in her trial, "she was not a thing from God." He sprinkled holy water over her and made the sign of the cross. With the good humour and stalwart good sense that marked Joan even in adversity, she taunted him: "Come forward boldly; I shan't fly away."[61]

Joan knew that witches were supposed to fly, and if she had been learned, she might have agreed with the Canon Episcopi of the ninth century; it laid down, as a matter of Church law, that night flying and metamorphosis of witches were hallucinations and anyone who credited such things was "beyond doubt an infidel and a pagan." The troubled witch-hunters of later centuries had difficulty explaining away this ancient tenet of the Church,[62] for belief in Sabbats visited by witches on broomsticks from far and wide became widespread, on the grounds that the devil had carried Christ himself to the top of the temple and tempted him to fly.

One of the diabolical powers most widely attributed to witches was the ability to suspend the natural order. When Joan's body was not guilty of unwholesomeness, magic powers to defy physical laws were attributed to it. The judges groped to lessen her force, asking her if she used charms or amulets. If she were dependent on some such instrument outside herself, she would be weaker in herself. In the battle at Jargeau, a town on the Loire that Joan retook in the giddy sequence of victories after Orleans during that summer campaign of 1429, she had fallen from a siege ladder. She was stunned by a rock thrown down from the fortifications. But her helmet shielded her from the full weight of the blow, and she recovered quickly. Her judges, alarmed by her invulnerability, asked her insinuatingly what she was wearing inside the lining of her helmet to protect her. She denied any charm.[63] At another time, she was accused of using a mandrake, the curiously anthropomorphic root by which sympathetic magic was practised on victims. Joan admitted she knew about its uses, but scoffed at the idea she would ever stoop to such a tool.[64]

Her captors were, therefore, thrown into a position inspiring greater fear: her powers were internalised, her faculties unassisted by external means. They were, for instance, terrified she would escape "by magic and trickery"[65] and expressed their fear in the numerous questions with which they plied her in the trial about her plans to set herself free. She was asked if her voices had promised her she would escape. She answered cryptically, exciting further suspicions: "That is not in your case; however I do not know when I shall be delivered. Those who wanted to get out of this world might well leave before me."[66] Twice more they asked her when she would be set free, and twice she answered that she would tell them when she could: "One day I must be delivered. But I want leave if I am to tell you; that is why I ask for a delay."[67] At the next session, two days later, they returned to the subject. Did she know by revelation whether she would escape? She demurred; they persisted; Joan admitted she did not know the day or the hour of her escape.[68] They were, it seems, trying to pin her down to a confession of knowing the future and of passing through solid obstacles by magic—both witch's faculties. In prison, she was asked how had she expected to escape from the castle of Beaulieu "between two pieces of wood." Joan retorted that if the porter had not seen her, she would have shut her keepers behind her, like a heroine of an adventure story. But "it seemed that it did not please God for her to escape then." Did God, or her voices, then give her permission to escape whenever she liked?[69] Again, the question is trying to catch Joan confessing to supernatural guidance for an act that was forbidden by the code of chivalry (though there was a contemporary debate about the obligations of prisoners and captors toward one another).[70]

Her first escape attempt from Beaulieu was not produced in the charges; but another try was the subject of cross-examinations in both a public and a private session. In the summer of 1430, Joan leapt from the tower of Beaurevoir castle, near Arras, where she was transferred by John of Luxembourg. Her questioner tried to make her admit either that she had tried to kill herself—a mortal sin—or that she believed, with the aid of her voices, that she could fly. With the ingenuous straight dealing that always marks Joan's replies to her judges' deviousness, Joan thwarted them by declaring that she threw herself off the tower of Beaurevoir in direct contradiction of her voices' commands, so that although she commended herself to God and Our Lady when she fell, she was wounded. Saint Catherine was "much angered" by her act. In the first session on her fall, she said she jumped when she learned she had been sold to the English and declared that she would rather "surrender her soul to God" than fall into their hands.[71] But this was a dangerous admission of a suicide attempt, and at the second session, she shifted her ground. She had wanted to jump free, she said, because she had heard that everyone over the age of seven in the nearby town of Compiègne was to die in the Burgundian siege, and she would rather die than survive that. Yes, she knew she had been sold, and she would also rather die than be held by the English, but Saint Catherine told her almost daily she must not throw herself off the tower, for God would help her and the people of Compiègne, too. Joan retorted—she obviously spoke to her voices with the same frankness she used with her judges— that if God was going to help Compiègne, she would like to be in on the act. Then Catherine told her she would be set free once she had seen the English king. "Really!" exclaimed Joan. "I did not want to see him."[72] Nor did her gaolers allow it: Henry VI had arrived in Rouen castle on 29 July 1430, five months before Joan, and stayed till the end of November the following year, when he was taken to Paris to be crowned king of France. But the king and his famous enemy were kept apart until Joan was safely destroyed.

For two to three days after her fall, Joan lay in bed, semi-conscious, without eating or drinking. When Catherine told her she must confess her fault and that Compiègne would be relieved before the next feast of Saint Martin that winter, she began to eat and to recover. On further questioning, she denied absolutely that she had hoped to kill herself. But her judges persisted: when she began to speak again, had she blasphemed against God and his saints, as it said in their evidence? With a pitiable lack of her usual fire, Joan faltered, saying she did not remember. Then she reiterated her patient trust in God and in her conscience, on which she always relied when tackled closely by her judges: "I refer myself to God, and to no other, and to my good confession."[73]

In the first draft of the charges, Joan is accused of boasting she would escape with the devil's help.[74] But when the leap from Beaurevoir appears in the final list, her enemies' words cut both ways: she sinned by trying to kill herself, though she knew she should not, because her voices had told her not to.[75] For their purposes at this point, disobedience toward her voices carries as great a penalty as obedience does in other contexts. Joan was either unruly or heretical; either a rebel to the promptings of her conscience or, on the many other occasions when she followed her voices' instructions, the tool of figments of an evil mind or of fiends themselves. This kind of double-think is rife in the charges; and it is endemic to the business of witch-hunting, for the very reason that the witch-hunter is the alleged witch's most committed believer.

By the time the story of Joan's leap from Beaurevoir reached the public, the elements had been scrambled to fit the shape of witchcraft stories. The Bourgeois de Paris reported: "she answered at once that . . . she would produce thunder and other marvels if she liked; that someone had once tried to molest her physically, but she had jumped from the top of a high tower without hurting herself at all."[76] One of the sources of this power to waive nature was, to both her friends and her enemies, her frequent communion. Both sides commented extensively on it, on her intense devotion to the Eucharist. By partaking of the Saviour, she ingested his strength, his goodness and his grace. In the fifteenth century, frequent communion was rare. In Italy, for instance, among the confraternities rising in popularity at that time among lay people with a marked pious bent, communion four times a year, with the important commemoration of Easter included, was considered unusual.[77] In England, only the Easter solemnity was normal for the laity.[78] Joan's circle at court far exceeded this. Albert d'Ourches, a knight who had known Joan at Vaucouleurs and saw her again later, testified at the rehabilitation that she had taken communion two days running with the dukes of Clermont and Alençon at Senlis in August 1429.[79] A contemporary account of her life, attributed to Jean de Colonne, is at pains to refute the charge of witchcraft and asserts that all Joan's miracles come from God. Her piety, he says, is proof of this. According to this historian, Joan communicated daily.[80] But to her accusers, Joan made the sacrament's goodness null and void by profaning it by her men's clothes. By inverting nature through her dress, she also inverted the sacrament, as in a Black Mass. It was fundamental to terror of witches that the holiest things could be twisted inside out. As the poem "From Handling Sin" by the English poet Robert of Brunne said, a bishop or a witch could recite the *Pater Noster* to very different effect:

> *The words certes been right nought*
> *But false belief maketh deed y- wrought.*[81]

Joan's ostensible piety was no defence. She could be using the Eucharist to strengthen her black arts. At her trial, Joan seemed to understand the heterodoxy with which frequent communion could be tainted. She did not vaunt her attendance as proof of her goodness. When she was asked if she received the host on other feasts as well as Easter, she ordered her interrogator to proceed with his next question.[82] The inquisitor, Jean le Graverent, accused her of communicating twice in a single day in his vitriolic sermon of July 1431.[83] Joan's love of the sacrament was profound; and by depriving her of it, her gaolers had a weapon with which they coerced her. She begged to hear Mass and take communion on the Easter Sunday that fell during her imprisonment;[84] they yielded to her desire only on the day of her execution.[85] To take communion one must be in a state of grace, which the status of idolater and heretic precludes. It is one of the Inquisition's most paradoxical customs that it allowed relapsed heretics communion.[86] Many witnesses, not all of them Joan's staunch supporters, gave evidence at the rehabilitation that she had been given communion before she died. Even Courcelles, for instance, one of the most lukewarm of the judges heard by the later inquiry, thought she had confessed and had received the Eucharist.[87] She was thus allowed one great desire, but denied another: she was not buried in holy ground and must be one of the tiny number of saints who have been forbidden consecrated burial by the Church itself.

Yet they failed to prove even to themselves that their victim was the thing of irredeemable pollution they had hoped. She died reconciled, with the body of her maker inside her. The image they sought to project onto Joan would not fit; they thundered in their public documents that she was "abominable to God and man," but in private, they were far from convinced. Little more than a fortnight after her death, Henry VI wrote a solemn letter, given and signed in the presence of Joan's leading prosecutors. It is a long protestation of their good intentions and legitimate conduct in the case of Joan, "a notorious woman, unfavourably known and under suspicion of having said, repeated, and spread . . . distinctly dangerous errors." In it, Henry pledged himself repeatedly and insistently to protect by legal measures and financial aid all those who took part in her trial, should anyone try to cite them before "our Holy Father or the General Council or any other court of law." Cauchon is mentioned by name as the first who should lean on the king's arm, should the necessity arise. As Henry was a child at the time, Cauchon himself must have been a prime mover of this remarkable open pardon, granted before the event of a charge. The bishop of Beauvais and his supporters against the Maid were very uneasy indeed.[88]

The pursuit of validating blessings continued: before the century was out, King Henry VII of England laid before Pope Julius II his earnest suit for the canonisation of his murdered predecessor and half-uncle, Henry VI, at whose tomb there had been many miracles.[89] His request was made after the verdict on Joan's heresy had been rescinded by the retrial of 1456, but three and a half centuries before her own canonisation was to be pleaded at the Vatican. Henry VI, who had signed his name to the burning of Joan the Maid, did not join the line of England's sainted kings. But Joan was not the reason. And the judges who had helped him as a boy rid his people of their terror of Joan were not pursued by justice themselves when their verdict was overturned. Many enjoyed illustrious careers, after the French recovery, on the French side. Although Joan's case had inspired sincere religious fear, the aftermath observed the political expediency of forgetting and, if not forgiving, at least overlooking.

HERETIC

> *There may come, and there are wont to come, to*
> *spiritual persons representations and objects of a*
> *supernatural kind. With respect to sight, they are*
> *apt to picture figures and forms belonging to the*
> *life to come—the forms of certain saints, and repre-*
> *sentations of angels, good and evil, and certain*
> *lights and brightnesses of an extraordinary kind.*
> *And with the ears, they hear certain extraordinary*
> *words. . . .*
>
> *Although all these things may happen to the*
> *bodily senses in the way of God, we must never*
> *rely on them or admit them, but we must always*
> *fly from them . . . for the more completely ex-*
> *terior and corporeal they are, the less certainly*
> *they are of God.*
>
> SAINT JOHN OF THE CROSS,
> "The Ascent of Mount Carmel"[1]

When Joan of Arc went to the stake, she wore over her shaven head a tall mitre like a dunce's cap. On the cap, the words of her crimes were inscribed in Latin, for her shame and the dread of the onlookers. She was "*Heretica, Relapsa, Apostata, Idolater.*" The scroll was painted with her "malign spirits," Belial, Satan and Behemoth. They were represented as Joan's beloved voices, the archangel Michael and the two saints Catherine and Margaret, who had had guided her vocation throughout.[2]

The Inquisition did not bring formal charges against a suspect; but its duty was the diagnosis and eradication of heresy. The plaintiffs could never be defended against specific accusations, because the actions that had brought them under suspicion were never set forth clearly by the accusers, but appeared only under the veils of their questions. Joan's trial has the nightmarish ambiguity, formlessness, confusing menace of *The Trial* or *The Castle:* she has no means of knowing where the interrogation is driving, what the concealed charge is. She had to defend herself for her life, but was never told where lay her wrong.[3]

This was the ordinary procedure of the Inquisition, but in the case of Joan, her trial was even more bewildering, since the assessors who travelled to attend the trial from monasteries and abbeys in the neighbourhood or from the University of Paris changed frequently.[4] Daily, she was faced with a new crowd of strangers, and they were supervised not by the regular representative of the Inquisition, the papal-appointed inquisitor for France, Jean le Graverent,[5] but by his deputy in Rouen, Jean le Maistre.[6] He was docile, it appears, to the political necessity of the trial: to invalidate Joan's successes from the standpoint of God's morality, to show that she had been the creature of the devil and not of the angels.

All the themes with which Joan's enemies struggled as they tried to establish the evil of her person were gathered up in one dominating argument of the trial: the nature of her voices. The different facets of her accusers' quandary are all present in their attempted analysis. Goodness was ambivalent, for evil was its frequent simulacrum; a witch possessed redoubtable faculties; the guidelines established to detect lewdness or its opposite were flawed. Above all, in an age of anthropomorphism, they were convinced that the supernatural could be manifest on earth, and they feared the physical metamorphoses of the devil. Joan saw and heard her visions with her material senses, and she never wavered from this assertion. If her body was as foul as it was to her judges, her cause spurious and her king a usurper, how could she be so privileged as to receive grace by its means? But, as we have seen, the point of intersection between holy and unholy was so cloudy that the conclusion was far from clear. In Joan of Arc's case, her historical image has been frozen at one with her voices: Joan never comes unaccompanied. Historians, artists, psychologists have had different ideas about her voices' character and origins and verity; some, though very few, think she lied about them; most sceptics hold that she believed in them but they had no objective reality. That Joan of Arc heard voices is nevertheless the fulcrum of her personality and the motive force of her story. But what is ignored by the stereotype is the shape of her adventure with her voices, the way she narrated the experience and the way her descriptions themselves changed as she struggled to express how the visions happened and, above all, how they, too, changed.

In Domremy, outside the modern basilica dedicated to her, is a group of statues: Joan and her three voices—Michael, Catherine and Margaret—rendered in full representational detail. This nineteenth-century sculpture, by André Allar, is cast in a more grandiose idiom than some other tributes to Joan in village squares throughout France, but its idiom belongs to the same school of rhetoric, which represents Joan's voices as individual and recognisable saints with particular identities and apprehensible, if glorified, bodies (35).

This way of conceptualising the mystery of Joan's voices is borrowed from her original enemies. They were the first to take pains to apply language to the task of understanding it. On the one hand, static literalism has destroyed the fluid pattern of her spiritual adventure. On the other, history often overlooks the reality that Joan's friends made no special claim on her behalf on account of her voices; in effect, the rehabilitation trial gives the impression of avoiding the subject. This is in strong contrast to the first trial that condemned her. Joan's judges come back to the question of her guidance at every single session, public and private, and again after the cross-examination was closed, when her insistence that she had again seen her "counsel" cost her her life.

What we know of Joan's voices comes from her replies, as one hostile leading question after another drubbed them out of her; we know nothing independently of that trial. No other witness's evidence, neither at the trial of vindication nor elsewhere, ever describes in Joan's words the form of her leading inspiration. One extant description, which dates from before the trial, is a letter from Perceval de Boulainvilliers, seneschal of Berry and a recruiting officer for the Lombard and Scottish auxiliary soldiers in the French army—in short, an important courtier in Charles VII's circle. On 21 June 1429, just over a month after the relief of Orleans, Perceval wrote to the duke of Milan, to whom he was connected by marriage, and reported on the recent, brilliant reversal of English fortunes in France. Joan the Pucelle was sent from God, he tells the duke, and then describes, in elegant terms and some detail, the circumstances of her birth and her arrival at court.

According to this first account of Joan's voices, she was running footraces with her friends in the fields of Domremy when a certain youth appeared and told her to hurry home to help her mother. She did so, but her mother denied sending the messenger. When Joan returned to her friends in the fields, a shining cloud came down before her eyes, and a voice speaking out of the cloud told her: " 'Joan, you must lead another life and perform wondrous deeds; for you are she whom the King of Heaven has chosen to bring reparation to the kingdom of France and help and protection to King Charles.' " But when the voice had finished speaking, the cloud vanished, and Joan was left "stupefied by so many marvels."[7]

Boulainvilliers's letter is the formal epistle of a learned and practised courtier: as we shall see later, he drew from classical authors to flesh out his story, not from any want of veracity, but according to the epistolary conventions of his day. What is noteworthy, however, about his description of Joan's voices—and he repeats that the "apparitions" continued in like manner—is that he did not give them any physical substance or personal identity. After the siege of Orleans, the character of her inspiration was recognised to be divine, but nothing more precise than a disembodied voice emanating from a cloud was known to a high-placed courtier. On the other hand, Dunois, who fought alongside Joan in the Loire campaign and possibly knew her better than most, gave evidence at the rehabilitation of 1456 that differs completely from Boulainvilliers's account and, unexpectedly, from Joan's own story. Dunois deposed: "This young girl swore that she had had a vision in which Saint Louis and Charlemagne prayed God for the safety of the king and of this city [Orleans]." Patron saints of France, both great and holy kings, Louis and Charlemagne were apt to the task; but the discrepancy between them and Joan's trial saints—Michael, Catherine and Margaret—is not explained. Of course, Louis and Charlemagne could have appeared in addition; or perhaps Joan adapted her counsel to suit Dunois, a French champion himself. Whatever the reason, Dunois's account still shows that, before the trial, Joan did not speak of her voices in the same terms as she used during it.[8]

Guy de Cailly, who had hosted Joan in his castle near Chécy on her first trip to Orleans and who had fought with her at the battle of Les Tourelles, was ennobled at her specific request in June that year. In the letters granting his title, the king declared that Joan had told him that Guy had also shared in her visions. These were of angels, who were not named. To commemorate this privilege, the Cailly were allowed to blazon angels' heads, with wings, on their coat of arms. This, continued Charles, was the closest approximation to what Guy, and therefore Joan, had seen.[9]

By the fourth session of her trial, when the questioning about her voices was resumed for the third time, Joan began to show signs of desperation. Finally, after several more questions, she referred her judges to her earlier examination of Poitiers. Thenceforward, she tried this stratagem again and again: "it is written down in the register at Poitiers" and "send to Poitiers where I was examined before" are phrases that recur frequently as, feeling more and more at bay, she tried to elude her judges.[10] Her stratagem has great pathos; that she could even hope that the English and their French supporters in Rouen, the capital of English administration in France, would be willing to consult (let alone give credence to) the evidence of a tribunal presided over by their opponents reveals the breadth of her political naiveté. What her reference to Poitiers does reveal, however, is that she spoke there of her voices. Yet the courtier Boulainvilliers does not characterise her experience in terms that correspond in any way to her later descriptions in her trial. The proceedings at Poitiers may have been kept secret. But this does not seem likely, as her virginity, her birth, family, early life, her spotless conduct, her test for virginity are all mentioned by other witnesses from that period. The discrepancy argues rather that the voices were not known to be specific saints to the people surrounding Charles and Joan in her heyday as the French champion. Except for Dunois, none of her comrades-in-arms who give evidence at the rehabilitation trial mentions the identity of her voices—not D'Alençon, not D'Aulon—nor does one of the priests, Séguin de Séguin, who saw her and spoke with her at Poitiers. For them, Joan was guided by her counsel (the word she preferred), and this counsel came from God. Her friends, it seems, were satisfied with this much. They relied on more substantive means, like her victories, to corroborate her divine vocation; when those failed, Joan's voice continued to mean as little to them as it had in the beginning.

To her enemies, the issue was very different. It appears from the records of the trial that they were obsessed with determining the extent of Joan's sensual experience of her voices, the extent of her bodily contact with them, the nature of their physical manifestation. If they could not prove her pollution by association with earthly beings, they would through her tangible experience of the other world. Joan was their plaything, she was lured into a gin she did not even understand to be there, which bit into her deeper and deeper as she struggled to express her truth in a language that she could not fully master and would yet be intelligible to her questioners. As they were adept in branches of learning she hardly knew by name, she took her lead from them, borrowed their images to render explicit the ineffable. The trap into which they prodded her closed inexorably.

When Joan first spoke of her counsel, at her second public session on 22 February, she was open, almost talkative. Undaunted in the presence of forty-seven judges and assessors, she declared that at the age of thirteen she had heard a voice. It was summer, toward the hour of noon, and she was in her father's garden. The voice came from the direction of the village church, and she seldom heard it without a light, a "great light." It seemed to her a "*digna vox*," a worthy voice; and the third time she heard it, she knew it was an angel's. Further on, she described how the angel instructed her, helped her find the king, but when her judges interrupted her story to ask again if she saw a light, she retorted: "Pass on to the next question." When they asked if it was an angel, she was again peremptory: "Spare me that. Continue."[11] At this early stage, she was not yet cornered. She also asserted, as we have seen, that Charles himself had had "revelations and apparitions, too," and that "her party knew the voice was sent to her by God, and they saw and knew the voice too, and . . . the king and several others, including the duke of Bourbon heard and saw them."[12] She claimed not exclusive privilege, therefore, but a form of divine guidance available to others. Yet by this stage, the single voice of the garden had already divided and become plural.

At her third public session, two days later, her cross-examiner, Cauchon's assistant, Beaupère, asked her if her voice had touched her to wake her and if she knelt down to give thanks.[13] Already Joan's experience is being manoeuvred into a world of concrete sensation. When pressed as to whether the voice was an angel's or a saint's, she still refused to specify: "This voice comes from God; I believe I do not tell you everything about it and I am more afraid of failing the voices by saying what is displeasing to them than of answering you." Again, the ambiguity: was the voice singular or plural? When asked again about the light, she gave an answer that is a model of mystical description: "The light comes in the name of the voice."[14] Teresa of Avila, a visionary with much greater mastery of theology and language than Joan, wrote a hundred years later that the highest kind of prayer was when the vision was not seen with the eyes of the body, but clearly seen and felt nevertheless: "He appears to the soul by a knowledge brighter than the sun." She wrote that the experience—which she did not consider a vision—was a little similar to the knowledge that someone is there in the dark, or to the blind man's sense of a presence, except that this analogy did not suffice, as the material senses are not in use at all. The light is known, not apprehended:

> It is not a dazzling radiance but a soft whiteness and infused radiance, which causes the eyes great delight and never tires them; nor are they tired by the brilliance which confronts them as they look

on this divine beauty. The brightness and light that appear before the gaze are so different from those of earth that the sun's rays seem quite dim by comparison, and afterwards we never feel like opening our eyes again. It is as if we were to look at a very clear stream running over a crystal bed, in which the sun was reflected, and then to turn to a very muddy brook, with an earthy bottom, running beneath a clouded sky. Not that the sun or anything like sunlight enters into the vision; on the contrary, its light seems the natural light, and the light of this world appears artificial.[15]

Though Teresa denied that perception of this grace involved the senses, she could not, as extraordinarily articulate as she was, express the phenomenon without recourse to the use of the senses—the eyes, the ears. This limitation, which is in effect a limitation of language itself, was the trap set for Joan. If Joan had said she had not seen or heard her voices, she would have seemed to deny them, to be an impostor; but grappling with the semantic problems strained her mental resources beyond endurance. She had no training in the imagery of mysticism, no knowledge of theological niceties; to distinguish between empirical and mystical knowledge, as Teresa later struggled to do, was indeed beyond her. Her canniness made her avoid at first the snares her judges laid for her. But soon she was to find herself committed to literalism and precision about her experiences in a way that had never been necessary when she had described them to her friends.

Her dictum that "the light comes in the name of the voice" cuts across the sensuous boundaries of ordinary empirical knowledge, and beyond that Joan would not disclose more: "I will not tell you everything. . . . This voice is good and worthy and I am not bound to answer you." She then added that she would like the points she did not answer to be given to her in writing, a sign that she sensed the questioning was already becoming dangerously perplexing for her. Beaupère ignored her request and persisted: did the voice have eyes? At this, the first gentle push into the theological maze where she would be finally lost, Joan, as yet unvanquished and mettlesome, replied, "You will not learn that yet," and quoted that motto from her childhood: "Men are sometimes hanged for telling the truth." When Beaupère insisted, she countered that she wished everyone could hear her voice as well as she did. Again she abrogated a claim to exclusive graces. Beaupère reverted to another line of questioning.[16]

At the fourth session, three days on, Beaupère tackled her again on the subject of her counsel, asking, Was it an angel's voice, a saint's, male, female? Did it come straight from God? It was then that Joan suddenly named Saint Catherine and Saint Margaret and added that they had appeared to her crowned richly and beautifully. "And to tell this, I have God's permission." Then she referred him to Poitiers.[17] From this exchange, it seems clear that in the interval since the last cross-examination she had prayed, probably with the help of her voice, and felt she was now free to name her saints. At the same time, she was still reluctant to continue any circumstantial description. Remembering that in earlier and similar conditions she had been believed and vindicated when she had been questioned, she hoped to fob off her new examiners with the happy results of Poitiers. When Beaupère persisted, she remained stubborn and would not answer his questions about her saints' dress, age, manner of speech, order of appearance. "I did not recognise them immediately," she admitted revealingly. "I knew well enough once, but I have forgotten."[18] But it is not really possible that she could have forgotten. In her own presentation of herself, the divine counsel guiding her was always in the foreground. It is much more likely that she did not know and that what she knew was, as she then added, that her voice gave her great comfort.[19] Again, however simple it is in contrast to the eloquence and sophistication of other, more lettered visionaries, this phrase recalls the essence of the mystical experience: the sweetness and the pleasure of it.

As Saint Teresa wrote about divine locutions: "The words are perfectly formed, but are not heard with the physical ear." It is like speaking, except that the mind is working, not listening. "Words lead to deeds. . . . they prepare the soul, make it ready, and move it to tenderness. They give it light, and make it quiet and happy. If it has been dry and disordered and restless, the Lord seems to remove its troubles."[20]

Then Joan mentions Saint Michael and says that it was he who had first visited her. But it was not his voice that mattered to her, but "his great comfort." She keeps trying to wriggle away from Beaupère's relentlessness: yes, she saw Michael before her eyes; he was not alone, but accompanied by many angels. But having plunged into this much detail, she turns back to the vagueness of her early assertions: she had done everything by the instruction of God. But Beaupère, seizing on her admission that she had *seen* Michael and his angels, drove home: had she seen them "corporeally and in reality"? And Joan answered, again recalling Teresa's ecstasy, "I saw them with my bodily eyes as well as I see you; and when they left me, I wept; and I would have had them take me with them, too." At that session, she would answer no more about them, except to add, in its closing stages, that Saint Margaret comforted her when she was wounded in the assault on the bridge fortress at Orleans and that she had known she would be hurt, for her saints—Catherine and Margaret—had told her beforehand.[21]

At the next session—still held in public, before fifty-seven judges and assessors—Joan was as uncooperative. When asked if Gabriel had appeared with Michael and Catherine and Margaret, she did not remember. She continued to insist she heard them daily, several times each day; but as to their form or their sex, she would not elaborate. She knew nothing, she affirmed, except by revelation and God's command. What part of them did she see? Their faces. At this point, Joan produces some of the cheeky answers that have made her famous for pluck, defiance, heroic unyieldingness. But the spitfire that, for instance, Shaw's play celebrates, the outspoken, unabashed country girl with a quick tongue in her head, had perhaps deeper reasons for her recalcitrance than the sheer high spirits Shaw's portrait assumes. She snaps back, when asked if they had hair, "It is well to know they have," or, when asked if Margaret spoke English, "Why should she speak English when she is not on the English side?" or, when plied with queries about Michael's body and dress and hair, "Do you think God has not the wherewithall to clothe him?" and "Why should it be cut off?" These responses reveal rather more desperation than the lighthearted cussedness so entertainingly rendered by Shaw. None of these replies provides any information at all about her visions. Each one is an evasion, neat but, as it would turn out, inadequate. At this stage, she does not know if they have arms or limbs, only that their voices are sweet and low and beautiful. The only remark she makes that rings sincere and describes her personal relation with her visions is again her reiteration that when she saw Michael—no, she did not know if he was carrying scales—she was filled with great joy.[22] This is the *dulcedo Dei*, the intense rapture of Julian of Norwich, or Richard Rolle.[23]

Two days later, in the final public session, her questioner returned to the theme: did Michael have wings, and did Michael and Gabriel have natural heads? Joan was weary; she kept on trying to answer that she had said everything she had to say on the subject, that for her they were real: "I believe it was they I saw as firmly as I believe in the existence of God." God had created them as she saw them, but further than that she would not be drawn.[24]

When the interrogations were resumed in Joan's cell, before a restricted number of judges, the same pattern manifests itself: Joan stalls at any deeper description of her voices' effect beyond their comfort to her; she talks of an angel, who is always the same one; she declares that angels walk among ordinary people all the time, and the only difference is that she can see them. Fatally, she told her new questioner, another lawyer from the University of Paris, Jean de la Fontaine, that she knelt before Michael and his angels when they appeared and kissed the ground after they had gone.[25] Her judges persisted with interrogation about the sign she had given the king at Chinon. Wavering between her resolve to keep her secret and a desire for surcease of torment by providing some answers to satisfy her questioners' craving, Joan told the story that we have heard, the story that grew more and more unwieldy, about the angel, and the crown, and the king's faith, and the fabulous ceremony in the great hall at Chinon. Her replies became incoherent and filled with contradictions and disavowals. But again, she was making certain fundamental points: that she saw the angel at Chinon and that many others, including Charles, saw the angel, too, at the same time; that the angel spoke to him; that her vision was real, since "He came from on high," but "entered the room by the door"; and that when asked if he came from earth, he stepped on the ground and uncovered his head to do reverence to the king. She named the courtiers and churchmen there who also claimed to have seen the angel. When asked what the angel at Chinon and his companions looked like, Joan was vague: "As far as she could see," some were winged, some crowned, and Saint Catherine and Saint Margaret were with them.[26] On the fourth day of cross-examination in prison, Joan was exhausted: when she was questioned yet again, about the light that came with her voices, she answered as she had always done and then added that if they were going to take her to Paris for a further trial, she wanted to be given a transcript of the questions and answers she had made hitherto. She could hand it over and say, "See how I was interrogated at Rouen," and need not be belaboured (*travaillée*) any more by questions.[27]

With a certain imprecision, Joan is borrowing attributes known to her from religious iconography—wings, crowns. Two of her predecessors at the stake, Margot de la Barre and Marion la Droiturière, condemned for witchcraft in 1390–91 in Paris in one of the first and therefore important judgements handed down by a secular court, confessed under torture to seeing the devil. When asked what he looked like, they replied he looked as he did in the mystery plays.[28] If their admission had not been fatal, such ingenuousness would be funny.

The Church had always used images to teach the rudiments of theology to the illiterate. As the poem *Dives and Pauper* says, paintings were "a token and a book to the lewd people that they may read in imagery and paintings that clerks read in the book."[29] It is not surprising that Joan should have fumbled for a recognisable feature. She is more convincing when she says that when the angel left her, she was "much vexed, and wept, and would have gone with him, at least her soul."[30] Again, Saint Teresa echoes her, writing that after rapture, the detachment "makes life much more painful" and leaves "this great distress."[31]

Joan's interrogators were inexorable. The last cross-examination of all, on 17 March, opened with the same question: in what guise, shape, size and dress did Saint Michael come to her? She replied, "In the shape of a most upright man." She held fast to her story; she would not waver from the truth she had beheld in front of her eyes. Accusingly they asked her why she had the angels on her standard painted with "arms, feet, legs and clothes." She told them she had already answered that. Later, at the very end of the session, true to the tradition of bewildering a defendant with chopping and changing, they jumped on her again with the same question, couched in a more insinuating form. Had she ever kissed or embraced Saints Catherine and Margaret? Yes, she said. Did they smell good? Yes, she said. Were they warm to the touch? Yes, she could hardly embrace them without feeling them. Where, head or feet? It was more respectful, she implied, to embrace their feet.[32]

The trap had long been set; now it was sprung. The forty-ninth charge in the judges' draft declares that her "cult and veneration" of her saints "seem to partake of idolatry and to proceed from a pact made with devils."[33] The fifty-first states that she had boasted Saint Michael came to her: "To say this of archangels, and of holy angels must be held presumptuous, rash, deceitful; especially seeing that it is not written that any man, however upright, nor even Our Lady, Mother of God, received such reverence or greetings."[34] Of the other signs Joan had been given through her voices, the judges declared: "These are less divine revelations than lies invented by Joan, suggested or shown to her by the demon in illusive apparitions, in order to mock at her imagination while she meddled with things that are beyond her and superior to the faculty of her condition."[35] She was further accused that though she proclaimed her belief in her voices as firm as her faith, "she reports no sign sufficient to know them by" and that she had not consulted a bishop or a priest about her voices to receive their approval.[36]

Joan had trespassed gravely. It mattered less what colours one flew than who bestowed these colours; the ritual was legitimised only by the legitimacy of the performer, not by the words themselves. Joan had never told anyone about her voices; she had not obeyed them because they had been approved by a man of the Church. She had not told her confessor, nor any of the high ecclesiastics she met later. Her voices had remained a private affair, and as a laywoman she had no right to trust in them without the formal permission of the Church. But it is important to recognise that her judges accused her of not producing "sufficient" signs to recognise the origin of her voices: the phrasing admits the slender possibility that her private experiences might have convinced them.

It did not, because the visions Joan described were too special and, at the same time, too mundane. Her contact with the supernatural was too intimate and too regular; it was not characterised by the raptures or other physiological wonders associated with the visions of earlier and contemporary mystics. It took place in a recognisable and almost human framework, belonging to earth below, not to heaven above; and the traditions of demonology in the church associated the imitation of reality with Satan, not with Christ. Each one of the questions put to her about her sensuous knowledge of her voices was linked to the lore of witchcraft, and though Joan knew about mandrakes and night flying and other sorcery, she does not seem to have recognised the import of the questions about kissing or touching her saints. At a Sabbat, the witches were supposed to worship the presiding devil, first praying to him, then kissing him, often first his left foot or his genitals or anus. Though he took on flesh and blood to appear before them or to sleep with them as an incubus, he was deathly cold to the touch.[37] Hence the interrogation about Saint Michael's clothes, which Joan had fielded well, and then about the "feel" of her voices. Though her answers did not commit her fully to the stereotype of the witch, she was, all unknowingly, deeply embroiled in a fundamental quarrel in Christian theology, and her innocent replies testifying to the reality of her voices were immuring her on the wrong side.[38] Just the year before, the Breton woman Pieronne was burned as a witch in Paris for taking a stand similar to

Joan's about the reality of her visions. The Bourgeois de Paris, who reported her death, wrote: "She affirmed and swore that God often appeared to her in human form and talked to her as one friend does to another; that the last time she had seen him he was wearing a long white robe and a red one underneath, which is blasphemous. She would not take back her assertion that she frequently saw God dressed like this." Pieronne also admitted that she had taken communion twice in one day; and, when questioned about Joan, then in prison, she was staunchly loyal: "what she did was well done and was God's will."[39]

The quarrel that worsted Pieronne and Joan concerned the way the supernatural is expressed. The Neoplatonism of the Renaissance would not have found them guilty of devil worship, because it recognised that the world of the spirit could assume a beautiful form, could materialise as a radiant image, in order to be grasped by the human mind, confined to human means of understanding. The sublime could be represented, through the appropriate sublime appearance that it assumed in order to be manifest. Plotinus wrote, in a text that influenced Renaissance thinking about visual images, "It must not be thought that in the Intelligible world the gods and the blessed see propositions; everything expressed there is a beautiful image."[40] When Pico della Mirandola reviewed the medieval theological attitude to the appearance of devils, "he held the correct Neoplatonic view that the spirits belong to the suprasensible world and only assumed visible form to enable them to have commerce with human beings."[41]

But Joan's judges did not hold that heaven could be made apprehensible to the human senses, through a change of form undertaken by the angels themselves. Sublime beings were not as protean: they could not alter their nature and become groundlings; only the profane had the cunning of multiple form. Their reasoning forbade the switch of categories necessary for bodiless creatures to descend and take on the lowliness of flesh for images to give substance. Angels, like Michael, or saints, like Margaret and Catherine, were insubstantial spirits until their resurrection on the last day in a glorified body; if they had substance, it was because they belonged to the lower, demonic class where the trammels of the flesh still held. This is the work of fearful minds, filled with phantoms they believe to be real: our existence here below is trapped by the world, the flesh and the devil and is incapable of receiving a ray of the other world's light; evil can penetrate to the soul through the senses, and good is exalted far above messages given and received materially. Demons farted, stank, gabbled and generally aped the fashion of the world; saints and angels soared far above the bodily metaphors that could capture them for human reality. During Joan's lifetime, the dualism buried deep in the Christian soul made all fleshly experience sinful.[42]

This traditional division gave birth to the figure of the blind seer. From the ancient myths to the present day, the idea that the eyes of the body are unnecessary to the sight of the soul has been expressed by the belief in visionaries like Tiresias, or the widespread convention of blind fortune-tellers, or the baseless tradition that Homer was blind. Even a contemporary prophet, the self-styled Pope Gregory XVII, crowned in Seville in 1978 as leader of a schismatic group adhering to the messages the Virgin Mary gave to four little girls in Garabandal in the 1960s, is blind; his blindness, the putting out of the material senses, emphasises the purity of his contact with the supernatural.[43]

Joan in all simplicity flouted the hierarchical structure of the intelligible and sensible world at a time when the sense of it was so developed that an unwritten code of conduct existed to conform to it at every level. Denis the Carthusian, a generation after Joan, displayed a characteristically fifteenth-century appetite for symbolism when he wrote that polyphonic music was not fitting in church because it was "broken" and only "whole" sounds chimed with God's presence.[44] The feeling that the inapprehensible is higher than the apprehensible and requires an appropriately more elevated response, as dictated by the Platonist hierarchy of a world below and another above, still dominates our thinking.

The historian Giambattista Vico, in the eighteenth century, surprises us when he praises the Neoplatonists for their rejection of abstraction in favour of the concrete: "It is . . . beyond our power to enter into the vast imagination of those first men whose minds were not in the least abstract, refined or spiritualised, because they were entirely immersed in the senses, buffeted by the passions, buried in the body."[45]

In the fullest sense, Joan was buried in the body. She used what she knew to express the unknown; her saints' reality was clothed in familiar robes and familiar images. More than her defiance of the Church's authority, more than her claims to know the future, more than her perhaps heterodox enthusiasm for the host, she was condemned for experiencing the other world as simply and as concretely as she experienced this world every day.

Michael the Archangel, Catherine of Alexandria and Margaret of

Antioch were the images most readily at hand to express the difficult concept of her visions. As J. H. Huizinga, the great historian of this period, has written: "It seems plausible to me that it was only fairly late, perhaps even only during her trial, that Joan linked her inspirations to the figures she knew best and cherished most among the saints."[46] There is nothing derogatory to Joan in this; it would reveal the same unsubtle literal-mindedness of her interrogators to find Joan false because she expressed herself, under duress, according to what she knew. She reached for metaphors that would be so close to her experience that the distinction between truth and its simulacrum would be effaced. Michael, Catherine and Margaret were approximations—hence the ambivalence about their appearance and the many references to an unnamed angel as well—but even as approximations, they came so close to rendering what she felt about her voices, that at times, when she talks of the consolation they bring her, she speaks with clear conviction.

The main characteristic of Joan's relationship with her voices is her loyalty to them: she exonerates them from everything that went wrong, saying either that they had not given her the command or that they had expressly ordered her not to—as with her leap from Beaurevoir. When, in the charges, the judges simply declared that she had followed her voices' instructions in everything, she corrected them angrily. "Everything *good* that I did," she insisted.[47] She had placed her counsel firmly outside herself; there is never the slightest hint that she heard an inner voice advising her. On one side, there was Joan with her own views, and on the other, there were her voices. Their identities never merge. It was a dynamic relationship, not a symbiosis. In fact, so externalised were Joan's voices that she twice claimed she could not hear them properly. In prison, she complained that "on account of the disturbance of people and noise of her guards" she failed to understand what Saint Catherine was telling her.[48] On the occasion when she was lying asleep in Orleans and was woken with a command from one of her voices to go to the attack, she could not make out whether her counsel had said "Fastolf," the English commander, or "Fort St. Loup," one of the English redoubts.[49]

So even if one believes that Joan's voices were not supernatural and objective phenomena, but the private projections of her imagination, it must be accepted that she herself never heard them except as external, separate entities who were independent of her and over whom she exercised no control at all.

The faces she chose for her voices were as well known to her contemporaries, both French and English, as a football player's or a tennis star's or a singer's are today. Michael was the emblem of French resistance. When the abbey of St. Denis, France's patron saint, fell under English administration in 1419, Charles as Dauphin ordered that Michael's image be painted on the standards of his soldiers instead. Mont St. Michel, the monastery rising on a rocky cone and defended by the sea on all sides off the coast of Normandy, was the last bastion in the north of France. Its defenders had successfully resisted attack; but, more significantly in a time of easily wooed allegiances, they had not changed sides. Pilgrimages to the shrine grew in popularity, and though Henry V, the English king, had forbidden them, pilgrims continued to run the English blockade without much trouble. Charles VI himself went there to cure his madness in 1394; and when he found some respite, he named his daughter Michelle in the angel's honour. Michael was a patron saint of the Barrois, where Domremy was situated, and his cult was popular in neighboring Lorraine and Champagne. There were two shrines to him locally, in the castle of Joinville built in 1414 and on a mountain near Toul, Joan's nearest cathedral town. This military saint, always represented in knightly armour, weapons drawn, his demonic assailant crushed under his mailed feet, had been the patron of Norman soldiers in their conquest of territory from England to the Holy Land; during the Goth invasion, he had appeared with legions of angelic soldiers at Monte Gargano in southern Italy. He was the natural, most apt choice for Joan to make for the standard-bearer of her political mission[50] (6).

The cults of Saint Margaret and Saint Catherine were flourishing in the fifteenth century; Saint Catherine, in particular, was probably the best loved saint of the day, her story told in painting cycles, poetry, mystery plays and votive figures all over France as well as in England, Italy and other European countries. As far afield as St. Mary's Church, Sporle, near Swaffham in Suffolk, there is a time-worn sequence of frescoes of her life, elaborating each of the many scenes with primitive skill but some detail. The richness of the story told proves that known hagiographies travelled widely in the fifteenth century and were retained by their hearers.[51]

Saint Catherine was the patron saint of Maxey, the village next to Domremy, and her ashes were transferred there for veneration according to the local nobleman's will in 1399.[52] Catherine was the name of Joan's younger sister, who died before 1429; probably at Joan's request, it was the name of the child she helped deliver at the nearby village of Burey when she first left home.[53]

Saint Margaret was, with Catherine, one of the three female saints (the third was Saint Barbara) in the large group of intercessors called the Fourteen Holy Helpers, who from the fourteenth century onward were the object of fervent hope and devotion, especially in the Holy Roman Empire. They were highly specialised: Saint Denis cured headaches and rabies; Saint Erasmus, colic and cramp; Saint Blaise, sore throats; Saint Pantaleon, tuberculosis; Saint Giles, epilepsy, insanity and sterility; Saint Vitus, his own dance and epilepsy. Saint Christopher was the patron of travellers, as he still is; Saint Eustace, of hunters; Saint George, of soldiers. Saint Barbara gave protection against lightning, fire and sudden death; Saint Cyriac protected against demonic possession; only Saint Achatius had no particular province.[54]

John Myrc, the fourteenth-century English poet, wrote in *Festial* that "St Margaret will con you more thanks for to make a mass said in the worship of her than to fast many evenings bread and water without mass."[55] This mechanical power, working independently of the votary's merits, and without recourse to God, was absolute and therefore frightening. William Tyndale wrote later: "We worship saints for fear, lest they should be displeased and angry with us, and plague us or hurt us. As who is not afraid of St Lawrence? Who dare deny St Antony a fleece of wool for fear of his terrific fire, or lest he send the pox among our sheep?"[56]

Saint Catherine was the patron of philosophers and students and wheelwrights; Saint Margaret's specialty was pregnancy and demonic possession. Each of the helpers had a vivid attribute, either of an exploit or of martyrdom, which gave them arresting and plastic qualities that made painters love them. Saint Catherine's famous symbol was the wheel with which she was tortured; Saint Margaret was inseparable from the dragon who swallowed her, but then disgorged her safe and sound. Even in a painting as attentive to realism as Hugo van der Goes's beautiful altarpiece at Portinari, Saint Margaret, watching the adoration of the newly born Christ Child, holds on a leash a huge, glassy-eyed, squamous sea-green monster. They were struck from the calendar, as a group, at the Council of Trent because their votaries' trust in their automatic intercession was heretical.[57]

Catherine of Alexandria died in 305, according to tradition. The twelfth-century *Golden Legend* compiled by Jacopus de Voragine reproduces the stories of saints in their most properly vulgar form. It tells us that she was a king's daughter. When the Emperor Maxentius ordered the wholesale slaughter of Christians in Alexandria, Catherine was brought before him and began a disquisition on her faith. Fifty learned orators were summoned to dispute with her; she confounded them all; each one was put to death for failing to defeat her. Maxentius then immediately proposed to Catherine. She spurned him for Christ, her "God," lover, shepherd and "only Spouse." A gigantic engine of destruction with four wheels was devised to kill her, but an angel laid it waste. Its huge blades, fitted to the whirring wheels, flew off into the crowd and killed several spectators. An angel eventually destroyed this "Catherine wheel" as well.

After further ordeals, Catherine died beheaded. Jacopus de Varagine ends his story with a eulogy of Catherine's intellectual powers. She thus becomes one of the few women saints to be revered for her brains. As a result, she often appears reading a book, the broken wheel at her feet, in paintings and statues of a date—the fifteenth century— when literacy was uncommon in lay society and even more so among women.[58] Her story was illustrated in *Les Belles Heures du Duc de Berri*, so although we have no way of knowing what Joan knew about her saints, we do know Saint Catherine's legend was current in her immediate circle at court. Catherine's statue was placed in Dunois's private chapel at Châteaudun soon after Joan's death. She was an intimate of angels. In one illumination of *Les Belles Heures*, angels appear in Catherine's cell and tend the wounds of her torture just as Joan's saints had comforted her after she was wounded in the fight at Orleans, helped heal her after her failure in Paris and strengthened her after her fall from Beaurevoir[59] (4).

Another accretion to the legend of Saint Catherine links her sympathetically with Joan. After her marriage to Christ, he appeared to her in a vision, and gave her his body in the Eucharist. Giovanni di Paolo painted the story of her life in an altarpiece some fifteen years after Joan's death, with predella scenes showing her mystic marriage and its counterpart, a miraculous communion. She was, therefore, a saint associated with eucharistic devotion. But Saint Catherine of Alexandria stood chiefly for independent thinking, courage, autonomy and culture. She was the saint chosen by young unmarried women in France.[60] Saint Margaret of Antioch, though her spiritual sister in the paintings of the helpers, was also her opposite number. Alexandria was the centre of classical allegorical studies, where the Bible, for instance, was read in the tradition of Philo Judaeus to uncover the secret meanings under the narrative surface. Antioch, the other great school of learning in the Byzantine Empire, was the seat of the literalist school, where mystical interpretations of the Alexandrians were shunned. Joan, therefore, unconsciously named her visions after the two poles of the Christian philosophical tradition.

Margaret was associated with motherhood; Catherine, with virginity. Margaret was prayed to for help in difficult deliveries because she had been born again unhurt from the belly of the dragon. Margaret's story, as it was known in the fifteenth century, was conflated from several legends and appears widely in both the English and the French contexts. Margaret Beauchamp, daughter of Joan's gaoler, the earl of Warwick, married the redoubtable English champion John Talbot; and in Talbot's campaign missal, they are portrayed side by side under the protection of their patron saints, Margaret and George.[61] In the French court as well, Saint Margaret inspired devotion. Isabella of Bavaria personally commissioned her life in illuminated manuscript for her library.[62]

According to a version of her legend, Margaret, or Pelagia, is one of the several saints who enters a monastery in the disguise of a man. This story clearly provides a vital link with Joan's unconscious, as we shall see later. Under another aspect, as Margaret of Antioch, she sees the devil, but her purity is proof against his assaults. She also refuses to marry, in this case Olybrius, prefect of Pisidir (5), who falls in love with her while she is keeping her sheep, again conforming to her successor Joan. She is thrown by him into prison, where she resists the successive torments of her atrocious martyrdom with a miraculous force so wonderful that five thousand bystanders are converted and themselves martyred. She is, finally, decapitated. Yet another story attached itself to Saint Margaret of Antioch: at the age of fifteen, she jumped off a high building in order to preserve her chastity.[63] But this incident is not told in the illuminated cycles of Margaret's life painted before or during Joan's life, and it is not to be found in verse or in paint in any milieu associated with her. The shape of the story, and its curiously exact echo in the Bourgeois de Paris's version of Joan's leap from Beaurevoir, might mean that the Margaret legend was known;[64] it might also mean that the content captures in a fundamental and memorable way the psychology of a young girl faced with an intolerable future—marriage in Margaret of Antioch's case, imprisonment by the English in Joan's.

Because Margaret of Antioch had been martyred by decollation, as the liturgical phrase would have it, she was also portrayed with a sword. Joan's voices were all three commonly armed: Michael carried an avenging sword, but the two women bore the swords of their enemies, swords which had afflicted them, which they themselves did not use. This was important to Joan, who saw herself as defending a cause against terrible foes even when she was going over to the attack.

Joan did not respect divisions, did not sift and classify according to the given laws of appropriateness. Her saints have bodies, talk French, wear clothes and can be held and touched. She could not see the incongruity—why should the soul not have ears and eyes? All unwittingly, she trespassed against a basic structural axiom in the Christian idea of the holy and sinned both against the classical idea of propriety, that abstractions should remain abstract and not take on material shape, and against the strong, enduring strain of Platonic idealism, which decrees that all things have their appropriate nature. Always artlessly, Joan displayed a profound and unerring ability to cross from the permitted to the impermissible and thus to define others' fears and assumptions, until the clarity became unbearable and she became a victim of her own illumination.

As an impossible object, a *coincidentia oppositorum*, a sinner against possibility and a practitioner of impossibility, Joan went to the heart of the ancient semantics of magic. There is a beautiful, riddling folk song, which lists the impossible tasks a lover sets his beloved. He begins:

> *Can you make me a cambric shirt,*
> *Parsley, sage, rosemary and thyme,*
> *Without any seam or needlework?*
> *Then you shall be a true lover of mine.*

In reply she sets him equal problems:

> *Can you find me an acre of land,*
> *Parsley, sage, rosemary and thyme,*
> *Between the salt water and the sea sand?*
> *Then you shall be a true lover of mine.*[65]

The song probably contains a memory of benign witchcraft: the posy of herbs could be the same chaplets that Margot and Marion in 1390 confessed to offering the devil, with the same nefarious significance Joan's judges tried to pin on her when she told them, in all innocence, that with the other young girls of Domremy she had hung garlands on the Arbre des Fées, the huge beech in the wood near the village, the focus of local festivities and reunions.[66] Through her voices, Joan found that "acre of land," in terms of the theology of the period. She joined what should not be joined, she touched what cannot be touched, simply and effortlessly, without seeing the problem.

One of the most sustained deployments of Platonic Christian dualism occurs in Charles Péguy's *Les Tapisseries de Sainte Geneviève et Jeanne d'Arc*, written at the beginning of this century by a poet who combined faith and socialism with complete sincerity. For nine hundred and sixty-nine alexandrines, set out in triplets that swing backward and forward as regularly as a pendulum swings to the rotation of the earth, Péguy rings changes on the theme of God's weapons against the devil's. Each sequence of metaphors begins *"Les armes de Jésus . . ."* or *"Les armes de Satan. . . ."* They reverberate as hypnotically as a litany, revealing the basic principles of the Christian idea of evil. Although Péguy is one of Joan's most fervent and most loquacious acolytes, the imagery he applies to the devil can be used to show, even though nearly five hundred years have passed, the way her enemies' minds worked against her. The trial groped toward a redefinition of her being that would show her to be counterfeit: not whole, not holy. To seem so and not to be so is far worse than to seem or to be unholy. The counterfeitness of her body was compounded by the distorted motives of her actions: what is holy obeys the laws of teleology; its aims are at one with its conduct. To work at cross-purposes is profane; to take communion without grace, to defy the natural order in an attempt to fly, to see what cannot be seen with the eyes of the body, to touch what is not tangible, all such thwarting of the given order of things comes not from heaven, but from hell.

Péguy speaks in the same philosophical tradition as Joan's execucutioners when he writes:

> *Les armes de Satan . . . c'est toute ouverture*
> *Que l'on n'a pas ouverte et toute fermeture*
> *Que l'on n'a pas fermée et toute quadrature*
> *Que l'on n'a pas quarrée et c'est toute arcature*
> *Que l'on n'a pas arquée . . . et toute horticulture*
> *Qui n'est pas pour la fleur, toute arboriculture*
> *Qui n'est pas pour le fruit, toute viticulture*
> *Qui n'est pas pour le vin, c'est toute agriculture*

Qui n'est pas pour lè blé, c'est toute apiculture
Qui n'est pas pour le miel, toute sylviculture
Qui n'est pas pour le bois . . .[67]

All creatures and all things have their purpose in God's design, and their form and their nature are made to fulfil it. When it is contradicted and disobeyed, then the devil shows himself in the rift. Joan's judges thought she defied this divine ordinance. But the question always remains: Who and what decides what is appropriate? How is the innate property of things defined?

In one paramount respect, Joan defied the quiddity of her sex and ignored what seemed its natural destiny. She went across prescribed boundaries, she became the opening that is not open, the square that is not squared, when she declared herself a maid but lived as a man.

CHAPTER 7

IDEAL ANDROGYNE

*The woman shall not wear that which pertaineth
unto a man, neither shall a man put on a woman's
garment; for all that do so are abomination unto
the Lord thy God.*

DEUTERONOMY 22:5

hen Joan of Arc, played by a student at the Jesuit University of Pont-à-Mousson in Lorraine, delivered her opening speech in Father Fronton-du-Duc's verse tragedy, *L'Histoire Tragique de la Pucelle d'Orléans*, on 7 September 1580, before Charles III, duke of Lorraine, she began with some questions. Phrased in alexandrines that anticipate Racine, they go nicely to the heart of the matter:

What indeed should I do? Who will be so kind and place me on the right path and take away my pain? Alas! Oh! Must I pervert all order? Must I, forgetting my sex, dress myself as a man?

Though the twenty-two-year-old university rhetoric teacher attributed doubts to Joan that she never admitted during her trial, he dramatised lucidly the problem that troubled Joan's supporters: how was her inversion of the God-given order to be justified? His Joan continued:

[Should I] follow thus a new life, soon to find myself pursued by everyone with justifiable accusations, and [should I] perpetrate a falsehood by daring too far? But, on the other hand, should the fear of men mean we do not keep faith with the God who made us?[1]

In the view of a partisan like Fronton-du-Duc, the conflict lay between the conventions of society and the commandment of God; to Joan's enemies, the two were not in opposition. Joan went to the stake because she refused to yield to the authority of the Church, as represented by the Inquisition that tried her. That defiance focussed on two counts: first, the truth of her voices; second, her male dress.

Standing up to authority has cost many a life, but to lose one's life for one's dress, to express one's separateness, one's inalienable self through one's clothes, is unusual. Yet Joan's transvestism was taken very seriously indeed by the assessors of Rouen, who condemned her for it, and also by herself. It ranked of equal significance for her with the truth of her voices. When she found, after her recantation, that she had forsworn both her "counsel" and her dress, she swiftly returned to her previous stand on everything. The visions and the dress were one and indivisible.

It is often overlooked, when the story of Joan's life is told, that she abjured. It is this abjuration and its reversal that show how deeply Joan cared about her dress. On Thursday, 24 May, she was taken to the cemetery of St. Ouen in Rouen, placed on a scaffold and harangued by Guillaume Erard in the harsh words, from John's gospel, "that the withered branch must be thrown in the fire else the tree cannot flourish." On the rostrum as spectators were Pierre Cauchon; the English and Burgundian prelates, the cardinals of Winchester and the bishops of Thérouanne, Noyon and Norwich; the regent, the duke of Bedford; the governor of Rouen castle, the earl of Warwick; and others among her enemies. The accounts of the scene as told later at the rehabilitation are very confused, and the contradictions have inspired volumes of controversy. Was Joan, who could not read, tricked into signing a document of recantation, which disavowed far more than she realised?[2] Later witnesses talked of parchments switched at the last moment, of Joan's signing a short declaration, although the abjuration printed in the trial records is very long. Guillaume Manchon, the notary, shows himself anxious for self-vindication in his evidence after her death. He says that Joan smiled as she signed. She had perhaps made her mark in a cross, a code sign she used, she had told her judges before, beside certain passages in her letters, to convey secretly to her readers that they should not be believed.[3] Another witness said she signed mockingly.[4] Whatever she signed, her signature committed her to judgement and she was condemned forthwith to perpetual imprisonment, on bread and water, in solitary confinement. She was then led from the platform. Confusion broke out, Warwick cursing Cauchon for letting the "witch" slip through his fingers with her life. They had wanted her dead; with her recantation, she won survival.[5]

This is the vindication witnesses' story. Historians of Joan have interpreted the scene in a variety of ways. According to one analysis, Joan was duped into signing a denial of everything she had maintained during her trial.[6] Cauchon manipulated her deliberately, because the Inquisition could not hand over a simple heretic to the secular arm for burning, but could condemn only a *relapsed* heretic, one who had recanted, but then repented of the recantation and returned to former evil convictions. When Joan was told what she had signed, how much of her very identity she had forsworn, she despaired and denied that she had meant any of it. Cauchon had anticipated this, and he now had Joan where he wanted, a nicely legal package, a relapsed heretic whom he could, without any illegality, turn over to the stake. Hence, his bracing words to the angry English after the scene at the cemetery.

Within four days, however, Joan had taken off the woman's dress issued to her and assumed her male costume again. Her male clothes may have been left for her in a sack on purpose to tempt her or even to force her. Some of the vindication witnesses say her female dress was removed. But whatever the exact events, when Thomas de Courcelles, then rector of the University of Paris and one of Joan's most hostile assessors, visited her in prison with seven others on the Monday after she had signed the recantation at the cemetery, she said she had yielded only "for fear of the fire." They asked her if she had heard her voices again. She said yes. In the margin of his notes, the clerk was moved to comment *"Responsio mortifera,"* the fatal reply.[7]

This reading of history, placing Joan as chick in the jaws of a fox, seeing her as the toy of devious cold-blooded death-dealers, is ingenious, brilliant and quite plausible; but it is also possible that the sequence of events, like so many in history, was a muddle. It was only by taking a certain course of action that Joan, that Cauchon, that the English discovered what they really wanted. Joan recanted, then found she could not bear the nonsense such a denial made of her past. Also, she protested that she would rather die than live in a dungeon for the rest of her days: she had not expected life imprisonment. Nor would she have suffered it, but most probably she would have been amnestied within the decade, as we know with sad hindsight.

Cauchon, from the beginning, had acted out the hocus-pocus of a fair trial. He had corresponded interminably with veritable catenae of living authorities in Paris for reactions to the charges and to the evidence. His laborious attention to due process and the ponderous legal phraseology of his epistles and summaries fail altogether to disguise the ardour that possessed him. One need only compare the language of the charges against Gilles de Rais some fifteen years later to see how impartial legal terminology can sound, even when the crimes are heinous, devil worship and child murder. Cauchon felt that he had to prove that Joan was either a witch or a hoax. The latter was preferable, and Joan's abjuration, as it appears in the trial record, was certainly approved, and perhaps composed, by Cauchon himself. In it, Joan confesses that she lied when she said she acted at the promptings of God, when she claimed to see angels and saints; that she had worn dissolute dress, contrary to all womanliness; that she had been cruel and bloodthirsty; that she had been a schismatic and an adorer of evil spirits.[8] She was made to admit not to effective action through witchcraft, but to self-deception and deception of others. If proved a hoax, Joan tainted with falsehood the whole French argument of legitimate rights to the French crown. So it might not have mattered to Cauchon that she should be burned rather than survive. A recantation might have sufficed. But the superstition of Bedford ran deeper, as we have seen. She was, in his eyes, "a limb of the fiend," not just a vainglorious liar. The English defeats were her fault. She was his excuse for failure, and it was therefore of cardinal importance to reduce her magic to ash. Cauchon and Bedford were struggling on different fronts: the former wanted to show belief in her was unfounded and hollow, the latter believed and wanted her destroyed. That conflict might have been the cause of the rage on the rostrum when Joan made her abjuration. For Bedford, she was a cunning and possessed woman, working her wickedness further to save her skin; for Cauchon, she was admitting she had lied and thus undoing all her power. Cauchon despised her and the French who followed her; Bedford paid her the tribute of belief.

In prison after her recantation, Joan realised she had signed away her specialness, and she wanted it back. And the outward sign of her uniqueness was her dress, both for Cauchon and for herself. Judge and victim understood each other well.

Joan's dress formed the subject of no less than five charges, so although we know nothing of Joan's appearance, we have detailed information about her clothes. The charge declared:

> The said Jeanne put off and entirely abandoned woman's clothes, with her hair cropped short and round in the fashion of young men, she wore shirt, breeches, doublet, with hose joined together, long and fastened to the said doublet by twenty points, long leggings laced on the outside, a short mantle reaching to the knee, or thereabouts, a close-cut cap, tight-fitting boots or buskins, long spurs, sword, dagger, breastplate, lance and other arms in the style of a man-at-arms.

The thirteenth article in the charges continued in similar vein, inveighing against her for attributing unholy commands to God Himself and for often dressing "in rich and sumptuous habits, precious stuffs and cloth of gold and furs":

> not only did she wear short tunics, but she dressed herself in tabards and garments open at the sides, besides the matter is notorious since when she was captured she was wearing a surcoat cloak of cloth of gold, open on all sides, a cap on her head, and her hair cropped round in man's style. And in general, having cast aside all womanly decency, not only to the scorn of feminine modesty, but also of well instructed men, she had worn the apparel and garments of most dissolute men, and, in addition, had some weapons of defence.[9]

The accusation breaks down in three parts: the unwomanliness and immodesty of her costume; the luxury of her state; the carrying of arms. Her transvestism offended; it was a potent strategy for change, as Fronton-du-Duc noticed when he poised his heroine on the edge of "a new life," symbolised by her donning the garments of men.

At the trial, Joan's questioners returned to the subject of her dress with as much persistence as they had used about her voices, and Joan proved again in return as intransigent and as niggardly with information. On 22 February, she told the story of how she had set out from Vaucouleurs for Chinon, in the "habit of a man," carrying a sword Robert de Baudricourt had given her, with a knight and a squire and four servants in her suite. But when Beaupère asked her, several times, why had she put on male dress, she baulked. She would not divulge who had advised it; she would not pass the responsibility for it on to anyone else. In her next reply, she added that "it was altogether nec-

essary to change her clothes."[10] But neither at this point in the trial
nor at any other time, until the very end, did she specifically give a
practical reason. She never said she had done it to live with greater
safety among soldiers, to preserve her chastity, or to ride a horse. No
pragmatic explanation was ever offered by Joan herself until after the
trial, when she had resumed her male dress in prison. Then she said
that if she was not to be transferred to a more seemly ecclesiastical
prison, a *prison gracieuse* with women to attend her, as was her right,
but was to be kept under the same unruly English guards, it was better
for her to live dressed as a man.[11]

Her tenacity to her dress beforehand had different roots. The
second time she was asked if she wanted a woman's dress, she answered:
"Give me one. I will take it and go: otherwise I shall not have it and
am content with this, since it pleases God that I wear it."[12] Her clothes
were connected in her mind with her mission and held there an exalted
place, above a mere practical measure. At the fourth public session, she
made her famous answer: "The dress is a small, nay the least thing."[13]
But Joan can hardly have meant this when she clung so fiercely to the
costume. Her reply must have been a clumsy attempt to lead her
accusers away from a crucial and sensitive area, for she added immediately "that she had put it on at the command of God and his angels,
as she had done in all things." She insisted on this—that her motive for
the dress was the gratification of God—three times. The subject again
came up in the sixth session, the last in public. Joan was at her most
recalcitrant. Had her voices asked her to wear her costume? "I do not
recall." Had the clerks at Poitiers questioned her about it? "I do not recall." Had the queen, Marie d'Anjou, sometimes asked her to change
her costume? "That is not in your case," replied Joan.[14]

Had she been asked to change when she was a prisoner at the
castle of Beaurevoir? Yes, the demoiselle of Luxembourg, the aged aunt
of John, Joan's keeper, and his wife, the lady of Beaurevoir, offered
her a new dress or the cloth to make a new one. But she told them she
could not accept because she did not have God's permission. As we
have seen, she added, becoming almost voluble, that if she had, she
would rather have changed at the request of those two ladies than of
anyone else in France, except the queen.[15] At the second session in
prison, she explicitly denied that Baudricourt had suggested her change
of clothing. She had done it of her own accord and not at the request
of any man alive. It was at this point, when pressed further on the

subject, that Joan made her pure protestation of faith in her voices, "Everything *good* that I have done, I have done at the command of my voices." She thus implied that they had ordered her. But she added quickly that she could not elaborate further about her dress, not until tomorrow when she would have been advised. She remained defiant when the judges pressed her to admit it was wrong. If she were free, she would do exactly as she had done, all over again, for it seemed to her that France had benefited greatly by it.[16] She was not questioned further in the following session, as she had expected; and in the charge, the turncoat Baudricourt is exonerated: he gave her male dress at her request, it says, *cum magna abominatione,* "with the greatest repugnance."[17]

Twice more, Joan was interrogated about her dress. She was bribed with the offer of Mass and communion if she would reassume female clothes. She was ambiguous in her answers. She first bargained, over several exchanges, for the right to hear Mass: "Promise me that I may hear Mass if I wear a woman's dress and I will answer you." Her examiner promised. Joan then prevaricated, saying she had promised the king not to change. But then, changing course swiftly and ordering her accusers to make her "a long dress reaching down to the ground, without a train," she said, "Then, on my return, I will put on once again the dress I have." She was playing for time. When the examiner tried to compel her to answer, one way or the other, she snapped back: "Give me such a dress as the daughters of your bourgeois wear . . . with a long surcoat and a hood." She continued to plead for her Mass, but proved incapable at making the simple switch of clothing.[18] So she never heard Mass; the dress was not, it seems, a trifle. The final draft of the charges reduced Joan's shilly-shallying to a clear statement: "The said Catherine and Margaret instituted this woman in the name of God, to take and wear a man's clothes; and she had worn them and still wears them, stubbornly obeying the said command, to such an extent that this woman had declared she would rather die than relinquish these clothes."[19]

Why was Joan so obstinate? Though it does not seem a small thing to deny her voices, it seems to us now contrary and self-destructive to cling to apparel so obviously offensive and even dangerous to her survival. But Joan was right not to belittle it by rejecting it casually. Through her transvestism, she abrogated the destiny of womankind. She could thereby transcend her sex; she could set herself apart and usurp the privileges of the male and his claims to superiority. At the same time, by never pretending to be other than a woman and a maid, she was usurping a man's function but shaking off the trammels of his sex altogether to occupy a different, third order, neither male nor female, but unearthly, like the angels whose company she loved (6).

There was a long tradition, some of which Joan must have known, of sexual obliteration through dress, and it had long been recognised as a special sign, both upsetting the natural order and yet approaching the *vita angelica*. Before Joan's capture, her own side was anxious about her transvestism, and learned arguments in her defence were put forward in two treatises written after the victory of Orleans, before her capture. *De Mirabili Victoria Cujusdam Puellae* is the debate attributed to the exiled chancellor of the University of Paris, Jean Gerson, a brilliant and scathing preacher who, with his blend of religion and politics, represents on the French side what Cauchon, though less distinguished, represents for the Anglo-Burgundians. The treatise is dated 14 May 1429, at Lyons, that is, six days after the victory of Orleans and just before Gerson's own death. It exults in the turn of events. Joan's claim to divine guidance has been proved, *post hoc propter hoc*, because it has brought victory. The essay also refutes the prohibition of Deuteronomy, declaring that the new dispensation has cancelled the old; special circumstances require special responses.

As Joan has been chosen by the King of Heaven to bear His standard and has cut off her hair in order to accomplish the salvation of the French, Saint Paul's ban is also overturned in her case. For in I Corinthians 11:14–15, he had condemned sexual ambiguity: "Does not even nature itself teach you that, if a man have long hair, it is a shame unto him? But if a woman have long hair, it is a glory to her: for her hair is given for a covering."[20]

This tract was only attributed to Gerson at the vindication. But its date, so close to Gerson's death—as well as its carelessness of style and the use of classical allusion, which Gerson, as a serious and puritanical Christian, had rejected—cast doubts on his authorship. (Joan is compared to Camilla, the Volscian princess of the *Aeneid*, and to the Amazons.) Gerson was also a severe opponent of the many visionaries of the day and was quick to censure individual claims to divine guidance outside the rituals of the Church. It is unlikely Joan would have won such partisan treatment from him.[21] Another contemporary reaction to Joan's victories, from Jacques Gélu, the distinguished archbishop of Embrun, also uses the argument that by their fruits ye shall know them. He, too, justifies Joan's irregularities by her success and sees her male dress as only fitting for a soldier.[22] A further disquisition on the arguments for and against transvestism, *De Quadam Puella*, ducks the problem of Joan's obstinacy by stating that as soon as she got off her horse after a battle, she resumed female dress. Thus it defends her on the grounds of convenience. More interestingly, this treatise, attributed to Henry of Gorinchem, a professor of the University of Cologne who died in the same year as Joan, denies the current rumour that she is a phantom, a "fantastic effigy" or a good or evil spirit, and declares that she is no ghost but a flesh-and-blood woman who eats and drinks.[23] In this, the treatise echoes the Bourgeois de Paris's first report of Joan: "A creature in the shape of a woman, what it was, God knows."[24]

The uncertainty points to a reality at the centre of transvestism for a woman: that it unsexes her and dehumanises her, but does not confer manhood upon her. She remains ambiguous. But in the process, she rises rather than falls. Yet her unsexed state requires the manners, customs and, of course, the dress of the male. There is no mode of being particular to the third sex, or to androgyny. But as the rejection of femininity is associated with positive action, it assumes the garb of virtue, in the classical sense, *virtus*. Semantically, virtue is associated with man (*vir*). Joan of Arc's greatest quest was for virtue; she identified herself with the forces of good, she fought for what she thought above all to be good, and she hardly wavered from her conviction that all that had happened to her and through her was good. In order to marry her self-image to her actions, she needed a framework of virtue, and so she borrowed the apparel of men, who held a monopoly on virtue, on reason and courage, while eschewing the weakness of women, who were allotted to the negative pole, where virtue meant meekness and humility and nature meant carnality. But as a woman, she could not be anything but counterfeit. This is what Cauchon's trial needed to prove: that her voices were illusions; her dress, a trick; her mission, a perversion of nature.

That a woman contravened the destined subordination of her sex when she wore men's clothing underlies many of the prohibitions against it. Transvestism does not just pervert biology; it upsets the social hierarchy. A fifteenth-century manuscript dating from Joan's time contains a proverb warning against masculine women: "A woman who talks like a man and a hen who crows like a cock are no good to have around."[25] A poem written by an anonymous contemporary of Joan of Arc states fiercely:

> *It is forbidden in the Bible*
> *That a woman be so bold,*
> *On pain of terrible torment,*
> *To commit the idolatry*
> *Of wearing on a single day of her life*
> *The dress that belongs to a man.*[26]

Christianity is unique among the world's universal religions in proclaiming the equality of the sexes—or rather the unimportance of sexual difference—before God. "There is neither Jew nor Greek, there is neither bond nor free, there is neither male nor female, for ye all are one in Christ Jesus," wrote Saint Paul in a text (Galatians 3:28) that is at the heart of the Christian philosophy. The democracy of souls is a central tenet of the faith.

But historically the Church has hardly borne it out, and among the stratagems its women members have used to overcome deep-seated prejudice have been virginity—the renunciation of sexual relations—and transvestism—the renunciation of sexual identity. Paradoxically, the Fathers also encouraged such methods, both openly and unconsciously. Saint Paul had proclaimed that faith abolished sexual difference and wrought a new asexual state, an ideal androgyny, which transcended gender and represented Christian virtue. But in the writings of the Fathers, this virtue is interpreted according to conventions about masculinity. Traditional female activities, like motherhood, or traditional female characteristics, crudely conceptualised by the Fathers to include gossip or flirtatiousness, were excluded from the virtuous prototype. Saint Jerome, though he criticised eunuchs, elsewhere exhorted women to a castrating asceticism: "As long as a woman is for birth and children, she is different from man as body is from soul. But when she wishes to serve Christ more than the world, then she will cease to be a woman and will be called man."[27] Saint Ambrose echoed the thought, using the term *manhood* with an even greater positive value: "She who does not believe is a woman, and should be designated with the name of her sex, whereas she who believes progresses to perfect manhood, to the measure of the adulthood of Christ. She then dispenses with the name of her sex, the seductiveness of youth, the garrulousness of old age."[28]

Christ, in whom all Christians, regardless of sex, were to be equally united by faith alone, is seen by the Fathers as man. But not man in the full sense of humanity, but in the particular, gender category of male. In the minds of the most eminent theologians, Christ himself does not transcend sexual distinction, and their arguments for his maleness still underpin the objections to the priesthood of women, who, being female, are considered biologically incapable of expressing the full humanity of the incarnate Jesus. Again, the problem is literalism, an inability to penetrate to the essential truth through the rind of realism. A female Christ offends a deeper sense of appropriateness than historical fidelity.

The prejudice against women, stemming from the cultural identification of the sex more closely with biological processes, with the body that is the divine spark's gaoler, raises enormous historical problems about the Graeco-Roman and Christian world's attitudes to menstruation, generation and parturition. The principal course that ambitious Christian women have taken to combat it has been virginity, and many virgins, like Julian of Norwich, Catherine of Siena, Mary Ward, having claimed special status for themselves by this means, were able to impose their desires on society in a way they could not have done otherwise. But the history of virginity as an expression of female independence and ambition belongs only partly to a book about Joan. Though she chose a life of chastity, she made her demands felt more particularly through her dress, through her maleness, through dispensing with the name of her sex and progressing to manhood.

Transvestism in women is only occasionally pathological. It is tempting today, when explanations from sexual deviation are popular, to say Joan of Arc was a lesbian. But the formula takes no account of cultural or social conditions and is totally inadequate. Historically, transvestism has often provided a device for a woman to make something of herself, a figure of speech to lay claim to greatness beyond the expected potential of her sex. Like many devices, it is practical and yet mysterious, convenient and yet magic, all at once, and its provoking, fascinating quality has made it a motif in tragedy, folklore, mythology, hagiography, ritual, romance and children's stories.[29]

The Christian tradition is rich with examples of the theme. An ancient text, the *Acts of Paul*, thought to have been written around 160 A.D. by an orthodox Christian, tells the story of Thecla, Paul's disciple, a beautiful young woman who is engaged to be married. One day, by chance, Thecla hears Paul preach chastity. She becomes enthralled. His words pierce home to her and convert her with all-consuming loving blindness. She rejects her suitor: many others follow her example. When Thecla's conversion and others' provoke riots, Paul is scourged and driven out, and a stake is prepared for Thecla, but "though a great fire blazed forth, the fire took no hold on her." She sets out to find Paul again, and when they meet, she begs to become his acolyte: "I will cut my hair and follow thee whithersoever thou goest," she says. Paul sternly refuses her, and her faith is tried in a picaresque sequence of ordeals. Finally, Thecla is baptised. Again the male motif returns: "She took young men and maids, and girded herself, and sewed her mantle into a cloak after the fashion of a man." Paul accepts her this time and sends her out to teach.[30]

Thus, in the *Acts of Paul*, the act of becoming a Christian is intertwined for a woman with the rejection of femininity, in Thecla's case accentuated by the seductiveness and eligibility ascribed to her.

The Passion of Saints Perpetua and Felicity,[31] a text of remarkable force and beauty, tells another story about a woman's struggle to overcome the denigration of her sex. Composed early in the third century in Carthage, the tale is written in the first person of Perpetua herself, a twenty-two-year-old patrician and mother of an infant boy whom she is still nursing at the time of her martyrdom. She defies her Roman father and refuses to deny Christ. Before the appointed day for her death, Perpetua dreams that she is stumbling over hard, winding roads on the way to the arena. A deacon, called Pomponius, is guiding her. He promises to help her, but when they reach the theatre, he disappears and she finds herself alone before an immense, angry and ignorant crowd. An "Egyptian" appears in the ring to fight her. He is huge and "very ugly." Assistants materialise at her side. She finds herself changed: "I was a man," she says. They rub her down with oil, like a Greek athlete before a contest. Then Christ appears, disguised as "a giant," and announces the games are to begin. Perpetua fights hard, wrestling with the Egyptian like a professional. In the final victorious struggle, she seizes his head and crushes his face onto the arena floor.

Her vision is about her conflict and victory over the devil, over the temptation of denying Christ. Her change of sex develops fluidly, within the dream, according to the natural workings of the unconscious. In this trial of her virtue, a prelude to the supreme ordeal of the arena, Perpetua puts off the weakness of her sex to assume the image that approximates in her religion to fortitude and grace—the image of manliness.[32] Saint Jerome, in a sermon for her feast day, explicitly draws this conclusion—and approves it. He comments that Perpetua dreamed she was a man in order to be more perfectly like Christ, as Saint Paul described in his letter to the Ephesians: "till we come in the unity of the faith, and of the knowledge of the Son of God, unto a perfect man, unto the measure of the stature of the fullness of Christ" (Ephesians 4:13). In this passage, Jerome displays the characteristic patristic bias: *man* means male, not the general state of humanity, transcending gender. When Perpetua dreamed she fought as a man, she was surely seeing herself not as male, but as not-female. In the realm of the spirit, in the theology of the incarnation, the category *man* should mean human, without value differences of age, race or sex. Joan, lacing herself into doublet and hose, cropping her hair in the pudding-basin style that had just come into fashion, never proclaimed herself a boy. Indeed she never once pretended she was male, since she referred to herself in the feminine gender, as La Pucelle, the Maid. But her dress declared her not-female, as Perpetua dreamed she was when she faced the greatest ordeal of all, the struggle with evil.

When Joan was criticised for wearing male dress, her supporters, like the queen mother, Yolande of Anjou, countered with the Gerson argument that the Old Covenant was dead and the Bible's ban on transvestism, like the law of circumcision, a legacy of the past. But they also cited the many female saints who had lived as men and who do indeed present a powerful group, so numerous that they must signify more than mere curios of sexual history. In one of the *Golden Legend* stories about Saint Margaret of Antioch, one of Joan's voices, she vows to remain a virgin and, on the night of her arranged marriage, escapes from home: "commending herself to God, and cropping her hair in the male fashion, she stole away secretly." Arriving at a monastery and adopting the name Brother Pelagius, Margaret lives there quietly as a monk until, in the dramatic turn of events characteristic of these stories, she is accused by another young woman of fathering her child. Margaret suffers the accusation in silence and is condemned to solitary confinement on bread and water for the rest of her life. She endures this uncomplainingly for years but, when she feels death at hand, decides to write a letter and reveal the full extent of her innocence. She is then recognised a woman and honoured as a saint.[33]

The structure of this story—the rejection of marriage, the change of dress, the life of a monk, the false charge and the deathbed vindication—is repeated in many other stories about monachoparthenics, or disguised female monks. Saint Euphrosyne, for instance, died in 470, after thirty-eight years disguised as the monk Smaragdus. Her relics were transferred to Compiègne, where Joan of Arc was captured in 1430, so her story and her cult might have been known to the Maid. The stories of Saints Theodora of Appollonia, Anastasia of Antioch, Hilaria, Theodora of Alexandria, Matruna of Perge, and Eugenia of Alexandria, most of them anchorites living at the acme of the fifth century's passion for world-denying rigours, all exhibit some similar features to the paradigm case of Joan of Arc. There is, unfortunately, little evidence for the incidence of holy transvestism in the realm of real women. Saint Jerome condemns it, in the fourth century, and a canon of the Synod of Ver in the ninth proves the existence of cases earlier than Joan of Arc: "If women who choose chastity in the cause of religion either take on the clothes of a man or cut their hair, in order to appear false to others, we resolve that they should be admonished and criticised, because we consider that they err through a great ignorance rather than zeal."[34]

Male dress symbolised an ascetic renunciation of the world. Femaleness is identified with beauty and luxury; and by forsaking vanity, these saints grow in virtue. Joan herself, however, did not assume male dress in any spirit of penance. She loved beautiful clothes. But Joan's claims to rank and status do correspond to Saint Eugenia's, for instance, who through the cultivation of manly virtue, eventually gained the position of provost:

> His [Christ's] rule I have wholeheartedly embraced, and out of the faith I have in Christ, not wishing to be a woman, but to preserve an immaculate virginity, I have steadfastly acted as a man. For I have not simply put on a meaningless appearance of honour but rather . . . I have acted the part of a man by behaving with manliness, by boldly embracing the chastity which is alone in Christ.[35]

Had Joan possessed more eloquence, she might perhaps have used equally sophisticated phrases to justify her male dress, instead of repeating, with determined but inarticulate clarity, that her dress simply pleased God.

Second—and in this respect the analogy is most fruitful—the disguise constituted a rejection of parental authority and, more precisely, of male domination. By becoming male, the female escaped subordination. Margaret, Thecla, Perpetua and, as we shall see, Uncumber, refuse to act according to their fathers' wishes about their beliefs or their marriages; the break is characterised by the change of clothes, just as the new life of a nun is marked by the cutting of her hair and the wearing of a veil. Dress can be used to solemnise rites of passage, initiations into new modes of being. Joan's reluctance, even anger, at the idea that she put on her boy's clothes at the suggestion of a man—Robert de Baudricourt—echoes the bid for autonomy of the female saints who lived in men's clothing.

Joan laid claim to her independence in a much more fundamental way before she met Robert de Baudricourt. At the age of sixteen or seventeen, she broke with her parents, exactly as described in the hagiographies of transvestite saints. She refused to marry the man they had chosen for her. She told the story under La Fontaine's examination, in the afternoon of the second closed session in prison, and it appears in most revealing form, buried in the middle of her account of how she decided not to tell her parents about her visions. In the morning, she had announced that she had told only the king and Robert de Baudricourt about her voices. Although they had not stopped her telling others, she had feared to do so, in case her enemies, the Burgundians, heard and prevented her journey. But, she added, she feared especially that her father would forbid her to go. Her cross-examiner immediately asked, Was it right for her to contravene the fourth commandment and leave without her parents' consent? Joan answered that she had always obeyed them, in everything except her departure, and that she had since written to explain, and they had forgiven her. Pressed on the point, she said that as God had commanded her to leave, she would have done so "even if she had had a hundred fathers and mothers and had been a king's daughter." Interrogated further, she added that her voices had not forbidden her to tell her parents, except that the knowledge would have caused them pain; "But as for herself, she would not have told them for anything in the world." Already, her conviction rings keenly, with a touch of pain, or even desperation, as she remembers how tightly she hugged her purpose to herself.[36]

In the afternoon, she revealed why. La Fontaine asked her about the dreams it was said her father had had about her before she left home. The phrasing is revealing: either Joan's father or Joan herself must have been the primary source. It is unlikely Joan's father would have boasted of such dreams; it is more probable that Joan herself would have nursed the knowledge and spread it, in order to justify her unfilial secrecy, for it must have been a harsh memory. She described to La Fontaine that "when she was still at home with her mother and father," her mother told her that her father said he had dreamed that " 'Joan his daughter would leave with men-at-arms.' Her mother and father took great pains,' Joan continued, 'to keep her and held her in great subjection; and she obeyed them in everything, except in the case at Toul about the marriage.' " Also, she went on, telling her prosecutors that her father had also said to her brothers: " 'Indeed, if I thought that it would come to pass as I fear regarding my daughter, I should like you to drown her, and if you did not do so, I would drown her myself.' " "[Her] father and mother practically lost their minds when [she] left for the fortified town of Vaucouleurs," Joan admitted.[37]

The simple words tell a dark story of anger and incomprehension, defiance and pain, in which the refusal to marry is mixed up with the desire to leave on her mission; together they provoke a murderous rage in her father. It was immediately after telling this that Joan snapped that she assumed male dress "by herself of her own accord, and not at the request of any man alive." The atmosphere of the D'Arc household at Domremy was worlds away from the edifying family cosiness applauded by Joan's hagiographers. Joan was, in fact, a runaway.

One of the strangest saints in the transvestite group is Saint Uncumber; and her legend uncovers the deepest meaning of the saints who adopted male dress. Uncumber was born Wilgefortis, *virgo fortis*, "the strong virgin," and she was one of the septuplet children of a king —of Portugal in some versions, of Lusitania in others. He wished her to marry another pagan, the king of Sicily. Like most of the saints in the group, Wilgefortis was pledged to a life of virginity. In despair at the proposed match, she prayed to Christ to help her keep her vow, and immediately a long silky moustache and beard grew to disfigure her. When the king of Sicily saw his bride, he declined. Wilgefortis's father, in the mortal rage characteristic of patriarchs in these legends, had his daughter crucified.[38] Wilgefortis's story spread throughout Europe, for perhaps it touched a widespread need before the age of easy divorce. She became known as a different kind of redeemer, the redeemer of women from men: Livrade in France, Liberata in Italy, Librada in Spain, Saint Débarras in Cauchon's own see of Beauvais, Ohnkummer in Germany, Ontcommere in Flanders, and Saint Uncumber, from the

Old English, which has now changed into "disencumber," the saint who helps to free women from unwanted husbands. Thomas More commented scornfully on her cult in Old St. Paul's: "for a peck of oats she will not fail to uncumber them of their husbands." Her beard, the sign of her masculinisation, served to alter her status: she escaped the subjection of women and attained the privileges of men.[39]

Joan might have heard of Uncumber, though it is impossible to claim that she provided a conscious model. But Joan certainly resembled her in her open femaleness. In both cases, the male trappings were used as armour—defensive and aggressive. It protected Joan—and Uncumber—against men, and it attacked men by aping their appearance in order to usurp their functions. On the personal level, it defied men and declared them useless; on the social level, it affirmed male supremacy, by needing to borrow its appurtenances to assert personal needs and desires. Copycat fashions today, from executive suits to the workers' look, the oversized boilersuit and faded dungarees, are an equivalent. They announce that women can do men's work, are as good as men, are up to men of every station; but men remain the touchstone and equality a process of imitation.[40]

Ironically, Joan's life, probably one of the most heroic a woman has ever led, is a tribute to the male principle, a homage to the male sphere of action. As Saint Margaret says, when she reveals in *The Golden Legend* why she cannot be the father of a child (the version Joan probably heard recited on many occasions): "I have the virtue of a man, and have *virtue of that sin* that was put on me."[41]

At only one point in her trial did Joan insist stoutly on her feminine skills. She did not shepherd animals in the fields, she retorted, and she challenged any woman in Rouen to better her at sewing or spinning.[42] Spinning is the quintessential sex-stereotyped activity. When Hercules is sold into slavery to Omphale, queen of Lydia, the badge of his degradation, of his emasculation, is a distaff. But when Joan made her boast, she was claiming higher social status, through an activity where, for once, women took precedence over men. A seamstress or spinster, though female, ranked higher than a cowherd; Joan responded to the distinction with the precision of a spirit level. She undoubtedly had what is termed upward mobility.

In the fourteenth century, another story of a heroine in male disguise was written in the form of a play, and it was performed, we know, in the 1370s, for the text was prepared as part of a series commissioned at that time by the Goldsmiths' Guild in Paris. We do not have a record of a later performance, and we cannot know how widely disseminated the tale itself was. But if Joan knew *La Fille d'un Roy*,[43] it would certainly have stimulated the elements in her imagination that were already working busily on certain dreams. It is a miracle play about a king's daughter who leaves her father's house and lives and fights as a knight.

Ysabel's mother dies giving birth to her, and her father refuses to marry again. When his advisors insist that the kingdom must have an heir, he vows he will marry only someone exactly like his dead queen. After searching the length and breadth of the realm, the counsellors return to say that the only woman who equals his queen in beauty and goodness is his daughter. He must marry her.

In despair, Ysabel the princess takes counsel and, advised to disguise herself as a man, escapes with a handmaiden. She becomes a soldier, entering the service of the emperor of Constantinople in his holy wars against the infidel. In one battle, she takes five kings prisoner and binds them together "like dogs in harness."[44] In return for this signal prowess, the emperor offers the strange knight the hand of his daughter, and they are married. After many vicissitudes and the miraculous interventions of Saint Michael and God Himself, the tangle is unwoven. Ysabel marries the emperor; his daughter separates from Ysabel to marry her father.

The miracle play possibly discloses the springs of transvestism in women: identification with the father and the prohibition against incest. In some of the versions of Uncumber's story, her father also wants to sleep with her. It would be interesting for a psychologist to pursue the reason that so many of the known historical cases are also illegitimate children—Mary Read, who became a soldier, then a pirate in the eighteenth century; Albert Nobbs, a waiter whose story George Moore told in a novella in the nineteenth.[45]

Where the daughter is a bastard, her change of external appearance may arise from a fear that she might meet her lost father and then neither know him nor be known to him, that she might, like the girl in Pirandello's *Six Characters in Search of an Author*, make love to her own father. The exchange of femininity for masculinity also marks a psychic identification with the lost father; in the case of Joan, when the rejection was voluntary, even longed for, it still had the effect of pushing her into imitative maleness, as if to defend herself against the strong emotions that clearly flowed between them. *La Fille d'un Roy* is a fascinating example of these unconscious impulses, for it reveals that the desire of a father for his daughter, or of a daughter for her father, can impel her to refuse her womanhood, to refuse to become the adult object of his lust and to retreat instead into a symbolic neutral state, neither fully man nor fully woman. By denying sexual differentiation, the grown-up state is never reached.

The girl child who makes believe by dressing up that she is a boy is a popular motif of children's fiction, and it is acceptable in a way that a boy in girl's clothing could never be for the same age group. In itself, this reveals our commonly held prejudices. Jo in Louisa May Alcott's *Little Women* has excited children, and especially girls, all over the world. Diana Trilling, the literary critic, has described her disillusion with Jo's girlish end: "Jo represented my own first encounter with a heroine of spirit; it was a love affair but one that ended in devastation when at the end of the book it was not Jo but her insipid sister Amy who got Laurie while Jo had fobbed off on her that old professor with a beard." Trilling goes on to diagnose shrewdly the problem of shifting ideals that the transvestite heroine poses. Held up for admiration at one moment, she is whisked away to defeat at the next: "For the reader aged nine or ten this outcome of *Little Women* established forever a fatal incertitude about what constituted a successful femininity since it was unmistakable that Jo was the vital centre of the book, yet the man I wanted for her, which was also of course for myself, preferred Amy's golden curls to Jo's gallant brown head."[46]

The state of suspension, of nondifferentiation, achieved by a transvestite girl was confirmed by the Christian tradition as holy. Sexlessness is virginity's achievement and a metaphor for martyrdom, as hagiography bears out. Transcendence of gender in most of these cases heralds a welcome or even a self-imposed death; transvestism becomes the transitive verb in a sentence of self-obliteration. Yet the martyrs of this kind saw their renunciation as a rebirth into an exalted state of original wholeness, where sex did not obtain. A Freudian would see this state as analogous to death, not life, because in seeking to cancel sexual difference, it seeks to arrest time and to deny the mutability to which all flesh is heir. Catherine Clément, a French analyst, in a brilliant essay on myth and sexuality, warns against the illusion that health can be discovered in the denial of fundamental laws, the law of sexual difference, the law of time and change. She quotes the case of Sidonie, an anorexic girl who told her doctor as she lay dying of starvation: "There it is, my problem, I want neither to get fatter nor thinner, to be neither boy nor girl, to have no more periods." She wanted, as Clément comments, to annul periodicity, "to play the disorder of androgyny against the order of the female cycle [called *règles*, or rules, in French], to be neither one thing nor the other, *neuter*."[47]

Apart from the minor but particular associations with Joan—the imagined, but possibly real absence of periods, the sexlessness enacted—the stasis implied by the image of female transvestism is apt. Joan, as we shall see later, is used as the figurehead for moral causes that proclaim the absoluteness of their way, their impregnability to moral relativism, which means their sovereignty over time. This again connects with the Christian concept of the holy, to which Joan in one way belonged so illustriously.

CHAPTER 8

KNIGHT

Embrouded was he, as it were a mede
Al ful of fresshe floures, whyte and rede.
Singinge he was, or floytinge all the day;
He was as fresh as is the month of May.
Short was his gonne, with sleeves longe
and wyde . . .

GEOFFREY CHAUCER,
The Canterbury Tales[1]

Joan of Arc broke with her parents and Domremy and ran away to the world, not from the world. Her male dress could have taken many forms, not least, like her models, that of a monk. But it did not; instead it betokened a specific worldly caste, the significance of which had great importance not only for Joan who chose it, but for her adherents who supported it and her enemies who would not tolerate it. Joan chose, with her brilliant instinct for effectiveness, to dress herself in two intertwined uniforms of positive virtue, maleness and knighthood. The advancement she achieved by this means was swift and illustrious. It was also deeply subversive. By assuming the forms that the interpreters of right and wrong, the dominating arbiters of society, usually understood to be right, by pretending to such dazzling effect, Joan posed a severe problem about the relationship of intrinsic to extrinsic virtue. She showed that one did not have to be a nobleman to be a nobleman. Some of her contemporaries were prepared to accept a flux of people into stable institutions without feeling threatened. But they were unusual for their time and for all times; a society feels stable when neither institutions nor people shift or change. Joan is the personification of mobility: she accepted neither her peasant birth, nor her female condition, none of the limitations society had provided for her circumscription. Instead, in an age of chivalry, she assumed its most successful guise and dressed herself and comported herself like a knight born to the role.

The exploits of Jean de Bueil, who fought with Joan of Arc, were told in *Le Jouvencel,* one of the most eloquent testimonials to the abiding fascination with chivalry of the fifteenth century. In it, the romantic hero declares: "Those who are not noble by descent are noble by the practice of the profession of arms they follow, which is noble in itself. I tell you that as soon as a man-at-arms has a helmet on his head, he is noble, noble enough to fight a king. Arms ennoble a man, whoever he may be."[2]

De Bueil is guilty of special pleading, for the niceties of social distinctions were felt so keenly that later on in the century, Louis de Bueil, fighting in a tournament before René of Anjou, duke of Lorraine, wondered if his adversary, Jean de Châlons, was of high enough birth to cross lances with him.[3] In Joan's day, there was considerable tension between the old nobility of long lineage and the new, who had won their titles recently by deeds of war. It was still possible to achieve knighthood by military prowess; chivalry provided a means of social advancement. When Suffolk, the English leader, was captured at the siege of Jargeau in June 1429 by one of the French soldiers with Joan of Arc, he asked his captor if he was noble. When the latter said no, Suffolk told him to kneel and dubbed him, then and there, a knight. Only then did he yield himself up. For an earl to have been taken by a commoner would have been degrading; consequently, for a commoner, winning such a prize in battle meant a sudden rise in the world.[4]

No society has ever accepted without grumbling new recruits in the old enclaves, and Joan was criticised for the grandeur of her attire and her suite, unseemly enough for a commoner, worse for a common woman. Joan had dash, valour and a gift for display, just as the flower of chivalry was supposed to have. In the first full biography of her life, written around 1500 by a Burgundian who found himself, willy-nilly, admiring Joan and her exploits, Joan's presence at the ceremony of touching for the king's evil is described: "The Maid, arrayed in white armour, rode on horseback before the King, with her standard unfurled. When not in armour, she kept state as a knight and dressed as one. Her shoes were tied with laces to her feet, her hose and doublet were shapely, a hat was on her head. She wore very handsome attire of cloth of gold and silk, noticeably trimmed with fur." This is Joan, around five months after she broke with her destiny as the daughter of a middle peasant of Domremy.[5]

To keep state as a knight was very costly: the horses, the weapons, the armour, the retinue (who in theory should be paid now and then), the pageantry, put it out of the reach of almost everyone except the sons of the aristocracy or military adventurers. Joan was neither, and she had nothing to her name. She transformed herself by her wits and by her astonishing ability to compel credence. Early 1429, a peasant girl in a homespun red dress calls at the castle of Vaucouleurs. A short while later, and a knight rides astride one of many chargers in her stable, carries bright weapons and armour, made to measure, her own banner with her choice of device streaming out behind her, her retinue behind her, her page, her squire in attendance upon her, her soldiers ready and equipped to follow her. She wrought this metamorphosis through her ability to embody an urgent set of symbols, and it was not accidental that, having this gift, she chose the compelling idiom of chivalry and codified her mission in its language. She knew the romance of chivalry from an early age, in spoken or perhaps dramatic form. One of her godmothers, Jeanne Thiesselin, said at the rehabilitation that she had heard stories of a *fée*, an enchantress rather than a fairy, "read in a romance."[6] Even in Domremy, there was some living tradition of reading aloud from literature other than religious. Chivalry had a very potent spell over her, as it had over many of her contemporaries.

When Joan was first told by her voices that she must leave her native village and raise the siege of Orleans, that she must go to Vaucouleurs and find Robert de Baudricourt, who would give her men to accompany her, her first response was that "she was a poor maid, knowing nothing of riding or fighting."[7] A horse seemed indispensable to Joan for the art of war, but quite beyond her reach. Yet horses, the first necessity for a knight, came Joan's way quite easily. Her first was bought for her by her cousin Durand Laxart. With a colleague, Jacques Alain of Vaucouleurs, Durand Laxart paid twelve francs for her horse; the money was reimbursed by Robert de Baudricourt later.[8] A second horse soon followed, very probably a finer specimen than the twelve-*franc* nag. As we have seen, the duke of Lorraine, Charles I, demanded Joan in audience. He was sick and hoped she might cure him. Joan rode to Nancy under safe-conduct and said that she wanted to go to

France. She refused to discuss his health with the duke, telling him only that if he gave her his son for her companion and men to follow her, she would pray for him.[9] According to one local witness at the rehabilitation, who remembered the story of Joan's meeting with the duke, he then gave her a black horse.[10] Joan herself does not say so. But it is highly significant that Joan requested the heir to the duchy of Lorraine to accompany her. For the "son" she demanded was René of Anjou, aged twenty in 1429. He was also the duke of Bar, the fief in which Domremy stood; and therefore, had vows of fealty been exchanged, he was Joan's local suzerain and she his vassal. René was married to the duke of Lorraine's daughter and had been adopted his heir that very year in March, news that Joan would very likely have heard. His mother was Yolande of Anjou, major influence of the Angevin party at court and a spur to Charles's flagging ambitions. Since she had married her daughter Marie to Charles and wished to see her as queen of France, these were identical with her own. At every point, René of Anjou stood in a vital connexion to the world of feudal relations which Joan was poised to conquer for a time, and when she requested his services, she showed her natural business-like instinct for success in these matters. René did not, however, join her until after her glory, at Provins, on 3 August 1429. If Joan had arrived at Chinon in the company of the Dauphin's brother-in-law, she knew she would have had no problem of access.[11]

Joan was terse with her judges when she described her first retinue: she had a knight, a squire and four servants when she set out from Vaucouleurs.[12] Twenty-seven years later, these men themselves were more forthcoming when they remembered the enterprise in which they had been so suddenly involved. Jean de Novelompont and Bertrand de Poulengy were the first men-at-arms to pledge themselves to Joan, and very proud they were of it later; they were also the first to bear the expense of that first journey to Chinon.[13]

The ride to Nancy, the eleven days across country to Chinon, and perhaps some riding practice there were enough, it seems, to teach Joan such horsemanship that she inspired wonder. D'Alençon saw her in the lists at Chinon: "After dinner the King went for a walk, Jeanne coursed before him, lance in hand. Seeing her manage her lance so well, I gave her a horse."[14] When questioned about her train at her trial, Joan said that she had five *coursiers* or (warhorses), given to her at the king's expense, and more than seven *trottins* (trotting ponies)[15]—not a splendid stable, perhaps, for someone who had been "*chef de guerre*," but not negligible, and besides, before the decline of her fortunes with the failure to take Paris in September, Joan might have been keeping greater state.

Her first sword—the other essential possession of any knight—was given to her by Robert de Baudricourt and was the only weapon she was carrying on her first journey.[16] She makes a point of this to her judges, as if to stress that all she had later obtained had been won on her own. But like her mounts, Joan's weapons, and her sword above all, had significance beyond their material value. To D'Alençon she had said, when they were introduced, "You are welcome. . . . the more that come together of the blood of France the better it will be."[17] The horse he gave her came from the stables of a man connected with the Blood Royal that Joan found holy, according to the spirit of chivalry that sanctified the secular aristocracy and made their battles just. Her principal sword, the one she used after Robert's was discarded, established for her an even more intimate link with the holy company of God's knights, and its finding is one of the stories that Joan tells at her trial with the greatest and simplest confidence.

The last stop Joan made on her historic journey to Chinon was at the shrine of Saint Catherine of Fierbois, a country chapel in which were kept relics of the saint whose voice Joan heard. It was a shrine that had begun to flourish again during the Anglo-French wars. The Saint Catherine of this chapel was the patron of escaped criminals and captives, particularly of prisoners of war fleeing the English. The chapel was hung with fetters, shackles, balls and chains and other tools of imprisonment from which the saint had miraculously relieved her votaries.[18] As Bertrand de Poulengy may have been in trouble for helping a man to escape from gaol, he may have known of the shrine and wanted to stop there, or Joan herself might have wanted to.[19] Not only the dedication of the shrine might have attracted her, but also the circumstances of its renewal. It was not until the late fourteenth century that the ancient chapel was rediscovered in the tangled woods that had grown up around it, and one of its most generous benefactors was Jean le Meingre, called Maréchal Boucicaut, whose feats of arms and deeds of piety earned him the accolade of perfect knight.[20]

A *Livre des Faicts*, written by a friend in 1407, holds up like *Le Jouvencel* Boucicaut's chivalry for the emulation of all. He lived austerely, but within the colourful world of tournaments and battlefields, just as Joan was to do; he renounced swearing and forbade it in his retinue, as Joan also was to do. However deeply in the thick of a fight, the marshal heard Mass, on his knees, twice a day.[21] Frequent attendance did not inspire suspicion of heresy unless there were other grounds, and the marshal's fervour was unimpeachable. It is not surprising, in this context, that Joan tells us that she heard three Masses at the shrine of Saint Catherine that day.[22] She could not have read the *Livre des Faicts* herself, but she had undoubtedly absorbed the image of this paragon among heroes.

It was there that Joan found her sword, in miraculous circumstances that, in the true spirit of chivalry, exalted and legitimised her acts of war. Instructed by her voices, Joan sent for it, from either Tours or Chinon, and it was found behind the altar and was covered with rust, which fell away from it as soon as it was rubbed, revealing five crosses along its blade. The words "Jesus" and "Maria" were inscribed on the edge. Joan denied that she had had the sword blessed, but said that she loved it because it came from the church of Saint Catherine, whom she loved. Three scabbards were made for it. One of crimson velvet and one of cloth of gold were gifts from the people of St. Catherine of Fierbois and of Tours. But she had had a sturdy leather one made.[23] Again, Joan shows herself in the practical, stern tradition of knighthood, spurning frivolous luxuries, and incidentally reveals a major feature of all new successful military champions: popular subsidy.

Just as Arthur found the magic sword Excalibur in the stone, so Joan divined her sacred weapons under the earth in a sacred place. The chosen hero must have a magic weapon. The cult of swords flourished still in her time and later; they symbolised, even more than the horse, the hallowed pursuit of peace through war. Bertrand du Guesclin, the great constable of France, a hero living still in the memories of Joan's generation, put a sword into the hand of Louis of Orleans as he was being baptised. God and battle were synonymous. The dukes of Burgundy claimed they owned a precious relic, the sword of Saint George; and King John, among the treasure he lost at sea in 1216, thought he had a sword belonging to Tristram himself.[24] Charles himself fought with the sword of Saint Louis. It was burned in the siege of La Réole in 1442. It is not surprising that when Jean Chapelain wrote his interminable epic, *La Pucelle ou la France Delivrée*, in 1656, he followed the structure of such myths and attributed Joan's sword to Charles Martel, the legendary hero and founder of French monarchy. Charles

Martel had left the sword, it was believed, behind the altar at St. Catherine for the second liberator of the fatherland to find. How Joan did divine its existence and send for it will never be known, though several circumstantial theories have been put forward.[25]

Even without such august antecedents, Joan's discovery of the sword under divine guidance perplexed and frightened her judges. She resisted their attempts to implicate her in blasphemous prayers about the use of it and eluded interrogation about its present whereabouts. The sword she had had at Compiègne when she was captured she had won from a Burgundian, she said, and it gave "good blows and good slashes." The sword she had hung up in thanksgiving in the abbey of St. Denis, along with a suit of armour, had been won at Paris, and was also different. Pressed, she refused point-blank to tell her judges where the Fierbois sword might be. It was too hallowed to be revealed.[26] Joan flew her own standard, which was a knight's prerogative. She denied at her trial that she bore a coat of arms or had even been granted one by the king.[27] Louis de Coutes, her page, affirmed at the rehabilitation that her rank had been granted by the king, and a document exists, dated 2 June 1429, which reports a grant of arms to Jehanne la Pucelle and gives her and D'Alençon command of the siege of Jargeau.[28] This document's authenticity is doubted. But in December 1429, at a parlous stage of Joan's fortunes, she and her family and all their issue in the male and female line were ennobled by Charles in perpetuity.[29]

Arms or no arms, Joan carried into battle the standard that she loved, she told her questioners, forty times more than she loved her sword.[30] Its design was dictated to her by her voices and came from God. They told her to paint the king of heaven upon it, holding the world between two angels, Michael and Gabriel. The field was white, which, as Joan's contemporary Christine de Pisan tells us, "men call in armoury silver the which colour of white is the most noble of all . . . it signifieth innocence and cleanliness."[31] It was sewn with fleurs-de-lys, and the words "Jesus Maria" were written upon it. Joan held it when she went into the attack, she said, in order "to avoid killing anyone." She insisted that she had never done anyone to death.[32] Cauchon and the other interrogators were very suspicious about her standard. Even the apparently innocuous and even pious use of the motto "Jesus Maria," on her letters and on a ring as well as on her standard, provoked her judges' fears of heresy. The cult of the Holy Name was fraught with controversy. Its chief proselyte, San Bernardino of Siena, had been summoned to Rome by Pope Martin V to defend his usage, and he had subsequently only permitted the monogram JHS or the names Jesus Maria to be painted beneath an image of the crucified Christ.[33] Joan was obviously ignorant of this complication, and again, unwittingly, she was heterodox. Joan's questioners also attributed to Joan superstitions about her standard that they themselves entertained. They accused her of believing it to have absolute efficacy on its own, of her casting a spell in it, so that butterflies, the familiars of witches, were seen fluttering in its furls at Château-Thierry.[34] When they asked her why her standard had been more prominently held at the coronation in Rheims than any of the other captains, Joan made her most famous, most eloquent reply, the reply that closes her trial: *"Il avoit esté à la paine, c'estoit bien raison que il fut à l'onneur"* (It had borne the pain, it was reason enough it should have the honour).[35]

The fifteenth century used emblems to express its values with a refinement that escapes us today; the sense of allegory and of the import of a device ran very deep; a motto or a family crest was not a hollow conceit, chosen for its sonority or charm. It embodied the owner's image of himself and his ultimate quest. By creating a personal poetic language, a knight could maintain the fiction that the internecine struggles of his house were gallant undertakings approved by God. Maréchal Boucicaut invested his characteristically ambitious and cruel enterprises on the field of battle with piety and courtliness by calling the chivalric order he founded the order of the *Ecu Vert à la Dame Blanche*. Alliances under such picturesque and meaningful titles were frequently made and, given the shiftiness of the times, as easily broken. But the very existence of the orders created an illusion of constancy. Louis of Orleans called his order after the porcupine, raising its prickles against Burgundy; Burgundy's famous order of the Golden Fleece recalled the Argonauts' heroism; the house of Brittany adopted the ermine as its symbol of chivalry; the house of Foix, a dragon; the house of Polignac, a golden apple.[36] These devices were added to the profusion of legends and coats of arms and insignia already blazoned on knights' banners and armour. A knight going into the lists presented a veritable catalogue of labels, each of them pointing to an aspect of his adopted character. John of Luxembourg, count of Ligny, Joan's captor, appears in a miniature painted around 1460 in full rig for a tournament: his horse's dagged caparison is resplendent with red dragons rampant, and a huge dragon spits from the crest of his helmet; he carries his family's coat of arms on his shield and another device on his banner.

Joan's standard, in which she invested so much pride and love, seems at first glance religious. But the images are underpinned by a powerful secular creed. Joan chose, through her voices, a political image: Christ pantocrator, Christ the King, ruler of all, including the world here below, on a field of lilies, the emblem of France as God's chosen country. Joan told her judges she had finally described her voices' instructions to Charles but *à contre-cœur*. Why "unwillingly," one wonders? Because the voices made plain that the ultimate king was always Christ, that the knight's responsibility lay with God and not with the earthly suzerain? Is it more likely that, by admitting to Charles that she had been designated a banner with lilies on it, she felt she was arrogating to herself prerogatives to which, as a common girl, she had no right and was exacting from her overlord rank and insignia that should be bestowed on her by him, not taken?

Certainly the lilies were a token of high esteem. But others outside the royal house could and did wear them, if granted by the king. They were emblazoned on the Orleans arms. In 1428, Charles even granted the right to quarter arms with those of France to John Stuart of Darnley, Lord Darnley, one of the Scots champions of the Valois cause. It was an inexpensive way for a hard-pressed suzerain to reward loyalty. In September 1429, Gilles de Rais, marshal of France and Joan's companion-at-arms, was awarded an orlure, or border of fleurs-de-lys, after his services in the Loire campaign and the victories of Orleans and Patay.[37]

The fleur-de-lys was associated with the legends of the earliest days of the Christian kingdom of France. According to the legend, Clovis, losing the battle of Tolbiac against the Alemanni, remembered the God of his wife, Clothilde, and vowed, as Constantine the Roman emperor had done before him, that he would be converted if God gave him victory. Forthwith the Alemanni were routed, and Clothilde, praying in her oratory, was visited by a dove with three white feathers in its beak. These formed the three-petalled lily, the heraldic emblem of France, and were substituted by Clovis for the three toads that had been the device on France's escutcheon since the legendary pagan king, Pharamond. The baptism of Clovis in Rheims cathedral and the conversion of the Franks is still taught in schools as the beginning of French history. In Joan's day, the claim of legitimacy through the divinely given fleur-de-lys was felt keenly. *The Bedford Book of Hours*, painted around 1423 for his duchess, depicts a version of the legend in exquisite, bright detail. God the Father, in a flaming aureole, gives the three lilies on a field azure to an angel, who then leaves the banner with a hermit. Queen Clothilde, attended by three gentlewomen in the horned headdresses of the fifteenth century, visits him; in the foreground, King Clovis, elegantly loricated in the overlapping steel plates that had recently come into style, receives the new blazon from his wife as one greave is fastened by a kneeling squire.[38] That the English depicted this legend in one of their prayerbooks shows how profoundly they longed to own title to the holy kingdom of France and how bitterly they must have resented Joan's simple, even cavalier takeover of one of its most powerful symbols. Interestingly, a further document, discovered at La Rochelle, declares that Joan had a different image painted on her standard, and though there is no evidence that she ever wore this coat of arms either, its contents are also related to the legend of the fleur-de-lys: on a field azure, a dove descending, with a scroll in its beak saying "From the King of Heaven."[39] It bears the same message: that Joan is called, in a characteristic chivalrous fashion, to accomplish worldly deeds on behalf of God's kingdom on earth.

A knight who was not born to the role but carved it for himself was carried forward on the fickle and swift enthusiasm of the people for whom he fought. Chivalry demanded that he repay in kind, and so we find Joan making gifts in the strong tradition of knightly largesse. To the nine-year-old daughter of her host in Orleans, Charlotte Boucher, she gave a hat of grey felt with a wide brim. It was hung with the fleur-de-lys and had been worn by Joan.[40] On behalf of the daughter of the man who painted her standard, she asked the citizens of Tours for a dowry, but when they refused, Joan gave her wine for her wedding feast.[41] As a true knight, Joan knew she must not forget her own people. At Château-Thierry at the end of July 1429, just after the coronation, Charles issued a decree: "In honour of and at the request of our beloved Joan the Maid, in consideration of the great, high, noteworthy and profitable service she had done us and does each day for the recovery of our sovereignty," he declared that he exempted the village of Domremy and its neighbour Greux from all taxation—*tailles*, *aides*, and other levies—in perpetuity. From then on, in the account books of the tax gatherers, against the names of Domremy and Greux it was written: "*Néant, la Pucelle*" (Nothing, the Maid).[42] Mark Twain, burning with love of Joan's gallantry, considered it an act of the grossest turpitude that this exemption was withdrawn in the

French Revolution. "She asked for nothing for herself, but begged that the taxes of her native village might be remitted for ever. The prayer was granted, and the promise kept for 360 years. Then it was broken, and remains broken today. France was very poor then, she is very rich now; but she had been collecting those taxes for more than 100 years."[43]

In a further, smaller way, but one that is just as revealing of Joan's chivalry, she sent a token to a lady most intimately linked with its proudest ideals, the widow of Bertrand du Guesclin. In the summer of 1429, just after her victory at Orleans, Joan met Guy de Laval, the grandson of Bertrand du Guesclin, the legendary liberator of France and gentle parfit knight, the constable whom Christine de Pisan perhaps described when she portrayed the epitome of chivalry in her influential book.[44] Guy de Laval, in the letter he wrote to his mother and his grandmother describing his meeting with Joan at Selles-en-Berry, evokes her with ardent admiration:

> And I saw her mounting her horse, armed all in white, except her head, with a little axe in her hand, on a great black charger, which at the gate of her lodging bridled hard and would not let her mount him; and then she said: "Lead him to the cross," which was in front of the church nearby, on the road. And then she mounted, without his moving, as if he had been bound. And then she turned toward the door of the church, which was close by, and said, in a womanly enough voice, "You, priests and people of the church, make prayers and procession for God," and then she turned back to her path, saying "Forward, forward," her standard unfurled and carried by a gracious page, and she had her little axe in her hand.[45]

It is a courtly picture, brimful with the charm of Joan's ambiguous state—the skilful knight, with the light voice of a woman. Later, in the same letter, Guy adds significantly that Joan told him that three days before her arrival, "she had sent to you, my grandmother, a tiny little gold ring, but that it was a trifle, and that she would willingly have sent you far better, considering your state."[46]

This is the quintessence of the chivalrous code, the core of Joan's identification with the romance of France's heroes. After Orleans, she did indeed hear Mass in the cathedral and dine with the people of the town, but the first gift that came to mind was for Anne de Laval, widow of the great constable Bertrand du Guesclin. She sent her a little gold ring as a pledge that she was carrying on the great and holy cause of France's peace and freedom. Joan adopted a religious vocabulary and imagery because they provided a readily available description of the world at the centre of her heart. But knightliness came before holiness.

Joan's judges were incensed by her worldliness. Her banner was bewitched and, at the same time, a typical effect of her vanity and love of luxury. The charges about her clothes were as vicious: the tragic detail that Joan was caught at Compiègne by the trailing panels of her golden surcoat and dragged by them from her horse inspired a sanctimonious sniff from her accusers. Such vaingloriousness was deservedly punished.[47] Joan was not unusual in enjoying rich dress, and besides, she was given it, according to the customs of the day. The imprisoned duke of Orleans, Charles, ordered a splendid costume for her as a token of his gratitude after the raising of the siege. At his orders, from the Tower of London, Joan was given two ells of "fine crimson Brussels" velvet, to be embroidered with nettles, the livery of the house of Orleans.[48] Charles himself knew all about finery. In one of his poems, he reveals his times' love of fashion, for he uses clothing as an image of the changing seasons:

> The weather has left off its coat
> Of wind, cold and rain.
> River, fountain and stream
> Wear, as a pretty livery,
> Drops of silver and gold,
> Everyone is getting dressed anew . . .[49]

His silver raindrops are not entirely a conceit since, on the eve of the battle of Agincourt, Charles bought a robe embroidered all over with 960 fine pearls; on the sleeves, the words of his song, "Madam, I am the most joyous of men," were spelt out with 568 more pearls, of which 142 provided the notation for the tune.[50]

The extravagance and the folly of the court fashions from the mid-fourteenth century onward continually excited the pens of moralists. "Poulaines," the later, English winkle-pickers, came first in vogue when Anne of Bohemia's suite brought this "Polish" fashion to the English court on her marriage to Richard II. Statutes were passed to limit their length; but the points grew longer and longer, until a chain was fastened to the tip for the wearer to hold while walking. They were even imitated in suits of armour.[51] Sleeves, cut in tongues, swept the floor; trains grew so long they were either tucked into girdles or held by pages; hennins, the steeple hats now obligatory as the medieval look, grew so high that at the château of Vincennes, Queen Isabella of Bavaria had the doorways heightened. Templars—latticed earphones—enclosed the hair; wimples, horns, cones all adorned women's heads; the liripipe, a long cowl wound round with the dagged ends falling round the shoulders in folds like a coxcomb, were men's equivalents. From 1360 onward, the Valois and Burgundian courts rivalled each other to create wild and eccentric fashions in what constitutes the first manifestation of the rapid changes in taste and style that have since become the norm.[52] The luxuriousness of the clothes can be seen very quickly in any of the paintings of the period, but we have become so accustomed to the lavish apparel of medieval sitters, or to the Virgin and saints portrayed in the gorgeous costumes of the past, that we forget people really were adorned like that, in damasks and satins and figured brocades.

Moralists inveighed particularly against the effeminacy of men. The vanity and immodesty of women were bad enough, but women were known to be foolish. The conspicuous luxuries of men were intolerable. Alain Chartier, chancellor of Notre-Dame in Paris, taunted bitterly in 1405 the softness in France: "He who does not want to get up to the sweet sound of a song, what will he do at the horrid noise of a trumpet? If a gown trails two feet on the ground and sleeves are wide to right or left and poulaines six inches long, what advantage will all this be when it comes to running away energetically from the enemy?"[53]

La Hire, one of the most ferocious and battle-worn captains who fought with Joan, had a scarlet mantle sewn all over with tinkling silver bells.[54] Philip de Cröy, of a renowned and learned Burgundian family, was nicknamed Clochette de Haynault after the little bells he hung on his horse's armour. Yet Christine de Pisan tells us: "He was the straightest lance of his day and a great performer of feats of arms."[55]

Clothes were capital; a good tailor as valuable, for instance, as an armourer; apparel signified social position. Joan knew this, and though she recalled the practical side when necessary, as with her tough leather scabbard, she wore the cloth of gold and the ornamental livery of her high state, whether donated or not. The mid-fourteenth-century consciousness of fashion was a discovery of a new method of social indexing and a very important one. Sumptuary laws revealed the abiding desire of the aristocracy to keep themselves apart and above the bourgeoisie who, by imitating their fashions, came close to usurping their place.

Philip VI, for instance, decreed that the common people could wear six-inch poulaines; the bourgeois rich, one foot long; and nobles, two feet long.[56] Such attempts to restrict social mobility prove fashion's power in this area, a power it still possesses. As Fernand Braudel has pointed out, luxury is a spur to social change; rulers, annoyed at the masses' mimicry, change the fashion and invent a new one, until that again is "stolen" and again a new mode is found.[57] This is a dynamic of progress, one that Joan, by changing her dress, used to her advantage until the fatal capture. Alain Chartier, her contemporary, was well aware of such manoeuvres. He decried it: "This most scandalous shame . . . when a varlet dressmaker and the wife of a man of low estate dare wear the clothing of a gallant knight and a noble lady." He hankered after the days when social status was instantly recognisable, when it was simple "to know the rank of a man from his clothes and not to confuse a nobleman with a mechanic."[58]

This is exactly one of the abuses Joan committed in the eyes of her condemners. Her male dress offended against canon law, natural law and, above all, social propriety. Henry VI, in a letter no doubt written by Bedford in June 1431 to justify Joan's execution, waxes furious at the scandal:

> She diverted the minds of men and women from the way of truth. She led them to a belief in fables and falsehoods. This is not all. She put on armour like a Knight or Equerry and designed a banner, and what is more outrageous, through excessive pride and presumption she has made the demand to have and to display the truly noble and surpassing Royal Arms of France. For this she was granted only partial permission.[59]

Even some members of her own side agreed with this. Joan was an interloper; she carried social advancement too far. When the archbishop of Rheims, Regnault of Chartres, turned against her, he gave as a reason "the rich clothes she has assumed."[60] Martin le Franc, a Burgundian, specifically refutes this charge in an early poem (1440) defending Joan. She needed her short coat and her finery, he says, to make war, just as a falcon must be freed from his long jesses in order to hunt.[61] But Le Franc's is a solitary voice; for the most part, Joan's style is glossed over by her enthusiasts. It should be borne in mind that the word used for *lust* in the medieval catalogue of the Seven Deadly Sins was the Latin *luxuria*, giving *luxure* in French. Indicting Joan for pomp and vanity stained her reputation in the same way as calling her a harlot. For the female, fettered by carnality, lust and luxury were synonymous.

The knightly code affected Joan even more fundamentally: Joan would never swear in court. The reason may be that she had sworn herself elsewhere, as a vassal. Every session opens with a bout of wrangling about her refusal, which ends in her agreeing to take a limited oath. At the first session, she would not put her hand on the Gospels, saying that there were things that she would only tell to Charles her king, revelations from God that he alone could hear. Eventually she yielded to her prosecutors and took the oath, but only on matters concerning the faith.[62]

Having made this condition, Joan kept to it as far as her resources would allow, and they were extraordinary. Time and time again in the trial, she retorted, "That is not in your case" or "*Passez outre*" (Pass) because the question went beyond the restrictions of religion and touched upon politics. "*Passez outre*" became a watchword for Joan, even more than her frequent "*Je m'en atends à Dieu*" (I wait upon God). It exemplifies the extent to which Joan had absorbed a male attitude, how well she had abjured the female's coquetry and winsomeness. She learned, to her cost, that all replies were a form of concession, and for a long while in the first sessions of the trial she was able to refuse to please, to refuse to project herself as her interrogators wanted, to produce again and again the intransigent "*Passez outre*." She surrendered, of course, by the third session in prison, after eight days of interrogation.[63] She then became embroiled in the long circumstantial and unconvincing tale of the king's sign, the crown and the angel at Chinon. But her speech is hobbled by her reluctance.

Shaw made Joan's defiance of the ordinary procedure of a trial the mark of her individualism and disdain for institutions' coercion. His image of the young, plainspoken peasant taking on the mighty pillars of the Church and sundering them like Samson has an eloquence that has made it stick in the minds of many as the true Saint Joan.[64] But it is an anachronism; Joan was not against compromise for purposes of modern self-determination. The reason she would not bend to the Inquisition and would not take their oath could be that she had pledged herself elsewhere and owed loyalty there. The judges at Rouen kept trying to make Joan admit that she would not answer certain questions because she had promised her voices not to. Joan never assented to this. For instance, on 13 March, in prison, when Joan was asked about the sign she gave the king, she retorted: "Would you be content if I perjured myself?" Had she promised and sworn to Saint Catherine that she would not tell this sign? "I have sworn and promised not to tell this sign, of my own accord, because I was too much pressed to tell it." Then she had told herself to promise not to speak of it further to anyone in the world.[65]

Her interrogators never asked her if she had promised, not Saint Catherine, but Charles. It seems extraordinary they should have failed to think of this, since the commonest oath of the time was the oath of fealty, made by a vassal to an overlord. Joan might have taken a private oath of this type to Charles. The holy kingdom on earth of God, embodied by the suzerain, coexisted beside his spiritual realm and its ruler, the pope, as the left-hand and right-hand parts on a piano form a piano score. At times, concord of sweet music, rippling peacefully in unison, can flow from the instrument; at other times, discord, angry clashes and a syncopated rhythm. Yet equal loyalty to both was owed by a Christian of the Middle Ages, and in times of stress the two-handed part became intolerable, and a choice had to be made, a choice and a submission. Joan tried to keep her faith with both, and it is a mark of her redoubtable strength of personality that she nearly succeeded. She insisted throughout that she would accept the pope or a Church council's judgement on the question of her heterodoxy, if only she were allowed to come before either,[66] but she remained equally adamantine that she would not be shifted over the private revelations she had concerning Charles, which had led her to Chinon and the momentous meeting with him (see Chapter 3).

She was bound, it seems, by her oath. Christine de Pisan, in her *Book of Fayttes of Armes and of Chyvalrye*, states quite firmly that one of the requirements of the oath of fealty is "that he [the vassal] shall never discover nor tell his secret of that thing that to him [the overlord] might be prejudiciable."[67] Later on she says that oaths must never be broken, unless the promised act is a greater sin. The sacredness of the bond between a knight and a lord cannot be overstressed. This was the age when words, images, legends and emblems formed the thin ice covering the dark pool of social chaos. It was mere camouflage, to mask bloodthirstiness as justice, as peace-making warmongering. But to break one's word meant kicking in this weak protection, refusing to maintain the illusion that order prevailed. Of course the men and the women of the fifteenth century did so continually; it was a period of treachery and impiety and falsehood; but at the same time, they usually pretended they performed such deeds in the name of a greater faith, a more binding loyalty.

Lorraine, Domremy's home province, was a stronghold of such ideals. It was the birthplace of one of the most beloved of the men who had spliced together love of God and love of battle, spirit and world, the crusader Godfrey of Bouillon, duke of Lower Lorraine. Godfrey was handsome, blonde, tall, unassuming, modest and devout, every inch the true knight, and his fame made him an example much farther afield than Lorraine. He sold his estates to raise funds for the crusade; and when elected king of Jerusalem, he refused, preferring the simple, gallant and saintly title *Advocatus Sancti Sepulchri*, defender of the Holy Sepulchre. He led to the Holy Land many other Lotharingian knights, including Rainald, count of Toul, from Joan's nearest cathedral town.[68] With the exception of Normandy, no other province stood closer to the romance of the crusades.

The crusader was a healing figure, for in theory he united in himself the two warring worlds—God and man; the warring allegiances—king and pope; the warring principles—right Christian conduct and the love of battle. He was therefore continually held up before the eyes of the medieval world, and many of Joan's models were cast in his image: Saint Michael was a knight and his victory over Satan "the first deed of knighthood and chivalric prowess."[69] Gentile da Fabriano, Joan's contemporary (d. 1427), painted the archangel as a beautiful young soldier, arrayed in the latest plate armour, his iridescent wings buckled under bosses on his shoulders like the cape of a knight; Jan van Eyck also painted a contemporary Saint Michael, an epitome of sexless angelical nature, in full knightly costume, on the panel Isabella of Castile bought for her private collection at Granada. Saint George, patron of England, and Saint Andrew, the battle cry of the Burgundians, were represented as soldiers in armour, often overcoming evil dragons by force of arms.[70] France had its especial patrons, too: Saint Martin of Tours, who, tearing his cloak in half to cover a beggar, personified the spirit of chivalry (though to have given him the whole cloak might seem more generous); Saint Denis, who, though a bishop, provided French soldiers with their battle cry and who, until the fall of the abbey of St. Denis into English and Burgundian hands, had been the country's patron saint; and Saint Maurice, who was martyred with the Theban Legion and especially venerated by René of Anjou (who had himself painted on his knees, with the figure of an elegantly armoured Moor behind him, by the Master of Moulins around 1480).[71] There is an exquisite carved head in the Musée d'Orleans, a fragment of what must have been a free-standing polychrome statue. The lips, lids, eye sockets and cheekbones are rendered with exceptional sensitivity, and the whole face is won-drously harmonious. It expresses a quality of recollected, poignant com-posure that is also visible in some of the statues of a similar date that Dunois commissioned for his private chapel at Chateaudun. Until re-cently, this head was thought to be a portrait of Joan, principally be-cause it is chaste, beautiful and, in spite of the heavy helmet—or perhaps because of this contrast between delicate feature and hammered metal—feminine. Now it is thought to be a head of Saint Maurice—an interesting example of how iconographic forms govern identification. Joan, whose knightly style took Saint Maurice among its models, was herself con-fused with him later.

In Lorraine itself, there was a local devotion to another equestrian saint, of whom Joan might have known, Saint Gengoult. Gengoult was said to have been an eighth-century soldier from Frisia who was in service to the king of the Franks and then left the life of fighting to dedicate himself to the Church. His wife's lover murdered him, and as a result, cuckolds have a patron saint. On his feast day in country dis-tricts, garlands of yellow flowers are placed on the thresholds of de-ceived husbands. He inspired special devotion in Lorraine, with a church dedicated to him in Toul and a statue in the fortified basilica of Saint Maurice in Epinal; it depicts him in a characteristic pose, mounted on a charger and bearing a sword.[72]

The life of a soldier and a sacred mission were not, therefore, in-compatible; such a calling would have been familiar to Joan. In the 1400s, the dream of the crusade was still very much alive, although the frontier of the fight against paganism was closing in.[73] The holy places were impregnably in the hands of the infidel; the front line was now drawn in Hungary, against the expanding Ottoman Empire's western borders. In 1396, the flower of Burgundian chivalry, led by the heir to the duchy, the future John the Fearless, met its destruction at the hands of the Turks in the battle of Nicopolis. John himself was captured, to be ransomed later at an enormous price by his father.[74] In the year of Joan's glory, Henry Beaufort, cardinal of Winchester and one of the prelates who later attended Joan's execution, was appointed by the pope the general of a crusade against the Hussite heretics of Bohemia.

But on 1 July 1429, the 2,750 holy fighters in the cardinal's army were wilfully diverted to serve in the French war for six months, much to the pope's displeasure.[75]

In such circumstances, the crusade ideal was destroyed to all practical effect. Yet the dream continued to be nourished by ritual, by literature, by the prevailing romance of chivalry's moral code. Christine de Pisan, who in most instances followed closely Honoré Bonet's earlier handbook on warfare, departed from him on the subject of the crusade. She leaves out the passages in which Bonet denounces war against the heathen for reasons other than the recovery of Christian territory or the redress of injuries to the faith.[76] The restoration of the holy places to Christendom was still the grail from which the knights of the Round Table wished to drink to prove their worth. Henry V spoke of his French campaign as a mere preamble to the great crusade during which he would rebuild the walls of Jerusalem; the duke of Burgundy seconded his desire with enthusiasm.[77] When Constantinople fell in 1453, Charles the Bold, duke of Burgundy, planned to win it back with a mighty army under his personal command. Nothing came of it. When Louis the Dauphin, son of Charles VII, fled his father's kingdom for his uncle's duchy of Burgundy, the excuse he gave was that he was joining the crusade against the Turk. In 1461, Louis's men were still under the apprehension they were leaving for the Holy Land and were seen polishing up their armour, as if on the point of departure.[78]

Joan subscribed to this collective fantasy. When she challenged the English to leave France before the battle of Orleans, she was using the conventional chivalric style of the formal defiance to combat. In it, she claimed for herself and her side divine right and then enjoined her enemies, saying that if they left France, they could fight side by side again in the holy war: "If you will give her [the Maid] satisfactory pledges, you may yet join with her, so that the French may do the fairest deed that has ever yet been done for Christendom."[79] Joan dictated her letters to a scribe, and they run on freely, following a rapid, casual flow of speech, full of repetitions and exhortations, taunts and cajolery, leaping live off the page. On the day of the coronation in Rheims, again she returned to the theme of the crusade. She wrote to the duke of Burgundy, chiding him for not answering her invitation to the ceremony and warning him not to anger the King of Heaven by doing battle against France: *"S'il vous plaist a guerroier,"* she writes, *"si alez sur les Sarrazins"* (If you like fighting, go ahead, fight the Saracens).[80]

The letters in Antonio Morosini's chronicle report that Joan promised Charles first victory in France, then conquest of the Holy Land.[81]

In a slightly different, more restrained style, possibly reworked by a clerk, Joan also challenged Jan Hus's followers in Bohemia and threatened them with a crusade:

> I, Joan the Maid, to tell you true, I would have visited you long ago with my avenging arm if the war with the English had not kept me here. But if I do not hear soon that you have mended your ways, that you have returned to the bosom of the Church, I shall perhaps leave the English and turn against you, to extirpate the dreadful superstition with my blade of iron and to snatch you from heresy or from life itself.[82]

The letter is written from Sully, on 3 March 1430, a time when Joan was deeply frustrated in her battle plans by Charles's diplomacy. She may also have been advised to forestall charges that she was a Hussite sympathiser by declaring herself their open enemy. The letter's authenticity has been disputed. But the Dominican witch-finder Johannes Nider corroborates independently that Joan, in her pride, sought to crush the Hussites as well as the English.[83] If her missive is genuine, its language of total intolerance, exactly reproducing the English invective against Joan herself later, represents a cruel irony.

Apart from the chivalrous impulse to save, which made the knightly code a secular system of salvation, it was also inspired by lofty ideal of magnanimity and self-sacrifice. Leaders should be bold and rash, careless of their own lives, eager to lay themselves down for their followers. Challenges to single combat were still frequent among princes, as gestures to settle quarrels without increasing the sufferings of the people and butchering armies in the process. In 1425, Philip the Good, duke of Burgundy, called upon Humphrey, duke of Gloucester, to meet him in the lists to settle his claim to the Lowlands after Gloucester had married the heiress, Jacqueline of Brabant, whom Philip himself had wanted to wed. In 1445, the duke of Saxony wanted to fight in single combat over the issue of the duchy of Luxembourg. As he lay dying, he was still vowing a duel to the death with the Grand Turk. A kind of bravura, of foolhardy recklessness was prized as the badge of great courage. A famous example was that of Sir William Felton, who charged a posse of mounted Castilians in 1367 single-handedly, armed only with a lance, and died on the instant. The Chandos Herald, one of England's arbiters of courtly conduct, praised him as the epitome of valour. As the historian Barnie comments: "Militarily, Felton's death was meaningless: in terms of a chivalric code based on an unbending sense of personal honour, there could be no finer way to die."[84]

Joan displayed the same glorious recklessness. She stormed the fortress of Les Tourelles at the siege of Orleans and returned to surge forward again after she had been wounded in the neck. Before Paris, she leapt into the fosse, trying to lead her men in an impossible assault; at the end, at Compiègne, after a series of military failures, she was still to the fore, braving enormous odds and terrible losses, but willing to bear the brunt of it. Her fearlessness was rousing and made her men follow her, as at the taking of St. Pierre le Moustier in October 1430, Joan's last reported victory. Jean d'Aulon, Joan's steward, was wounded in the first assault and retreated with the other forces. But seeing Joan left behind almost alone at the ramparts, he rode back to her and asked her to retire with them. "After taking her helmet from her head, she answered that she was not alone and that she still had fifty thousand men in her company, and that she would not leave that spot until she had taken the town."[85] The attackers' spirits rallied at this fresh vision of Joan's, and they filled the ditches surrounding the town with faggots to make a bridge and took it by storm.

Chivalry was a social code based on intense reliance on individual action; it was an institution designed to make heroes. But such heroes necessarily break out of the containing structure of the institutions that foster them, by dint of the very exceptional deeds that are expected of them. Then, like the archetype outlaw Robin Hood or companions-at-arms of Joan like La Hire or Poton, they are forced outside the conventional family of God, king and subjects to prey on the very body politic they were groomed to save.

Even before Joan was captured, the process of exclusion was already taking place. Her desire, backed by soldiers like Dunois, to build on the coronation with a military campaign in the capital and in Normandy, was completely overridden, and the army was disbanded. As early as Paris—September 1429—she was acting independently of the king and his advisors' wishes. As a freelance, she lost the battle for the capital because her assault was called off by Charles, against her instinct and desire. When she was taken at Compiègne in May 1430, only a year after Orleans, she was fighting as a "free captain" at the head of two hundred men, one of whom was her brother Pierre, who was captured with her. The absence of effort to ransom her or save her also shows how far she had travelled down the doom path to banditry, from her position as heroine at the centre of the kingdom's loving embrace. Chivalry needed an identifiable, unambiguous villain; it needed the barbarian at the gate, the Grand Turk, the heathen.[86] It did not fit with the growing sense of diplomacy in public business in the fifteenth century or with the subtle manoeuvring of Charles VII, a man who liked the parley table and truces, which made Joan angry and which she could not understand. She was a firebrand: her king was a slow fuse, stealthy and patient. Charles never entered a battle, not at least during Joan's campaigns.[87] Her traditional, honoured form of heroics was useful; but once the duke of Burgundy had come to the conference table, as he did for the edict of Compiègne, signed on 29 August, there was no further use for a fire-eater like Joan. She felt it keenly, as her letter to the inhabitants of Rheims reveals.

On two counts, Joan grievously flouted the laws of chivalry, thus endangering herself in a world that still paid them lip service and bringing about part of her condemnation. She attacked Paris on the feast of Our Lady's Nativity, 8 September, and fighting on a holy day was strictly prohibited except, as Christine de Pisan wrote, in defence:

> To undertake a day of battle upon a holy day it is not well done nor it appertaineth not though that at this day been the Christian people of so feeble and so little faith and of so little reverence towards God and to his saints that men of arms maken now force so that they see their advantage for to ride, skirmish, steal, and to go forth to the pillage and the robbery as well upon an Easterday or the Good Friday or upon some other a great and solemn day as upon other days, which thing ought not by now manner to be done.[88]

Christine was indignant because, as in so many other things that chivalry pretended to proscribe, the rule was not respected. Yet it is surprising that Joan, who made an issue of not fighting at Orleans on Ascension Day, assaulted Paris on the Virgin's birthday. Was it a sign of desperation, born of the month or so of inactivity since the coronation? Was it a strategic choice, to take the Parisians by surprise? At her trial, she was surly. Asked if it were a good thing to attack on a holiday, she merely replied, "*Passez outre.*"[89] Later she simply denied point-blank that she had sinned mortally in making her attack.

Joan was also accused of ordering the death of a prisoner of war, the knight Franquet d'Arras. She remembered the story clearly and defended herself.[90] He had confessed to murder, theft and treachery and was tried for over a fortnight. She arranged to exchange him against a prisoner of the English, a Parisian, but when she discovered her man was dead, she gave up Franquet d'Arras to the bailiff to do as he saw fit. Franquet was forthwith executed.[91]

There was a current controversy about the treatment of prisoners and two of the contemporary experts differ. Honoré Bonet, in his *Arbre des Batailles* of 1387, justified the killing of prisoners, but Christine de Pisan disagreed, declaring prisoners could not be slain while the battle continued. In the case of the protracted civil war in France, she advocated sweet handling of prisoners, because ill-treatment stiffened the enemy's morale and desire to fight.[92]

Joan probably erred toward severity when she turned over Franquet d'Arras and ceased to grant him the privileges of a prisoner of war. But it was not a clear crime on her part, and it is characteristic of the time that her interrogators made so much of it, issuing long diatribes about her bloodthirstiness. By the time the story is told by the chronicler Monstrelet, Joan is described as attacking Franquet in person bodily and chopping off his head at a blow.[93]

The knight personifies righteousness; and in this historical guise, Joan was seen by her panegyrists and her artists as a direct descendant of other equestrian saviours—Saint George, in particular, England's equivalent palladium, who crushes evil at the point of his spear and flies his banner of truth and justice over evil's broken form. The most interesting development of this ancient dialectical theme at the basis of chivalry and of its many evocations in sculpture was made by the Princess Marie d'Orléans in the last century, in a small bronze group now standing in the town hall of Orleans (34). Marie was the daughter of King Louis Philippe, and she sculpted Joan, another daughter of France, several times before her early death in childbirth at the age of twenty-six in 1839. Her more famous statue of Joan at prayer stands outside the town hall and is decked with flower garlands at the culmination of the annual procession celebrating the relief of 8 May. But in her equestrian group, she adapts the ancient theme of dragon killing with originality: Joan, on her warhorse, steps delicately aside to avoid the supine body of an enemy Englishman and gazes down at him with an expression of solemn and intense compassion that has nothing maudlin in it. Iconographically, the group belongs to the long tradition of combats between good and evil, but the content has been remoulded and contest transmuted to pity. Joan herself was easily moved to tears, disliked bloodshed and, as we have seen, claimed she had never killed anyone. Her interrogators did not bring forward any specific evidence of murder or slaughter, except for Franquet d'Arras, so it is probable she was true to her word. Joan's page, Louis de Coutes, gave evidence at the rehabilitation trial that after the capture of Beaugency, where almost all the English defenders were killed, Joan "was greatly distressed by such slaughter. Once when a Frenchman was bringing in some English prisoners, he knocked one of them on the head and left him for dead. When Joan saw this she dismounted and received the Englishman's confession, raising his head and comforting him as much as she could."[94]

The angel who first appeared to her taught her, Joan told her judges, "the pity that reigned in the kingdom of France."[95] Pity was the ruling passion in the ethic of chivalry; it ranked above courage. It was the mainspring of the knight's actions, or at least it was meant to be. The pity of France's plight was to be matched by pity in the breast of France's saviour. Joan was never more a knight than when she used the word *pity* to express the emotion with which she set out on her mission. However cruel the warfare, however oppressed the peasantry by their betters' quarrels, chivalry clung to the idea, as its central sustaining fiction, that compassion governed all its enterprises.

The ideals of chivalry ennobled the business of warfare and aligned the warrior on the side of right. Joan had the hero's essential quality, an unshakeable conviction in her rectitude and the rectitude of all her motives, her passions and her enterprises. This is what she meant when she said she came from God: she came from true rightness that could never slip into wrong. But such commitment is often seen as fanaticism and even madness by the opponents of a cause; and in Joan's case, her chivalry, like her voices and her dress, formed part of her aberration. The hostility she aroused is not really surprising; what is more so, and also more interesting, is how her gallantry and her courage and her independence and her defiance were made acceptable to established authorities who would themselves be subverted again by those very qualities of hers, how the story of Joan of Arc came to be told so it could be heard without anger or fear.

THE AFTERLIFE OF

JOAN OF ARC

CHAPTER 9

THE VINDICATION

Now we begin to understand the old motto No-
blesse Oblige. Noblesse means having the gift of
power, the natural or sacred power. And having
such power obliges a man to act with fearlessness
and generosity, responsible for his acts to God. . . .
Some men must be noble, or life is an ash-heap.

D. H. LAWRENCE,
Movements in European History[1]

fter her capture, Joan was forgotten by her party by commission, not omission. She was deeply embarrassing to them:
a champion held on suspicion of heresy. The only person
whose voice we hear raised on her behalf that year is that of
Jacques Gélu, archbishop of Embrun. He had formerly defended her
transvestism; and in 1430, he wrote to Charles, enjoining him to recover
Joan at all cost. To neglect her fate would be "culpably ungrateful."[2]
Yet no ransom attempt was made, in an age when ransoms were the
custom. Joan would have vanished from the triumphant story of the
Valois recovery in France if it had not been for two mighty social
forces: political necessity and family feeling. In her case, these were
intertwined because Charles had given Joan an enduring mark of his
esteem, which sealed his approval and created a faction deeply interested
in rescuing her name. This seal was the coat of arms granted to Joan's
brothers, permitting them the noble name of "du Lys."[3]

After their sister's death, the family did not retreat into oblivion,
but attempted and succeeded in capitalising on her exploits in a number
of shrewd, ambitious and not entirely honest stratagems, some of which

they originated, others they accepted for the greater contending advantages of church and state. Shadowy but self-serving, Pierre and Jean and Isabelle in particular have not come down to us wrapped in the same glow of sincerity and truthfulness as their marvellous Joan.

Pierre and Jean joined Joan in Tours after her success at Chinon and Poitiers. Jacques, Joan's father, came to Rheims for the coronation. Pierre was fighting with her at Compiègne and was taken prisoner at the same time. He was soon ransomed though, either with his wife's dowry or with an advance from a knight called Philibert de Brécy; it was raised against revenues from the bailiwick of Chaumont, which Charles levied and for which, in freedom, Pierre became responsible.[4] When the duke of Orleans was himself ransomed in 1440, he rewarded the brother of his city's liberator with an island, the Ile aux Bœufs, lying midstream in the Loire. There Pierre lived as a *châtelain*, a member of the duke's chivalric order of the porcupine. Jean made a career for himself, too, as provost of Vaucouleurs, captain of Chartres and again provost of Vaucouleurs until 1468.[5] Isabelle Romée left Lorraine to live in Orleans, where her daughter's memory was honoured, on a pension from the burghers. Yet their loyalty to her successes was not matched by comparable feeling in Joan herself.

The first time she mentioned them at her trial was in reply to the questioning about the whereabouts of her holy sword. She said she thought her brothers had everything she owned, all her goods, her horses, her sword and other things, worth in all more than twelve thousand *écus*.[6] She returned to this when she was being questioned about her retinue. Again, she mentioned the sum of ten to twelve thousand *écus* and added that for the purposes of waging war, it amounted to very little. She said that her brothers had it, but added with asperity that everything she possessed rightly belonged to the king.[7]

Inferring hostility from this comment might be exaggerated, if other remarks about her brothers did not reveal Joan felt exploited. Joan had exchanged her birthright as a peasant for an independent career in a just war; she shows continual annoyance and no pleasure in her father's and brothers' appearance on her trail. They had thought of drowning her, after all, and there are no signs they helped her in any way before she became successful. Her animus against them erupted clearly when she was asked in her trial about her coat of arms. She made it plain that the king had granted her brothers a shield azure with two lilies and a raised sword, but not at her request. She had not accepted this blazon for herself, and it did not originate in a vision or any instruction of her voices. She repeated twice that the grant of arms to her brothers was none of her doing. She thus detached herself firmly from any identification of her mission with her brothers' rise to the nobility and disassociated them from her divine guidance.[8] From the moment the grant was made, Pierre and Jean styled themselves with the high-sounding title "du Lys"; Joan never changed her name from La Pucelle.

Yet when her affections were engaged, she was always generous and spontaneous. She uses the word "love" quite freely for her standard, her saints, the king and Charles, duke of Orleans, the poet-soldier who had been a prisoner in the Tower of London since the battle of Agincourt. She consistently presents herself as easily touched to the quick, with a heart fast to kindle and eyes to weep. So the absence of avowed love for her family has to be weighed against the other loves she did voice; and only then can one see clearly the exchange Joan made of one family against another, when she altered her dress and struck out on a new life.

There was only one moment when Joan spoke with something approaching family feeling, even nostalgia or tenderness, and that was when she snapped at Cauchon that he had taken a ring from her, a ring given her by her brother. The Burgundians had taken another from her, one her parents had given her in Domremy, which, like her standard, also had the words "Jesus Maria" inscribed on it.[9] In the last interrogation session in prison on 17 March in the afternoon, her questioners returned to this ring. She told them she did not know if it was gold, for it might be brass, and she thought there were three crosses on it as well as the holy names. La Fontaine probed as to why she liked to contemplate this ring before going into battle. Joan gave a gentle reply: "For pleasure and for the honour of her father and mother; and she, having that ring on her hand and on her finger, touched Saint Catherine who had appeared to her."[10] So that although Joan commemorated her parents, she also recalled her more special contract, that to her saints and especially to the one who in medieval painting was identified with a ring—Catherine, who had become Christ's bride.[11] There was a custom, as there still is at shrines today, of giving Fierbois pilgrims rings that had touched the saint's relics.

Joan's mistrust was justified by events. In 1436, only five years after her burning, Pierre and Jean appeared in Orleans with a young woman in armour on a horse. They asserted she was Joan, miraculously saved from the fire by a last-minute substitution. Claude des Armoises, an Amazon adventurer who had fought in Italy before, impersonated Joan of Arc so effectively that the ever-willing citizens of Orleans feasted her and Joan's brothers generously and, in gratitude for the marvels of 1429, granted them delightful bursaries and free lodgings. In 1440, after an equally successful progress through France, this profitable circus was disbanded, when Claude des Armoises was unmasked in Paris after a full confession. Claude's role is raffish and engaging; she retired and married and gave birth to children whose descendants still try to claim she really was Joan of Arc.[12] Joan's brothers' role is less appetising, especially when one finds them, in 1456, coolly adding their names to their mother's formal pleas for the reopening of their sister's trial and the rescinding of the condemnation that sent her to the stake. When the rehabilitation hearings were called, neither Pierre nor Jean gave evidence. Their opportunism was probably too much to stomach, even for that tribunal. But they, and the interested parties masterminding the reha-bilitation, were still eager to use Joan's career to their best advantage. If she were declared innocent, they stood to gain prestige, and so they joined in the struggle over her memory that began in 1450 when Guillaume Bouillé, the dean of Noyon, petitioned Charles to show the trial of Joan of Arc to have been fraudulent.[13]

Joan had intertwined her destiny so successfully with Charles's that he carried the burden of her activity on his behalf and its implications long after she was dead. The long, interrupted history of the different tribunals that met to repeal the sentence on Joan of 1431 reveals the enormous tension between secular and spiritual authority that had to be fought out throughout Charles's reign. In 1452, Guillaume Bouillé expressed a widespread anxiety when he exclaimed: "What a disgrace for the royal throne it would be if in the future our adversaries could repeat that the King of France had kept a heretical woman in his army!"[14] The Inquisition had declared a heretic the young girl who had led Charles to victory in Orleans and to his coronation in Rheims; Charles, who owed so much to her, was successfully made to feel uneasy that his hard-won position was tainted by the means used to secure it, that his prophet was false. The uneasiness was shared by the churchmen who were Charles's followers or who had returned to him after the recuperation of his territories in northern France: Paris in 1436, Rouen in 1449. The stain spread by the judgement on Joan needed to be cleansed; and in 1450, Guillaume Bouillé received his orders. Charles wanted the English who had "rigged" Joan's trial discredited and his good name thereby rehabilitated.[15]

But there was another aspect of the posthumous retrial of Joan, which perhaps Charles in 1450 did not foresee: if the Church quashed its own decision of 1431, it was proving itself to be the highest authority, with power to sanction Charles's right to the throne or not. This was less palatable, especially as Charles was engaged in a prolonged struggle to establish the monarch's and the nobles' rights in the ecclesiastical sphere in France and to weaken the reach of the papacy into his kingdom. In 1438, he proclaimed the Pragmatic Sanction of Bourges, arrogating to himself and to some feudal lords powers to intervene in the appointment of bishops and abbots. Charles did not enjoy the prospect of the Inquisition, the limb of the papacy, asserting its sovereignty in any matter at all.[16]

But the Inquisition had, in the case of Joan, a double-edged sword: it was itself disgraced if it revoked the sentence at Rouen of 1431, but it could also prove Charles's dependence on the Church's prescripts if it pronounced him absolved of Joan's disgrace. Thus the representatives of the Church in France pressed for Joan's absolution for their own political ends, and Charles, though he wanted his prophet cleared, squirmed away.

The first inquiry, held on 4 March 1450 by Bouillé, called only seven witnesses.[17] Too many people who had taken part in Joan's condemnation were still alive and were now working for Charles. Bouillé's very own bishop, for instance, Jean de Mailly, had attended the trial and the burning and had signed Henry VI's general letters of protection to all who took part in the trial. It was perhaps more embarrassing for these survivors than Bouillé had foreseen. The first inquiry was hastily dropped.[18]

The next request for a new investigation came from the papal legate in France, Guillaume d'Estouteville, a cardinal and a cousin of Charles. He was anxious, he professed, to clear Charles's honour by restoring Joan's. When D'Estouteville first arrived in France from Rome, Charles reduced him to "absolute confusion and despair" by his anger and coldness. Charles had not been asked to approve the appointment, an act he considered his right as king. But when the pope finally conceded the point, D'Estouteville was received in February 1452. The reiteration that only the Church could clear Charles's past was a powerful weapon;

and on 2 May, the second inquiry into the trial at Rouen began. It was hasty and hardly thorough. Key figures at Joan's trial who were still living in the city itself were not called as witnesses. The very archbishop of Rouen, Raoul Roussel, had attended Joan's trial and shown no signs of obstructing its development. He could hardly appear before a tribunal in his own diocese. One of the canons of the cathedral who helped D'Estouteville draw up his questions had actually signed the certificate of Joan's relapse into heresy. The second inquiry's main objective was to declare null and void the proceedings held in the English capital of Rouen by Anglo-Burgundian sympathisers. D'Estouteville quickly despatched this business, declared the hearings over on 22 May and granted indulgences to all who took part in the procession of 8 May held in Orleans in honour of the raising of the siege and its heroine.

In July, Charles, mollified by Joan's vindication and his release from guilt, received the legate at last.[19] But the proceedings had not satisfied Rome's plans, and Jean Bréhal, the inquisitor in France, reopened the trial yet again, emphasising that Joan had been "wickedly burned to dishonour the king," which was tantamount to stating that Charles was still dishonoured and still in need of the Church's grace. Bréhal began his researches and two years later travelled to Rome to petition the pope, Nicolas V, to open official hearings. For the inquisitor, a repeal of an earlier inquisitorial trial had to be a solemn and weighty affair. At this stage, in a stratagem that united several interests, Bréhal approached Joan's mother, Isabelle Romée, and her sons Pierre and Jean, who were in Orleans, and organised that an emotive and anguished plea to the pope should be presented by the family. Nicolas died while the suit was still under consideration in the Vatican, so it was his successor, Calixtus III, who authorised the commission to sit and "in the final instance to pronounce a just verdict."[20] Isabelle Romée in person made the formal request for her daughter's rehabilitation on her knees in the Cathedral of Notre-Dame in Paris on 7 November 1455, and she presented to the commissioners the papal rescript "with great sighs and groans" and "pitiable plaints and mournful supplications."[21]

In spite of the personal tragedy of the D'Arc family and the extraordinary and stirring presence of Joan's mother at this moment, the aim of the trial of rehabilitation was always political, and the main result of the proceedings, announced on 7 July 1456, was the annulment of the sentence, not the proclamation of Joan's holiness. The choice of male dress was not explained or exonerated; her voices were not declared authentically divine. The charges of 1431 were declared trumpery, cooked up by English hatred. As Malcolm Vale, Charles's biographer, sums up, "The definitive sentence did not pronounce on her orthodoxy or her sanctity."[22] Although Isabelle Romée had specifically asked for the judges of her daughter to be cited in reparation, they do not appear in the condemnation of the trial they had held in 1431, neither those who were dead, nor those who were still alive and could have been punished. Jean le Fèvre, one of the assessors in 1431, was even a sub-delegated judge at the hearings of 1456; he could not be expected to pass sentence on himself. Joan's innocence was not the target of the repeal; the issue was the power of the Church over the king. Joan's closeness to God had served as a bulwark in 1429 for his claims to legitimacy; so in 1456, the institution that held the key to knowing who was close to God and who was not used her again to rock and then to stabilise the secular arm. Expiatory crosses were ordered to be put up in Rouen and Orleans; on the bridge at Orleans where she had fought her great victory, a monument was to be raised to its memory (31). But a further directive was given that no other images or epitaphs to Joan be set up at Rouen or elsewhere. When documents of her trial—the articles of condemnation and the sentence—were formally burned by the public executioner in Rouen in July 1456, the ceremony clinched the repudiation of the English and the purification of the French who had worked with them at Rouen. Joan was incidental to the political purpose of making it seem that the archenemy, the devil-ridden English, who had done so much evil in France, were responsible for the kangaroo court that had condemned her.

But these intrigues were concealed from the people, and the ban on Joan's growing cult was a dead letter. Joan became the emotive, preeminent heroine of the Hundred Years' War and the full-blooded talisman of the changed French fortunes. She was the *"fille de Dieu"* she had said she was, a holy heroine, brimful of divine inspiration, and the dry tomes of the several trials that said one thing and then another were of little consequence to anyone but their composers. The two main impetuses to the flowering of her fame after 1456 were the veneration in which her memory was held in Orleans and the desire of her self-styled posterity to cling to her nobility.

Orleans, the proud and loyal city, had a long tradition of inter-twining civil and religious ceremony. In the year 1422, no less than six processions had been held to rally the townspeople by a public display;

"stations" were made at the town's many fine churches.[23] The commemoration of the deliverance of the city in 1429 became customary on 8 May, as it still is; and in 1498, a banner and standard, painted to resemble Joan's, were first carried by ordinary citizens in procession through these stations.[24] The bridge monument was finally erected in 1502, at the expense of a devout family of Orleans and of the town's aldermen. It showed Joan in armour kneeling with Charles VII at the foot of the crucified Christ. The Calvinists, triumphing briefly in the town in 1562, destroyed the statues in a bout of anti-Royalist and iconoclastic fervour; but on their retreat, they were patched up from the remains, and the body of Christ that had previously hung on the cross laid across the knees of his mourning mother.[25] About a decade later, around 1580, the aldermen commissioned another tribute to Joan, a special portrait which still hangs in the town hall of Orleans (25). This Joan of Arc is entirely unrecognisable to modern eyes: she wears a Renaissance dress with slashed sleeves and a cross-laced bodice, a handsome necklace of large gold links and a dashing hat crested with ostrich plumes. The only vestige of Joan's military prowess that remains is the sword she holds raised with her right hand. The inscription salutes the "return" to France of "Jeanne de Vaucouleurs" and greets the new queen of that time, Louise, wife of Henry III, as another fortunate Pucelle.

A few years later, Orleans's citizens ordered another banner made for the annual procession; it showed their own duke and an armed Joan kneeling at the feet of the Virgin, with a panorama of the city in the background and the town's two patron saints, Aignan and Euverte, on either side (7). The particular circumstances of Joan's story and personality were eclipsed by the greater moment of promoting the self-pride of the famous Catholic and Royalist town, at a time when it was again being threatened, by the religious wars between Huguenot and Catholic.

But this civic piety intersected another dominant theme in French society: during the political upheavals of the religious wars of the sixteenth century, the aristocracy's complacency was shattered and their standing and value in society reappraised with a deeply sceptical eye among themselves and others. In reaction to the questioning of their rights, the nobility tried to assert that it was the possessor of those qualities implied by the word *nobility* itself. Many nobles were stripped of their rights, which included enormously desirable privileges, above all, exemption from tax. Small wonder they strove to prove themselves worthy of their former titles. One curious offshoot of this distress and the search for self-justification was the rediscovery of Joan of Arc, not just as a cypher of Charles's integrity or Orleans's grandeur, but as a person. Through the efforts of a small group of self-styled aristocrats who wanted to validate their titles, Joan of Arc was rescued from a minor place in the chronicle of France's medieval wars, and became a cynosure in the history of ideas about virtue, about women and about heroism.

Joan's first apologists and biographers were men who were caught up in the prevalent anxiety about nobleness and its meaning, who wanted to use her family's ancient ennoblement to vindicate themselves and retain their privileges. They were living at a time of change, when the old criteria were becoming obsolete, when chivalry still fascinated, but its principles had become antiquarian. Incursions into the old aristocracy had been made throughout the sixteenth century by men who had amassed wealth and then acquired territory from failing noblemen, by men who simply bought their ennoblements and by men who traced their families back and found some connexion with an ancient lineage, like the du Lys. The debate as to what true nobility might be flourished in the pages of numerous sixteenth- and seventeenth-century tracts, broadsides and pamphlets. Some moralists argued that innate virtue alone constituted nobility, and noblemen who fell short of the required standards should forfeit their titles. Others argued another, more traditional view, that ancient *race* alone could entitle a man to nobility. The reality of the situation did not fail to be recognised: it was apparent that peasants, however virtuous their lives, were not to be elevated to the ranks of the aristocracy and that noblemen, however vicious their behaviour, were not to be degraded, either. Although the opinion prevailed that the nobility, on the showing of titled people, had no special claim to virtue, the coveting of titles that appeared to confer it continued anxiously throughout the century.[26]

As the century progressed, definitions were drawn more precisely, and precedents established in law to clarify the different grounds for a claim and reduce the proliferation of self-styled aristocrats. The effect was that ancient titles were strengthened considerably, and an old creation, like the grant of arms ennobling Joan's family with the title of du Lys, became the most covetable claim of all. Two hundred years was considered the appropriate antiquity necessary for the title of "*gentil homme*," the highest group of all, ranking above a "noble."[27] Behind this stress on antiquity's confirming nobility lay a deep hankering for a golden age, when heroes were heroes and heroics were possible, when ancient virtues were constant and clear and the rift between noble action and noble men had not opened for all to see. Joan of Arc provided that healing image, that balm of illusion. It seems surprising, this alliance of a saint with snobbery, but snobbery itself is often a distorted tribute to the search for an inviolable fount of virtue.

Joan of Arc was remembered by men who wished to assert the justice of their claim to nobility through descent from someone who enjoyed an unimpeachable right to the title, in its social and its moral value. In 1612, a certain Jean du Lys petitioned the king, then Louis XIII, that as the principal branch of the family of Joan of Arc had died out, he might take over their coat of arms, the lilies of France. He claimed that he bore the cadet branch's arms, a shield azure with a golden bow, set with three arrows. This is the first mention anywhere of any such armorial bearings, and when Louis allowed Jean du Lys to quarter them with lilies, he authenticated in retrospect a coat of arms that was entirely spurious.[28] But then the claim itself was hollow, since no descendants of Joan of Arc's brothers have ever been traced by genealogists. But Jean du Lys was by no means alone: the clan of the du Lys was large and ambitious, and they expressed themselves in promoting Joan's cult.

After her death, until the opening of the seventeenth century, there were only a handful of accounts of Joan, principally in the chronicles and collected biographies about the great women of history. They constitute no special body of work addressed specifically to her phenomenon. There were only one or two chronicles exclusively dedicated to extolling her character or telling the story of her life. She is, for instance, the heroine of the fanciful *Chronique de la Pucelle*[29] and of a mystery drama about the raising of the siege at Orleans,[30] but such documents remained in manuscript and did not achieve a wide circulation. However, among the first truly influential works about Joan were two books published within a year of each other. They were printed, and contributors were invited from all over the cultivated world.

These books were the creation of men who claimed descent from Joan. Jean Hordal, a professor of civil law and canon of the new Jesuit University of Pont-à-Mousson in Lorraine, where local connexions had already inspired interest in Joan's story, published in 1612 in Latin *The History of the Most Noble Heroine Joan of Arc, Virgin of Lorraine,*

Maid of Orleans.[31] Fronton-du-Duc's play about her had been performed twenty-three years before. Hordal's enterprise is self-consciously learned, crammed with allusions to the classics and the Fathers, but it does display genuine knowledge of Joan's trial and rehabilitation. It vindicates her of the charges of cruelty and transvestism with indignant eloquence, compares her to doughty women of antiquity and more recent history and emphasises the resounding successes of her undertakings, rather than her spiritual mission or supernatural faculties.

Jean Hordal claimed to be descended from Etienne Hordal, who had raised a chapel in the *bois chesnu* near Domremy where Joan had communed with her voices. Etienne Hordal's name and the du Lys arms were found engraved on the fragment of pediment discovered buried in the undergrowth in 1869 by Monsignor Dupanloup, bishop of Orleans and one of the most assiduous promoters of Joan's cult.[32] In 1467, Etienne Hordal had married Helwige, or Hauvy, du Lys, daughter of Pierre, Joan's brother, or so it was held by the Hordal family tradition.[33] The Hordals were active in keeping Joan's name and fame alive: another member of the family, Jean's cousin, was dean of the Chapter of Toul Cathedral. He raised a statue to her there in 1560, an extraordinary honour for a champion who had hitherto only been exculpated from the charge of witchcraft and heresy and whose sanctity had hardly been discussed, let alone confirmed.[34]

In June 1596, Jean Hordal ordered an inquiry to establish the veracity of his title to nobility through descent from Joan. The duke of Lorraine, who counted among his many titles the lordship of Domremy, granted it.[35] So Hordal dedicated his book about Joan to the duke and, in his opening eulogy, expressed his gratitude to the house of Lorraine for granting him and his family the right to bear the du Lys arms; he proudly declared how deeply attached he was to Joan herself, the ancestral guarantor of his proud descent. Hordal reproduced in his book, for the first time, the document by which Joan and her brothers and their posterity had been granted noble rank in perpetuity, in the male and female line. Before this, Joan's one description at the trial of her brother's arms is the only evidence, and it is not as all-embracing, or as unequivocal, as Hordal's version. The latter may even be a forgery.[36]

Hordal himself expressed his private doubts about his descent in a letter to a close friend and putative relation, Charles du Lis, who was writing other books about Joan and had contributed to Hordal's own work. Charles du Lis confirmed Hordal's doubts and added that his own claim was also very shaky, since in spite of diligent research carried out by himself, in collaboration with the historian Etienne Pasquier, he could come no closer to Joan herself than the Claude du Lis who was curé of Domremy and Greux in the early part of the previous century, a good hundred years after Joan's death.[37]

Hordal, du Lis and Pasquier belong to one of the most ambiguous of the social groups striving to attain noblemen's rank, for teachers and lawyers and administrators—the basis of the *noblesse de robe*—were regarded with a high degree of suspicion, since they possessed an occupation other than the bearing of arms. Pasquier himself did not claim to be noble, and he even wrote that "the nobility of *robe* was regarded as bastard by the people."[38] By contrast, he devoted a whole chapter to praising the rise of Joan of Arc's family to the nobility. Here was the true, complete recipe, he proclaimed: inborn natural virtue, feats of chivalry and a royal charter nearly two hundred years old: "No service ever made to France can be compared to the Maid's; never were letters of nobility of such weight and stature as these."[39]

Charles du Lis, like Jean Hordal, was undaunted by the vagueness of his descent, and his performance of family *pietas* continued unabated. In 1613, the year after Hordal's biography, he published his *Collection of Inscriptions and Poems in Honour of the Pucelle of Orleans*,[40] the crowning achievement of a lifetime of indefatigable pamphleteering on the subject of his ancestress. This collection is of incalculable importance in the development of Joan's cult. Charles du Lis had the bold and brilliant inspiration to invite eminent men and women of letters from all over the cultivated world to praise Joan, by submitting entries to his competition for the best verses to set upon her monument. The Dutch philosopher Hugo Grotius invoked her as an Amazon of antiquity; François de Malherbe, the French poet and theoretician, contributed two epigrams; Marie de Gournay, the belles-lettriste who was adopted by Montaigne as his daughter, wrote Joan a stirring quatrain; Flemish, Italian and Spanish authors all responded to Charles du Lis's invitation. In Flanders, Rubens was moved to paint his little-known full-colour portrait of Joan, kneeling in armour as she did in the monument for which du Lis was asking inscriptions. Charles du Lis established a further link between Joan, the city of Orleans, its deliverance at her hand and his own family when he claimed, in another of his pamphlets, *On the Extraction and Family of the Pucelle of Orleans*, that a member of the du Lys family had taken part in the annual procession commemorating the liberation of the city.[41] His only source was, it seems, an old servant of Jean du Lis, Joan's brother, who in 1550 claimed that a representative of the family had always attended. In his enthusiasm for a family tradition, he expanded this solitary and improbable witness to "journalists and historians of the time."

The procession had been disrupted by the wars of religion, and thus it represented, in 1610 when Charles du Lis made his statement, another lien on a peaceful, Catholic, orderly past, as did the monument to Joan for which he invited inscriptions.

Civil disturbances and corresponding upheavals in class definitions had brought Joan of Arc to the fore, to play for the first time the role she is to play throughout history, that of personifying certain causes with a consoling lack of ambiguity. Kneeling opposite her king on the bridge of Orleans, Joan stood for the ancient stable relationship of the monarch, the Catholic Church and the nobility who had proved their virtue by deeds of war in the days when the present painful ambiguity about what constituted nobility had not existed. The industrious burrowings in fantasy genealogies, the convenient unearthing of documents, the panegyrics to Joan by Jean Hordal and Charles du Lis made them the proud inheritors of that "secret seed of nobility" that one moralist claimed was transmitted from generation to generation.[42] In another way, also, Joan transfused her alleged posterity with ancient blood. As her putative descendants and her eager votaries contemplated the figure of their forebear and their champion, her contours were discreetly shaped to encompass another rich complex of images, themselves durable metaphors of the courage and the nobility that was so deeply desired.

CHAPTER 10

AMAZON

It's bad enough to be a girl, anyway, when I like boys' games and work and manners! I can't get over my disappointment in not being a boy; and it's worse than ever now, for I'm dying to go and fight with papa and I can only stay at home and knit, like a poky old woman.

LOUISA MAY ALCOTT,
Little Women[1]

The name *Jeanne d'Arc*, Joan of Arc, is an invention. Joan never used it. At her trial, according to the old French transcription, her first words were that in France she was called "Jhenne," but at home she had been known as "Jhannette." She knew nothing of her surname, she declared.[2] A month later, when this statement was read out to Joan, she corrected herself. Her family name was "Darc," she said, or "Rommée," because in her part of the world, girls took the names of their mothers. But this later emendation is interpolated in only one manuscript copy of the trial, and its authenticity has therefore been questioned.[3]

Joan's choice of name for herself has nevertheless been ignored. To call her the Maid or the Daughter of God, as she liked to do, sounds false and precious to contemporary ears. Preference for the name she was given by posterity runs so deep that its genesis and development have never been investigated. Yet this style, "of Arc," is a fascinating, even disturbing example of how culture works on history to recreate its protagonists in familiar forms. *Arc*, with its multiple meanings of "bow," "arch" and "curve," places Joan at the centre of a web of imagery associated with the power of women since antiquity.[4] The bow is the weapon of the Amazon, and when Joan of Arc was first written about, in *Breviarum Historiale*, the tract attributed to Gerson, and in Hordal's and du Lis's works, it was principally as an Amazon that she was presented.

The name *D'Arc* was established only gradually. In the trial and rehabilitation documents, Joan's name is written *Darc;* but until the early seventeenth century, this surname was pronounced to end either with an open vowel or with a voiced *r*.[5] The particle *de* is an invention. It is a sign of noble birth, and its appearance was made possible by the absence of apostrophes in medieval and Renaissance French names (for instance, Dallenson for D'Alençon in many documents). The grant of the du Lys arms in 1430 to Joan's family spells her name *Day*.[6] Michel de Montaigne, travelling through France in 1580 on his way to Italy, visited Domremy. He described Joan's family home by the church, writing that it was decorated with a frieze of her adventures: "The front of the little house where she was born is painted all over with her exploits; but the paintwork has badly worn with time." Montaigne called her "this famous Pucelle of Orleans, who called herself Jeanne, Jane Day, or Dallis."[7] *Dallis* renders the title "du Lys"; *Jane Day* presumably transcribes phonetically the way Montaigne pronounced her name.

The arms of lilies borne by Joan's brothers corroborate, by omission, the speculation that *Arc* is a later reading. Christine de Pisan, discussing the coats of arms a noble of new creation might adopt, describes clearly the visual punning behind most bearings: "they take arms at their own will and such a device as them pleaseth whereof some ground and founded the same upon their name, as one that is called Peter Hammer he shall take one, two, or three hammers for his arms. And as another called John Pye he shall in likewise set the figure of certain pies upon a shield for his arms."[8]

If Joan's family name had signified to her own contemporaries anything as distinctively associated with military prowess as a bow, her arms would surely have borne its image. Yet, as we have seen, when Jean du Lis in 1612 petitioned the king to alter his coat of arms from bows and arrows to fleurs-de-lys, it was the first time any such armorial bearings, punning on the name *D'Arc*, were ever mentioned.[9]

The superficial reason for the shift is clear: when Joan began to be written about by classicists like Jean Hordal and Charles du Lis in the late sixteenth and early seventeenth centuries in France, her written name *Darc* was rendered into Latin, *Ioanna Darcia*, in which the *c*, when read, has to be pronounced, effectively uncovering the hitherto obscured meaning of her surname. Once the *c* was sounded in the Latin, it began to be sounded in the French. In Charles du Lis's collection of inscriptions in her honour, there appear the first conceits playing on her name and on her coat of arms. Thus one scholar praises her, embroidering the hitherto concealed pun:

> *Arcia quae fuerat, fit Martia; Lilia servans,*
> *Nobiliore nota, Lilia facta fuit.*

The wordplay is picked up in French by another author:

> *Jehanne Darc comme un arc celeste*
> *Dardant ses traits sur les Anglois*
> *Tira de la tombe funeste*
> *Le glorieux nom des François . . .*
> *Le Roy chérissant ces gens-d'armes,*
> *Changea leur Arc en un beau Lis . . .*

(Joan of Arc, like a bow from heaven / Shooting her arrows on the English, / Drew from the deadly tomb / The glorious name of the French . . . the King, holding these soldiers dear, / Changed their Bow into a beautiful Lily . . .)[10]

The deeper reasons for the change lie in the way Joan was conceived by her earliest reporters. Her exploits were so extraordinary that in order to grasp and interpret them, writers relied on earlier, more familiar formulae. The letter of Perceval de Boulainvilliers, for instance, an important document written when Joan was still alive, uses classical typology to communicate her importance.[11] He describes multiple marvels attendant on her birth and childhood: the cocks in the village crowed when she was born, just as they do for the birth of the emperor Augustus in Suetonius's *Twelve Caesars*; her flocks were never preyed on by wolves, for savage beasts became tame at her call; and she lived at one with nature, just like all shepherd heroes of antiquity, from David to Orpheus. These phrases are figures of speech, designed to promote belief in Joan's mission. In Boulainvilliers's letter, Joan first hears her voices when she is running against other girls from her village. Speed on the racetrack is the defining mark of the Amazon, or Atalanta, figure.[12] The well-read courtier had the model in mind, for his words echo Virgil's description of the swiftness of Camilla, champion of the Volsci who resisted Aeneas in Latium. Virgil wrote: "She might have skimmed over the tops of uncut cornstalks without ever harming their delicate ears as she ran, or upheld her way through the midst of the sea supported on heaving waves without once wetting her swift foot-soles on its surface."[13] Boulainvilliers's less poetic approximation describes Joan: "She moved with such speed in the second and third races that they thought she hardly put foot to earth, so that one of the girls cried out, 'Joan . . . I saw you fly just next to the ground.' "[14] When Boulainvilliers's humdrum effort was received at court by the duke of Milan, his secretary, a poetaster called Antoine Astesan, recast the letter in classical hexameters and, recognising Boulainvilliers's allusions, compared Joan openly to "the queens of the Amazons of old, Penthesilea or Oritesia," to Tomyris, and then to the original prototype, Camilla. He then offered his explicit thanks to Virgil, his model and inspiration, and compared the exploits of which he had written to the deeds sung in the *Aeneid*.[15]

Astesan sent his effort to Charles, duke of Orleans, in 1435, as a newsletter of recent events in France, and after Charles was released from the Tower, he travelled to Italy and there met Astesan in 1449. Befriending him, Charles brought him back to France, where he appointed Astesan his secretary, to translate the duke's poetry into Italian, his native tongue.[16]

In Joan's closest circle, therefore, in the heart of the house of Orleans, to whom she had given her most intense loyalty, there existed a popular portrait of her youth, which preferred to draw on classical sources about the warrior-maiden Camilla and her scions before her, the Amazons and Artemis, and not to base itself on the evidence Joan gave at her trial. If such a document can be found so close to the very circle in which Joan lived, so soon after her death, it is even less surprising that farther afield accounts of her life become more approximate and rely even more on a body of established tradition and not on her case's particularities.

An early account of Joan was written for a collection of lives of illustrious women by an Augustinian friar called Philip of Bergamo, who published it in 1497 in Valencia.[17] The brief entry claims to be based on an eyewitness's story, but it is dotted with blatant errors. (The rehabilitation is, for instance, attributed to the efforts of Louis XI, not Charles VII.)

Joan's strength and feats of speed and skill are applauded. Again the language recalls, in its vocabulary if not its stylishness, the Latin of the classical masters. But what is more significant is that the engraver, who appended a small woodcut portrait, seized on the association and depicted Joan as a Greek maiden, bearing her bow and quiver, even though Philip never refers to her as anything but "*Ianna gallica pulcella*" (Joan, the little maid of Gaul).[18] To any classically trained reader, Joan immediately and even unconsciously stepped into a category of women made familiar by mythology and history. The phonetic coincidence of her name with this type's predominant emblem was a true godsend, received probably unwittingly by those who read Joan's story. Anyone with any claim to culture at all in the fifteenth century in Europe was familiar with Homer and Virgil and Ovid at least; other texts, in which Diana, the maiden of the chase, and Penthesilea, queen of the Amazons, appear, were also widely known and their stories related and depicted. This compelling and dangerous myth underlies the development of Joan's personality and her gradual rise to prominence as the most modern and the most famous of European heroines.

In the *Iliad*, the Lady of the Bow was Artemis,[19] and after the *Iliad*, Diana in Virgil's *Aeneid*[20] and Ovid's *Metamorphoses*.[21] Artemis-Diana was an inexorable goddess, one of the cruellest in the dark classical pantheon, and her cult probably echoes a lost ancient chthonic mystery of death and rebirth. After Actaeon the hunter had seen her bathing naked, she turned him upon the instant into a stag, so that his own pack of hounds set on him and tore him in pieces; after Jupiter had raped Callisto, one of her beloved nymphs, Artemis banished her forever from their gang of virgin girls. Another of her nymphs, Chione, was shot down with arrows when she boasted she had a son by Apollo while Artemis remained barren. Feeling Athens was neglecting her cult, Artemis fashioned the Calydonian boar, a monster of destruction, to ravage the Greek countryside. She was beautiful, chaste and cold as the moon, and, as Plath has written, she

> . . . *has nothing to be sad about*
> *Staring from her hood of bone.*[22]

The bow she carried was a crescent: the arc of Joan's name. Associated with speed of foot, suppleness of limb and violent death, Artemis-Diana lived for the chase, with living and dying animals her familiars. She stood above all for fierce autonomy, for which her unassailable virginity was the sign. She was linked with all women through the moon, the timepiece of menstruation, though she herself was proudly childless.

Her followers were made in her image. Callisto, as described by Ovid, was "one of Diana's warriors, wearing her tunic pinned together with a brooch, her tresses carelessly caught back by a white ribbon, and carrying in her hand a light javelin or her bow."[23]

Though she is not one of her companions, Daphne, too, chose Diana's way until Apollo's pursuit and her metamorphosis into a laurel tree: "fleeing the very word 'lover,' [she] took her delight in woodland haunts and in the spoils of captured beasts, emulating Diana, the maiden goddess, with her hair carelessly caught back by a single ribbon."[24]

The effect is not forbidding, but seductive: few of Ovid's other creations have the hoyden grace of Diana and her imitators. Their tantalising quality is recognised in the stories: Apollo loves Daphne at first sight (though he wants to do her hair better); and Meleager, on the Calydonian boar-hunt with Atalanta the fleet-footed, is attracted precisely by her ambiguity: "An ivory quiver, containing her arrows, hung from her left shoulder and rattled as she moved, while she carried her bow as well, in her left hand." Such was her attire—she had features that in a boy would have been called girlish, but in a girl they were like a boy's. "As soon as the hero of Calydon saw her, he fell in love."[25]

In Virgil, the type of maiden warrior evokes erotic languor less openly than in Ovid, as might be expected, but the appeal of the figure remains. After a glorious and heroic sequence of bloody exploits in the field as the champion of Turnus against Aeneas, the invader of Latium, the death of Camilla brings the campaign to a climax; after this, all is bleak loss of hope and defeat, and an elegiac tone prevails in the canto. When Camilla falls, Italy falls, too. Virgil centres on her a passionate sympathy for the conquered. She represents their courage and their glory. Camilla "was of Volscian race and led her cavalcade of squadrons a-flower with bronze."[26] She fights, giddy with excitement, never losing her speed or her skill: "Camilla rode armed with her quiver, exulting like an Amazon, through the midst of the slaughter, having one breast exposed for freedom in the fight. From her shoulder's level twanged the golden bow, the weapon which Diana uses."[27] She and her maidens "were like Amazons of Thrace, who, warring in their brilliant accoutrements, make Thermodon's streams echo to the hoofbeats, as they ride, it may be with Hippolyta, or else when martial Penthesilea drives back in her chariot from war, and her soldier-women, shrieking wild battle cries, exult as they wave their crescent shields."[28]

The Amazons, with their two most famous queens, Hippolyta and

Penthesilea, were Diana's chief votaries, their cult celebrated in particular at Ephesus, site of one of Diana's greatest temples. They lived by her example, spurning men, tracking game, rejoicing in battle, inverting biology and flouting nature, for which in some sources the chief sign is their right breast, severed according to legend in childhood so that they can draw the bow without hindrance. Some etymologists have traced the word to *a-mazon*, the breastless one.[29] Camilla herself was dedicated to Diana as a baby. Her father Metabus, disgraced in his native city, wrapped her in his cloak and fled, his enemies in pursuit. When they reached a river in full flood, Metabus lashed the infant Camilla to a spear, vowed her to Diana, and hurled her across the torrent, swimming across himself behind and finding her safe on the other bank. She was raised on the milk of wild beasts and from her babyhood bent the bow and threw the javelin. Men and the mothers of men sigh for her, but "she found complete happiness in Diana alone, and cherished unendingly her love for her weapons and her maidenhood, touched by none." As the goddess tells us herself in the *Aeneid*, Camilla was "dear to me before all others."[30]

Later texts, by Diodorus Siculus, Pliny the Elder, Justin, Apollonius of Rhodes, and Plutarch, expand on the stories of Amazon society, on their war against men, their sex-segregated organisation, the conduct of their love affairs and their eventual, inevitable massacre at the hands of their chosen enemies, sometimes personified by Theseus, sometimes by Hercules, always by a hero incontrovertibly male.[31] Though it may seem anachronistic to quote it here, the most resonant synthesis of the Amazon cycle was made by Heinrich von Kleist, in his poetic drama *Penthesilea*, written in 1808. There has decayed into the very fabric of the play all the rich stuffs of the ancients to express the psychological meaning of the Amazon: virgin, bride and devourer; unbreakable bow dealing death with its arrows; impregnable womb, in whose shed blood lies life; the forbidden entrance; the mother who must, in her son's eyes, remain a maid. In Kleist's play, Penthesilea, the queen chosen as bride of the god of war, leads her forces into battle with the Greeks during the siege of Troy. Their aim is not to support the Trojans, but to capture as spoils of war the lovers by whom, in Artemis's temple at Themiscyra, the Amazons will conceive the children who will grow up to be their next generation.

Penthesilea sins against her own people's code, because she elects Achilles through love, rather than allowing hazard to choose her lover for her. Alight with passion, she pursues him in battle. She is conquered by him, unknowingly, and he, touched to the heart by her courage and her beauty, is enslaved by her. But when she discovers that she is his prisoner, that she no longer holds the preeminent freedom of an Amazon queen, her senses become deranged; and in a murderous bacchanal, she tears him limb from limb, loving him in the slaughter as much as she would in her rose-petalled grove's bed of love. By this blood offering, she reinstates herself in the majesty of autonomous virginity, according to the Amazons' oracle which she had earlier flouted by her love. When Penthesilea awakes to reality again and discovers her loss, she kills herself.

The rose garlands with which the Amazons adorn their captive-lovers, the wounds with which Penthesilea gashes Achilles in his death throes form overlapping and potent metaphors of the central death image of all, the closed womb, the virginity of the Amazon. But virginity according to the antinomy of life-death symbolism is the promise of fruitfulness, and so the maiden warriors seeking out their mates to conceive children are symbols of the most blissful eroticism, nymphs made more appetising by disdain, the emotional correlative of the strength given them by their inviolateness. After Achilles' death in the play, "It was proclaimed: free as the wind are women who can do so great a deed! Free as the wind—no more subservient to the male!" Kleist is faithful to the symbol's dangerousness and subversion. In Joan's case, however, the Amazon figure's story was borrowed but her significance changed.[32]

There are two common places for Amazons to appear in early Renaissance literature and culture. The first is alongside other great women of history in the biographical collections that were a current and popular form of belles lettres; the second is as the female counterparts of the *Neuf Preux*, or Nine Worthies, a conventional group established in the late fourteenth century of heroes of old, champions of their people—Hector, Alexander, Joshua, David, Julius Caesar, Judas Maccabeus, Arthur, Charlemagne, Theseus—the identities vary from one work of art to another. It is here, in these selfsame contexts, that the earliest eulogies or tributes to Joan appear. Some of the Nine Female Worthies, or Neuf Preuses, are heroines of the Bible—Esther, Judith, Jael, Deborah; some are classical, some religious, some contemporary, like Joan.[33] These are the earliest comparisons Joan invited, her earliest companions in art. In her day, there was no alternative stock of knowledge about human behaviour to draw on in order to understand the prodigy of her rise, her success, her nature, and she was assimilated into Amazon folklore in order to pluck out the heart of her mystery and thereby to tame her.

Christine de Pisan in 1429 compares her favourably to Joshua, to Hector, to Achilles, three of the Nine Worthies and bywords in her day for prowess: "And she is the supreme captain of our brave and able men. Neither Hector nor Achilles had such strength!"[34]

Elsewhere in the same poem, she uses the convention of the Nine Worthies openly, declaring that Joan surpasses them: "I have heard of Esther, Judith and Deborah, who were women of great worth, through whom God delivered His people from oppressions, and I have heard of many other worthy women as well, champions every one, through whom He performed many miracles, but He has accomplished more through this Maid."[35]

A brief account of Joan's career, attributed to Jean de Colonne and also written in 1429, Joan's *annus mirabilis*, compares her as well to Deborah, Judith, Esther and Penthesilea and declares she surpasses them in all virtues.[36] Gélu also saw Joan as a new Deborah.

Such allusions would have been immediately recognisable to a contemporary audience. The Neuf Preuses were a convenient group for writers who wished to treat the female sex or for artists who wished to portray secular women, escape the bonds of religious iconography and let their imaginations explore the female form and its beauties. The Neuf Preuses were an especially popular subject in the Valois court: among Charles VI's effects, sold by the English in Paris in 1422, were several tapestries telling one version of Queen Penthesilea's story, in which she fights with Priam against the Greeks and is killed by Achilles, and other Amazon tales.[37] In 1402, when restoring a wing of the castle of Coucy in Picardy, Louis of Orleans, the king's brother, added a chimney piece with the carved figures of the Nine Female Worthies in the chamber next to the great hall where the Nine Male Worthies also stood. Significantly, he followed the scheme laid down by the learned and prolific poet Eustache Deschamps and added Bertrand du Guesclin, hero of the battles against the English, Joan's special love.[38] As Huizinga comments: "In this way he [Deschamps] linked the cult of the ancient heroes to the budding sentiment of national military glory."[39] Godfrey of Bouillon, the perfect crusader knight, had already taken his place beside his peers, Hector, Charlemagne and David, in some of the recorded groups,[40] and the inclusion of Guesclin reveals how the shared culture of chivalry dominated the thought patterns of the Orleans-Valois circle and how they held paragons in common. Joan was not unusual in her desire to pay homage to the memory of the great constable when she sent his widow a ring. She herself was acceptable in the same circle because she conformed to ideas about the possibilities of female excellence and valour that were already held. Antoine Astesan, the same poet who celebrated Joan's life in verse for his patron Charles of Orleans, described Charles's father's sculptures in another Latin poem.[41]

Nor were these ideas confined to Joan's supporters. Philip of Burgundy commissioned a tapestry of ten male and nine female Worthies to be worked in gold and silver thread; and another, for the rich sum of 2,000 *livres* (a fifth of Joan's eventual ransom), of the females alone, was also to be woven in gold and Cyprus silver. When Henry VI, the baby king, made his botched attempt at a triumphal entry into Paris in 1431, he was preceded by a procession of devices and figures, including the Worthies, male and female, performed by actors. The Bourgeois de Paris was scathing about the skimping at the banquet, but very struck by the ingeniousness of some of Henry's pageantry: there was a masque of three mermaids, and "in the middle of them was a lily whose buds and flowers spouted out milk and wine for everyone to drink who wished or who could. Above, there was a little wood where wild men frolicked about and did very pretty tricks with shields."[42]

There is an actual historical content to the stories preserved by the emblematic figures, like the *Neuf Preuses,* who were so popular in fifteenth-century France. When Cleopatra sailed on her flagship in the thick of the battle of Actium, she acted according to the principles of Eastern royalty, which did not debar women from war, but expected their leaders, kings and queens, to attend the field. Achilles's own shield depicted women defending a city wall; Plato allowed women to be warriors in his republic, if they so desired.[43] But a female enemy nevertheless sharpened Greek desires for conquest; and at the battle of Salamis, the presence of Artemisia (who ranks occasionally among the *Neuf Preuses*) as captain of one of the Persian ships incensed the Greeks, just as Joan's appearance in the defence of Orleans angered the English.[44] They offered a special reward for her capture alive, again, as the English were to do for Joan. The particular insult of defeat at the hands of a woman turns into special respect for that woman; both reflect the assumption that only manliness is equivalent to strength and a woman's victory is a travesty of the natural order, worthy of either horror or respect.

Historical examples existed in sufficient numbers to keep the historians excited, but were few enough to remain worthy of remark. Boccaccio's *De Claris Mulieribus* was one of the most influential collections of women's lives of all.[45] After him, throughout the Renaissance, accounts of Amazons, past and present, became more frequent and more fertile. Joan's contemporary, Aeneas Sylvius Piccolomini, Pope Pius II (d. 1464), whose classicising names betoken his humanist erudition, wrote of Wlasta, the Czech national heroine of the eighth century, also liberator of her country. In his memoirs, when he talks of Joan, he compares her to Camilla.[46] Travellers to the Americas brought back tales of Amazon tribes, glimpsed or heard of, throughout the sixteenth century. Similarly, as Africa was explored by the first Europeans, Amazon societies were described in Ethiopia and in present-day Zimbabwe. It was an abiding source of fascination, and the facts discovered were aligned to coincide with other travellers' and historians' tales of female kingdoms. The distinguishing characteristics of different tribes' social structures were blotted out by an overwhelming interest in the figure of a woman warrior: the mere sighting of a native girl carrying a weapon could lead an explorer to posit yet another homeland of Amazons.[47]

One of the most authentic and earliest descriptions of such a kingdom comes from the vivid account of Brother Gaspard of Carvajal, a Dominican monk who accompanied the conquistador Francisco de Orellana on his exploration of the Amazon basin in 1542. An Indian prisoner was taken by the party in a village remarkable for its central building, a very tall temple raised on two carved lions and situated around a well for ritual libations. The prisoner told the Spaniards that his tribe was subject to a female suzerain living in the interior with her female following,

> that the only service which they rendered them was supplying them with plumes of parrots and macaws for the linings of the roofs of the buildings which constitute their place of worship, and that (all) the villages which they had were of that kind, that they had that thing [the temple] there as a reminder, and that they worshipped it as a thing which was the emblem of their mistress, who is the one who rules over all the land of the aforesaid women.[48]

The Spanish continued to navigate up river and arrived at another village, where they did battle and found among their most formidable opponents some ferocious women who

> [are] very white and tall and have hair very long and braided and wound about the head, and they are very robust and go about naked, with their privy parts covered, with their bows and arrows in their hands, doing as much fighting as ten Indian men, and indeed there was one woman among these who shot an arrow a span deep into one of the brigantines, and others less deep, so that our brigantines looked like porcupines.[49]

When the prisoner is later questioned, he tells the explorers that his rulers live without men, but in order to propagate their race, they raid neighbouring Indian villages and carry men off until they conceive by them. The men are then banished; sons who are born are either killed or sent back to their fathers, while daughters remain with them, raised with great solemnity and instructed in the arts of war. It is the same story Diodorus Siculus told, several hundred years earlier, that Kleist used three hundred years later.

It is impossible to know now whether the Amazon tribe Carvajal described existed. His narrative is vivid and the truth of it borne out in other areas. There is every likelihood he wrote down what he saw and heard, but the tribe, so white, so tall, has never been found again. With regard to Joan, the significance is that stories of Amazons gained wide currency in his own day, though they were not always believed. The stories even gave their name to the great river Orellana had travelled. The existence of such preeminent warriors reinforced the fascination with the phenomenon, and they smoothed the triumphal passage of Joan of Arc into this particular branch of secular hagiography.

The collections in which Joan first appears are often dedicated to eminent women of the day, and frequently their avowed purpose is to establish the legitimacy of some cause: the monarchy, the Catholic victory over the Huguenots in the wars of religion. This tendency becomes more marked as we move through the sixteenth and into the seventeenth century. In Symphorien Champier's *La Nef des Dames Vertueuses*, four volumes of lives of women collected by this Lyons doctor in 1503, Joan occupies a short chapter, which dwells on her prowess in the field and ends with the declaration: "For this reason she is aptly compared to Penthesilea."[50] The following year, Antoine Dufour completed his collection of ninety-one illustrious lives, *La Vie de Femmes Célèbres*, which he composed for the queen, Anne of Brittany.[51] Dufour was born in Orleans; and on 8 May 1502, he delivered the annual pane-gyric on the anniversary of the raising of the siege. Later in his career, he became bishop of Marseilles. Anne, his patron, was a learned woman with a bibliophile's passion, and she had taken over Charles of Orleans's great library at Blois. Among the many books she had printed in the course of her patronage was Boccaccio's *De Claris Mulieribus* in 1493 in a French translation. Dufour's book drew on it extensively, exactly reflecting Anne's curiosity and her tastes. It is lively, erratic, full of interesting material and wild guesses, and it mixes up, without any sense of classification, women of history, of legend, of antiquity, of his own day, of the Bible, of pagan mythology with a syncretist's genuine obliviousness to anachronism. Joan ranks here, in a three-page summary, alongside most of the Nine Worthies and such assorted heroines as Mariamne (the wife of Herod), Minerva, Isis, Dido, Niobe, the Sibyls, Saint Thecla, Saint Helena, Patient Griselda, and many Amazons, some from classical literature, some from contemporary history.

One of Dufour's innovations in the genre is a biography of the goddess Diana. She appears neither in Boccaccio, though Dufour was using him as a model, nor in Symphorien Champier's work, which he probably also knew. His portrait of the goddess reveals Dufour at his most delightful:

> Taking the valuables of her late father and the rings of Latona, her mother, at the age of sixteen, she escaped into the woods, accom-panied by twelve beautiful young virgins. . . . since then no man can meet her in the forest. She did a thousand kindnesses. She had a bow and quiver, and lightly she hunted among the rocks and crags and mountains. And she sang so sweetly that birds and wild beasts lay down to rest at her singing. She lived full of joy, so much so that through long familiarity with animals, she tamed four beau-tiful white stags, who bore her in a chariot.

With her group of young virgins around her, she qualifies, according to Dufour, as the first abbess and the founder of the monastic ideal. Her device was that "a whole body makes a beautiful soul." He ends his paean with the wistful remark: "If she had not been heathen and damned, great praise would be her due."[52] Dufour's eulogy of Joan at Orleans is lost, but his written sketch of her tells the story of her divine mission, her insight into Charles's fears, her finding of the sword and other miracles that make her "almost divine." He calls her "Joan dubbed 'of Vaucouleurs,' " and says she was "small in stature, brief of speech, weighty in judgement, light-footed, agile, good, pious and chaste, bold and generous." Dufour does not insist on her skills with horse and lance or make classical comparisons.[53] But Joan appears, helmeted and armed on a white charger in the coloured vignette illustrating the manuscript. The armour she wears is the Renaissance suit kept in the castle of Amboise by Anne of Brittany and believed to have belonged to her. Joan appears, therefore, like a warrior after the antique.[54]

From then on, the lives of Joan proclaim her deeds of valour in the classical idiom: in 1516, Valerand de la Varenne, a doctor of theology at the University of Paris, tried to redress the errors of Joan's judges, his predecessors in that seat of learning, by writing an epic of over three thousand mediocre lines: *On the Deeds of Joan the Maid, the Great Warrior of France*. The great warrior's life is told from copies of the trial and rehabilitation which La Varenne was lent. Little of note distinguishes it, except that in order to increase the atmosphere of wholesomeness, Joan's father dies of grief after her burning. The poem is dedicated to the archbishop of Rouen, another effort to reclaim innocence and redeem the past.[55]

In this and other books Léon Tripault, a councillor in Orleans, published another *res gestae* of the liberator of his city in 1583,[56] and André Thévet told her story in *True Portraits and Lives of Illustrious Men* of 1584[57]—the image of Joan has not just crystallised but petrified: she is always represented, in both the text and the engravings that accompany it, as a classical warrior, wearing various sorts of armour and carrying different weapons. The image bears no relation to the facts of her life, even when the author has read the trial in manuscript. First, Joan's male dress is glossed over. She is armed and cuirassed as a practical measure. No inquiry is made into the disturbing and deep ambivalence of Joan's need to wear male dress far from the battlefield, in the prison cell, at the communion table. Her transvestism is, in a spirit of uncomprehending chivalry, made light of. Second, Joan always has long hair, and the specific description in the trial charge, that her head was shorn like a fashionable boy's, is simply ignored in the texts and the pictures. The image most often reproduced is the town hall of Orleans's portrait, with its gay plumage and full skirts. When Joan is mounted, this costume is sometimes caught up to reveal full leggings to permit her to ride astride.[58] The distinguishing plumes remain, usually indicating the temporary and expedient nature of her full armour, as in the two engravings by Gaultier, which both Jean Hordal and Charles du Lis used in their books. "Troy would still be standing," Gaultier wrote under his equestrian image, "if such a figurehead had led their troops." "Under the girlish clothes," he inscribed on the other, "there hides a Mars-like virgin."[59] By mid-century, Joan of Arc had been reestablished through these efforts as a national saviour of the glorious French monarchy, but her personality had been stolen away under the particular influence of an Amazon of Renaissance culture.

A profound metamorphosis of the classical Amazon, the death-dealing virgin votary of Diana, took place in the work of the Italian Renaissance poets on the *chansons de geste* of medieval France. In their epics, Boiardo and Ariosto and Tasso borrowed two great heroes of French chivalry—Roland from the early twelfth-century *Chanson de Roland* and Renaud de Montauban from the slightly later *Quatre Fils Aymon*—and retold their exploits in magnificent style, which gave the genre a new and extraordinarily hardy popularity.[60] (In the seventeenth and eighteenth centuries, such stories of chivalry still predominated among the titles of the widely disseminated Bibliothèque Bleue.)[61] One particular development of significance was their treatment of the warrior maid as a romantic heroine. She was to remain a figure of bewitchment in European literature for nearly two hundred years: the heroines Marfisa and Bradamante in Boiardo and Ariosto, Clorinda in Tasso, Britomart and Radegunde in Spenser's *Faerie Queene*.

All the erotic vitality of Ovid's Atalanta or Daphne charges the figure of their descendants, these female knights of Renaissance fantasy, these mounted maidens in disguise who accomplish remarkable feats of chivalry; but their chastity no longer expresses an inexorable renunciation of men, for much of the drama of the epics centres on the love of the protagonists. The Amazon is no longer fearsome, except in the field or at the tourney; she is susceptible to languishing, and her love represents the most elevated ideal to which the heroes can aspire. The outward sign of the radiant beauty that is the catalyst of love is her hair. In a seminal passage, Tancred, one of Tasso's heroes, at last finds Clorinda, whom he has sought ever since he saw her face reflected in the water with which she once cooled his forehead. Disguised as a knight and hidden under a visor, she is jousting with him, and he, charging her with lance, knocks off her helmet: "And, her golden locks loosed in the wind, a young woman appeared in the field."[62]

This episode, characteristic of the emotional dynamic of epic poetry, is the origin of Joan's sixteenth- and seventeenth-century long, wavy chevelure. If the warrior maid bore arms, she also remained the ideal feminine. Nothing so radical as Joan's rejection of the female mode of life belongs to Clorinda or to Britomart. They live as knights, but their knightliness, like their chastity, no longer expresses rejection, but invitation, within the special context of the love ideal centring on non-fulfilment, which is one of Christianity's most important legacies to European society.

The influence of the Italian epics on the cult of development of ideas about Joan of Arc is quite specific and can be clearly traced to Lorraine, to the period when the court at Nancy reached its apogee and began to struggle to establish a separate identity distinct from the French kingdom. The ducal court's rivalry with the other princely milieus of the day, in Italy and in France, also acted as a spur. Hordal's homage to Joan, published at Lorraine's university at Pont-à-Mousson, opens with invocation to her by Catherine de Cailly, Charles du Lis's sister, saying Joan far surpasses Bradamante, Ariosto's fabulous heroine.[63] Claude Deruet, one of the circle of inventive and delightful painters around the duke of Lorraine in the first half of the seventeenth century, painted Joan as a romantic Amazon. Deruet travelled to Italy in 1613 and there refreshed the inspiration that had already marked him in his early work as an apprentice to another Lotharingian painter, Jacques Bellange. In 1606, Henry II of Lorraine married Margaret, daughter of the duke of Gonzaga Mantua; the duke was a patron of Tasso, chief exponent of the epic art. Her entry into Nancy as duchess was celebrated with the pageantry that the Valois court had perfected, under the inspired guidance of Marie de Médicis, who was Margaret's aunt. Not to be outdone, the court of Lorraine built fantastic triumphal arches, painted all over with figures taken from the classics, under the strong influence of Ovid, the native poet of Mantua. Deruet helped Bellange, the chief painter on the project, and though Bellange's work is not extant, a memory of the elaborate edifices lingers perhaps in the background fairy palace of Deruet's later enchanting painting, *A Banquet of Amazons*.[64]

The Amazon is one of the chief themes of painting in Lorraine at this time: one might say it is almost obsessional in Deruet, if the

lightheartedness of his style did not argue a more frivolous interest. The
duchess was herself personified as a hunting princess, and in the four
magnificent allegorical tableaux of the Four Elements, now in the Museum of Orleans, Deruet scattered innumerable female cavaliers. In *Le
Feu*, they caper in the wide courtyard of a graceful and splendid palace,
illuminated by the exploding fireworks of a festivity that probably took
place one night in Nancy (9).

When Lorraine was invaded by French troops in 1633, Louis XIII
and Richelieu made a triumphant entry into Nancy. Deruet changed allegiance. Without self-consciousness, he used the same imagery to celebrate his new sovereign, Anne of Austria. He posed her on an exquisitely
caparisoned and lavishly groomed white horse beside three goddesses
who include Diana, wearing breastplate and plumed headdress and
carrying her javelin and shield.[65]

Deruet was ennobled by Louis XIII and lived in grand style, receiving the king and queen in his own home in 1633. His fascination
with Amazons is superficial, avoiding all hints at profound comment on
sexual nature. His aim seems purely decorative, and he emerges as a man
frankly enjoying the pleasures of such fancies as an Amazon orchestra
conducted with a baton of roses, as a voluptuary taken with something a
little piquant, but harmless.

Deruet's lightness of touch does not prevent his preoccupations'
being revealed. In a painting either by Deruet or by Jean de Caumont
(d. 1659) after him, Joan is identified by her "du Lis" coat of arms and
in the long inscription is described also as "Pucelle d'Orleans" and
"Amazone de France." Along the blade of her unsheathed weapon, the
painter wrote, "This sword saved France"; and in the background,
knights in armour are skirmishing. She wears her long, loose hair under
her plumed hat over a manly cuirass, as usual (24).[66] But it is a typical aspect of Joan's story that the public's imagination did not halt at this
portrait and that when Deruet's painting of Roger and Bradamante riding together was engraved and disseminated, they were identified as
Joan and Dunois. As in the case of the head of Saint Maurice, the die
is so firmly stamped on Joan that the impression remains, while the
original is forgotten.

Jean Chapelain, who spent thirty years working on the twenty-five
cantos of his epic poem about Joan on commission from the duke of
Longueville, count of Dunois, and a descendant of the house of Orleans,
modelled himself explicitly on Tasso: instead of Jerusalem's delivery,

he described France's. His *La Pucelle ou La France Delivrée* was published in a sumptuous edition in 1656; five others followed quickly after, though the work was viciously lampooned by contemporary stylists like Boileau. It is unreadable today.[67] When Denis Foyatier's bronze was unveiled in Orleans in 1855, the equestrian Joan, with her flowing hair under the classic helmet, seemed to the poet Théophile Gautier "a new Clorinda." The comparison seemed apt; he probably did not know how apt.[68]

Can the sleave woven by the Amazon triad, by Diana-Penthesilea-Clorinda, be unravelled and its meaning teased out of it? The lasting entrancement of the figure leads Jungians to see an archetype, a mystery in which the desired *coincidentia oppositorum* has been effected, in which yin and yang, female and male, are in balance and equally expressed. The rejection of the male world by the Amazon argues the wholeness of her own psyche.

When Jungians, in their quest for union, see a completing and healing image in the androgyne, they are blind to the self-mutilation of the figure, the death wish that drives the ambiguous girl to wish to obliterate her sex (see Chapter 7), that brings Kleist's Penthesilea, by the mortal logic of unconscious, to maul and maim first Achilles, whom she loves, and then herself.[69] The Amazon dramatises sexual difference, but gives the palm to the male: for their physical skills, courage, accuracy of aim, speed of foot, endurance in battle, not for their psychic choice, are Hippolyta and Penthesilea praised.[70] Nothing could be a clearer symbol of how the figure embodies a rejection of the feminine than the severed breast. Astonishingly, this custom appears to have been invented at some later date: no Amazon in a Greek vase painting or sculpture of classical times is mutilated in this way, and the authors who describe this custom are comparatively late: Justin, Diodorus Siculus, Galen. They also provide the mistaken etymology of Amazon. As Robert Graves has pointed out, the *A* may be emphatic, so that the word may mean "many-breasted," as indeed was the Amazons' special goddess, Diana of the Ephesians.[71]

The widespread fantasy of the Amazons' eradication of a breast in infancy (usually by burning, not surgery), so that they could pull the bow with greater ease, extends the murder that lies at the heart of the myth and is exemplified in the earliest Greek accounts, both written and visual, of the appalling Amazonamachies, the massacres of the women's tribes by the great heroes, Hercules and Theseus. It is murder, and it is self-murder: a sacrifice of the body, in the most bloody fashion, to preface renewed strength in the victors. The self-slaughter of the Amazons' warrior ways and their terrible engagements with their destroyers represent a ritual combat between feminine and masculine elements, reduced to a confining apartheid, in which the male is shown ultimately to prevail. The analogy of this in Joan's case is her martyrdom, as will be seen.

The war zone changes in the epics; though the heroes meet the armed maidens in the field, the conflict is concentrated in their hearts, and battle provides only the external metaphor of the struggle. At the end of Ariosto's *Orlando Furioso*, for instance, Bradamante, who has loved and been loved by Ruggero throughout the poem, declares that she will promise herself only to a man who can beat her in a fight. By parrying her assaults and remaining entirely on the defensive, Ruggero manages to hold his ground; and though Ariosto's love of ingenuity and dramatic reversals takes us through a few more phases of the plot, their wedding is eventually celebrated with great pomp.[72] The bridal ending of the poem is a much more convincing image of union, of the *coincidentia oppositorum*, than the single figure of the Amazon, if only because the courtly convention, dependent on Christian teaching about the necessity of chastity in true love, has hitherto kept apart the lovers, representatives of male and female. Where consummation had been death for Penthesilea, for Clorinda it is defloration, one of its analogues.

The valour of Clorinda and Britomart and their likes serves to enhance the valour and the nobility of the knight who wins them: we are very far from Actaeon's scattered limbs in the goddess's desecrated grove. Joan of Arc would never have survived in memory as a figure of good if in history's eyes she had remained a faithful follower of Diana. It is not her androgynous aspect that has been obscured through fear, but rather the sharpness of the Amazon threat has been sweetened. Joan's Amazonian likeness had to be softened to be countenanced at all; her transvestism, her armour, her inviolability had to seem something that in the final conclusion was offered on the altar of male supremacy. That is why, when Joan is rehabilitated, her joy in battle is made little of, and one story is repeated and repeated until it gains widespread credence: all she wanted to do after Charles's coronation was to go home and look after sheep again, but she was prevented by her battle-loving colleagues. That is why so many of her fervent apologists have given her inamorati, so many Ruggeros and Rinaldos to win her favour. In

Schiller's tragedy *Die Jungfrau von Orleans*, Joan falls in love with an English soldier and dies in battle beside him; Temistocle Solera's libretto for Verdi's opera follows Schiller's plot, except that Joan falls in love with the Dauphin himself, with whom she sings a characteristic rapturous duet; in a forgotten play of 1829 by N. J. C. de Hedouville, both Dunois and *Bedford* sigh for her;[73] in Jean-Joseph Olivier's opera (1870), La Trémoille, Charles's devious advisor, takes on the role.[74] Of course literary conventions of the day demand such reshaping of the story; and in our own times, acquaintance with the ambivalent impulses of human nature has attributed Joan a poignant conflict of emotion. In Thomas Keneally's intense and admirable novel, *Blood Red, Sister Rose*, Joan rushes on D'Alençon with blows, curses and drawn sword when she finds him in bed with a whore. She feels like weeping for jealousy but tells herself, preemptorily, to think of his wife: "Be sad for that poor dark business-like duchess at Saumur."[75]

Transvestism can accentuate sexuality, not eliminate it, and the Amazon, in her apparent rejection of men, can be seen to affirm sexual difference and male superiority.[76] Joan's life, as said before, is a tribute to the traditional sphere of man, as opposed to woman, so that Amazon independent virgin that she was, she became a suitably versatile talisman for a host of causes conducted by men, military and political. Yet at the same time, because she was undeniably female, she was a figurehead for the women's side in one phase of the lasting struggle, the continuing duel, between Queen Penthesilea and Hero Achilles.

CHAPTER 11

PERSONIFICATION OF VIRTUE

Perfection is terrible, it cannot have children.

SYLVIA PLATH,
"The Munich Mannequins"[1]

The anthropologist Carl von Sydow borrowed the botanical term *ecotype*, describing a plant that travels, adapts itself and develops differently according to its surroundings, and applied it to migrant cultural figures, who take root and flourish in different places in different guises.[2] The Amazon is one such ecotype, and Joan is one of its species; another is the Virtue, the allegorical figure who personifies an abstract moral quality (12). She is very close to the Amazon, the burnet as it were to the Amazon's dog-rose, in the same thick and bristling hedgerow of classicising medieval culture, and Joan again is one of the many flowers on its thorny stems.

Whereas the Amazon belongs to a mythological and historical tradition, the Virtue reveals something fundamental about our thought patterns. But we are so accustomed to the convention of female personification of virtue that it has become largely invisible. Yet it is the principle that gives us to this day Britannia on coinage or in song; Liberty in the harbour of New York; Justice on the Old Bailey, her eyes blindfold, the balance and sword in her hands; the draped female symbols of mourning on tombstones; that makes it possible for girls to be called Hope, Faith, Charity, Prudence, Liberty and Unity, and impossible for boys; that gave Joan of Arc an intelligible context and helped us not to forget her.

The issues of feminism were alive in the fifteenth century as they never were again until the late eighteenth century and the present day, although the debate was restricted to educated circles, clerical and lay. This *querelle des femmes* centred on the long medieval poem, *Le Roman de la Rose*.[3] It is difficult, reading it today, to enter into the minds that were inflamed by this allegory, for its use of established literary conventions makes it ineffably remote. But the *Roman de la Rose* was as influential as Dante's *Divina Commedia* for over two hundred years after its composition and as controversial as Darwin's *Origin of Species*. It is extant in *three hundred* manuscripts. Begun in the first half of the thirteenth century by Guillaume de Lorris, it was completed between 1275–80 by Jean de Meung, and it is Meung's larger contribution (eighteen thousand lines—Lorris only wrote four thousand) that stirred the fury of his readers. Lorris had established the imagery: enclosed at the heart of the garden of love, a flowering earthly paradise, is a rose, which the Lover longs to pick. His adventures take place in a dream; he meets allegorical qualities of soul who give him help and hindrance, and the drama of obtaining the lady's favour is drawn by different personifications of her fluctuating inclinations.

Lorris's poem is a rich expression of the medieval visionary tradition, fashioning an entire cosmos from the interior of a single individual's mind, but the energy and realism, which make Dante, for instance, still accessible today, is absent. In Meung's elaboration, courtliness is forgotten and the rigid framework for inner experience provided by the allegory weakens under the poet's vigorous disputatiousness about money, the authorities, the Church and, of course, women. Meung savages the entire medieval world's pretence at chivalry: he lifts up the smooth slab of all the traditions of compassion, justice and love to show the lice busy grubbing underneath.

Meung's misogyny was particularly popular; and in 1400, Christine de Pisan wrote *Le Dit de la Rose*, refuting it with spirited indignation.[4] Jean Gerson supported her publicly.[5] Belief in the virtuousness of women was bound together with the ideals that Meung attacked: the authority of the Church, the sacred monarchy, the practice of chastity, the genuine learning and noble aspirations of the establishment. Both

Gerson and Christine produce Joan as their living embodiment. Twenty-nine years after her defence of women, Christine came out of her retirement, as we have seen, to pen her praise of Joan of Arc, a supreme example of the virtues she had extolled in her sex: "Oh! what honour for the female sex! It is perfectly obvious that God has special regard for it when all these wretched people who destroyed the whole Kingdom—now recovered and made safe by a woman, something that 5,000 *men* could not have done—and the traitors have been exterminated."[6] That God had chosen a woman to save France and thereby shown the whole sex his love was an argument that appears in subsequent feminist literature and made Joan a favourite subject among women themselves. She appears in books dedicated to women, as we have seen; the first biography of Joan alone, written around 1500, for King Louis XII and Louis de Graville, one of Joan's companions-at-arms, was probably instigated by Anne de Graville, his daughter, a woman who like Christine had a pronounced taste for learning and an independent spirit. She herself wrote (a version of Boccaccio's *Palemon and Arcita*), and when she married the man of her choice, against her father's wishes, she called their daughter Jeanne.[7]

Martin le Franc, in *Le Champion des Dames*, a work directly inspired by the quarrel about *Le Roman de la Rose*, takes Joan's part against her detractors. Their arguments focus on her belligerence, her transvestism and her condemnation by the Church. Le Franc's champion rebuts them.[8] In the same year as the printing of *Le Champion des Dames* (1530), a morality play appeared on the same subject: *Le Bien et le Mal des Dames*.[9] In Lyon in 1546, another broadside against the enemies of women was published. With extensive use of numerology and riddles, *Le Mirouer des Femmes Vertueuses* concentrates on Joan's prophetic faculties. Joan, the spirit of action, and Griselda, the personification of passivity, provide examples of the wide-ranging quality of women's virtues.[10]

In 1547, Guillaume du Bellay, lord of Langey, a village north of Orleans, took his secretary, François de Billon, and perhaps his other protégé, François Rabelais, to Rome. There Billon, incensed by what he saw as the dominating misogynist accent of Rabelais's work, sprang to the defence of women and became one of the most enjoyed and widely read supporters of the sex in this later stage of the *querelle des femmes*. *The Invincible Strength of the Honour of the Female Sex* expressly sees Joan as the victim of men and a rallying point for Frenchwomen. He attributes—wrongly—the erection of the Orleans monument to the townswomen's enthusiasm:

> O poor maid, who so gloriously and with your suffering avenged the oppressions of the French: the wrongs and the hurts, the contempt and the rough handling suffered for such a long time by such an infinite number of French ladies, will they ever be avenged by someone like you? Who would have had a statue raised to you on the bridge at Orleans, if it had not been for the noble women of the city who urged it so strongly?[11]

But the most fierce, fanatical and bizarre feminist tract of the times was the work of Billon's contemporary, Guillaume Postel, a hermetic philosopher, a priest and at one time a Jesuit, whose mixture of lunging inspirations and dazzling dexterity of learning is indeed bewildering. The title is self-explanatory: *The Very Wonderful Victories of the Women of the New World. And how they should govern the whole world by reason, and even those too who will be Monarchs in the Old World.*[12]

Postel stood high in the favour of François I and the queen, who considered him a "wonder of the world." He was certainly extraordinary: a jackdaw assimilating information and reassembling it in a nest of strange construction, strewn with numerology, the cabbala, astrology, comparative religion, alchemy, assorted strands of ancient wisdom, to prove that, by the logic of pure reason, a woman should now prevail. He had found the female Messiah who would inspire this rebirth in the shape of a Mère Jeanne, an Italian visionary who had adopted him and whose revelations he used for both *Les Très Merveilleuses Victoires* and for a subsequent book about her alone. Unlike most of the female prophets we have encountered so far, Mère Jeanne was illiterate but had absorbed the chiliastic ideas that had circulated in Europe throughout the medieval period, particularly from Joachim of Flora and his followers. She fasted continually, meditated for long intervals, sometimes all night, lived a life of stern virginity and austerity and had discarded all possessions. She worked in hospitals in Italy and did other good works, among which the rearing of Postel should no doubt be counted. She prophesied that she would become pope and reform the Church, that the Turks would be converted and that, at the millennium, all would be saved. Postel himself was an ardent monarchist as well and saw Joan's affirmation of the Valois line as God's seal of approval; but his heresies, not least his belief that Mohammed was a true prophet, cost him his liberty. He died in prison in St. Martin des Champs in 1581.

Postel dedicated *The Very Wonderful Victories* to Marguerite of France, duchess of Berry, and he asked her in particular to look closely at his chapter on Joan of Arc, as the supreme representative of female virtue. Postel is caustic about the efforts of his predecessors in female biography. He will write about women who have distinguished them-selves, not through vice, but through virtue. Joan embodies the "sov-ereign feminine power in this world." His story concentrates on her prophecies and their realisation, particularly Charles's recovery of France and the expulsion of the English, and he concludes, "God not only shows himself under a male species omnipotent among his own and the God of wars and battles; he shows himself even more clearly in the weakest and most feminine person than in a male; but so it had to be, that the perfect religion should be completed in its perfection and led by the same female sex." As he continues this argument, he jumbles Joan of Arc with Mère Jeanne, his mentor, whom he sees as her direct descen-dant, if not her reincarnation.[13]

Postel's trumpet call for a rule of women should not be dismissed as quackery. He is certainly writing on the extreme fringe of a cultural tradition in France in his day that was already marginal, and he is unarguably unique in what he has to say. But his outlook and the passionate reverence for Joan of Arc that it inspires were shaped in many ways by other, more commonplace thinkers and unveil a nexus of arguments which, like the Amazon tradition, kept the figure of Joan before our eyes because they made her understandable as a special, but nevertheless recognisable phenomenon. This nexus is present in all the writings mentioned, in Symphorien Champier, in François de Billon; it provides the foundation of the concept of female virtue. It becomes part of the central current of culture only when a certain catalyst, like the debate over the *Roman de la Rose*, or Rabelais's inheritance of Jean de Meung's ribaldry, forces the orthodox—like Christine de Pisan or Jean Gerson—to consider it. Otherwise it remains on the periphery, where it is susceptible to curious treatment, like Postel's. The very exclusion of women from central consideration, their continual treatment as a thing apart—of which the collections of illustrious lives themselves, however praiseworthy their intention, are a symptom—reinforces the problem, by creating an intellectual situation in which the cause of women is argued by recourse to fringe sciences, heterodox philosophies, areas of thought considered unsound by the dominating intellectual world.

Women and their champions, finding little support in the Augustinian and Thomist theology for their spiritual equality, had throughout the Middle Ages mined the seam of gnosticism that taught, in its various different forms, the acquisition of knowledge often made manifest—and here is the key—in the female figure of wisdom.[14]

As Sophia in Greek, as the *shekinah* (spirit of God) and the *hokmah* (wisdom of God) in the Bible, as Athene-Minerva in the classical pantheon, Wisdom retained a feminine aspect in the mystic Christian tradition fed by the Neoplatonist streams that flowed from Hellenistic Alexandria and its school of biblical exegetes in early Christian times. In Proverbs, Wisdom builds her house of seven pillars (Proverbs 9:1 ff.); in Ecclesiastes 24:9, she speaks of herself in the exalted lyricism as God's eternal bride: "He created me before the beginning of the world, and I shall never fail." The prophet then comments: "Her thoughts are more than the sea, and her counsels profounder than the deep." (Ecclesiastes 24:29).[15] The gnostic initiate often sought to possess Wisdom by union with her as lover or as child. Gnostic rites, as practised, for instance, by the Valentinian sect in the second century, were often cast in the form of nuptials,[16] and constantly led their practitioners into trouble with the Church.

Above all, gnostic teachers were dangerous, because they were self-appointed prophets. Many, as we have seen, were women, and their vaunted independence made their position more perilous. Concomitantly, heretical groups sometimes proclaimed a revolutionary egalitarianism, perhaps in revolt against the inferiority of women in orthodox theory and practice. The tract *Schwester Katrei*,[17] written in the first person of the eponymous Sister Catherine, establishes that a woman can reach the highest knowledge of God, until her essence is commingled with his as a dewdrop is lost in the ocean. Not only that, but she can reach this state under the gentle guidance of her confessor and can then reverse roles and become his teacher in turn. Written before 1337 and wrongly attributed to Meister Eckhart, this work won a wide readership, and it is entirely characteristic of *illuminati* yearnings in its assumption of female equality. The tradition is tenacious, still present all over Europe in the seventeenth century and able to voice its revolutionary content in England under the commonwealth. Christopher Hill has pointed to numerous incidences of women's equality among the sects that then proliferated. There was a firm link, in the mind of revolutionaries like Mary Cary, between the equal status of men and women, democracy on earth and democracy of access to spiritual riches. In her *New and more exact Mappe or Description of New Jerusalem Glory* of 1651, she wrote, recalling the text of Joel: "The time is coming when not only men but women shall prophesy; not only aged men but young men, not only superiors but inferiors; not only those who have university learning but those who have it not, even servants and handmaids."[18]

The intellectual relation of programmes like that of Mary Cary to the gnostics of the ancient world and the Neoplatonists of the Renaissance is beyond the reach of this book. But from the point of view of feminism, Neoplatonism, with its particular emphasis on the higher world of ideas and their emanations in this world, kept before the eyes of Christendom the convention by which visions of the ideal were expressed in the feminine. This in turn affected the conception of the feminine itself, because it lent women an affinity with virtue uncharacteristic of the central argument of Christianity, that Eve had lost the human race. It made a learned defence of women easier, even for the orthodox.

Although the Bible provided individual stories that could be used in praise of women, the schoolmen's cupboards were almost bare of supporting arguments. When an author dyed in the patristic tradition, like the Jesuit Pierre Lemoyne, takes up the female cause, he can apply the language of theology to his theme, but must overlook its misogynist tenets and avoid the use of authoritative quotation from the Fathers, to which his training would lead him in any other area of inquiry. Lemoyne published his interesting compendium, *The Gallery of Strong Women*, in 1647,[19] and he dedicated it to the queen regent, Anne of Austria, mother of Louis XIV, with a fulsome preface about the wisdom and strength of a woman's rule. His album of viragoes perfects the genre of women's collected lives: Lemoyne mingles figures from the past with contemporary examples (as recent as Mary Stuart and Jeanne Hachette, the Catholic heroine of the siege of Beauvais in 1472) with mythological and classical characters, in a recipe that is by now familiar. He has a pious and pedantic touch and is characteristic of the growing Neoplatonism of his time in wishing to leave nothing of the great heathen tradition out, while remaining at the same time unexceptionably loyal to Christianity alone. He strives to maintain the continuity of ideals between the ancient wisdom and the faith and to effect a synthesis between the two currents of European culture, pagan and Christian, but always to give the better part to Christianity. Thus Joan, La Pucelle d'Orleans, should not only be identified with the Amazons, he declares, for to do so neglects the divine inspiration that guided her. The spirit that breathed in her breathed in Deborah and David. The sword in her hand reminds him of the double-edged flaming sword of the angel leading the chosen people. Her special courage comes from God, independent of her sex; it is the kind of enthusiasm—Lemoyne means this in the exalted Greek sense of divine possession—that transcends questions of gender. He proclaims vehemently the irrelevance of maleness or femaleness in the case of such greatness as Joan possessed and relates her to the Platonic world of absolute ideas, unmodified by questions of sex. "As for Heroic Virtue," he writes,

> it is certain that these faculties are not different where the sex is different. They have the same foundation everywhere and are capable of the same forms. The light that descends into the spirit of man is not purer nor does it come from a higher sphere than the light that descends into the spirit of woman, and this equal light, coming from the same source, can kindle an equal fire of equal strength in the heart of both. . . . It is not therefore the difference of sex that makes for the difference in the soul's faculties, since these are equally perfect in man and woman; and as they can be imbued with the same light and penetrated with the same fire in one case and the other, let us proceed freely and willingly to the conclusion to which this argument leads us and agree that women can be disposed by this light and by this fire to the chief functions of Heroic Virtue.[20]

This is an arresting paean to Joan. It dismisses the idea prevalent in all the previous literature, even in the earlier collections of heroines, that her activities were exceptional only because she was a woman. Lemoyne also marks a point in Joan's historiography where the Amazon identification is decaying: for her contemporaries, it had been an apt analogy; for their followers, Hordal and du Lis's contributors, it had sunk so deep that it underlies all their thinking, even to the point of establishing her name; but for a cultivated priest with mystical and even alchemical leanings, it was not sufficient tribute to her virtue. Lemoyne responded to the sexism of the Amazon figure. He wished to divorce Joan from it and place her above, in that androgynous zone that is, as we have already seen, Christian mysticism's metaphor for angelic purity.

In this respect, Christian mysticism comes closer to encratite heresies, the fierce early schools of ascetic thought that were tainted with gnosticism and were, in most cases, anathematised. In the fourth century, the learned Priscillian taught ascent to holiness through austerity and self-denial, in order to partake of the divine nature, which "transcends all sexual differentiation." But he allowed women to practise his rule as much as men, a freedom that lunged him into obloquy and helped toward his undoing.[21] (Priscillian, a deeply holy man, is Joan of Arc's true father, for he was the first Christian to be tried by the Church for heresy and witchcraft and condemned in 385 to die, and she is the only canonised saint to have been handed over to be burned at the stake by the Church itself, the Inquisition.)

All these elements come together and relate to Joan over the question, How is the concept of virtue represented? At the basis of the feminists' material, of Postel's fancies, of Lemoyne's propositions, even of *Le Mirouer*'s use of magic numbers, is a Neoplatonist web of ideas linking spiritual virtue with revelations of the higher world expressed in the feminine, both verbally and visually. It is, however, a defeminised feminine, closer to the angels than to mortal women, which relates it to the gnostic-ascetic tradition. (The name of the archangel Michael—and angels play a great part in gnostic teachings—means "Who is like God.")

There is a semantic foundation to virtue's expression in the feminine, since abstract qualities—beauty, peace, justice and, at the negative pole, anger, lust, envy—are almost without exception feminine in gender in Greek and Latin. But whereas the memory of gender fades in modern usage in most cases (nobody in France thinks of *la table* as female, and in England gender has all but disappeared for the naming of anything other than people), the femininity of abstract nouns has remained alive. The reasons behind this semantic phenomenon are difficult and obscure; but they certainly cannot be that women possess such qualities more abundantly or remarkably, nor that femininity itself is more abstract, lending itself to the general, masculinity to the particular. That would be putting the argument the wrong way around and allowing usage to speak for origins.

The startling aspect of the widespread use of female personification is that it runs contrary to gender use in almost all other ways. The feminine gender in the Romance languages is, for instance, associated with the small-scale, by contrast to the male's larger size. Thus in

French, an insect is *une bête*, and the ant is *la fourmi;* but the tiger is *le tigre* and the lion, *le lion*. The feminine is also the gender label of auxiliary objects. Tools are "helpmeets" to *homo faber: la tronçonneuse*, the chain saw; *la moissoneuse*, the mower. The feminine gender of *la Beauté* (beauty) or *la Justice* (justice) or, indeed, any of the abstract nouns common in languages that share a Greek and Latin past conflicts with these two traditions, in that the words signify large, encompassing absolutes. In this, they would appear related to the usage that grants the feminine to material concepts of mighty, even boundless dimension: *la terre*, the land; *la mer*, the sea. But this is complicated, since contrasts in size between two words—for river, *le fleuve, la rivière;* for the sea, *l'océan, la mer;* for the world, *l'univers, la terre*—maintain the traditional standard of comparison in the same area of reference, and the usage does not obtain throughout the Roman languages. The sea, in Italian, is *il mare;* the river, *il fiume*, rarely has a female name: *il Tevere* (the Tiber) or *l'Arno*, unlike *La Seine* or *La Tamise* (the Thames).[22]

The most fundamental way in which feminine abstractions contradict the apparent rules is in the abstraction itself and the abstraction's autonomy. The feminine in Indo-European languages is never the matrix from which the masculine is derived but always, on the contrary, the modified version of the masculine form. The feminine is also subsumed into the masculine, and not the other way around. In a French sentence of which the subject is six women and a male child, the correct grammatical agreement would be masculine. Similarly, in a language like English, in which only personal pronouns are inflected according to sex (with a few exceptions, like "ship" or "country"), the male category includes the female in its meaning or is intended to do so, at least. This relegation of the female to a dependent, ancillary role has provoked much discussion recently about its effect on the conception of femaleness itself.[23]

The continuing use of the masculine to express general truths about humanity, and the feminine only to particularise the female, has contributed to the ideology that women are different, worse than separate, peripheral. The feminist Christabel Pankhurst tried to combat the inbuilt tendency of official language in this respect and, in her first publicised meeting, took her first militant step and proposed that whenever the word *he* was used, it should be understood to mean *all*.[24] In order to rank beside men, in order to shed that otherness which makes her a subspecies and not the thing itself, not the genuine article—as if a woman did not carry the full quiddity of humanity in herself—the female should use language for her own ends.

The problem does not lie in our Western languages' system of gender classification itself; and feminists who wish to abolish the grammatical differences are seeking to forge a primitive and monolithic language with lesser flexibility, less accuracy and less capacity to express distinctions that are, through both the precision of their meaning and the range of their associations, emancipating in themselves. In creating greater discrimination and subtlety in language, not in reducing it, shall we arrive at greater fairness (*freedom* is too absolute an ideal to use the word here). The problem lies in the semantic usage of male and female linguistic categories, and the prejudice is more marked in English, where the gender system is comparatively weak, than it is in the Romance languages, where it is strong and where it does not conform to sexual characteristics alone. For instance, in French *la personne*, *la victime*, *la bête* are always feminine, whether the person, victim or animal in question is male or female. It is much less unusual in French to hear whole sentences or read whole paragraphs with general application to humanity, written in the feminine, than in English, where such thoughts are only expressed in the feminine if they apply exclusively to females. For instance, *"Une personne qui se croit folle pourrait être la victime d'une idée sociale de la folie"* is a sentence in which the language effortlessly expresses the universality of the thought. When this sentence is rendered into English, trouble immediately occurs: "Someone who considers himself (?) mad . . ."? "A man (?) who considers himself (?) mad . . ."? Resorting to the plural—the only way in English to embrace both sexes in the meaning ("People who consider themselves mad . . .")—a different problem occurs: the sentence no longer refers to a hypothetical person, a nonspecific example, but implies the existence of such people. "Someone who . . ." leaves the question of the person's actual existence open.

The occasional disjunction of sex and grammatical gender in French is proven by the remarkable inversion that occurs with words describing the organs of sexual difference. Women's are usually masculine—*le sein*, *le con*, *le vagin*, *l'utérus*—and men's feminine—*la pine*, *la verge*. There are exceptions: *testicule* is masculine, for instance. But the very absence of a strict rule implies that the significance attached to grammatical categories is not always strictly biological.

This semantic freedom could be used fruitfully. Unfortunately, in

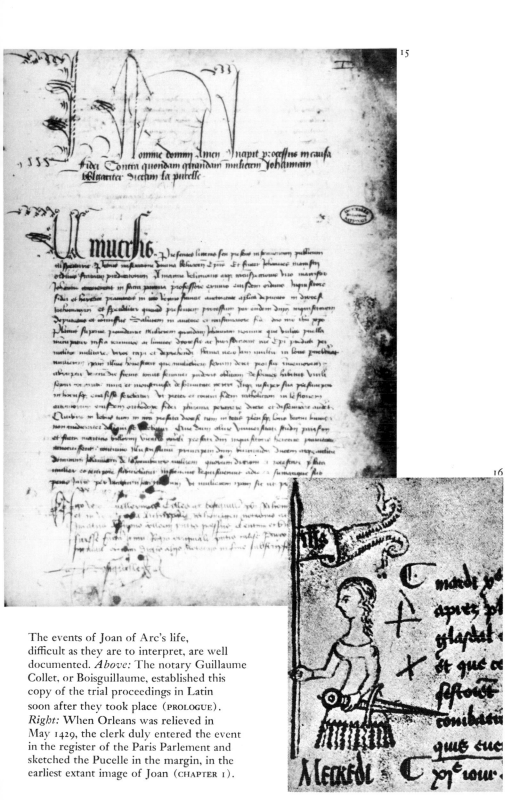

The events of Joan of Arc's life,
difficult as they are to interpret, are well
documented. *Above:* The notary Guillaume
Collet, or Boisguillaume, established this
copy of the trial proceedings in Latin
soon after they took place (PROLOGUE).
Right: When Orleans was relieved in
May 1429, the clerk duly entered the event
in the register of the Paris Parlement and
sketched the Pucelle in the margin, in the
earliest extant image of Joan (CHAPTER 1).

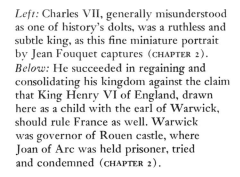

Left: Charles VII, generally misunderstood as one of history's dolts, was a ruthless and subtle king, as this fine miniature portrait by Jean Fouquet captures (CHAPTER 2). *Below:* He succeeded in regaining and consolidating his kingdom against the claim that King Henry VI of England, drawn here as a child with the earl of Warwick, should rule France as well. Warwick was governor of Rouen castle, where Joan of Arc was held prisoner, tried and condemned (CHAPTER 2).

Above: In 1407, assassins ordered by the duke of Burgundy cut down Louis of Orleans, the king's brother, in a Paris street, and, as this contemporary miniature shows, severed his right hand to prevent him, even in death, from practising the witchcraft they feared and suspected (CHAPTER 2).

Below: The bastard of Orleans, later count of Dunois, portrayed in full knightly array with the bend sinister over the fleur-de-lys on his shield, was the duke of Orleans's illegitimate son and remained loyal to the king's cause throughout the campaign in which Joan fought (CHAPTER 2).

Above: In Chapelain's lengthy seventeenth-century epic, *La Pucelle, ou La France delivrée*, Joan's recognition of the Dauphin at Chinon takes on the appearance of a latter-day Annunciation, by an angel to a new Messiah (CHAPTER 3).

Above: In order to grasp the extraordinary life of Joan of Arc, historians turned to earlier models: in *Le Champion des Dames*, by Martin le Franc, she was compared to Judith, who killed the tyrant Holofernes to save her people (CHAPTER 11).

Right: The Virgin Mary, in her comparatively rare aspect of the Biblical Tower of David and sword of strength, also provided a traditional framework for the concept of heroic virtue. This image of the Virgin in armour, commissioned for an altarpiece by the Teutonic Knights in Joan's lifetime, was later quite naturally confused with Joan of Arc herself (CHAPTER 11).

Above: A painting after Claude Deruet, attributed to Jean de Caumont (d. 1659), invokes a plumed Joan of Arc as the Pucelle d'Orléans, the Amazon of France and a second Judith (CHAPTER 10).

Right: A portrait commissioned by the aldermen of Orleans pays little attention to the male dress that the historical Joan chose to wear (CHAPTER 9).

By the beginning of the
nineteenth century, Joan
of Arc was identified with
the spirit of national
defence. *Right:* She
metamorphoses into a new
Minerva, Goddess of
Peace, in an engraving to
Schiller's influential epic
drama, *Die Jungfrau von
Orleans. Below:* An
anonymous artist, in the
year of Waterloo, imagined
the flower of French
womanhood pledging
patriotic faith at the foot
of Joan's Orleans statue
(CHAPTER 12).

26

27

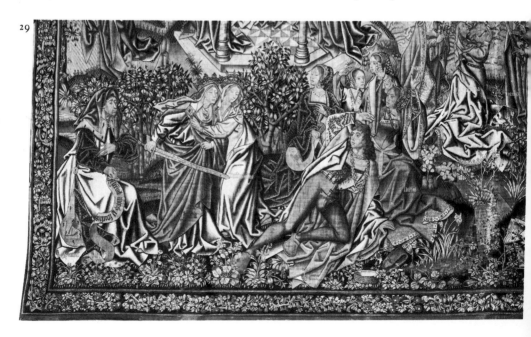

28

Above: A miniature in Martial d'Auvergne's *Vigiles* illustrates Joan's celebrated moral zeal when she drove *filles de joie* from the army camp. The artist was probably inspired by the traditional figure of avenging Justice, who, as in this later Flemish tapestry (*below*) of the Seven Deadly Sins, rushes with drawn sword upon Everyman to rescue him from the toils of Lust and her handmaidens, but is restrained by Mercy (CHAPTER II).

29

Above: Voltaire brought obloquy upon himself for his daring and farcical comic epic, *La Pucelle d'Orleans,* in which, among other absurdities, an amorous winged ass plays an important role (CHAPTER 12).

Below: At the beginning of the nineteenth century, few monuments had been raised to Joan, and her image had not been standardised. This engraving shows the Republican-style standard-bearer of Gois fils in Orleans (left), the expiatory cross and fountain at Rouen (background), the fountain and plumed bust at Domremy (right) and the kneeling figure from the bridge monument at Orleans (bottom right) (CHAPTER 9).

32

Above: Commissioned by the minister of the Interior, the romantic sculptor François Rude established in 1852 an eloquent and influential version of Joan as the peasant maid hearing her voices (CHAPTER 12).

Equestrian portraits of Joan of Arc provided
sculptors with a satisfying challenge as well as a
handsome commission. *Above:* At Chinon, the
animalier Jules-Pierre Roulleau in 1893 created
a histrionic effect of a horse at full tilt by poising
its flying hooves on the prostrate wounded
(CHAPTER 13).

33

Left: The Princess Marie
d'Orleans, daughter of
Louis Philippe, rang an
interesting change on the
Saint George and the
dragon theme, when she
sculpted Joan of Arc gazing
with pity on a dying
Englishman (CHAPTER 8).

34

Domremy, Joan's native village, became
the focus of her cult. Within decades of
each other, Church and State set up rival
statues to her memory. *Above, left:* André
Allar's group outside the basilica shows
Joan receiving the orders of heaven through
her voices (CHAPTERS 6 and 13); *above,
middle:* but Antonin Mercié's secular Joan
raises her sword with the help of a
strictly non-religious personification of
France (CHAPTER 13). *Above, right:* At her
family home in the village, a state shrine
was created; while, *below,* in the basilica,
the painter Lionel Royer created a cycle of
frescoes stressing Joan's role as a holy
saviour, as in this imaginative version of
the battle of Patay. In fact, Joan did not
fight in that battle, but was bringing up the
rear (CHAPTER 12).

Domremy. - Maison de Jeanne d'Arc.

39

Left: Sarah Bernhardt was only one of many famous divae who have played Joan of Arc, here in Jules Barbier's popular play, with music by Gounod, which she performed in 1890 (CHAPTER 12).

Below: For his lavish silent film of 1916, Cecil B. De Mille chose the famous opera singer Geraldine Farrar, and, with scenes of heroism and carnage, stirred associations with France's sufferings in World War I (CHAPTER 13).

40

41

Left: Paul Claudel's
poem, *Jeanne au Bûcher,*
illustrated here by a
Decaris mezzotint, saw
her martyrdom as the
martyrdom of his
country, during both
world wars (CHAPTER 13).

Right: The sculptor
Maxime Réal del Sarte,
one of the most ardent
adherents to the extreme
right-wing movement,
the Action Française,
also saw Joan as a figure
of his country at the time,
and carved her as a huge
Mother of Mercy
(CHAPTER 13).

42

43

Above: This tableau vivant of 1900, with Joan and her "counsel" and the village church on the painted backcloth, was performed when the campaign for Joan's recognition as a saint and not just a national heroine was gaining ever wider support (CHAPTER 13).

French, neologisms are almost always masculine now, even if the word's components are feminine, as for instance in *autoroute*.[25] The feminine gender is losing ground and, with this weakening, will lose its semantic flexibility and be used only with the biologically feminine.[26] Then it will perhaps become associated with the kind of prejudice endemic in English, where the feminine of nouns in current use sometimes belittles them: "songstress," "authoress," "poetess," "suffragette."

In European languages, the use of the feminine to embody different aspects of goodness is in this context remarkable, and the phenomenon was seized on, in most cases probably unconsciously, by numerous women in Christian history, either as visionaries or authors or patrons or artists, and also by their male counterparts, until it became a firm ordinance, capable of working in reverse: the mere appearance of a queen like Elizabeth in the sixteenth century stirred immediate associations in her audience with glorious virtues;[27] the bare-breasted champion of the barricades in Delacroix's famous image of Liberty as late as the 1830 revolution stood for all the Republican ideals.[28]

But the convention runs counter to prevailing ideas about women's inferiority, weakness and greater inclination to sin. Cesare Ripa, who produced a famous handbook for painters, *Iconology, or a Description of the Universal Images*, in Milan in 1602,[29] professed himself frankly puzzled by the discrepancy and then proceeded to record faithfully the perpetuity of the tradition, from classical times onward. After telling his readers that *Fortezza* (Strength) should be depicted as an armed woman with a broken column and a lion at her feet, he digresses to explain:

> She should be a woman, not to declare that a strong man should emulate feminine ways, but to make the figure suit the way we speak; or because, as every virtue is an image of the truth, the beautiful and the desirable, in which the intellect takes its delight, and as beauty is commonly attributed to women, one can use them to represent them conveniently; or, rather, because just as women, depriving themselves of those pleasures to which nature inclines them acquire and keep the reputation of special honour, so should the strong man, with the risks to his own body, with the dangers of his life, and with his spirit on fire with virtue, give birth to reputation and fame of high esteem.[30]

The equation of armed struggle with chastity, itself synonymous with virtue, holds throughout the tradition. Ripa was describing a very

ancient phenomenon. Athene is a virgin and is also virgin-born, springing fully armed from the head of Zeus. Saint Paul uses boxing and
athletic metaphors when he describes how he overcame sensual temptation in 1 Corinthians 9:25, the *locus classicus* of ascetic militancy. In
the same vein of classicism, a beautiful relief in the Villa Medici in
Rome represents Virtus as an armed maiden. One of the most influential
works of early Christian culture was the *Psychomachia* (Struggle in
the Soul), written by Prudentius, a civil servant from Saragossa, at the
beginning of the fifth century.[31] It is the first Christian allegory in
verse, and it dramatises temptation as a gory and ruthless battle between
the vices and the virtues. Chastity leads an army of virgins, including
Humility, Patience and Reason, against the daughters of Sodom, led
by Libido and Luxuria. A series of mortal hand-to-hand combats takes
place, with virtue triumphing all the way.

The battle of the Virtues and Vices became a leitmotif of medieval
sermons and art and eventually of drama and pageantry.[32] One of the
streams on which the personification of virtues as women was carried
was the illustration of the *Psychomachia* itself, and one of the most
original early versions was included in the *Hortus Deliciarum*, the
encyclopaedia devised, organised and edited, text and pictures, by Herrad of Landsperg.[33] This extraordinary and imaginative abbess intended
her *Garden of Delights*, whose making took from 1160 to 1190, to
contain all human knowledge in her time. The iconography she devised
was uniquely her own, and though the manuscript is lost, copied
sketches remain. In Herrad's imagery, the protagonists of the conflict are
dressed in twelfth-century armour, doing ferocious battle. They appear
either sexless or female. But in later *psychomachiae*, clear female personification dominates.[34] The Seven Liberal Arts—Grammar, Arithmetic,
Logic, Music, Astronomy, Geometry, Rhetoric—are also pictured as
women, following the structure Grammar herself lays down. The entry
about the Ladder of Perfection shows Caritas at the summit, also personified as female. This scheme became traditional.[35] Meanwhile Herrad's contemporary, the prophet Hildegard of Bingen, was recording
the visions she had received since the age of five. Some concerned the
state of world affairs, and others were apocalyptic. In one, she saw
the Celestial Beatitudes as maidens in the triple-girded citadel of Heaven
—personifications of Generosity, Abstinence, Piety, Peace, Truth, Dis-
cretion and the Beatitude of Eternal Life.[36]

When the Arts, Sciences, or Virtues and Vices were represented, as in the sculpture programmes of French cathedrals or in the pageants organised for kings' and princes' entrées, they were often accompanied by examples from the real, as opposed to the ideal, world: Tubal-Cain as the exponent of Music; Euclid, of Geometry.[37] For the Virtues, examples were taken from history and the Bible. This is the point where the tradition of personifying the virtues as female intersects with the convention of female Worthies and female biography and in turn brings us back to Joan.

The four cardinal virtues are Prudence, Justice, Temperance and Fortitude; Fortitude is the cardinal Virtue who most frequently wears armour. Her attributes are a spear and shield, sometimes a broken column, sometimes a lion, all borrowed from Hercules.[38] Other Virtues, especially in *psychomachiae*, are also armed; indeed, the breastplate became a visual synonym for inviolability. Chastity often wears full armour; Justice always carries a sword. They are daughters of Wisdom, avatars of Athene, the goddess of Wisdom and of Peace, whose uniform they wear. Judith is Fortitude's most common exemplar, and Judith, often one of the Women Worthies, is one of the common comparisons used of Joan in contemporary accounts and eulogies and in later works. Judith, who by guile overcame Holofernes, the Assyrian general, cut off his head, put it in her maid's bag and carried it out of the camp: she is a preeminent armed maiden, so redolent of the terror expressed by the figure that Sacher-Masoch used the words "The Lord hath smitten him by the hand of a woman" (Judith 16:6) as an epigraph to his celebration of inflicted pain, *Venus in Furs*.

A medieval audience was accustomed to understanding emblems, and Judith was one, connoting strength and chastity, with which they were familiar. An idea could be compressed visually in a way that is inaccessible to us now: the Bourgeois de Paris, for instance, very much enjoyed some mysteries performed by children in Paris to celebrate the English victory of Verneuil. They were "very fine," he tells us, and were performed "without speaking or moving, as if they had been statues against a wall." He does not describe the subject matter, except to say that it was taken from the Old and New Testaments.[39] In the processions that greeted each fresh reversal of Paris's fortunes and entry and reentry of its master ruler—the duke of Burgundy, the duke of Bedford, Henry VI or, later, Charles VII—figures were costumed with unmistakeable attributes. In 1603, the allegories and personifications on the triumphal arches greeting James I to London were very elaborate indeed, but John Dekker became impatient when asked to explain the designs he, Ben Jonson and Thomas Middleton had devised: "Having told you her name was Justice, I hope you will not put me to describe what properties she held in hands, since every painted cloth can inform you."[40]

This language has currency still today. As the great art historian E. H. Gombrich has observed:

> We are used to making a clear distinction between two of these functions (of an image)—that of representation and that of symbolization. A painting may *represent* an object of the visible world, a woman holding a balance, or a lion. It may also *symbolize* an idea. . . . the woman with a balance will symbolize Justice, the lion Courage or the British Empire. . . . As soon however as we leave the ground of rational analysis we find that these neat distinctions no longer hold. . . . For where there is no clear gulf separating the material, visible world from the sphere of the spirit and spirits, not only the various meanings of the word "representation" may become blurred but the whole relationship between image and symbol assumes a different aspect. . . . We are all apt to "regress" at any moment to more primitive states and experience the fusion between the image and its model or the name and its bearer. Our language, in fact, favours this twilight region between the literal and the metaphorical. . . . It so happens that Indo-European languages tend to this particular figure we call personification, because so many of them endow nouns with a gender which makes them indistinguishable from names for living species.[41]

A derogatory slant to "primitive" and "regression" is not appropriate to such an important aspect of aesthetic response and religious belief. Both in creation and in appreciation of art, receptivity to the content of an image, without splitting it from its external sign, is an essential primary stage; otherwise no artefact could be enjoyed without intellectual consent: a nonbeliever could not be stirred by the crucifixion, for instance. The acceptance of sacramental forms clothing religious mysteries is also a crucial part of faith: if a Mass were seen simply as an act performed by a man in costume on a rostrum, its meaning would be entirely lost.

In Joan's case, the process was reversed: by accidents of her chosen way of life and even of her dress, she conformed so exactly to the prototype that her claim to the virtues she so closely resembled was corroborated.

Her judges implied this when they asked her, without expanding further, whether there was a painting of Justice, Peace and Unity in the house of her host in Orleans. They believed either that she had modelled herself on such Virtues or, more plausibly, since the question follows immediately upon another about portraits and images painted of her, that she had already been identified with such Virtues in her lifetime.[42]

Afterwards, Joan is constantly depicted as Fortitude or Justice's new epiphany on earth. The similes occur again and again in the femiist literature and its illustrations. In Martin le Franc's manuscript of *Le Champion des Dames*, Jeanne la Pucelle stands beside Holofernes's tent, while Judith, holding his head by his hair, stows it in her maid's proffered bag[43] (22). On Jean Hordal's title page, Fortitude and Virginity, both armed, stand on either side of the title, with Joan above them, as she appeared in the Orleans bridge monument.[44]

One of the stories told about Joan after her death may have been developed under the influence of circulating ideas about the Virtues, imitated from the *Psychomachia*. In Prudentius's poem, Pudicitia is one of the doughtiest knights: "And then, it's the virgin Chastity, who, ready to do battle, appears on the grassy plain; she shines in her resplendent armour." Sodomita Libido assaults her, trying to blind her with sulphurous firebrands, but Chastity stones Libido, disarms her and runs her through the throat. She then harangues the victim: Judith and the Virgin Mary provide her with examples of women's purity and victory over lust.[45] Her sword, contaminated by Libido, is washed in the river of Jordan and dedicated to God, according to an old soldier's custom, Prudentius tells us.[46]

Some of the art works inspired by the battle of the Virtues or the *Psychomachia* depict this scene with variations. The sixteenth-century Brussels tapestry cycle of the Seven Deadly Sins in Hampton Court, for instance, shows Homo, a fashionable youth of the day, dressed in doublet and hose, fallen into the toils of Luxuria, a beautiful and lascivious girl. Justice, with drawn sword, attacks the couple, but her avenging arm is restrained by Mercy, who is by her side (29). At the rehabilitation trial, a similar cameo is related by both Joan's page and the duke of Alençon. Naturally, the event could have taken place and need not have been invented. But it is possible all the same that the form the stories took was shaped by the existing assimilation of Joan with the heroic virtues of Chastity, Fortitude and Justice. Louis de Coutes, her page, told the tribunal: "She would not allow women with the army. Indeed, once, near the town of Château-Thierry, when she saw the mistress of one of the soldiers, who was a knight, she chased her with a naked sword. But she did not strike the woman. She warned her gently and kindly that she must never appear in soldiers' company again, or she, Joan, would do something to her that she would dislike."[47] D'Alençon's account was more violent: "Joan was chaste, and she loathed those women who follow the soldiers. I once saw her at Saint Denis, on the way back from the king's coronation, chase a girl who was with the soldiers so hard that she broke her sword."[48]

For Jean Chartier, who may have written his chronicle before 1456 and the rehabilitation evidence, the breaking of her sword ended Joan's power. It was her magic sword, her Samson's hair, found by prophecy in the shrine of St. Catherine, and after she attacked the prostitutes and shattered it, it would neither let itself be mended nor lead her to victory in battle again. Chartier is alone in condemning Joan's action in this fashion; the story is told forever after in praise of Joan's invincible virtue.[49] Henri Wallon, in a pious and learned nineteenth-century biography, bases himself on Chartier, but cannot resist adding: "She cared more for the honour of her sex than for the sword of St. Catherine."[50] In the miniatures that illuminate the 1484 manuscript of Martial d'Auvergne's poem, *Les Vigiles du Roi Charles VII*, the incident forms part of a series celebrating her greatest exploits. On her white warhorse with her sword raised and *filles de joie* scattering with their clients in front of her, Joan is the very image of relentless Pudicitia or avenging Justice[51] (28).

Joan's historical conduct, in both her valour and her knightly semblance, assimilated her with ease to the traditional representation of Virtue; in turn, she came to be a cypher denoting the potential of virtue in women and of the virtuousness of whatever cause she was used to represent. The layerings of the image resemble a cartographer's superimpositions of mapping paper to show the shifts in boundaries, the erosion of coastlines; each configuration is not exactly the same as the one beneath, though the territory charted retains the selfsame identity. In Joan's case, the land mass that always remains, however dimly one can perceive it through the overlays, is virginity and its paramount importance.

The virtues are maidens—indeed, in many of the schemes, including the *Psychomachia*, Chastity is their chieftain, although in theology Charity is the highest of the three theological virtues, themselves higher than the cardinal. To indicate that their maidenliness is proof against all sexuality, these maidens sometimes appear with wings and are thus assimilated to the angels, who have no sex. The only one who cannot be winged is Charity, for she is often distinguished by the many children who suckle at her breasts or cling to her knees. As this is an irrefutable sign of femaleness, angelic nature is denied her. Wings abolish gender; they reinforce the crucial character of virtues when personified as female: that Virtues nevertheless belong to the world of ideas, where sex has no place. Discrepant Charity can be seen in the series of medallion reliefs by Giovanni d'Ambrogio and Iacopo di Piero on the Loggia dei Lanzi in Florence, sculpted in 1380–86. As a mother, she cannot also be a virgin (unlike Mary), so she remains anomalous.

Angels are also, in the medieval world, God's soldiers; like the fighting virtues, they are armed for the contest against the devil's followers.[52] The metaphor of chivalry tugs with such force at the minds of the age that even the Virgin Mary sometimes appears at the time in full armour, in her aspect as the Tower of David, "whereon there hang a thousand bucklers, all shields of mighty men," one of her titles from the litany of Loreto that is taken from the Bible (Song of Solomon 4:4). The Virgin is like the bride, "fair as the moon, clear as the sun, and terrible as an army with banners" (Song of Solomon 6:10). In the Albrecht altar painted in Mary's honour before 1440, possibly while Joan was alive, the Virgin wears mail shirt and breastplate, gauntlets and leg pieces of armour under a voluminous mantle. Her fine, wavy blonde hair spills down her back. Behind her stand two knights with rainbow wings carrying shields. It is not surprising that she, like so many other images, was identified as Joan of Arc. The sixteen-panel painting was commissioned by the Teutonic Knights, who deflected enthusiasm for crusading in the east and battled against the heathen nearer home, in Prussia and Lithuania, an interest that Joan shared, as we have seen[53] (23).

This idea of goodness rests on virginity, expressed in the imagery of war: Joan of Arc corresponded to the formula. Because she was in her body undefiled and whole, the metaphors of holiness, or of moral good used by a culture terrorised by sensual sin, could be applied to her quite smoothly, enhancing her power and her appeal, when she was alive and long after she was dead. She is an epiphany of virtue's many faces: pure Wisdom; the Virtues themselves—Fortitude and Pudicitia; parthenogenetic Minerva;[54] unsullied Diana; the virgin Amazons; Judith the tyrannicide; each of them a mirror of angelic nature. Joan la Pucelle, the Maid: on that single note of overwhelming resonance, the idea of her perfection, including its political sphere of reference, to which we shall now turn, has been built.

Joan did not convince the people of her time by demonstrative reason, but by imaginative projection on her part and on theirs. It is natural for different ages to look for different explanations of mysterious historical events and characters; but it is not necessary in Joan's case to posit that she was a royal bastard kept conspiratorially in the wings until the judicious moment, that as a child she was schooled by travelling monks to adopt her mission, that she was the tool of high politics; nor are the numerous other supposedly practical and rational solutions needed. The central problem of her story is, Why was the girl believed and followed? And the answer lies in the configuration of people's minds. Joan was a familiar face, but it had hardly ever been seen in the real world before. That was the miracle.

CHAPTER 12

CHILD OF NATURE

Falsehood's fallacious words are full of guile,
But hers are pure and simple as a child's.
If evil spirits borrow this disguise,
They copy innocence triumphantly.
I'll hear no more. To arms, Dunois! To arms.

FRIEDRICH SCHILLER,
The Maid of Orleans[1]

oltaire and Joan of Arc died on the same day, 30 May. In 1878, the French government considered that feelings were rising so high it was necessary to ban all demonstrations, processions or other public commemorations for that day, the centenary of Voltaire's death and the 447th anniversary of Joan's execution. Violence in the streets had already marked the rivalry between the enthusiasts of Voltaire, identified with anticlericalism and revolutionary fervour, and the adepts of Joan of Arc, monarchists, patriots, Catholics.[2] For in 1878, in the turbulent aftermath of France's crushing defeat by Prussia and the loss of Alsace-Lorraine to Germany, symbols of national integrity were beyond price, as they had been in another time of humiliation, the Hundred Years' War. All colours wanted Joan for themselves.

Joan of Arc had become a serious political symbol, a hope of future restoration and unity, revered and truly loved with an earnestness not present in the earlier encomia, however eager. In Lorraine, at the house in Domremy that had been identified as the D'Arc family home (37), there were 2,000 signatures in the *Livre d'Or*, the visitors' book, in 1870, the first year of the war. In 1878, there were 4,500.[3] In those days, Domremy was accessible only by train to Void, with a thirty-three-kilometre ride after. In 1873, services were already improved, but it remained a pilgrimage for committed people. The signatures invoke her help, as at a shrine of a wonder-working saint. As Joan had not yet been canonised, the inscriptions in the *Livre d'Or* often pray for official recognition of Joan's sanctity.[4] But, above all, they implore deliverance of France from its enemies. These are sometimes identified with the French themselves, who failed to vanquish the Prussians just as the Armagnac party had failed to keep the English at bay, or with the Prussians, who are seen as the exact descendants of the English. " 'I fear only betrayal,' " writes one. " 'But whether they will or no, the English will be thrown out of France, except those who died there.' Joan! Pray that it might be so with the barbarians from the north who have invaded our Fatherland!' "[5] Another pilgrim, a certain Antoine de la Tour who visited the shrine six times, inscribed a thirteen-verse poem in her book (long poems are very common in the *Livre d'Or*) and prayed, rather despondently:

> She *will not come; for a long time we no longer see here at home*
> *Angels come back to earth;*
> *But God could send, if He wants to give her back to us,*
> *Her genius to our commanders and her spirit to us all.*[6]

Here and there, throughout the century, Voltaire is not forgotten and receives his share of hate:

> *Praise to the chaste Maid!*
> *Undying shame to the famous writer*
> *Who, steeping in mire a divine pen,*
> *Shamelessly profaned such beauteous fame!*[7]

Why this animus against Voltaire, father of liberty? Why would the celebration of his centenary insult the heroine of liberty herself?

In the aftermath of the 1870s, Voltaire had committed an unpardonable crime: he had failed to take Joan of Arc seriously. Hardly known today, and hardly read, is *La Pucelle d'Orléans*, the poem in twenty-one cantos of heroic couplets that Voltaire began in 1730 and finally published in his own version in 1762, after several pirated and garbled editions had appeared in London and Paris.[8] But its neglect is a pity, for apart from its almost unique status as the only comic treat-

ment of the legend of Joan of Arc—a light relief in the midst of all the
solemnity about her—it is a wickedly funny, racy, bawdy, clever and
skilful piece of mischief. It guys Chapelain's egregious *La Pucelle* and,
through him, parodies the conventions of the Italian epics with a light
touch that neatly points up their absurdities. The magic horse of Ariosto,
the Hippogriff, loses his enchantment when he appears as a winged
ass (30). The obsession of the epics with their heroines' virtue touches
bathos when Voltaire bluntly writes of Joan: "And the greatest of the
rare exploits/Was to preserve her maidenhead for a whole year."[9] In
the poem, Joan is promised to Dunois, but only after a year has passed,
during which her virginity, the guarantee of the country's safety and
of her victories in battle, has to be closely guarded. She is put to the
test many times, by many different suitors strayed from the castles
and fairylands of the epics, and she very nearly fails in the last test,
when she is passionately wooed by the ass: "To this speech, perhaps a
little bold,/Joan felt a righteous indignation:/To love an ass, to give
him her flower!/But oh! heavens, this ass, what an ass it is!"[10] At the last
moment, Joan is saved by the handy presence of Deborah's lance at
her bedside and the vigilance of Dunois at her keyhole.

For all his trifling, Voltaire seized on the crux of the legend: that
Joan's virginity was essential to her role of saviour. But in the eighteenth
century, the terror of vivisection by an outside power did not exist as
it did in the nineteenth, and Voltaire could afford to poke fun. It is
fascinating that his humour dated so quickly, that it could not work in
the unsettled world that so closely followed upon his death and indeed
owed so much to his teachings. The climate of romantic patriotism
that prevailed all over Europe at the end of the eighteenth and through
the nineteenth century made Voltaire's *La Pucelle* a lapse in the worst
possible taste, the equivalent of slipping a banana skin under a cripple.
At best, during France's troubles, it was ignored. Frivolity was quite out
of keeping: Joan became the raw material of noble aspiration and idealis-
tic conceptions. From the first Consulate of Napoleon till the apogee of
her cult was reached in 1920 when she was canonised, she grew in
importance and popularity, expressing in her life and her person a host
of causes held very dear by a great many people.

During this period, the understanding of who Joan of Arc was
changed fundamentally. The concept of goodness and its wellsprings
was modified according to the precepts of romanticism; the modern
idea of nationalism was gathering force; a new kind of attention to

history was being paid. The great historian Jules Michelet based his work on a thorough knowledge of contemporary sources to evoke Joan in 1844 with resonant enthusiasm in one volume of his *Histoire de France*.[11] The circumstances of her life were examined by modern historical methods when Jules Quicherat, a young and sceptical scholar chosen by the Société de l'Histoire de France, edited and published the records of her trial and rehabilitation, in 1841–49.[12] The result, five volumes of documents relating to Joan of Arc's career according to contemporary or near-contemporary sources, is a model of impassioned learning. It did more than any other work to bring the historical Joan before the eyes of the world, for through Quicherat's editing and annotation, Joan's speech, tone of voice, behaviour, as well as the reactions she inspired in person, came across with an immediacy that the tributes of the sixteenth and seventeenth centuries had not even attempted, even when the authors had gone to the manuscript material. It was in 1869, the year after Quicherat's edition of the trial and rehabilitation was translated, that Monsignor Dupanloup, bishop of Orleans, called for Joan's canonisation.[13]

Quicherat's *magnum opus* was carried forward on the surge of enthusiasm for medieval history that is one of romanticism's traits. The mid-nineteenth century was a time when the rationalist pooh-poohing of the Middle Ages and its thought was angrily rejected by the new literati, and Quicherat presented a characteristically reverent rediscovery. It was as much a product of the new curiosity as Chateaubriand's *Génie du Christianisme*, which in 1802 defied the philosophers' scepticism with a work of religious apologetics, or Victor Hugo's novel, *Notre-Dame de Paris*, set in the city just after Joan's time and published in 1831. The romantic quest for a new truth about human behaviour by searching the past turned upside down the enlightenment's view of time. It sought in the mysteries and thought and people of the past to find wisdom in a way that the concern with the present, and indeed with the future, of philosophers like Voltaire, Rousseau and Diderot had rejected, their conception of progress having been literally identified with a forward march. The *Encyclopaedia*, under the rubric "*Charles VII*," had given Joan of Arc respectful notice ("that extraordinary girl") and hailed her as the rallier of the French. But it had firmly attributed her exploits to natural gifts, not divine intervention.[14] Voltaire's later extended squib posed a violent challenge to romantic historians and historical poets, to which many responded with heartfelt eloquence. The grace they saw in Joan was equal in magnitude to the grace her earlier champions had also seen; but it was different in kind, because it conformed to new ideas about virtue and its sources.

The cosmology of grace was changing: virtuous beings no longer inhabited the ideal, supraterrestrial world of ideas, manifesting themselves now and then as a boon for the flesh-locked mortals below. The angelic was pulled down to earth, literally, stripped of wings, halo, ethereal bodilessness, and located in the human sphere, the world of the senses, in nature, and particularly in *natura naturans*, the world of the soil. Joan remained special, attuned more sensitively than other beings to the promptings of the holy; but the holy was different. And the difference between the sixteenth-century view of holiness, which had cast her as Amazon, avenging Justice and avenging angel, and the nineteenth-century stress on union with nature suited her historical persona perfectly. Joan was in actuality a daughter of the soil; this section of her biography, which had meant little to earlier historians of her life, was the keystone of the romantic edifice of ideas about nationhood, native virtue and individual liberty.

The first person to create Joan in the image of a romantic heroine was Friedrich Schiller, whose epic drama, *Die Jungfrau von Orleans*, was first performed in Weimar in 1801. Schiller wrote it as a direct answer to Voltaire: "O virgin . . . mockery has dragged you through the mire. . . . But fear not. There are still some beautiful souls that burn for what is great."[15] Schiller was writing before Quicherat's edition of the trial. His immediate inspiration was a dashing equestrian portrait, perhaps of Joan, galloping on a white horse and brandishing a sword, exhibited at Wurtzburg.[16] For his text, Schiller took elements both from Shakespeare and from Voltaire, but while Shakespeare presents Joan's conjuration of spirits as demonic, Schiller has her as a force of nature, the sap of creation itself; whereas Voltaire burlesques Joan's magic virginity, Schiller makes it the agent of her tragic fall. God arms and inspires Joan, giving her an enchanted helmet to protect her against all enemies, unless she falls in love (26). When Lionel, an English soldier, meets her in battle, Joan loves him at first sight and becomes altogether helpless therefore. The play ends with her death on the field, followed by a momentary resuscitation so that she can die in full glory before the assembled court.[17]

Schiller's drama immediately inspired numerous French versions.[18] One of the most successful, by Alexandre Soumet, was first performed at the Odéon in Paris in 1825 with Mlle Georges; twenty-one years later, Rachel played in the title part, perhaps the first of the scores of famous great interpreters of Joan on stage.[19] *Die Jungfrau von Orleans* is hardly ever performed today, nor are any of its large progeny, except for Verdi's opera of 1845, *Giovanna d'Arco*,[20] and Tchaikovsky's *The Maid of Orleans* of 1878,[21] though neither of them count among the composers' most celebrated works. In both, the stress on the peculiar enchantment of the countryside is very great: the peasantry among whom Joan grew up represent a mixture of forces, the elemental and ghostly, deriving from nature's powerful, unpredictable mysteries, and the solid and honest, deriving from the labourer's simplicity and toil. In both, the wood at Domremy and the villagers' relationship to its mysterious dark groves provide the setting of the first act and set the tone of the drama. In Verdi, Joan hides herself among the trees to pray to her voices, as is her custom, but her father, suspecting her of a secret rendezvous, follows her. Seeing her contact her spirits, he denounces her as a witch. In Tchaikovsky, Joan's rural background receives a greater lyrical emphasis: the first act dramatises the peasants' trials in Domremy during the civil war and ends with a beautiful aria, in which Joan solemnly bids adieu to the forests, rivers, fields and trees of her childhood.

Charles Gounod's later musical version of Jules Barbier's play, *Jeanne D'Arc*, enjoyed a huge popular success when it was performed at the Gaîté Théâtre in 1873 with Lia Félix, Rachel's sister, and again in 1890, when Sarah Bernhardt took the role (39). The idyll of Domremy here reaches heights of bliss; and at the end, when Joan has to leave her family home, "wrapped in a luminous ray of light, alone, with a kind of horror . . . she cries out a desperate farewell to her father's room and seems ready to leave. The curtain falls."[22] Queen Victoria, hearing it in England, declared it "so lovely."[23]

The appeal of Joan's free spirit broke international jealousies; and in England, the heroine of France inspired audiences in a way not to be expected from the liberator of the traditional enemy. A pantomime based on her life was played at Covent Garden in 1795, but when Joan, in the last act, was carried off to hell by demons, the audience booed. For the second performance, the demons were hastily recostumed, and she was borne heavenward by angels.[24]

Robert Southey tells us this story in the preface to his epic poem *Joan of Arc*.[25] Written in 1793 in a white heat provoked by Voltaire's insults, *Joan of Arc* expresses the revolutionary socialism of the young Southey. He saw in Joan a figure of the noble unspoiled culture of the soil, from a time when industrialisation had not withered the social organisation created spontaneously by labouring people. In his poem, Joan is a Rousseau-like force of nature, alert and obedient to the inner promptings of the innocent human heart. The poem is too long for a modern reader to enjoy (around six thousand lines), but it has passages of lyrical energy and is, above all, the fascinating prototype of the secularised Joan of Arc. Southey abolishes the personal God and re-places Him by Nature—"creating wisdom."[26] Joan herself is nourished as a flower or a tree; her strength, her heroism, her visions come from the country in which she was born. Its sensuous and palpable forms and surfaces clothe an undefined spiritual energy which flows more purely and more powerfully in some beings than in others.

Southey makes a fundamental break with medieval conceptions of the supernatural, by finding it in the natural and by looking at it with-out fear. Joan's voices are not corporeal visions of saints or angels; they come to her like weather, "in the glory of the tempest."[27] Nor do they possess the ambivalence that in Schiller led Joan's father to suspect them of diabolical origins. Nature's essence is of itself good, whatever its form, because the created world is all goodness. Joan is like Rousseau's solitary wanderer: after rhapsodies on the beauties of her homeland, she says:

> *Here in solitude*
> *My soul was nurst, amid the loveliest scenes*
> *Of unpolluted nature.*[28]

Southey moves from his paean to nature to hymn the uncrushable human yearning to be free. Joan, daughter of the earth, is also the champion of the people and the enemy of tyrants, according to a charac-teristic revolutionary identification. After the victory of Orleans, Joan exults:

> *. . . easier were it*
> *To hurl the rooted mountain from its base,*
> *Than force the yoke of slavery upon men*
> *Determin'd to be free.*[29]

Southey filled ten books with his poem, but stopped after the corona-tion of Charles. His optimism inspired Hazlitt to comment that it was "a work in which the love of liberty is inhaled like the breath of Spring, mild, balmy, heaven-born!"[30]

Southey showed a daring in these ardent days far beyond the later conservatism that so incensed Byron,[31] and Southey's *Joan of Arc* is full of sallies—somewhat fanciful since he did not have access to the trial or other documents—in defence of revolutionary liberties as being fought for in America in the War of Independence and in France during the Revolution. He gives Joan a companion-at-arms called Lafayette, merely in order to be able to exclaim, "Lafayette, name that freedom still shall love,"[32] and so to pay tribute to one of the few Frenchmen who fought in both revolutions.

When Thomas de Quincey, who sustained his radical enthusiasm far longer than Southey, first read Michelet's account of Joan's life, he was transported; his essay on Joan is one of the most beautifully written and imagined pieces of modern English prose.[33] Michelet's portrait was fervent, brightly painted and passionate; but as a historian, however inflected his use of material, he had to keep to the source he had so carefully sifted. Nevertheless he had leaped impulsively into grand rhetorical generalisations. Joan for him was the very spirit of his country: "The Saviour of France had to be a woman. France herself was a woman. She had the same fickleness, but also the same lovable sweetness, the same easy and charming compassion, the excellence of her first response at least. Even in the mist of her pleasure in empty elegance and exterior refinement, she remained at heart closer to nature."[34]

De Quincey leaps even higher, springing from the same excitement about freedom, patriotism and unpolluted nature. Michelet to him is the leader of a magnificent school of French historians:

> All these writers are of a revolutionary cast; not in a political sense merely, but in all senses; mad, oftentimes, as March hares; crazy with the laughing gas of recovered liberty; drunk with the wine-cup of their mighty revolution, snorting, whinnying, throwing up their heels, like wild horses in the boundless pampas, and running races of defiance with snipes, or with the winds, or with their own shadows, if they can find nothing else to challenge.[35]

But De Quincey's flights of imagination regarding Joan carry him into an empyrean of touching dreams and affectionate wit and poignant elegy. Again, the countryside is the cradle of the saviour. He opens with a comparison of Joan to King David, once a shepherd boy, and then mourns:

The poor, forsaken girl, on the contrary, drank not herself from that cup of rest which she had secured for France. She never sang together with the songs that rose in her native Domremy, as echoes to the departing steps of the invaders. She mingled not in the festal dances at Vaucouleurs which celebrated in rapture the redemption of France. No! for her voice was then silent; no! for her feet were dust.[36]

De Quincey defends her passionately: his Joan was unforgivably ignored by posterity; his Joan was brutally treated and unjustly tried; his Joan never recanted at all. When he reaches the end of her life, he enters into her spirit and evokes her last dream. It is of Domremy, her village, the crucible in which her metal was tempered and refined: "Joan saw Domremy, saw the fountain of Domremy, saw the pomp of forests in which her childhood had wandered. That Easter festival . . . that resurrection of springtime . . . were by God given back into her hands."[37] De Quincey then haunts Cauchon, on his deathbed as he lies tormented by images of Joan with "wasted features." When Cauchon faces Christ, his judge, who asks if anyone will speak for him, "all are silent." But then Christ finds him a counsel, someone to take his part: "Who is this that cometh from Domremy? Who is she in bloody coronation robes from Rheims? Who is she that cometh with blackened flesh from walking the furnaces of Rouen? This is she, the shepherd girl, counsellor that had none for herself, whom I choose, bishop, for yours. She it is, I engage, that shall take my Lord's brief. She it is, bishop, that would plead for you. Yes, bishop, SHE—when heaven and earth are silent."[38]

But De Quincey was less fluent and less convincing over the question of Joan's inspiration. He resorted to the English essayist's flippant mode to cloud over his indecision: "Fairies are important, even as in a statistical view certain weeds mark poverty in the soil, fairies mark its solitude."[39] The problem of belief is airily waved aside: "On a fine breezy forenoon I am audaciously sceptical, but as twilight sets in, my credulity grows steadily, till it becomes equal to anything that could be desired."[40]

The problem was not troublesome for De Quincey; he seems quite happy to be vague. For others after him, the origins of Joan's voices were a central problem, dividing in the later part of the century the devotees who wished to claim her for the Church and those who wished to keep her on the side of personal expression. The clash concerned the nature of obedience, just as it had in her trial in 1431. Was Joan the instrument of an external design, or was she the actor of an internal inspiration?

Alphonse de Lamartine put the humanist case at its most vigorous in his long biographical essay on Joan, which appeared in his magazine, *Le Civilisateur*, of 1852 in two consecutive issues.[41] He had read Quicherat's volumes, and the tragic story of Joan's trial and her indomitable heroism stirred the romantic poet deeply. His is a fast-moving, highly coloured and admirable piece of historical reconstruction, with brilliant touches of gore and voluptuousness as he conjures the decadence of the Burgundians, the cruelties of the time. Joan for him was inspired entirely through qualities of individual character. She is a heroine, not a saint, and he links her, according to the principles of romanticism, with the past—the stamp of the ancient Gaul is on her. "And besides our forefathers knew it," he writes: "Woman, inferior in her senses, is superior in her soul. The Gauls attributed to her an extra sense, the sense of the divine. They were right."[42] Her peasant stock gives her strength: she has "this nobility of heart and brow found more in people who till their fathers' lands than in those who labour in the workshops of others."[43] This primitivism underlies his confident explanation of her voices: "Should one be amazed that such a concentration of thought in a poor, young, ignorant and simple girl should finally produce a state of transport in her, that she should have heard with her ears those internal voices which spoke unceasingly to her soul?"[44] Politely, without scorn or contempt, Lamartine thus dismisses a theistic interpretation and claims Joan of Arc for romantic humanism in a way that is still the most widespread, widely held, sympathetic attitude to Joan. But Lamartine takes us a little further, for in her blend of higher intuition and sense of mission, he sees a figure of France and so aligns himself with the prophets of nationalism, who equated national liberties with personal self-expression: "The idea of a young girl leading armies into battle, crowning her young king, and liberating her country was born from the Bible and folktales together. It was the poetry of village fireside vigils. Joan of Arc made it the religion of the fatherland."[45]

The movement from Domremy to the battlefield, from the exiguousness of the peasant cottage to the epic dimensions of the deployed and victorious army, from girl child to personification of France, from home to homeland, is one that governs the structure of Michelet's,

Verdi's, Tchaikovsky's, and Schiller's works about Joan. It is present as well in lesser nineteenth-century attempts, like Casimir Delavigne's two poems about her life and her death, published in his collection of historical memories, *Les Messéniennes* (written in 1819 in response to the French defeat by the English at Waterloo, the new Agincourt[46]), and is Dumas Père's historical novel of 1842.[47] In all these, the story begins with the humility of thatch (often compared to Bethlehem) and rises in a crescendo to the glory of banners and trumpets, climaxing with Joan's death (often compared to the salvation of Christ on the cross). The long, weary months of inactivity after the coronation in July, the defeats, the protracted imprisonment and neglect after her capture are obscured by the need for a dramatic rhythm. The secular Joan of Arc is a figure of optimism and promise: her life proves the scale of heroism open to everyone.

Life in Domremy was not entirely invented: the published sources of Joan's trial and rehabilitation conjured up rustic festivities oddly consonant with operatic views of picturesque peasantry. The moral significance attached to this image has powerful political consequences, as we shall see, that take it far beyond Domremy. But the actual image was drawn from Joan by her accusers' fascination with village ritual. The evidence gathered in Joan's native village by the agents of Cauchon before she came to trial talked of a certain beech tree where on Laetare Sunday, the mid-Lent festival, garlands of flowers were hung up by the villagers as votive offerings amid music and dancing and picnicking. This tree stood on the land belonging to the lords of Bourlémont in the middle of the *bois chesnu,* near a spring with powers of healing. Joan told her judges: "Sick people drink from this spring, and go and gather its waters to regain their health."[48] The tree was sometimes called L'Arbre des Fées, sometimes L'Arbre des Dames, and it was said that fairies lived by it. Joan's godmother had told her she had even seen fairies there, but Joan herself never had, and when she hung up garlands and sang with the others near the tree, she did not do it in honour of her voices. She knew from her brother, however, that people thought she received her messages near this tree, because people identified her with the prophesied saviour who would come from a *bois chesnu.*[49] She could have danced there with the other girls from the village, but she preferred to sing. It was a beech, she confirmed, but added, puzzlingly, that from it came *"le beau mai."* Later Joan admitted that she had heard a mandrake grew near the tree.[50] But she tried to extricate herself from the drift of the questioning by asserting that she no longer took part in the dancing or the ceremonies after she received news of her mission.

Joan's judges were trying to implicate her in wise-woman magic of the countryside and in pagan rites and witchcraft. Fear of the power of these ancient customs was very alive, and the rehabilitation paid more attention to reversing this charge of superstition than to other matters. Both Joan's friends, Hauviette and Mengette, in their mid-forties in 1456, stressed the innocence of the gatherings round the fairies' tree. "We used to eat there and dance and play. I have known them [girls and boys] bring nuts to the tree and the fountain."[51] Gérardin of Epinal, a farmer, remembered that parents baked loaves for their children and sent them off to picnic under the tree, "to do the Fountains," as the villagers called the rustic ritual.[52] His wife Isabellette added that once the Bourlémonts themselves had joined the villagers on one of the feast days.[53] The beauty and majestic size of the tree were remarked on by Edmond Richer in his book on Joan of Arc of 1628: its great branches hung down to the ground all around, creating a dry chamber within.[54]

What was potentially *maleficium*, a druidical worship of trees, was folklore to later generations, innocent and charming and childlike. On account of that innocence and charm, the metamorphosis of Joan into ideal child-peasant marks the last serious change in the concept of virtue represented by her. Innocence entails the full possession of rights: no crime has been committed to incur the penalty of curtailed liberties. One cannot rob someone who is innocent of the full expression of his freedom without being in the wrong oneself, without admitting aggression against him on one's own side and, with aggression, guilt.[55] Innocence is a philosophical and moral position of immense strength; it presents an image of integrity needed in times of crisis in a nation. The armed maiden of the Renaissance was reborn in the nineteenth century as a guileless child. One of the most fundamental changes that occurred, as a legacy from the enlightenment and a visible social force of transformation, was that the concept of nobility was divorced from the class of nobles. The writ of chivalry was run; high birth, learning, sophisticated mores, military skills, all were stripped away by the post-Rousseau prescript about moral integrity. Culture no longer was seen to confer grace on the children of original sin; in nature, we are born pure, and the chains of man-made societies are not only political, but of course moral, too.[56] At the basis of some of the most nauseating and banal representations of Joan lies this thoroughly revolutionary idea, which struck at the long Augustinian belief in original damnation; it was deeply democratic. But Joan, when she mutates according to its principles, does not represent a total break with concepts of virtuous strength in the past.

The Amazon is a figure living outside man-made society, flourishing in a semisavage state and closely linked with the forces of nature, forests and their wild denizens. Joan's purity had been always associated with her sympathy to all natural things. Boulainvilliers reported that no sheep was ever lost when she was guarding them and that no wild beast even came near to devour one;[57] Antonio Morosini's chronicle quotes letters written in 1429 that stress Joan's occupation of shepherdess, as a badge of her simplicity;[58] the Bourgeois de Paris reported, with a different emphasis, that she had magic powers over nature: wild birds came to her call to eat from her hand, as if tame.[59] Occasionally, rustic or noble savage elements creep into the traditional iconography to emphasise Justice's aloofness to the commerce of the world. There is, for instance, a German soapstone figure of the sixteenth century, now in the collection of Anglesey Abbey, Huntingdonshire, that shows Justice with her traditional sword, but dressed—or rather half-dressed—in a tunic of leaves, like the Wild Men whom the Bourgeois saw in Henry VI's pageant.[60]

The writer Jacques Audiberti (d. 1966) in his *Pucelle*, first performed in Paris in 1950, plays with this tradition when he portrays Joan of Arc split between two actresses, one a shrivelled, silent peasant grovelling by the hearth and the other a radiant, vigorous, splendid "natural" specimen, full of health, of energy, bursting with laughter, *"le rire éclatant, cascadé, un peu démentiel"* (bursting, cascading laughter, a bit crazed).[61] At one point in the play, this Joan—the projection of one of our fantasies—declaims the power of the natural physique: "I don't need a broomstick. Our sinews and our limbs, however little we exploit their natural vigour . . . allow us to leave the ground in ever growing leaps and bounds."[62] *Rusticité* is at the foundation of her strength, her Amazonian prowess, and it is in this context an analogy of her unassailability, her inviolability, which itself can be understood on another facet of the same prism, as a state of sexual immaturity, the condition of the child.[63]

Nineteenth-century hagiography emphasised Joan's bucolic origins.

Péllerin of Epinal, the famous Lorraine printers of coloured woodcuts showing popular heroes, events, legends and folklore, have demonstrated over the years such a sure-footed sense of the common denominator of popularity that their product, *les images d'Epinal*, has come to mean "cliché" or "stereotype" in French. In 1909, they printed a best-selling booklet of highlights from the life of Joan of Arc, then declared Blessed.[64] The familiar cycle is set: the first woodcut shows Joan carrying a distaff and kneeling to Saint Michael. She is surrounded by sheep and goats on the wooded edge of a field. In this fashion, the *bois chesnu* is indicated by the trees, but the important pastoral message is not omitted. From then on, the usual salient points are made: the recognition scene at Chinon is on the cover; the triumph at Orleans and Joan's heroism after her wound are the subject of two drawings; the victory of Patay, the coronation, her capture, trial and death fill the rest of the pages. Péllerin were not of course aiming at innovation. They were following the accepted patterning of a perfect heroic life: their slant falls in the same way as in the stained glass of Orleans cathedral, quite fine turn-of-the-century compositions by L. Jac-Galland and E. Gibelin.[65] Their shepherdess's upturned face is tenderly held in Saint Margaret's hand, in a pasture filled with violets, lilies and even mushrooms. The wall-to-wall frescoes of Joan's basilica at Domremy hardly altered the schema of "essential" scenes. Lionel Royer, who won a prize at the Salon in Paris in 1913 for these poor works of historical *verismo* (38), introduced, as only fitting in a church, a different scene to emphasise Joan's piety.[66] Her first communion at Domremy, little girls in white on the altar steps, approaches the theme of Joan's innocence and childlikeness in a novel way. Puvis de Chavannes, who decorated the Panthéon in 1876–80 with scenes from Joan's life, and Maurice Boutet de Monvel (d. 1913), an interesting illustrator who published a children's book on Joan that is a classic today and still selling, both begin with sheep.[67]

Puvis, who represents the summit of official, accepted art at that date, elaborated a parallel with Saint Geneviève, patron saint of Paris, the badge of whose early sinlessness is also a solitary and pastoral life. The imagery Puvis uses of the little, simply clad Geneviève keeping her sheep is identical to holy pictures of Joan at the same period and relates back in time to medieval illuminations of Saint Margaret of Antioch in the pastures with her flocks when the lecherous prefect Olybrius rides by and sees her (5).[68] Sheep inspired innocent, healthy thoughts, tinged at the same time with the supranormal—the keen-sighted, the wise and the silent—for it was not forgotten that angels had appeared to shepherds when Christ was born. The Child Jesus, in the late nineteenth century, is conflated with a cult of the Good Shepherd. Jesus as a boy in a rustic tunic surrounded by sheep is a new inspiration of the time, brought into being by the new worship of simplicity.

It would be impossible and tedious to enumerate the late nineteenth- and early twentieth-century images of Joan that insist on her simplicity by associating her with youth and pastoral labour and present this combination as indisputably and unambiguously admirable. Books, statues throughout France (32), holy pictures all use the formula; often the essentially democratic, even revolutionary concept that underlies it is spoiled by sentimental treatment.

Yearning for a child's purity also informs the works of some of Joan's finest apologists. Michelet added a personal footnote to his panegyric, grieving that "no one today wants to be either childlike or good."[69] Fifty years later, Mark Twain, another impassioned defender of individual liberties, created a Joan of Arc who is the epitome of the "marvellous child."[70] Of all Twain's books, he claimed to like this the best, although it contradicted in a fundamental way his atheist, determinist and antimonarchist philosophy. He writes Joan's story through the eyes of her page, Louis de Coutes, a type of Huck Finn transposed to the fifteenth century, and Joan emerges as a prototype of the democratic hero: unlettered, "natural," rising by innate qualities of personality alone to a position of wisely exercised power. The historian William Searle has pointed out that Twain's favourite daughter Susy died in 1896 of cerebrospinal meningitis at the age of twenty-four.[71] Twain had almost completed his *Joan* and had been reading it aloud to her. Her death sharpened his vision of Joan as a child taken before the world could sully her. "He ended by representing her, in effect, as a saint in a world without God. . . . the search for a means of transcendence in a world apparently abandoned by God has become the pre-eminent spiritual quest of our time."[72] Twain confessed his bafflement in a powerful essay he also wrote about Joan; to him, she is "the Riddle of the Ages": "We can understand how the possibilities of the future perfect peach are all lying hid in the humble bitter-almond, but we cannot conceive of the peach springing directly from the almond without the intervening long seasons of patient cultivation and development."[73]

This was the sceptics' problem; and it forced them into positions that, in their own terms, were illogical. Anatole France, whose *Vie de Jeanne d'Arc* (1908) is still very entertaining today, found his habitual rationalism in conflict with his enthusiasm for Joan as a heroine. He aimed to show that all about her could be understood through reason, but had to posit that in her acceptance of the supernatural origin of her voices, she herself was irrational to an extent he would normally despise. Joan, in this account, was manipulated by political agents among the clergy into believing that her role was divinely ordained and her voices and successes in battle were miracles, though all of these belonged to the natural order. He explained away his heroine and her supporters as credulous children, inspired by fantasies that had no value nor substance and were based on political intrigue. Yet at the same time, he responded with fierce emotion to the heroism of Joan's character and mission. For Anatole France as well, Joan was a type of wonderful child, in whom education and enlightenment would have wiped out the poetic enthusiasm and passionate idealism that carried her forward.[74]

The clearest and most popular expression of Joan of Arc as an inspired child of the people coincides in time and place with other forces that bore on her changing political role in France. A young woman, Marie-Edmée Pau, wrote *Histoire de notre petite sœur Jeanne d'Arc*, which was dedicated to the "children of Lorraine."[75] Pau was from Nancy, the capital of Lorraine, and she used her classmates as models for the drawings with which she illustrated her text. Her own face appears in the last few pictures of Joan as she embarks on her mission and bids her native land farewell. The snub-nosed baby girl has grown up into a dark, straight-browed, stern but sweet-faced young woman who raises her right hand in a gesture of farewell like a blessing. Marie-Edmée Pau never saw the publication of her book, which went through four different editions between 1873 and 1879. At the age of twenty-five, in 1871, she died of fever contracted on her mission to help the wounded in the Franco-Prussian War. She first joined when her brother, who was in the army, went missing; she searched for him for a month and, after finding him a prisoner, persuaded the Prussians that as he had lost his right hand, he could be released without danger. After six months at home, they both left to rejoin the fighting. Pau took with her parcels of clothes for the soldiers made by a group of her friends she had organised under the name of Joan of Arc. One of the curious services she also performed for the lines was to draw portraits of the dying, so that their families could be sent a last image of the loved one.

Before the war, she had given drawing classes in Nancy, and the style of her illustrations reflects the art nouveau school flourishing in the city. She frames salient scenes from Joan's life, often in sinuous circles or ovals ornamented with intertwined stems of flowers, leaves and grasses. Domestic happiness and rustic pleasures figure very strongly, with Pierre teaching Joan how to herd sheep and her guardian angel instructing her in the beauties of nature. In the evenings, the village children gather round the hearth of *"la vieille Merline,"* a crone with a repertoire of legends, folktales and old romances, who kindles Joan's yearnings. When her mother wants to teach her to sew, because the "weaker" sex should, Joan rebels: "The most difficult things are the most beautiful, and I would prefer to do beautiful things."[76]

Pau's naiveté is knowing, but the moral idealism of her simply told but skilful story is inspiriting. Without help, it could have been a success; but after her adventures at the Prussian front and her death, it was taken up by the local clergy, led by the bishop of St. Dié, and became one of the many elements in the cult of Joan that centred on Domremy in Lorraine. After the province was ceded to Germany in 1871 in the treaty following France's terrible defeat at Sedan on the Meuse on 1 September, Joan's role as the rallying figurehead of national integrity was renewed with new implications in the modern world.

The cult of Joan's childlikeness has one side effect that suited edifying purposes well. It threw the emphasis onto her upbringing and her parents. The nineteenth century saw many enraptured and tender evocations of home life at Domremy, with Joan learning her prayers at her mother's knee (authenticated by the trial)[77] and helping with the domestic chores (also implied by her evidence).[78] These interests correspond with the development of the cult of the Child Jesus and the new social interest in the state of childhood as a distinct phenomenon in itself, reflected in novels on both sides of the Channel—Hugo and Dickens. In Joan's case, the preoccupation has left a monument, quite unforgettable in its awfulness. In Joan's mother's native village of Vouthon, near Domremy, a statue has been raised to Isabelle Romée. The work of a notably ungifted sculptor called Maurice Cochinaire, it shows the immature Joan ferried forward by her very much taller mother. The dedication reads, *"A la Gloire des Mamans"* (to the glory of mamas, and continues, *"Derrière les saints cherchez leur mère"* (behind every saint, look for the mother). It was unveiled in 1961 and therefore counts among the most recent homages to Joan.[79]

The Vouthon monument stands at the culmination of a long period in which Joan's specialness was seen as her innocence's aptness to take on the impress of goodness about her. That goodness came from God or from an institution identified with Him—in this case, the family.

CHAPTER 13

SAINT OR PATRIOT?

*"The pinnacle of Joan of Arc's life is her death,
and the stake in Rouen."*

PAUL CLAUDEL,
"Jeanne d'Arc"[1]

Beside the bridge in Domremy, just across from the D'Arc house, on one of the prettiest sites of the village near the lush water meadows and the rushing Meuse, is a white marble group showing Joan, exalted and radiant. She is enfolded in the fleur-de-lysé mantle of a queenly figure, who, wearing a pearl-embroidered coif on her looped hair, represents France in its medieval form, the fifteenth-century realm. With her help, Joan lifts to the sky an avenging sword (36).

Antonin Mercié began this group in 1890, at the instigation of Jules Ferry, a prominent statesman from Lorraine and an active positivist and socialist. The statue refuses all divine associations for Joan's achievements: secular France, it says, provided the passion and the inspiration that guided her.

Mercié's sculpture was installed in 1902, eleven years after the Church's choice of statue, the Allar group, had been erected at the entrance to the basilica on the ridge in an equally beautiful position above the rich valley (35). His statue makes the exactly opposite point: Joan, dressed as a peasant, kneels in an attitude of alarm and humility, one hand shielding her face, the other outstretched in wonder before her three voices, who are raised high above her on a brick wall and are cast in precious bronze in contrast to her white marble. Catherine holds out a sword, Margaret a helmet, and Michael, slightly higher than the others and spreading tremendous wings, raises himself to his full height, points with his index finger of his right hand toward heaven and holds aloft her cross-staff banner in his left. Joan here is God's humble instrument. Thus the opposing power blocs contending for Joan's patronage confided their quarrel to imperishable stone in her very homeland.

The nineteenth-century contest between the faithful and the sceptics for the possession of Joan was dramatised far beyond the banks of the Meuse in the savage anticlerical movements that shook the France of the Second Empire and the Third Republic.[2] Joan was no stranger to this struggle for power in French history. As we saw, the repeal of her trial was promoted by ecclesiastical interests striving against Charles VII's independent ambition. Similarly, at the beginning of the nineteenth century, Napoleon's desire to reconcile himself with the Church led to a restoration of her cult, firmly expressed in nationalist terms. As first consul, on 10 Pluviôse, of the revolutionary year XI (30 January 1803), Napoleon authorised the celebration of the 8 May feast at Orleans, suspended during the Revolution, and a new monument to Joan (31). "United, the French Nation has never been conquered," he declared. "The Illustriousness of Joan of Arc has proved that there is no miracle that cannot be accomplished by the genius of the French when the National Independence is threatened."[3] Lest anyone mistake the import of such a monument in traditionally Royalist Orleans, Joan was represented by the sculptor Gois fils (d. 1836) as a species of Marianne, spirit of the Republic, seizing a flag from an English soldier.[4]

After the proclamation of the Third Republic in 1870 and the fall and exile of Napoleon III, the clash was articulated with greater ferocity. Its ever-widening implications were voiced during the violent and protracted Dreyfus case and in discussions that led to the disestablishment of the Church in France by the "Separation" of powers, made law in December 1905.[5] Joan had high symbolic value in these upheavals: she represented France for both sides, but a different France, with a different identity, and both were determined to claim her for their own.

It is entirely appropriate that the feud between Church and state regarding Joan should be immortalised in her birthplace, because the idea of nationality as an attachment to the earth itself lay at the roots of the nineteenth-century concept of nationhood. Domremy is not just a memorial to Joan of Arc; it is a testimonial to the idea that a man derives his identity from the soil that gives him birth. The peasant child derived virtue not from inexperience and innocence alone, but from the land itself.

The romantic atavism of such ideas often takes a very dangerous political form, in which a golden age of folkloric ignorance acts as a pretext for reaction, to maintain or promote a present repression. The historian Barrington Moore, Jr., in *The Social Origins of Dictatorship and Democracy* has described this cluster of ideas: paternal affection for country rituals, celebration of natural virtue and a harking back to an agricultural harmony and to a lost harmonious hierarchy in agricultural labours. He calls it Catonism, after Cato the Elder (234–149 B.C.), who cultivated stern virtues, repudiated foreigners as decadent and admired the untutored mind. Moore relates the philosophy to the fascist movements of Western Europe beginning at the end of the nineteenth century.[6] The ambivalence of such a philosophy is its most marked peculiarity; and it does not necessarily lead to fascism. It can be progressive or conservative, democratic or authoritarian; Gandhi, Mao Tsetung and Khrushchev were all Catonists. The ecology movement today, in many ways its present representative, attracts a social cross section, from the city-dwelling socialist and even revolutionary to the small-holding peasantry, traditionally the most reactionary of groups. Yet a celebration of "roots" also often appears alongside biological and historical determinism, which is intrinsically conservative and frequently oppressive.

Joan of Arc, as distaff-bearing shepherdess, belongs in this philosophical place; and she was put there by the efforts of her most worshipful partisans. When Margaret Murray wrote her famous but nonsensical rehabilitation of witches, *The Witch Cult in Western Europe*, in 1921, the identification of Joan with a supposed ancient agricultural people's religion, wise and effective and democratic, but which a tyrannical Church had tried to stamp out, was so complete that Murray maintains Joan really was a witch of this creed, practising magic in the name of the goddess Diana alongside another initiate, Gilles de Rais.[7]

The D'Arc house at Domremy reflects the struggle that made Joan a figurehead of this dubious populism. It was first bought as Joan's family house, *la maison de la Pucelle*, in 1583, when the tradition identifying it with the D'Arcs was well established. Louise de Stainville, mother of Jean IX, who was governor of Nancy, count of Salm and lord of Domremy, was the buyer.[8] It was already a tourist attraction, since Montaigne had visited it in 1580. At the beginning of the seventeenth century, Etienne Hordal built a chapel near the Arbre des Fées in the *bois chesnu* above the river valley. Domremy's cult then fades from view. But later, Nicolas Gérardin, a descendant of one of Joan's godsons and a vineyard keeper, came to prominence as the owner of the house when, for reasons of patriotism, he refused to sell it in 1815. A Prussian count had offered him 6,000 *francs*. Gérardin was himself a veteran of the Napoleonic Wars, during which he had been wounded, and so the story of staunchness in the face of rich temptation made him a hero; several plays were put on in Paris and Orleans dramatising his stand: *La Maison de Jeanne d'Arc* by René Perrin and another by M. de Rougemont, also in 1818.[9]

The interest of the Prussian shamed the Département des Vosges. It bought the house from Gérardin in 1818, for the rather smaller sum of 1,800 *francs*, and allowed him to live there as custodian. In 1820, the house was ceremonially opened. A triumphal arch bearing an equestrian Joan was erected at the entrance, and pavilions with pennons flying were pitched on the banks of the Meuse. Sensitive to the feminist content of Joan's story, King Louis XVIII ordered that a free school for young girls from nearby villages be established there. It was administered by the Sisters of Portieux until 1888; its large clinical buildings, raised on either side of Joan's low cottage, altered the latter's humble appearance to an extraordinary degree.[10]

Visitors came, signing the *Livre d'Or* and, in the wake of the defeat of Napoleon, appending suitably anglophobic comment on the enemies of Joan of Arc. A certain Félix Etienne, "French, body and soul," wrote in September 1853:

> *Children of the leopard, you whose cruel laws*
> *Drenched the pyre in the blood of the innocent,*
> *Let your criminal hands forever be anathema,*
> *Shame is the path that you must tread!*[11]

But, as we have seen, it was the commemoration of Voltaire's death in 1878, converging with defiance of the Prussian occupation of Alsace and much of Lorraine (though not Domremy itself), that brought Joan's cult in Domremy to a climax. The duchess of Chevreuse, an active, pious, determined and rich woman of a type indispensable to the growth of new forms of piety, undertook to defy the famous mocking smile of the great philosopher. For Joan's anniversary of 30 May, she brought down to the house Marie d'Orléans's statue of Joan standing recollected at prayer. One cast of this sculpture was already the focus of the annual pilgrimage at Orleans. In July, the duchess organised another demonstration, this time monarchist, and brought fifty crates of flowers to adorn the village. About 15,000 people attended. This was the year that signatures of pilgrims to Domremy doubled to 4,500. Meanwhile the bishop of St. Dié, Monsignor de Briey, was busy raising money for a shrine to Joan. The site, in the *bois chesnu* near the original chapel, was bought, and Paul Sédille, previously known for his design of Les Grands Magasins du Printemps in Paris, was commissioned to design a basilica. Plans were made for a chapel at Vaucouleurs, too; statues and projects for statues were commissioned and sometimes erected all through the eighties and nineties, not only in Domremy, Greux, Pont-à-Mousson and Nancy, but further north, in places associated with Joan: Crotoy, where she was taken on her last journey to Rouen, Rheims, Chinon (33). Journals dedicated to Joan were started (*L'Almanach de Jeanne d'Arc* in 1891; *L'Etendard de Jeanne d'Arc* in 1888; *Les Voix de Jeanne d'Arc* in 1891). It is a very good indication of the tensions alive in attitudes toward Joan that, of her journals, *L'Etendard* was started by the future bishop of Dijon, who sided with the state against the Vatican, and *Les Voix* by the Abbé Mourot, an ardent monarchist and conservative.[12]

The pious were not Joan's only fans: the idea that she should be commemorated by a public holiday was first proposed by Dr. Robinet, the sceptical mayor of the seventh arrondissement in Paris, a historian of the Revolution, who formed in 1888 *le Comité républicain de la fête civique de Jeanne d'Arc*.[13] Joseph Fabre, deputy from the Aveyron and one of Joan's ardent historians (his *Jeanne d'Arc* was published in 1882 and his five-act play performed in 1891), officially tabled the bill, and the Senate accepted it in 1892, in spite of fears that the Catholics would take it over.[14] Charles Péguy, though a believer, developed a brand of mystic socialism that escaped the taint of reaction associated with Catholicism after Pius IX's *Syllabus of Errors* in 1864 had openly declared the Church's antagonism to all relaxation, republicanism and liberalism.

In their differing ways, Péguy, the believer, and Anatole France, a vigorous unbeliever, laboured with their immense works—Péguy's two masterpieces (*Le Mystère de la Charité de Jeanne d'Arc* and *Les Tapis-*

series de Ste Geneviève et Jeanne d'Arc)[15] and France's work of biographical scholarship—to keep Joan aligned with progress, not reaction, as a means of national liberation and strengthening.[16] The theatre of their struggle became the Dreyfus case, which convulsed France during 1894–99, with implications long after. Their opponents were those who did not want the wrongful condemnation of Dreyfus for treason to be reversed. Such an admission that the army's justice had miscarried would reveal that social institutions were fallible, and this would weaken the state. For Péguy and France, on the other hand, Joan personified the freedom of the individual and her trial and condemnation the crushing oppression of government; Dreyfus, an outsider because he was a Jew, just as Joan had been thrust outside normal society as a witch, provided a parallel. Both Joan and Dreyfus were innocent victims of political machinery that has no regard for those individual rights that are, according to the principles—if not the practice—of democratic socialism, absolute and inalienable.

But for the enemies of Dreyfus, Joan was the symbol of the absolute authority of the state, as represented by the king whom she had so faithfully served, whatever his shortcomings; she stood for an idea of Patria dependent on military strength and established order, both of which Dreyfus's vindication appeared to threaten.[17] The passions of the anti-Dreyfusards worked themselves up to fanaticism, much of which was expressed through the inflammatory activities of the Action Française, a seedbed of the kind of nationalism that would develop in time into fascism.[18]

The Action Française grew out of the Ligue de la Patrie Française, an anti-Semitic association founded in 1899 to combat the Ligue des Droits de l'Homme, founded by Dreyfus supporters. It derived its popular support from a curious blend of nationalist radicalism from the intellectual right with a nostalgic and fanatical yearning for the restoration of the monarchy. This unwieldy synthesis was achieved by the efforts of a remarkably energetic and wholly antipathetic figure, Charles Maurras. Maurras's hatred of republicanism was so intense that during World War II he preferred collaboration to helping the Gaullist resistance. At his trial, he maintained the republican struggle had betrayed France far more grievously, and, at the age of seventy-seven, he was condemned to life imprisonment for treason. It was a terrible end for a man who had dedicated his life to patriotism, but it was a natural outcome of his ideology that the pursuit of justice knows no master and no laws.[19]

Soon after the founding of the Action Française at the turn of the century, Maurras declared that legal methods could be abandoned.[20] He had an ability to inspire, and his followers were obedient. Although he was himself sceptic, he was sympathetic to Catholicism, because it was committed to fight socialism, because it was royalist and because it was the true, ancient, legitimate faith of France, as he saw it, unlike Protestantism or other "foreign" creeds. He was not a man of faith, but he was a man of the Church. It represented high authority.

The Action Française was very popular with Catholics, in spite of its architect's unbelief. It spread its ideas through public meetings and lectures and through its own paper, of the same name, which became daily in 1908 and was financed by Léon Daudet, son of the novelist Alphonse, who had written so tenderly of French country matters. The first lecture was on Joan of Arc, given by the medievalist Auguste Longnon. Maurras proclaimed that Joan, the palladium of the cause, stood for three things:

> *The [national] Heritage maintained*
> *And the Fatherland saved*
> *By the monarchy restored.*[21]

She was the heroine not of "Democracy," but of the "Nation," and she came from *"cette bourgeoisie rurale"* which is "conservative, sane, vigorous and radical." Although Maurras himself was usually contemptuous, he admitted, of saints elected by the people, in Joan's case, "Church and Fatherland have gathered the flower of flowers. . . . This historical image will necessarily rise to attain more and more the level of model and law."[22] Maurras's rhetoric is wearisome to read, turning back on its own highly dubious premise as if it were an irrefutable universal, beyond argument, that militarist monarchy is "the natural order."[23]

Philip, duke of Orleans, the closest in line to the throne, was not attracted by his virulent supporter; and the Church, for a variety of political reasons, not least of which was the Action Française's atheist tinge, censured the movement in 1926. Maurras's writings were replaced on the Index, as they had been in 1914, and his newspaper as well.[24] But this was too late to drag Joan from the clutches of Action Française ideology.

In the name of nationalism, a programme of armed expression developed, which went further than the moral demands of resistance to aggression allows. Yet many distinguished people were attracted by the heroic atmosphere of the Action Française. François Coppée provides an instance of the union of ideas typical of the highly respectable membership of the original Ligue de la Patrie Française. Man of letters, Catholic, committed anti-Dreyfusard, Coppée included a poem about Joan in his collection, *Les Récits et les Élégies*, soon after the Prussian victory. Joan is praying in a cemetery filled with the crosses of the recent dead, while an old man grieves at France's weakness and lack of arms. Then:

> *Monsieur Saint Michael now answered the prayer*
> *That the naive warrior maiden murmured under her breath,*
> *And when she arrived in the place of rest,*
> *The crosses that had been made for the numerous graves from*
>   *two cut branches*
> *By a miracle suddenly turned into swords. . . .*[25]

With these new forged weapons, Joan rearms her countrymen.

Joan's name was linked with demands for violent support and disorder on behalf of authoritarian measures, the recipe made familiar in Germany in the thirties. The Action Française newspaper was sold on the streets by the Camelots du Roi (the King's Hawkers), a group of young men, aristocrats and workers dedicated to the monarchist cause. Their first president was the sculptor Maxime Réal del Sarte, a virulent anti-Dreyfusard[26] (42). One of his statues of Joan of Arc stands in the castle chapel at Vaucouleurs. When the Camelots heard that François Thalamas, a professor at the Lycée Condorcet who held a rationalist view of Joan of Arc, was teaching at the Sorbonne, a systematic campaign of disruption of his classes was begun. Thalamas was beaten up; Jewish lecturers were prevented from reaching their classrooms; riots broke out between police and students through the winter of 1908–1909.[27] Georges Bernanos, political polemicist and novelist of supernatural themes, was then in his early twenties and was sentenced to five days' prison for his Camelot rage. There were other disturbances, particularly around Joan's statue in the Place des Pyramides.[28]

Many other writers associated with the right-wing reaction to France's weakness regarding Germany throughout the period from the end of the Franco-Prussian War till the end of World War I, wrote in glowing terms of Joan's simplicity, inspiration, mission and origins among the people: Maurice Barrès,[29] Léon Bloy.[30] She was for them a symbol of national unity that could transcend ideological differences. She was *"une sainte pour tous"*[31] (13). Old hands of the Action Française, Thierry Maulnier and Robert Brasillach (the latter shot for treason after World War II), were still writing about her in the thirties and forties.[32] Yet at the same time, in spite of their master Maurras's adherence to both Vichy and Joan of Arc, her statues were thrown down in the public squares of occupied France by the Germans.

The same paradox about the liberator, who is also oppressive and conservative, can be seen in the women's movements of the turn of the century. Joan of Arc was a favourite figurehead of feminists. Sarah Moore Grimké, the American suffragist, translated one of the French biographies of Joan and published it in Boston in 1876.[33] In England, Christabel Pankhurst was known as the Maiden Warrior, and her followers wore badges of her in which she looked like Joan of Arc. When Mrs. Pankhurst was released from Holloway in 1908, the victory procession of the Women's Social and Political Union was led by one suffragette dressed as Joan in full armour. Christabel sometimes quoted Joan in her speeches, called one of her war orphans "Joan" and in 1916 demanded—rather oddly—to know why a statue of Joan had not been erected to celebrate a century of peace between France and England. Although the women's suffrage movement had its roots in socialist principles of equality, some of its leaders, like Christabel herself, became associated later with right-wing opinion, principally represented by the recruitment drives in World War I, which were shamefully militarist. But the campaigns of moral reform, the temperance and chastity movements which rallied women against men who subjugated them by intoxicated violence and sexual abuses, also had a strongly authoritarian side.[34]

The claim of the pious on Joan, a heroine for all seasons, was weakened by her unacknowledged sanctity. Monsignor Dupanloup, the conservative bishop of Orleans and a doughty antagonist of the secularisation of education in France—"a profound and vast enterprise of impiety"—invited twelve bishops and archbishops and then delivered a famously eloquent panegyric on 8 May 1869. At the end, he informed his cathedral that he had placed the petition for Joan's canonisation before the Vatican. But nothing happened for a time. A steady letter-writing campaign to the Vatican was begun: the bluest aristocrats—the count of Chambord, the prince of Joinville, the duke of Aumale—were enlisted and, in 1888, the case was first presented to the Sacred Congregation.[35]

In 1894, after enormous socialist gains in the elections of 1893 and under subsequently strong pressure from clerical groups in France, Leo XIII recognised that Joan could be used as a rallying point to reclaim French souls straying toward socialism and atheism. Joan was declared Venerable. This lowly degree did not satisfy her promoters. The petitions continued, and in 1909, Pius X, Leo's successor, and himself a saint now, declared her Blessed. The debate about her full sanctity was still fierce and focussed on one issue: was her allegiance to God above all other loyalties for her, or was her type of heroic virtue of this world? In 1888, the devil's advocate, whose task, in canonisation proceedings, is to argue the case against the candidate, compared her to Christopher Columbus, someone who had achieved great things, but not altogether for the glory of God. But in 1920, the devil's advocate's case was withdrawn, and Pope Benedict XV finally authorised the canonisation of Joan of Arc.[36]

Both the beatification and the canonisation were responses to pressure from groups like the Action Française who wished the Vatican to make a firm stand against the rapid secularisation of France and the spread of unbelief in the Christian world in general. Yet at the same time, Joan was once more a figure who bridged division: the French Catholics who, at Leo XIII's suggestion, adopted the pragmatic solution of *le Ralliement,* and recognised the Republic as the *de facto* government of France and thus accepted the idea of working with it, saw in Joan a symbol that Church and state could work together.

The problem that it was the Church itself that had condemned her in the first place was overcome with characteristic craft by the canonisation, which reclaimed her for God: the Rouen judges were adherents to the schismatic Council of Basle, it was declared. Nevertheless, Joan is not a "Martyr" of the Church; she is not officially designated a witness to the faith at the hands of its enemies. In the calendar, she is simply a "Virgin." The canonisation decree relies heavily on the evidence of the rehabilitation and does not quote Joan in person at all. It mentions the extraordinary marvels of her skills in horsemanship, the supernatural signs at her death, her heart unconsumed in the ashes. Her loyalty to the Church itself is necessarily stressed: her confessor was "always at her side," we are told.[37]

On 20 November, the same year as Joan's sanctity was proclaimed, the papal nuncio was returned to Paris, after a coldness of sixteen years, and Church and state were reconciled in appearance. On the five-hundredth anniversary of the relief of Orleans, 8 May 1929, the government chose to break the diplomatic ice with the Church. Both the papal legate and Gaston Doumergue, the president of the Republic, as well as Raymond Poincaré, président du Conseil, were to attend. Elaborate precautions were taken to keep them apart, on separate podia, with exact attention to equal etiquette for both. By a coincidence, Cardinal Lepicier, the legate, and Poincaré were both born in Vaucouleurs, and the strict formality of this subtle reconciliation was broken when Doumergue changed the protocol of the day and sought out the legate to tell him:

> My lord cardinal, my presence here today and that of my government means that the French Republic is neither atheist nor antireligious, but traditionalist. . . . Like all great nations, France knows that it must adapt its traditions to present necessities. But it also knows that it cannot deny those traditions without forswearing itself. And it rejoices, here in Orleans, in Joan of Arc who is at once a national heroine and a saint of the Church, to find again its traditions, national and Christian.[38]

No one has recently worn Joan's favour more fervently than Général de Gaulle (b. 1890), who was dyed in the thought of Barrès and Péguy from his youth at the turn of the century. The cross of her home province of Lorraine became the symbol of his movement of independence (14). He never lost his keen attachment and vivid identification with her. This presidential tradition was revived in 1979, at the 55oth anniversary celebrations of the raising of the siege, when Président Giscard d'Estaing, alongside dignitaries of the Church, attended both the procession in Orleans and later the inauguration of the restored Place de Vieux-Marché in Rouen, where Joan was burned. She has now become a safe symbol of the country's grandeur, for all sides, in spite of differences.[39]

The partisans of Joan in the Action Française did not uncover a central truth about Joan, any more than did the socialists or the sceptics who have given her their love. She is not intrinsically anticlerical or Church-abiding, though elements in her life can make her seem both; she is not intrinsically right-wing or left-wing, because nationalism itself can go either way. She has come to represent the nation to French men and women. It is Michelet who in 1833 first uses the word *nationalité* in the sense of the "existence or wish for existence of a group of men," Michelet who so frankly identified Joan with France.[40] Joan's following, whatever way it wished to express nationhood, agreed on the characteristics of her innate virtue that make her a suitable and beloved figurehead. Bernanos, in an essay, puts the central image most clearly. Remembering Péguy, who had just died, he writes: "Ever since then, one would have liked Joan of Arc to belong only to children." She is "this little France, who is so fresh, so mischievous, who is awfully afraid of being burnt." When she realises she must face the stake, "she replied with a cry of distress—a child's dear cry, whose flight through the air one would like to kiss, a cry of appeal which would have brought the sword of any knight leaping from its scabbard; the cry of innocence which from age to age would be answered by the furious thunder of the French guns."[41]

This is patriotic, sentimental, easily discarded as pious tosh—in times of peace. But in times of trouble, it leaps straight to the heart. Given a danger to the body of the nation, the image of Joan of Arc's integrity works, as it worked in 1429.

When virtue is pictured as innocence and innocence equated with childlikeness, the implication is obviously that knowledge and experience are no longer media of goodness, but have become in themselves contaminating. This is a very despairing outlook, in its way as black as Augustine's original sin, for it supposes that original goodness will in all likelihood be defiled. As Schiller wrote, "children *are* what we *were*. They are what we should again become."[42] It surrenders the attempt to represent virtue in a mature phase. Joan of Arc *was* young. There is that most pathetic of replies in her trial, "About nineteen, I think."[43] But her youth drew no comment in her own day. D'Alençon, her companion-at-arms, was only twenty-five, but no one remarked on that, either; he had been nineteen at the battle of Verneuil when he was captured; Dunois was twenty-four in 1429; the duke of Burgundy, John the Fearless, was twenty-five when he commanded the army at the crusade of Nicopolis. As a result of that catastrophe, he did not allow his son Philip to fight at Agincourt beside him at the age of nineteen, which greatly distressed the youth.[44] Nor was Joan's age a shock for generations afterward. It is only in the nineteenth century that it stirs the imagination and appears so appealing, so tender, so noteworthy and that the soft, blunt features of a "typical" peasant child make their appearance.

What does this child saint represent? Joan is not the only one of these times: Saint Thérèse of Lisieux, died 1897, canonised 1925, is another prototype, with her adoration of the Child Jesus, her early death at the age of twenty-four, and her devotional metaphors literally culled from child's play:

> For some time past I had indulged the fancy of offering myself up to the Child Jesus as a plaything, for him to do what he liked with me. I don't mean an expensive plaything; give a child an expensive toy. . . . But a toy of no value—a ball, say—is all at his disposal: he can throw it on the ground, kick it about, make a hole in it, leave it lying in a corner, or press it to his heart.[45]

Under the influence of Maurras, whom she read, the Little Flower's favourite saint became Joan (though in her lifetime Joan was not yet a saint). She wrote a book about her for her fellow sisters in the Carmel at Lisieux to read.[46]

The Saint Joan of recent hagiography, and Saint Thérèse, the Little Flower, both give comfort. They provide for adults a simple image of perfection. They eliminate complications; by remaining child-ish, they do not present their votaries with moral dilemmas or ambiguities. Such a saint represents a reduction of conflict. Joan tending her sheep, the innocent country girl called by God, becomes simple. One of the most tantalizing puzzles of European history disappears under the cloak of primal innocence. This feels reassuring. Creating simplicity often makes the heart leap; order has been restored, the crooked made straight. But order is understanding that things cannot be made simple, that complexity reigns and must be accepted. Infantilism is extrinsic to Joan, however young she was; it is projected upon her by adults who fear the absence of such clear and simple goodness in themselves and through themselves, who fear its disappearance in everyone and there-fore feel a need to experience it in reality by finding it in someone who lived. We have again a translation of a personal intimation of good-ness into the "real" world: an incarnate idea. But to conceive goodness as youth is also an admission of defeat, for it disallows the maturing of virtue and it expresses a fear that change, which is inevitable, will be for the worse. The young Joan of Arc, the sweet-faced child of hagiog-raphy, represents the Western attachment to changelessness and our terror of flux.

At one level, her martyrdom is a consummation of her unbending trueness to herself, a concept that underlies the essence of heroism. As a heroine, she could not be deflected from her path, even unto the last test.

She was loyal to her voices, and because those voices can be seen as her interior spirit, by those who reject the explanation from supernatural causes, she can be a heroine to believer and unbeliever alike. But at another level, her death in the fire is the only triumph in an ideological climate where change means deterioration, a gradual haemorrhage of grace from the state of first innocence, the pure child.

It is astonishing how many of Joan's apologists like her dead. Without this badge of blood, this self-obliteration in the ideal, her glory would be the less. She was cut off before she could be proven weak, and in that cutting off is the redemption of sin for others. Her stake is likened to Christ's cross: through it, her virtue can be transmitted to others and save them. Her perfection is preserved by her climactic end in violence, just as a goldsmith in the process of annealing heats the metal in the fire till it glows and then plunges it in water to seize all the heat's virtue, now transmitted to the gold, and uses them for his purpose. Dumas explicitly wrote: "Joan of Arc is the Christ of France; she has redeemed the crimes of the monarchy, as Jesus redeemed the sins of the world: like Jesus, she suffered her passion; like Jesus, she had her Golgotha and her Calvary."[47]

The idea of sacrifice is not, of course, exclusively Christian: it is widespread in the mythology of Greece and Rome. Joan has her martyred counterparts in the virgin girls and boys who were offered to the Minotaur in Crete, until Theseus killed him, and in Iphigenia, who was laid on the altar of Artemis's rage, in order to lift the calm that prevented the Greek fleet's setting sail for Troy.[48] Joan of Arc is a figure of sacrificial death, of redeeming goodness in its plentitude at the moment of its ceasing to be. The idea is fundamental: even humanist interpreters of her life use the concept. Lamartine also wrote that her martyrdom was the necessary culmination of her true heroism: "God decreed for her a complete fate. There is none without the wickedness of men, without martyrdom for one's country."[49]

Such a completion is built into our aesthetic response, so that even when God has been banished from the picture, when Joan's martyrdom is not seen in theological terms as adding to the store of grace, it is seen to add to the sum of beauty in the world. For De Quincey, a woman on the scaffold was the greatest sight in all the world, eclipsing Luxor, St. Peter's on Easter Sunday or the Himalayas: "Sister woman," he continued, "though I cannot consent to find a Mozart or a Michel Angelo in your sex, cheerfully and with the love that burns in depths of admiration,

I acknowledge that you can do one thing as well as the best of us men—
a greater thing than ever Milton is known to have done, or Michael
Angelo—you can die grandly, and as goddesses would die, were goddesses mortal."[50]

The disorder and formlessness of life are given shape by art; the
limits of the work of art itself impose a structure that does not necessarily reproduce truthfully the circumstances of the subject; the mirror
of art is faithless. Joan's life, to meet the demands of art, is likewise
organised by dramatists and by historians and biographers with a dramatic sense, according to Aristotelian theory: first the glory of the hero
with an overarching conviction of personal mission, then reversal, the
destruction of hopes and, usually, extinction. But in Joan's case, the
moral message of the form resembles that of the Catholic Mass. There is
no hubris in the strict sense, for the drive toward self-destruction lies
in a laudable consent to the divine will and God's call, which raises up
the hero-victim, paschal lamb or virgin girl, for the time required to
accomplish the vocation. There is no defiance of the gods, nor is the
destruction of the hero a defeat, but a victory.

While the Mass follows the tragic structure closely, and may indeed
provide the link between the theatre of the ancients and our own when
it developed in the early Middle Ages, it parts with tragic drama altogether on the level of meaning.[51] The sacrifice of Christ, renewed in
the ritual, and its mimesis, in such martyrdoms as Joan's, are intended
to achieve not catharsis, but salvation. These aims are not even related on
a scale of degree. Joan's life and death do not serve, in any version in
any medium ever made, to warn against an ambition such as she entertained. Her story is always intended in the contrary sense of tragedy:
to exhort and to indoctrinate others to revere her high example. She is a
heroine in the sphere of moral action; in literature, she does not inspire
cautionary pity and fear, but incites us to imitation. She is admonitory,
not minatory.

It is an interesting difference, and it depends on the idea of Joan's
total innocence: she is not tragic in the strict sense of the *Poetics*, because she does no wrong and does not bring her end on herself. Schiller,
perceiving this, gave Joan a flaw: her love for the Englishman. But
usually, the evil represented by the sentence to the stake is entirely external to her; it never touches her purity from the inside. The more
terrible it is, the more powerfully it reinforces the idea of her innocence,
assailed and yet unvanquished.

In Cecil B. De Mille's spectacular film *Joan the Woman* (40), made in 1916 with Geraldine Farrar for the large budget of $300,000, the pyre piled up under Joan's frail body fills the whole marketplace. It would burn an entire army and would most certainly have set fire to the city. But the enormousness of the auto-da-fé acts, in a silent film, to underline the moral enormity of Joan's death.[52]

The finest work of music inspired by Joan's story is probably Honegger's *Jeanne au Bûcher*, the oratorio written by Paul Claudel and first performed in Basle in 1938.[53] It was filmed by Roberto Rossellini, with Ingrid Bergman in the role of Joan. The stake is Joan's crucifixion here, too, the moment of the consummation that saved France then and a metaphor of France's martyrdom during World War I (41). During World War II, Claudel added laments on the tragic divisions of France, giving Joan's heroism contemporary meaning.[54] Without her death, Claudel stated firmly in explanation, there would be no witness to the truth of Joan of Arc:

> What Joan could not achieve by force of arms, she is to consummate with her blood. What she began with this sign of the cross-staff in her peasant's fist, bearing the names of Jesus and Mary, this will be made effective by the red oriflamme of the stake, springing from under her feet like a whirlwind of irresistible wings. It is this triumphant gust carrying right up to the feet of the Crucified the soul of an innocent victim; it is the breath of this purifying and unifying fire that will reestablish and free communications, that will teach France again to breathe and to make of these vast available resources of different wills and intelligences a single consciousness and a single aim.[55]

Joan annihilates herself in the fire, with loving desire. Claudel bases his language on the Minnemystic, of the ecstatics, of the Middle Ages and the Renaissance, who, like Pico della Mirandola, declared: "If by charity we, with his devouring fire, burn for the Workman alone, we shall suddenly burst into flame in the likeness of a seraph."[56] Claudel writes:

> She embraces the holocaust. She willingly throws herself into the flame with which she was threatened. It is not enough to say that she accepts it; she espouses it: Brother Fire, the great joyful, irresistible flame whose praises Saint Francis of Assisi once sang. It is the vehicle she needed, no longer the fat carthorse on which she once made her way to Vaucouleurs, but the great pair of wings,

eagle and dove, to the cry of "Jesus," which will carry her up even to the gates of paradise: this flame, this luminous, triumphant exhalation of flesh and smoke.[57]

In Martha Graham's ballet *Seraphic Dialogue* (1955), Joan dances into the fire's embrace again as with a lover. Saint Michael then enfolds her to him and closes the gates of the glittering skeleton-like centrepiece of the set. The angel from heaven takes the angel from the world with fatal love, and the passage is effected by her tender surrender to pain.[58] Even Robert Bresson's *Procès de Jeanne d'Arc* (1959), a film that concentrates on Joan's trial only, has all Bresson's still, slow, intense absorption with the pure image and his dislike of accented dramatic interpretation of word or gesture. Yet it, too, rises to the scene of her burning through a sequence of careful frames of her pain—her shackled feet in their worn-out boots, her bound hands—and reaches an unwonted pitch of elemental passion, with birds whirling about the stake as the drums on the sound track roll.[59]

The erotic element in this cleaving to extinction is clear, and its presence, particularly charged in Claudel and Honneger's oratorio, helps make it sublime. As the harsh outcry of Joan's accusers, sung as if by animals, defiles her, she raises her crystal-clear, high, young tones in witness of her goodness, and the ancient conflict between purity and impurity is renewed with intense and moving beauty.

If the central presence of sexual pleasure-in-pain in the Christian concept of martyrdom is recognised, martyrdom can at least be understood in its psychological place, without being trivialised. A link with the structure of erotic sensation is not cheapening in itself, but its existence at the heart of the cult of innocence as sainthood should cast light on that cult. We are back with the Amazonamachies, the defloration of the unattached female in death, the only eternal preserver of the maiden state. Saint Thérèse of Lisieux, the epitome of childlike goodness, longed for suffering as proof of her total gift of herself to the single state of loving God alone: "But above all," she wrote,

I long to shed my blood for you, my Saviour, to the last drop. Martyrdom was the dream of my youth. . . . a single form . . . would never be enough for me, I should want to experience them all. I should want to be scourged and crucified as you were; to be flayed alive like St Bartholomew, to be dipped in boiling oil like St John, to undergo all that martyrs ever underwent; offering my neck to the executioner like St Agnes and St Cecily, and like my favourite St Joan of Arc, whispering your names as I was tied to the stake.[60]

The Little Flower, with her affirmations of suffering, found her first popularity among the soldiers of World War I.

Claudel's willing, sacrificial Joan belongs in this long and strong tradition, yet the intellectual bad faith of his argument cannot be overlooked, for Joan's execution at the stake also bears witness to the cruelty of her captors, to their superstition, to the ruthless political exactions of the times, to folly, weakness and a host of other infirmities to which our flesh is pliant. That perhaps is a great truth of a kind, but it is not the truth Claudel intended. Joan free, Joan alive, even Joan captive and sentenced not to death but to imprisonment brims over with the same quality of goodness as she ever testified to in the flames. Death does not set the seal on her innocence; her life is the measure of her character. It is better to live for a cause than to die for it. Yet this simple axiom has been obliterated in our necrophiliac culture's ideology of heroism. When we admire and praise Joan of Arc for the honesty and commitment of her death, we must be careful to distinguish between praise of her courage and glory in the manner of her death. Our training inclines us to find in death a victory more astonishing and more permanent than, say, an escape from the castle of Rouen into survival. Our inherited morality, so flexible in some areas, is rigid and unforgiving about recantation and allows no honesty to victims who survive the rack or the stake or thumbscrew or the lamp or the unlit cell because they withdraw and abjure.

The position of Joan of Arc did not involve the lives of others; a recantation made "for fear of the fire" would have harmed no one except the reputation of the French who had sponsored her, and it could have been restored with more victories, as indeed it was. But it is tacitly fundamental to our concept of Joan's heroism that she died to testify to her truthfulness. Claude des Armoises, who pretended to be Joan of Arc for a few months in 1436 and 1439, excites enormous indignation, not only because her adventurism is so rank, but because the very idea of survival appears to taint Joan's life with insincerity.[61] If through a putative royal birth Joan escaped the stake, and another witch was substituted for her and burned in Rouen that May day in 1431 in order to console the populace, as the supporters of the dame des Armoises argue, then Joan's testimony to the truth of her mission seems weakened on all counts, not least by her refusal of death. Claude des

Armoises's claims have spilled far too much ink, ever since Caze first credited it in 1805, for the story was unmasked as soon as it began; its appeal lies with the ever-proliferating numbers of conspiracy theorists.[62] But at the same time, if Joan had survived, it should have been happy news for her friends, and the rebuttals should not be inspired by anger that anyone dare impute anything but a gloriously painful martyrdom to Joan.

Simultaneously, Joan's resoluteness in death when, knowing that such a declaration would cost her her life, she proclaimed she had heard her voices again (the *responsio mortifera*), is often diminished in the interests of promoting her childlikeness. Some rehabilitation witnesses, trying to exculpate Joan from the moral disgrace of her attachment to male dress, suggested that she had been tricked into wearing it again by Cauchon. He removed her woman's dress, they declared, and left her boy's clothes in her cell (see Chapter 7).

This interpretation fails to account, however, for her other proud affirmation that she had also heard her voices again, an equally serious reversal of her earlier disavowals, which had included forswearing her male costume. But the substituted dress is a very popular trope in Joan's story and is often used to powerful pathetic effect. Marco de Gastyne, for instance, in his scrupulous and exciting reconstruction of 1926, *La Merveilleuse Vie de Jeanne d'Arc*, one of the last of the silent films, concentrates on this stealthy exchange of clothing, made while Joan sleeps in innocence, and shows it to be the immediate pretext used to burn her. Though his film is very moving, this version of the story pictures Joan as much less heroic, much less eager to die for her principles and her vision. It adds the piquancy of terror and unwillingness. She is cheated, designated, a lamb to the slaughter, not "Cato's daughter."[63]

Our concept of a fitting end unites ideas about morality and aesthetics within a framework of a shared idea about time. The life and death of Joan of Arc have been told since 1431 according to ancient laws of narrative in the West: the hero must die before his time. But this is only one way to tell a story or construct a moral tale: the life of Buddha encompasses a normal death that does not detract from his witness to truth.

The Japanese entertain a wise concept, very different from the Christian concept of redemption. Like our idea of martyrdom, it has application to both theology and aesthetics and through them shapes the moral view of the universe. Their word is *Utsuroi,* and it means, at face value, the point of change. It locates beauty at the moment when it is altered. It implies an acceptance of flux and of transition, for it means that it is not the beauty of the cherry blossom that gives the highest pleasure, but the knowledge of its evanescence. The fugitive emptiness between one palpable state and another; the shadow's leaping lack of substance; the ephemeral dappling of light under trees; variations that are undone on the instant—all these answer to the idea of *Utsuroi.* It depends on an understanding that time is not linear, not one event after another in a chain, but an overlapping sequence of the same shapes, as in a shaken kaleidoscope.[64]

Joan's story has been told and told again, and, with the exception of Péguy's illuminated use of circularity in his *Mystère* recitative, the narrators have obeyed the aesthetic law of a beginning, a middle and an end, with its moral import that what is desirable is unambiguous, firm, unchanging and intellectually retrievable from the seething flux of history and time.

This has resulted in another, serious limitation, which has weighty repercussions for our inheritance. Because Joan of Arc is a woman, her story has been told within the terms of the available lexicon of female types, which is restricted. We are very inelastic in our mental attitudes and conform unknowingly all the time to conventional classification systems. With many phenomena, including women, attitudes are confined to certain *topoi,* and breaking out beyond them is difficult. It is, for instance, difficult for people brought up to count in a decimal system to grasp the octal system used today by computers, by which only the numbers 1 to 7 are used, so that 10 symbolises the number 8 in the decimal code, and 11 represents the number 9. The octal system is used to facilitate programming without wastage in the computer's binary logic, but its extremely alien air to noninitiates proves how rigid our cerebral equipment is. By imposing accepted codification upon her uniqueness, whether unconsciously or no—and for the most part authors obeyed the unspoken rules of narrative and female semantics unwittingly—the figure of Joan herself becomes restrictive, another example of heroic virtue that confirms conventional notions of the heroic. Only by paying attention to her unique experience, and by acknowledging that it is at the same time universal, since the experience of every individual is unique, can the mould of received ideas be broken, and only when that mould is shattered can Joan of Arc escape from the confinement of order handed down from generation to generation into the splendour of the unaccountable, the particular and the anarchical. Joan of Arc, in her different manifestations, stands for the opposite of *Utsuroi* and for the yearning in the West for stasis and constancy and comprehensibleness. The conflicts in Joan's story are disregarded; they spoil the simplicity of her heroism. Maurice Maeterlinck, in his poetic drama of 1940, is the only writer who dramatises her despair when she leapt from the tower at Beaurevoir.[65] Her abjuration is almost always omitted altogether. Such doubts undo the hope against fallibility we seem destined to hold. She answers a need that heroes should be people of undeflected purpose, though it would be agreed by most that such people are usually dangerous. She stands for an integrity that is not subject to decay, that was saved from spoiling by a glorious end, and so she can act as the talisman of people or of nations who feel themselves endangered. She has been set up as a stable monolith in an unstable world, and yet all the different uses to which she has been put prove only the vanity of our widespread refusal to accept that it is impossible to trap the idea of virtue within boundaries that will not alter.

Bibliographical Notes

A full bibliography of Joan of Arc and the questions raised by her life would be impossible here; it would treble the size of this book. I have therefore limited myself to giving references to authors I have consulted and suggestions for further reading in the appropriate passages' notes. For a complete bibliography of materials about Joan of Arc until 1894, the reader should consult *Le Livre d'Or de Jeanne d'Arc* (L.A.).

ABBREVIATIONS

Ayroles — *La Vraie Vie de Jeanne d'Arc.* 5 vols. Paris, 1890–1902.

Barrett — *The Trial of Jeanne d'Arc.* A complete translation, with introduction by W. P. Barrett. London, 1931.

Bourgeois — *A Parisian Journal, 1405–99.* Translated by J. Shirley. Oxford, 1968. From *Le Journal d'un Bourgeois de Paris*, edited by A. Tuetey. Paris, 1881.

Ditié — *Ditié de Jehanne d'Arc.* By Christine de Pisan and edited by Angus J. Kennedy and Kenneth Varty. Oxford, 1977.

Douglas Murray — *Jeanne d'Arc, Maid of Orleans.* Set forth in the original documents and edited by T. Douglas Murray. New York, 1902.

L.A. — *Le Livre d'Or de Jeanne d'Arc.* Bibliographie raisonnée et analytique des ouvrages rélatifs à Jeanne d'Arc, edited by Pierre Lanéry d'Arc. Paris, 1894.

NCE — *New Catholic Encyclopedia.* Edited by the Catholic University of America, Washington, D.C. London, 1957.

Pernoud, *Retrial* — *The Retrial of Joan of Arc: The Evidence at the Trial for Her Rehabilitation.* Edited by Régine Pernoud and translated by J. M. Cohen. London, 1955.

Q. — *Procès de condamnation et de réhabilitation de Jeanne d'Arc dite la Pucelle.* Publiés pour la première fois d'après les manuscripts de la Bibliothèque Nationale, suivis de tous les documents historiques qu'on a pu réunir et accompagnés de notes et d'éclaircissements, par Jules Quicherat. 5 vols. Paris, 1841–49.

Rankin-Quintal — *The First Biography of Joan of Arc.* With a chronicle record of a contemporary account, translated and annotated by Daniel Rankin and Claire Quintal. Pittsburgh, 1964.

Scott — *The Trial of Joan of Arc.* Being the verbatim report of the proceedings from the Orleans manuscript, translated by W. S. Scott. London, 1956.

Tisset-Lanhers — *Procès de condamnation de Jeanne d'Arc: Traduction et notes par Pierre Tisset avec le concours de Yvonne Lanhers.* 3 vols. Paris, 1870.

I have chosen between the two English translations of the trial (Barrett and Scott) according to how I judged the accuracy of the tone; the translations of the rehabilitations (Pernoud and Douglas Murray) are both unfortunately incomplete and inadequate in other ways, and the first two volumes of the new French edition by Pierre Duparc for the Société de l'Histoire de France came out in 1978–79, too late for me to use during my research.

I give the date of the session in my references to the trial, so that anyone using a different edition can look them up without difficulty.

CHAPTER I MAID OF FRANCE

1. Quoted in Sister Rosamund Nugent, "Portrait of a Consecrated Woman," in *Greek Christian Literature of the First Four Centuries* (Washington, D.C., 1941), p. 25.

2. The date of her birth is frequently given as 6 January 1412, as if it were known. This is based on Perceval de Boulainvilliers' letter to the duke of Milan (Q. 5:116). But this letter is filled with literary and artistic flourishes, and the Epiphany, the Fête des Rois, is so neatly apt a birthday for Joan of Arc that without other supporting evidence it cannot be taken as certain. See Jules Quicherat, *Aperçus nouveaux* (Paris, 1850), pp. 1 ff. Joan seems not to have known her date of birth. She says she is "about nineteen" on 21 February (Tisset-Lanhers 2:41).

3. Guy de Laval's letter, Q. 4:105–11.

4. Bourgeois, pp. 263–4.

5. 3 March, Tisset-Lanhers 2:95.

6. Comte François de Rilly, "Existerait-il un véritable portrait de Jeanne d'Arc?" *Bulletin de la Societé des Amis du Vieux Chinon*, vol. 6, no. 6 (1961–2), pp. 283–5; Louis Réau, *Iconographie de l'Art Chrétien* 2(3):737–9; l'abbé Paul Guillaume, "Les Fausses Jeanne d'Arc en effigie," *La République du Centre*, 8 May 1964. An equestrian Saint Maurice, now in the Musée de Cluny, Paris, was also identified with Joan of Arc for a very long time.

7. J. Huizinga, *Men and Ideas: History, the Middle Ages, the Renaissance*, trans. James S. Holmes and Hans van Marche (London, 1960); G. B. Shaw, *Saint Joan* (London, 1975), p. 221. The thirst to know more about Joan has uncovered certain corporeal relics: a single black hair, pressed into the seal of a letter to the people of Riom, is often produced as evidence of her unknown colouring. Though the story still circulates, the hair is no longer there, no trace of its imprint remains in the wax, and no one remembers anyone who actually saw it, but only people who knew of someone who had seen it. A suit of armour, now in the Musée de l'Armée, was long alleged to have been hers. Her height was calculated from it at just over five foot. Historians have also reckoned her height from the ells of cloth given to her by the duke of Orleans to make her livery after the raising of the siege. But the armour is of a much later date, and the duke's present is no indication of how much cloth was used. See Le Comte C. de Maleissye, *Les Lettres de Jeanne d'Arc et la prétendue abjuration de St. Ouen* (Paris, 1911); W. S. Scott, *Jeanne d'Arc* (London, 1974), p. 148; for the kind of armour Joan would have worn, see Adrien Harmand, *Jeanne d'Arc, ses costumes, son armure* (Paris, 1929), pp. 219–60; Charles Ffoulkes, "The Armour of Jeanne d'Arc," *Burlington Magazine* 16 (December 1909): 141–46; Régine Pernoud (preface) and Frédérique Duran (photographs), *Dans les pas de Jeanne d'Arc* (Paris, 1956).

Deborah Fraioli, "The Literary Image of Joan of Arc: Prior Influences," from a paper given at the Colloque d'Histoire Médiévale in Orleans in October 1979, and to be published in *Speculum* shortly, gives fascinating insights into the preconceptions of Joan's contemporaries.

8. 22 February, Tisset-Lanhers 2:46.

9. Article VIII (Estivet), ibid. 2:166–7.

10. Pernoud, *Retrial*, p. 225.

11. Ibid., pp. 219–24.

12. M. G. A. Vale, *Charles VII* (London, 1974), pp. 60–9. See below, Chapter 9.

13. Mary Douglas, *Purity and Danger* (London, 1966) and *Natural Symbols* (London, 1973), especially chapter 5, "The Two Bodies," pp. 93–112, are my chief inspiration for these thoughts. For the important place of virginity in the Christian scheme of virtue and its relationship with female achievement and excellence, see John Bugge, *Virginitas: An Essay in the History of the Medieval Ideal* (The Hague, 1975), especially pp. 50 ff., 127 ff. See also Marina Warner, *Alone of All Her Sex* (London, 1976), for the place of the Virgin Mary in the cult of virginity, especially chaps. 3–5.

The etymology of the word *virgin* is not known for certain. There is an often repeated guess that it comes from *vir-egeo*, "I lack a man." But this is undoubtedly wrong. The most plausible argument derives *virgin* from the Greek ὀργή (*orge*), "impulse" or "passion," and from the verb ὀργά-ω (*orga-o*), "to swell, to be puffed up." This is the same root as that for *orgy*, and both are related to the Sanskrit *ūrg*, *ūrgá*, *ūrgás* meaning "fullness of power, sap, energy." This possible root gives both *virga* (a rod or stem) and *virgo* (a young girl).

14. See under individual saints' feast days, in Jacopus de Voragine, *The Golden Legend*, ed. and trans. Granger Ryan and Helmut Ripperger (New York, 1941, 1969). See also William Caxton, trans., *The Golden Legend of the Lives of the Saints*, 8 vols. (London, 1900).

15. O. B. Hardison, Jr., *Christian Rite and Christian Drama in the Middle Ages* (Baltimore, 1969), pp. 35–79; B. L. Manning, *The People's Faith in the Time of Wyclif* (London[?], 1919).

16. Douglas Murray, p. 309.

17. Ibid., p. 205; Pernoud, *Retrial*, pp. 176–7.

18. Pernoud, *Retrial*, pp. 197–8.

19. Ibid., p. 201.

20. Ibid., p, 134.

21. Ibid., p. 75.

22. Ibid., p. 177.

23. Ibid., p. 149.

24. Ibid., p. 96.

25. Ibid., pp. 90–2.

26. René de Cériziers, *Jeanne d'Arc, ou L'Innocence affligée* (Paris, 1639), pp. 176–7.

27. Ibid., p. 181.

28. Evidence of Jean Pasquerel, in Pernoud, *Retrial*, p. 140.

29. T. E. Crane, ed., *The Exempla or Illustrative Stories from the Sermones Vulgares of Jacques de Vitry* (New York, 1971).

30. Evidence of Jean d'Aulon, in Ayroles 4:215.

31. *Almanach de Gotha* (1822), p. 63.

32. Jules Michelet, *Histoire de France*, vol. 5 (Paris, 1844), p. 53.

33. See Peter Brown, "Society and the Supernatural: A Medieval Change," *Daedalus* (Spring 1975), pp. 133–51.

34. Pernoud, *Retrial*, p. 176.
35. Johannes Wier, "De Praestigiis Daemonum," in Julia O'Faolain and Lauro Martines, *Not in God's Image* (London, 1973), pp. 212–3.
36. Katharina Dalton, *Once a Month* (London, 1979), pp. 25–34; Paula Weideger, *Female Cycles* (London, 1979), pp. 17–25; Penelope Shuttle and Peter Redgrove, *The Wise Wound* (London, 1978), pp. 19–94; see also Rosemary Dinnage, "The Starved Self," *New York Review of Books,* 22 February 1979.
37. 24 February, Tisset-Lanhers 2:60.
38. Evidence of Jean Tiphaine, a doctor, in Pernoud, *Retrial*, p. 163.
39. Martin de Saint Gilles, *Commentaries on the Amphorions of Hippocras* (Geneva, 1971), ed. Droz, quoted in Marie-Christine Ponchelle, *L'Hybride*, in "Bisexualité et différence des sexes," *Nouvelle Revue de Phychoanalyse,* no. 7 (Spring 1973), pp. 49–61.
40. 21 February, Tisset-Lanhers 2:38.
41. 12 March, ibid. 2:126.
42. 24 March, ibid. 2:148.
43. See Song of Solomon 7:3, 6:8, and Genesis 24:43, where *'almah* is used of Rebecca before her marriage to Isaac; and Isaiah 7:14 and Matthew 1:23 where the same word is used of the Virgin Mary.
44. In Old French, out of a sample of 1,394 uses, *pucelle* specifically means "virgin" in 1.79% of cases and the Virgin Mary herself in 2.01%. In Middle French, it is used more often to denote a virgin (13.25% of a sample of 83 uses) and Mary herself (19.28%). A. Grisay, G. Laris, and M. Dubois-Stasse, *Les Dénominations de la femme dans les anciens textes littéraires français* (Liége, 1969), pp. 156–66.
45. Eustache Deschamps, *Poésies morales et historiques*, ed. G.-A. Crapelet (Paris, 1832).
46. E.g., Baltimore Museum, 71.264: an early fourteenth-century ivory casket covered with Arthurian scenes. Ivory mirrors, also bridal presents, are sometimes decorated with the same motif.
47. Grisay, Laris, and Dubois-Stasse, op. cit., p. 159.
48. "Effeuillée comme la rose, secouée comme la prune, mangée comme le rat des champs, fânée comme la fleur de l'anémone pulsatile," from Georges Duby and Armand Vallon, eds., *Histoire de la France rurale*, vol. 2, *Le Temps des malheurs*, by H. Neveux, J. Jacquart et al., under the direction of E. Le Roy Ladurie (Paris, 1975), p. 500.
49. Quoted in Bugge, op. cit., p. 127.
50. Pernoud (Neveux), *Retrial*, p. 88; Douglas Murray, pp. 269–70.
51. N. Valois, *Jeanne d'Arc et la prophetie de Marie Robine, mélanges Paul Fabre* (Paris, 1902), pp. 452–67.
52. *Gallorum pulli throno bella parabunt.*
    Ecce beant bella, fert tunc vexilla Puella
    in Ayroles, 1:495–9; see also Q. 4:478 for the Scots chronicler Walter Bower, who attributed the same lines to Merlin.
53. Keith Thomas, *Religion and the Decline of Magic* (London, 1973), pp. 467, 471, 682–7; Rupert Taylor, *The Political Prophecy in England* (New York. 1911), pp. 1–47, 83–107.
54. See Rose Rigaud, *Les Idées féministes de Christine de Pisan* (Neuchâtel, 1911).
55. *Ditié*, pp. 43–4, 69; *Chronique d'Antonio Morosini*, ed. G. Lefèvre-Pontalis (Paris, 1902), 4:316–27, lists the differently attributed prophecies of Joan's day, including cryptograms; see Yvonne Lanhers, "Jeanne d'Arc vue par ses contemporains," *Bul-*

letin de la Société des Amis du Vieux Chinon, vol. 8, no. 3 (1979), p. 278; Deborah Fraioli, "The Literary Image of Joan of Arc," paper kindly lent by the author.

56. 24 February, Tisset-Lanhers 2:68.

57. Durand Laxart was married to Jeanne la Vauseul, daughter of Joan's mother's sister, Aveline of Vouthon. For the little we know of him, see Tisset-Lanhers 2:48.

58. Pernoud, *Retrial,* pp. 66–7.

59. Ibid., pp. 75–6.

60. Other prophecies circulated and were brought to bear on Joan's emergence from the obscurity of Domremy. All concerned a virgin. Mathieu Thomassin, who wrote *A Chronicle of the Times* soon after 1456 for the then Dauphin Louis, Charles's son, quotes another verse in connexion with Joan: "*Descendet virgo dorsum sagittarii et flores virgineos obscurabit.*" (A virgin will descend on the back of the archer, and the virgin flowers will be darkened). "*Ex nemore canuto eliminabatur puella*" ("Out of the oak wood will be brought forth a maid"), wrote Merlin, according to the Inquisitor Bréhal. The lines he cites come from Geoffrey of Monmouth's *De Prophetiis Merlinii,* but Bréhal had edited to fit them to Joan's case; see Deborah Fraioli, op. cit., and Galfridi de Monemuta, *Vita Merlini,* eds. Francisque Michel and Thomas Wright (Paris, 1837), pp. 69–70. So many prophecies associated with Joan indicate the strength of a confused oral tradition, transcribed in different forms by different hearers. See Q. 3:334. Ayroles 1:495–9 gives a translation in modern French of Bréhal's *Recollectio* on the subject of prophecies concerning Joan.

61. Pernoud, *Retrial,* pp. 153–74.

62. Three officials of the court, Nicolas Taquel, Guillaume Manchon and Jean Massieu, gave evidence that Nicolas Loiselleur gained Joan's confidence by pretending to be a local Lorraine man and confessing her in gaol. They alleged he was spying for Cauchon, who was a close friend, and while Joan confided in him, Warwick and Cauchon eavesdropped in the room next door. The notaries reported that they had refused to accept as evidence Joan's conversation in these circumstances. Thomas de Courcelles, independently of the court officials, corroborates this cruel deceit, saying that Loiselleur visited Joan "in disguise" and heard her confession. There is, of course, a problem about the authenticity of some of the rehabilitation testimony. (Ibid., pp. 38–40; Tisset-Lanhers 2:413–14, 3:23–4.)

63. Raymond Mauny, "Le Viol de Jeanne d'Arc dans sa prison," *Bulletin de la Société des Amis du Vieux Chinon,* vol. 8, no. 3 (1979), pp. 343–5; Douglas Murray, p. 257.

64. Carl Dreyer's film (1927–28) was recreated in 1952 by the film historian Lo Duca. The original negative had been destroyed, and the few prints that survived had deteriorated in quality. While researching something else, Lo Duca found another negative and, with the help of lip readers, reconstructed the script of Dreyer's film, which had been written in collaboration with the interesting writer Joseph Delteil, author of the poetic *Jeanne d'Arc* (Paris, 1925). He also added a new sound track, with the famous Albinoni *Adagio* at full yearning volume, Vivaldi, Scarlatti, Bach and Palestrina. Dreyer himself had used only plain chant. The version we see today is therefore partly Lo Duca's creation. Dreyer did, however, give him his written permission, and certainly the extraordinary intensity of his images is enhanced, not lessened, by the ecstatic, almost fanatical religious music.

65. Evidence of Maugier Leparmentier, Jean Fabri, Guillaume de la Chambre, Jean Riquier, Pierre Cusquel, Isambart de la Pierre, in Pernoud, *Retrial,* pp. 187–9.

66. Ibid., p. 190.

67. Ibid.

68. The chaplain is converted from his bigotry and shrieks desperately: "I will go pray among her ashes. I am no better than Judas: I will hang myself" (G. B. Shaw, *Saint Joan* [London, 1975], scene VI, p. 142).

69. Douglas Murray, p. 212.

70. Pernoud, *Retrial*, p. 190.

71. *Comme on voit quelquefois entre un faisceau d'espines*
    Une rose rougir en ses feuilles crespines.
    R. P. Fronton-du-Duc, *L'Histoire tragique de la Pucelle d'Orléans* (Pont-à-Mousson, 1581), Act V; L.A., no. 654; q.v. F. Bouquet, *Jeanne d'Arc au château de Rouen* (Rouen, 1865), p. 164: "*Cor superata flammas, superatque Maria Draconem.*"

72. Rev. Francis M. Wyndham, *The Maid of Orleans: Her Life and Mission* (London and Orleans, 1894), p. 82. P. V. Delaporte, S.J., *Récits et légendes* (Paris, 1893), is a collection of poems written expressly against freethinking atheists and materialists. It ran to several editions in that time of passionately taken sides. In a poem called "Le Cœur de Jeanne d'Arc," a messenger arrives at Domremy to give the news of Joan's death to her mother. Isabelle Romée decides to visit Rouen and the site of her daughter's martyrdom. There, in the remains of the pyre, she finds "*un reste de chaleur*"—her heart—which she carries off. This then becomes, in Delaporte's poem, an image of the Church living still in France:
    > *Partout te [l'Eglise] suit l'exil, l'insulte, l'esclavage;*
    > *Tu passes et tu vis partout. C'est qu'en tout lieu,*
    > *Dans ton sein immortel bat le cœur de ton Dieu.*

    Curiously enough, a similar story is told about Shelley's heart. His friend Trelawny arranged his cremation on the shore in Italy, as he had wanted. He wrote later: "The fire was so fierce as to produce a white heat on the iron, and to reduce its content to grey ashes. The only portions that were not consumed were some fragments of bones, the jaw, and the skull, but what surprised us all, was that the heart remained entire. In snatching this relic from the fiery furnace, my hand was severely burnt; and had anyone seen me do the act I should have been put in quarantine" (*The Oxford Book of Literary Anecdotes* [London, 1977], p. 195).

73. René Char, *Jeanne qu'on Brûla Verte* (Paris, 1956): *Taille en rectangle vertical comme une planche de noyer. Les bras longs et vigoreux. Des mains romanes tardives. Pas de fesses. Elles se sont cantonnées dès la première décision de guerroyer. Le visage était le contraire d'ingrat. Un ascendant émotionnel extraordinaire. Un vivant mystère humanisé. Pas de seins. La poitrine les a vaincus. Deux bouts durs seulement. Le ventre haut et plat. Un dos comme un tronc de pommier, lisse et bien dessiné, plus nerveux que musclé, mais dur comme la corne d'un bélier. Ses pieds! Après avoir flâné au pas d'un troupeau bien nourri, nous les regardons s'élever soudain, battre des talons les flancs de chevaux de combat, bousculer l'ennemi, tracer l'emplacement nomade du bivouac, enfin souffrir de tous les maux dont souffre l'âme mise au cachot puis au supplice.*

    Voici ce que cela donne en trait de terre: "*Verte terre de Lorraine—Terre obstiné des batailles et de sièges—Terre sacrée de Reims—Terre fade, épouvantable du cachot—Terre des immondes—Terre vue* en bas *sous le bois du bûcher—Terre flammée—Terre peut-être toute bleue dans le regard horrifié—Cendres.*"

    Reprinted in René Char, *Recherche de la base et du sommet* (Paris, 1971), pp. 50–1. Cited by kind permission of the author.

CHAPTER 2   A DIVIDED REALM

1. *Quele chose est tant dure comme*
   De perdre son propre pais
   De qui l'amour plus douce a homme
   Est que rien, s'il n'est fol niais?
   O naturele amour non faincte,
   Qui d'or fin est plus precieuse . . .
   Robert Blondel, *La Complainte des bons Français*, in Héron, ed., *Société de l'histoire de la Normandie* (1891–93), vol. 1, chap. 17, p. 93.
2. Mary Douglas, *Natural Symbols* (London, 1973) and *Purity and Danger* (London, 1966), passim, for relationship of body image to society.
3. Bryan Wilson, *The Noble Savages: The Primitive Origins of Charisma and Its Contemporary Survival* (London, 1975), pp. 94–5.
4. See Georges Duby and Armand Vallon, eds., *Histoire de la France rurale*, vol. 2. *Le Temps des malheurs*, by H. Neveux, J. Jacquart et al., under the direction of E. Le Roy Ladurie (Paris, 1975); Marcellin Defourneaux, *La Vie quotidienne au temps de Jeanne d'Arc* (Paris, 1952); George Holmes, *Europe: Hierarchy and Revolt, 1320–1450* (London, 1975); Maurice Keen, *Pelican History of Medieval Europe* (London, 1969); P. S. Lewis, *Later Medieval France: The Polity* (London, 1968); Denys Hay, *Europe in the Fourteenth and Fifteenth Centuries* (London, 1966); Kenneth Fowler, ed., *The Hundred Years War* (London, 1971), especially Philippe Contamine, "The French Nobility and the War," pp. 135–62; E. Perroy, *The Hundred Years War* (London, 1962).
5. Règine Pernoud, *Jeanne devant les Cauchons* (Paris, 1970), p. 8.
6. Defourneaux, op. cit., p. 167; Bourgeois, p. 355, describes the *écorcheurs*' continuing activities in 1444.
7. Defourneaux, op. cit., p. 229.
8. Philip Ziegler, *The Black Death* (London, 1969), pp. 26–7.
9. P. S. Lewis, *The Recovery of France in the Fifteenth Century* (London, 1974), p. 28. Jules Michelet, *Histoire de France*, vol. 5 (Paris, 1844), pp. 216–17, wrote a fine threnody for the times: "*Les Anglais avaient beau se retirer, la France continuait de s'exterminer elle-même. Les provinces du Nord devenaient un désert, les landes gagnaient; au centre, nous l'avons vu, la Beauce se couvrait de broussailles, deux armées s'y cherchèrent et se trouvèrent à peine. Les villes où tout le peuple des campagnes venait chercher l'asile, dévoraient cette foule miserable et n'en restaient pas moins desolées. Nombre de maison étaient vides, on ne voyait que portes closes qui ne s'ouvraient plus, les pauvres tiraient de ces maison tout ce qu'ils pouvaient pour se chauffer. La ville se brûlait elle-même. . . .*"
10. Duby and Vallon, op. cit., p. 74; Holmes, op. cit., p. 109.
11. Symon des Phares, *Recueil des plus célèbres astrologues*, ed. E. Wickersheimer (Paris, 1929), p. 243.
12. Blondel, op. cit., pp. 69–70.
13. Fernand Braudel, *Capitalism and Material Life 1400–1800*, trans. Miriam Kochan (London, 1973), p. 129.
14. Q. 5:105:11.
15. Georges Bataille, ed., *Le Procès de Gilles de Rais: Les Documents* (Paris, 1965), Intro.
16. Pierre de Giac had been drowned in 1427; see M. G. A. Vale, *Charles VII* (London, 1974), pp. 39, 41.

17. André Bossuat, "The Re-Establishment of Peace in Society during the Reign of Charles VII," in Lewis, *Recovery*, p. 65.

18. Perceval de Cagny is the chief source on D'Alençon's life; Q. 4:1–93, for his adventures during Joan's career; see Vale, *Charles VII*, pp. 74–88, 154–62, 217, for vicissitudes of his relationship with Charles.

19. Vale, *Charles VII*, p. 87.

20. Pernoud, *Retrial*, p. 106.

21. Q. 4:317. This scene was the unusual subject of a painting done by Edward Toudouze (d. 1907) and presented at the Salon in Paris in 1905, as a cartoon for a tapestry commissioned by the Grande Chambre du Parlement de Rennes. It is a magnificent neo-Renaissance work, complete with *trompe l'œil* setting between marble Corinthian columns. "Jeanne d'Arc et sa Légende," exhibition at Musée des Beaux Arts de Tours, April–May 1979, fig. 12.

22. "Chronique de la Pucelle," Q. 4:240; "Journal du siège," ibid. 4:175.

23. Vale, *Charles VII*, pp. 35–40; Andrew Lang, *The Maid of France* (London, 1908), pp. 21–23.

24. Bourgeois, pp. 325, 330–31.

25. P. S. Lewis, "Decayed and Non-Feudalism in Later Medieval France," *Bulletin of the Institute of Historical Research* 37 (1964): 167.

26. La Hire's nickname has been derived from *ira*, Latin for "rage." This is apt, if picturesque. It probably comes rather from the name of a tool used for tamping down paving stones. For Vignolles's and Xaintrailles's exploits, see Duby and Vallon, op. cit., p. 51; Michelet, op. cit., p. 218, who tells us that La Hire gave his name to the Knave of Hearts in French; Robert Boutruche, "The Devastation of Rural Areas," in Lewis, *Recovery*, pp. 34–5.

27. Defourneaux, op. cit., pp. 192–3.

28. Michelet, op. cit., p. 207.

29. Ibid., pp. 47–9; Siméon Luce, *Jeanne d'Arc à Domremy* (Paris, 1886), pp. xxxv ff, l–lxxxviii; Tisset-Lanhers 2:38; Edward Lucie-Smith, *Joan of Arc* (London, 1976), pp. 8–10; Jules Quicherat, *Aperçus Nouveaux* (Paris, 1850), pp. 1–13; however, Tisset-Lanhers 2.48 gives 1301 and the treaty of Bruges as the date the Barrois Mouvant was made over to the king.

30. Article IV (Estivet), in Tisset-Lanhers 2:163.

31. Michelet, op. cit., p. 50; Luce, op. cit., p. xxi.

32. Luce, op. cit., pp. xxix–xxx; Lucie-Smith, op. cit., p. 9.

33. For the enormous and pedantic literature on the subject of Joan's provincial origins, see L.A., nos. 658–84. Michelet wrote that Joan had "*la douceur champenoise, la naiveté mêlée de sens et de finesse, comme vous la trouvez dans Joinville*" (op. cit., p. 48).. Luce also argued fiercely that Joan was from Champagne. Emile Hinzelin, in *La Lorraine, Pure Gloire de France!* (Paris, 1918), gives a poet's passionate plea for Joan's Lotharingian nationality. One of the texts most commonly quoted as early evidence of Joan's Lotharingian origin is Villon's "Ballade des Femmes de Jadis," written around 1450. A victim of nineteenth-century sentimentality about the Middle Ages, its tone has been completely misunderstood, for it is a comic poem, in keeping with Villon's throwaway cynicism and defiance of life's horrors, and not a pious elegy on the transitoriness of things. After Héloïse, for whom, Villon tells us, Abelard was castrated, and Buridan, who was tied up in a sack and thrown into the Seine, and Berthe au Grant Pié (Big-Foot Bertha), Villon turns to Joan. Her end is no less bathetic:

Et Jehanne la bonne Lorraine
Qu'Englois brulèrent a Rouan
Où sont-ils, où, Vierge souveraine?
Mais où sont les neiges d'antan?

(And Joan the good girl from Lorraine, whom the English burned at Rouen . . . Where are they, where, sovereign maid, but where are last year's snows?). François Villon, *Oeuvres poétiques* (Paris, 1964), ed. A. Longman, p. 23. I am extremely grateful to Mrs. Rhoda Sutherland for her comments on this poem in a letter of 26 January 1977: "Did Lorraine suggest itself to him primarily for the rhyme, or is there some possibly snide reference to the region she comes from? An upstart provincial, who didn't last long. . . . This poem, in my opinion, is not meant to be romantically nostalgic, but satiric and comic."

34. Tisset-Lanhers 2:42.
35. Pernoud, *Jeanne devant les Cauchons*, p. 97; Luce, op. cit., p. xxx.
36. Luce, op. cit., p. lxxiv.
37. Pernoud, *Retrial*, p. 63; Douglas Murray, p. 222.
38. Luce, op. cit., pp. lxxii–v.
39. Ibid., pp. 287–89; Tisset-Lanhers 2:45.
40. 22 February, Tisset-Lanhers 2:45; evidence of Bertrand Lacloppe, in Douglas Murray, p. 218; evidence of Gérard Guillemette, in Pernoud, *Retrial*, p. 69.
41. 24 February, Tisset-Lanhers 2:64.
42. Ibid., p. 64.
43. Pernoud, *Retrial*, p. 65.
44. 24 February, Tisset-Lanhers 2:60.
45. 7 June, ibid., p. 365.
46. Pernoud, *Retrial*, pp. 60–1; Douglas Murray, pp. 218–19.
47. Pernoud, *Retrial*, p. 110.
48. Beaupère maintained that her *"conseil"* originated in "natural" causes (Pernoud, *Retrial*, p. 197); Pierre Maurice told Joan that people often distinguished words in the sound of bells (7 June, Tisset-Lanhers 2:365). This type of rationalist view has a long history: John Lingard, a Catholic priest, wrote in his *History of England* (London, 1823) that Joan "mistook for realities the workings of her own imagination. . . . An impartial observer would have pitied and respected the mental delusion with which she was afflicted" (5:78, 90).
49. Duby and Vallon, op. cit., pp. 144–5. Bells were associated too with benevolent magic and were consecrated to make them powerful against evil spirits and against storms raised by demons. See Keith Thomas, *Religion and the Decline of Magic* (London, 1973), pp. 34, 85.
50. 15 March, Tisset-Lanhers 2:137.
51. *Je donnerais Versailles*
Paris et Saint-Denis
Les tours de Notre-Dame
L'clocher de mon pays!
Traditional French musketeers' song.
52. 3 March, Tisset-Lanhers 2:92–3.
53. Ibid., p. 92.
54. Ibid., p. 92–3.
55. Article XVI (Estivet), ibid. 2:178, 3:34.
56. André Bossaut, "Le Parlement de Paris pendant l'occupation anglaise" (*Revue His-*

torique, 229, 1963), pp. 19–40; see also B. J. M. Rowe, "The Grand Conseil under the Duke of Bedford, 1422–35," in *Oxford Essays in Medieval History, presented to H. E. Salter* (Oxford, 1934), pp. 207–34, for Bedford's government.

57. John Barnie, *War in Medieval Society: Social Values and the Hundred Years War, 1337–99* (London, 1977), p. 17.

58. Lent 1435, Bourgeois, p. 300.

59. Louis of Luxembourg, bishop of Thérouanne in Normandy in 1431, attended only one of Joan's interrogations, but was present at her abjuration and her death. He became archbishop of Rouen in 1436, pipping Cauchon to this coveted post. A cardinal in 1440, he left France after Charles's complete recovery and became bishop of Ely, where he lived sumptuously and died in 1443 (Tisset-Lanhers 2:414).

60. Daniel Rankin and Claire Quintal have promised a biography of Pierre Cauchon, which I await eagerly. Meanwhile, for this extraordinary man, see Tisset-Lanhers 2:388–91; Albert Sarrazin, *Pierre Cauchon: Juge de Jeanne d'Arc* (Paris, 1901); P. H. Denifle and E. Chatelain, *Le Procès de Jeanne d'Arc et l'Université de Paris: Memoires de la Société de L'Histoire de Paris* (Paris, 1897), pp. 1–32, especially pp. 16–17; P. Wolff, "Le Théologien Pierre Cauchon de sinistre mémoire," *Economies et Sociétés au Moyen-Age, mélanges offerts à Edouard Perroy* (Paris, 1973).

61. Rankin-Quintal, pp. 54–64, 98.

62. Tisset-Lanhers 2:11–12. The *livre* and the *écu* were both worth 20 *sous tournois*. The *écu* was the gold coin.

63. The three were William Haiton, secretary of King Henry VI's commander (17 times); William Brolbster, a priest from London (3 times); Richard Praty, dean of the Chapel Royal and chancellor of Salisbury cathedral, bishop of Chichester in 1438 (number of attendances not clear). The others were William Alnwick, bishop of Norwich; Henry Beaufort, cardinal of Winchester; John Carpenter, rector of Beaconsfield and a member of Henry VI's staff; Robert Gilbert, later bishop of London; and John Hampton, a priest (Tisset-Lanhers 2:384–5, 387, 402, 421; Vale, op. cit., p. 48). A brilliant discussion of English involvement in the trial is contained in M. G. A. Vale, "Jeanne d'Arc et ses adversaires: la victime d'une guerre civile?", a paper given at Colloque d'Histoire Médiévale, Orleans, October 1979.

64. Tisset-Lanhers 2:385–6. Like a true villain, Beaupère had a mutilated hand; in 1423, he had been injured by bandits on the road between Paris and Beauvais. History does not record a hook, but he did have to obtain a papal dispensation to continue his holy office, since Thomas Aquinas had ruled that the priesthood was barred to the crippled.

65. Douglas Murray, p. 176.

66. Cf. J. Huizinga, *The Waning of the Middle Ages* (London, 1972), p. 36: "Institutions in general are considered as good or as bad as they can be; having been ordained by God, they are intrinsically good, only the sins of men pervert them. What is therefore in need of remedy is the individual soul."

67. "*Celui qui veut échapper à la vie servile ne peut en principe travailler. Il lui faut jouer. Il lui faut s'amuser librement, comme l'enfant: libéré de ses devoirs, l'enfant s'amuse. Mais l'adulte ne peut, comme l'enfant, s'amuser, s'il n'est privilégié. Ceux qui n'ont pas un privilège sont reduits à travailler. Par contre, le privilégié doit faire la guerre. De même que l'homme sans privilège est reduit à travailler, le privilégié, lui, doit faire la guerre. . . . Aux temps de Gilles de Rais, la guerre est toujours le jeu des seigneurs. S'il désole les populations, ce jeu exalte les privilégiés*" (Bataille, op. cit., p. 51).

68. Blondel, op. cit., pp. 94–6, 100–4, 114–16.

69. See Shakespeare, *Henry IV, Part II*, Act IV, Scene 5, Henry's last speech to the future Henry V:

> *God knows, my son,*
> *By what by-paths and indirect crook'd ways*
> *I met this crown; and I myself know well*
> *How troublesome it sat upon my head . . .*
>   *It seem'd to me*
> *But as an honour snatch'd with boisterous hand,*
> *And I had many living to upbraid*
> *My gain of it by their assistances;*
> *Which daily grew to quarrel and to bloodshed,*
> *Wounding supposed peace.*

70. Blondel, op. cit., p. 131.

71. Alain Chartier, *Le Quadrilogue invectif*, ed. E. Droz (Paris, 1923).

72. "*Que appelle-je guerre? Ce n'est pas guerre qui en ce royaume ce mayne, c'est une privée roberie, une larrecin habandonné, force publique soub umbre d'armes et violente rapine que faulte de justice et de bonne ordonnance fait estre loisibles. Les armes sont criées et les estendars levez contre les ennemis, mais les exploiz sont contre moy a la destruction de ma povre substance et de ma miserable vie . . .*" (ibid., pp. 18–19).

73. Ibid., p. 26.

74. "*Se le cheval par batre et flageler et le beuf force d'aiguillonner durement tirent hors leurs voitures des effondrez et des mauvais passaiges, ainsi croy je que le flael de divine justice . . . nous doye esmouver a prendre couraige pour nous horsgecter de ceste infortune*" (ibid., p. 40).

75. "*La juste venjance que Dieu prent de noz faultes*" (ibid., p. 4).

CHAPTER 3 THE KING AND HIS CROWN

1. Act III, Scene 3.

2. John Lydgate, *The Fall of Princes*, Book IX, ll. 3222–3, quoted in John Barnie, *War in Medieval Society: Social Values and the Hundred Years War, 1337–99* (London, 1977), p. 9; Maurice Keen, *The Laws of War in the Late Middle Ages* (London, 1965), chap. 5. passim.

3. Edouard Perroy, *The Hundred Years' War* (Paris, 1945; rep. London, 1962); M. G. A. Vale, *Charles VII* (London, 1974), pp. 3-44.

4. 22 February, Tisset-Lanhers 2:47, 56; 1 March, ibid., p. 86. Article XVII, ibid., p. 179.

5. Le Maistre appeared reluctant to take responsibility for the trial and began presiding in Rouen at Cauchon's side as judge only at the session of March 13. Cauchon, on 22 February, had asked Jean le Graverent, Le Maistre's superior, to insist that Le Maistre deputise for the inquisitor in person. See Tisset-Lanhers 2:410, 3:57–8, for the evidence at the rehabilitation of Le Maistre's hesitations.

6. 10 March, ibid. 2:107–9.

7. Ibid. 1:115–17, 2:108–9.

8. Ibid. 2:109.

9. 12 March, ibid., p. 112.

10. 13 March, ibid., p. 121.

11. 13 March, ibid., p. 120.

12. 7 June, ibid., pp. 363–4.

13. Pernoud, *Retrial,* pp. 38–47, quotes the evidence of the notaries Guillaume Manchon, Nicolas Taquel and Boisguillaume about the conditions in which they took down the evidence. All three asserted their honesty in recording the proceedings and putting their signatures to the completed sheets of the drafted manuscripts of the trial. But given the political climate in 1450 and 1455, it is not surprising they wished to make it clear they had acted under duress and with extreme scrupulousness.

14. Q. 4:277–8.

15. Vale, *Charles VII,* pp. 21–2, 51–3.

16. Ibid., p. 32.

17. Jean de Terre Rouge (Johannes de Terra Rubea), *Contra rebelles suorum regum,* ed. J. Bonaud (Lyon, 1526), quoted in Ernst Kantorowicz, *The King's Two Bodies* (Princeton, 1957), pp. 219–20; see P. S. Lewis, "Decayed and Non-Feudalism in Later Medieval France," *Bulletin of the Institute of Historical Research,* 37 (1964): 174.

18. Pierre Marot, "La Génèse d'un roman: Jean Caze, l'inventeur de la 'bâtardise' de Jeanne d'Arc," lecture, Colloque d'Histoire Médiévale, Orleans, October 1979, discussed the origin of the tradition in the phantasmagoric imagination of Pierre Caze, author of *La Verité sur Jeanne d'Arc* of 1819.

19. See L.A., nos. 195, 1786.

20. See 21 February, Tisset-Lanhers 2:38–9, when Joan declares that she was born at Domremy and that her parents' names were Jacques Darc and Isabelle Romée; she says this just after she had made a tremendous business of taking an oath, because she did not want to have to reveal certain things. Her birthplace and parents' names caused her no difficulty, however.

21. Shakespeare, *Henry VI, Part III,* Act III, Scene 1.

22. For recognition scene, see evidence of Simon Charles, in Pernoud, *Retrial,* pp. 82–3.

23. 22 February, Tisset-Lanhers 2:56.

24. Pernoud, *Retrial,* p. 83.

25. G. B. Shaw, *Saint Joan* (London, 1975), Act I, Scene 2.
    BLUEBEARD: We can easily find out whether she is an angel or not. Let us arrange when she comes that I shall be the Dauphin, and see whether she will find me out.
    CHARLES: Yes: I agree to that. If she cannot find the blood royal I will have nothing to do with her.
    Cf. Jean Anouilh, *L'Alouette* (Paris, 1953), pp. 87–8.

26. Ayroles 1:53 ff.

27. See Kantorowicz, op. cit., pp. 341–2.

28. Janet Nelson, "Inauguration Rituals," in *Early Medieval Kingship,* eds. P. H. Sawyer and I. N. Wood (Leeds, 1977), pp. 50–71.

29. See Marc Bloch, *The Royal Touch, Sacred Monarchy and Scrofula in England and France,* trans. J. E. Anderson (London, 1973).

30. "Le Miroir des Rois," exhibition at Musée de la Monnaie, Paris, February 1978.

31. Bourgeois, p. 270; cf. Richard II's entry into London in 1377, quoted by Vita Sackville-West, *Joan of Arc* (London, 1973), p. 297.

32. Damien Walne and Joan Flory. *Oh, What a Beautiful Lady! The Message of Fatima* (Devon, 1976).

33. Jean d'Aulon's evidence, in Pernoud, *Retrial,* p. 126; Louis de Coutes's evidence ibid., p. 135.

34. 27 February, Tisset-Lanhers 2:78. The military historian Ferdinand Lot considers that there were around 3,500 men at Orleans (*L'Art militaire et les armées du Moyen Age* [Paris, 1961]); but Marcellin Defourneaux, *La Vie quotidienne au temps de Jeanne d'Arc* (Paris, 1952), p. 186, considers that the garrison at Orleans numbered

700 in toto and the assailants 3,500 at most. See also Rankin-Quintal, pp. 54–9, 77–8. Numbers in medieval history are notoriously difficult and variable. A tendency to exaggerate is more common than the opposite.

35. Jean Gerson, *De Quadam Puella*, Q. 3:298.

36. *Ditié*, pp. 32–3.

37. Ayroles 1:40–52.

38. Felix Sejourne, quoted in *Animadversiones, Aurelianem Beatificationis et Canonizationis Servae Dei Ioannae de Arc Puellae Aurelianiensis Nuncupatei; Positio Super Introductione Causae* (Rome, 1893), and quoted and translated in William Searle, *The Saint and the Sceptics: Joan of Arc in the Works of Mark Twain, Anatole France, and Bernard Shaw* (Detroit, 1976), p. 171.

39. *Chose est bien digne de memoire*
    Que Dieu, par une vierge tendre,
    Ait adès voulu (chose est voire!)

    Sur France si grant grace estendre.
    O quel honneur à la couronne
    De France par divine preuve!
    Car par les graces qu'Il lui donne
    Il appert comment Il l'apreuve . . .
    Ditié, pp. 30, 42.

40. Pernoud, *Retrial*, p. 105.

41. The role played by popular acclaim in Joan's acceptance as a saviour is extremely problematic. Thomas Keneally, in his novel *Blood Red, Sister Rose* (London, 1974), develops imaginatively a thesis suggested by Anatole France: Yolande of Anjou, mother-in-law of the Dauphin, used agents to groom Joan for the role and then organised a claque of support through informers and more agents to rally the people to accept Joan. But this is fanciful, rather than factual; possible rather than probable. Vale, op. cit., gives strong arguments for the influence of the Anjou family at court. Dunois's evidence and the accusations that Joan allowed herself to be adored by the crowds show that the enthusiasm she excited was enormous, from the very first days after she entered Orleans.

42. The need for miraculous affirmation is even reflected in the freethinker Shaw's play, in which a scene actually takes place by the banks of the Loire:
    DUNOIS (looking at the pennon): The wind has changed. (He crosses himself) God has spoken. (Kneeling and handing his baton to Joan) You command the king's army. I am your soldier.
    Act I, Scene III (London, 1975), pp. 84–5.

43. Charles, duke of Orleans, was born in 1391, taken prisoner at Agincourt in 1415, and kept in the Tower of London for twenty-five years. There he continued to write tender, melancholy ballads and, on his return to France, created a literary court at Blois. He died in 1465 and was the father of Louis XII of France. Joan's desire to bring him back was not helped by the rivalries of the great French lords: Charles did nothing to ransom his first cousin. It was the duke of Burgundy who arranged his freedom. Vale, *Charles VII*, pp. 77–8; 22 February, Tisset-Lanhers 2:54; 12 March, ibid., p. 116, where Joan says she would have taken many English prisoners to exchange for Charles of Orleans, then sailed to England to fetch him back, but that she needed three years' freedom to accomplish it.

44. Pernoud, *Retrial*, p. 124.

45. Bourgeois, p. 233.

46. Régine Pernoud, *Joan of Arc*, trans. Edward Hyams (London, 1964), p. 97.

47. Pernoud, *Retrial*, pp. 127–34.

48. Ibid., p. 128.

49. Evidence of Simon Charles, in Douglas Murray, p. 292; Pernoud, *Retrial*, p. 84.

50. On the battle of Orleans, see "Journal du siège," Q. 4:94–167; J. F. C. Fuller. "The Relief of Orleans," in *The Decisive Battles of the Western World* (London, 1954), 1:477–97; Lang, op. cit., pp. 120–40, gives a lucid account; see also Pernoud, *Retrial*, pp. 70–107.

51. "Journal du siège," Q. 4:159–62, 169. Dunois's evidence, in Pernoud, *Retrial*, pp. 106–7.

52. Morosini, *Chronique d'Antonio Morosini*, ed. G. Lefèvre-Pontalis (Paris, 1902), referring to the duke of Burgundy's reaction to news of the relief of Orléans: "*C'est son intérêt que les Anglais, qui sont puissants, soient quelque peu battus*" (3:37).

53. Charles Wayland Lightbody, *The Judgements of Joan* (London, 1961), p. 99.

54. 27 February, Tisset-Lanhers 2:78. This declaration was ignored by the assessors at Rouen, who charged Joan with "cruel thirst for human blood" (ibid., pp. 159, 179). But she was not accused of committing any specific murders, killing anyone herself, only of allowing the knight Franquet d'Arras to be killed (ibid., p. 203).

55. Ibid., pp. 185–6; Barrett, pp. 165–6.

56. 1 March, Tisset-Lanhers 2:82–3.

57. See Henri Wallon, *Jeanne d'Arc* (Paris, 1876), for reproduction of the document giving Joan this command.

58. "Journal du siège," Q. 4:170–3.

59. Ibid., pp. 174–6.

60. Monstrelet, "Chronique," Q. 4:372–4; Louis de Coutes gave evidence that Joan was "greatly annoyed" not to lead the advance guard (Pernoud, *Retrial*, p. 137).

61. 15 March, Tisset-Lanhers 2:133.

62. Pernoud, *Retrial*, p. 106.

63. Dunois's evidence, in Pernoud, *Retrial*, p. 108. Joan fell on her knees before Charles and begged him not to delay his crowning any longer, at Loches, in June 1429 ("Journal du siège," Q. 4:167–68).

64. Pernoud, *Retrial*, p. 109.

65. "Journal du siège," Q. 4:180–4.

66. Ibid., pp. 185–6; Monstrelet, "Chronique," Q. 4:380.

67. Nelson, op. cit., pp. 51–61.

68. See Morosini, op. cit., 3:161; Lang, op. cit., p. 183.

69. Q. 5:128.

70. Dunois's evidence, in Pernoud, *Retrial*, p. 108.

71. Q. 5:186.

72. "Journal du siège," Q. 4:187; Monstrelet, "Chronique," Q. 4:381.

73. Marc Bloch, *Les Rois haumaturges*, is the masterpiece on the development of the custom of touching for the king's evil. See also Marc Bloch, "Two Pieces of Political Iconography," *Journal of Warburg and Courtauld Institutes* 27 (1964); and Georges Peyronnet, "Un problème de légitimité: Charles VII et le toucher des écrouelles," lecture, Colloque d'Histoire Médiévale, Orleans, October 1979, speculated that the secret verbal formula, transmitted from king to king at death, had not been given to Charles VII by his father and that, therefore, Charles made no attempt to heal the evil, but only made the pilgrimage. Charles VII's chroniclers do not dwell on the ceremony he performed with the eloquent eulogies that Shakespeare placed on

the lips of Malcolm in *Macbeth*, describing the miracles of Edward the Confessor. Shakespeare was trying to flatter James I, who himself was fascinated by the supernatural powers of mystic kingship (*Macbeth*, Act IV, Scene 3).

74. Keith Thomas, *Religion and the Decline of Magic* (London, 1973), p. 231.

75. *"Mes chiers et bons amis les bons et loiaulx franczois de la cité de Rains, Jehanne la pucelle vous fait assavoir de ses nouvelles et vous prie et vous requiert que vous ne faictes nulle doubte en la bonne querelle que elle mayne pour le sang royial; et je vous promeit et certiffi que je ne vous abandonneray point tant que je vivroy et est vroy que le Roy a fait trèves au duc de bourgoigne quinze jours durant par ainsi qu'il li doit rendre la cité de paris paisiblement au chieff de quinze jours. Pourtant ne vous donnez nulle mervoille si je ne y entre si brieffyement; combien que des treves qui ainsi sont faictes je ne suy point conteinte, et ne scey si je les tendroy; maiz si je les tiens ce sera seulement pour garder l'onneur du Roy . . ."* (Le Comte C. de Maleissye, *Les Lettres de Jeanne d'Arc et la prétendue abjuration de St. Ouen* [Paris, 1911], pp. 6–8).

76. 24 February, Tisset-Lanhers 2:57; 13 March, ibid., p. 124; 15 March, ibid., p. 136; Perceval de Cagny, Q. 4:86–88.

77. Bourgeois, pp. 240–1, attributes Joan's failure principally to the violation of a holy day.

78. André Bossuat, "The Re-Establishment of Peace in Society during the Reign of Charles VII," trans. G. F. Martin, in P. S. Lewis, ed., *The Recovery of France in the Fifteenth Century* (London, 1971), pp. 60–81.

79. Bourgeois, p. 268.

80. Joan described the circumstances of her capture (23 May 1430), on 10 March, Tisset-Lanhers 2:105; for map of the terrain at Compiègne, see Lang, op. cit., p. 235. Perceval de Cagny and later chroniclers after him accused William of Flavy, the garrison commander at Compiègne, of closing the town gates against Joan, so that after her skirmish with the besieging forces, she could not gain readmission. See Q. 4:34, 92, 261, 273. This treachery has never been established.

81. Q. 5:168.

82. Bourgeois, p. 268; Norman Cohn, *Europe's Inner Demons* (London, 1975), p. 41.

83. Bourgeois, p. 266.

84. Ibid., p. 268.

CHAPTER 4 PROPHET

1. © Editions Gallimard (Paris, 1946), p. 325.

2. The Armagnac prisoner in Paris whose death decided Joan to deliver Franquet d'Arras up to the local magistrate may have been one of the organisers of an internal Parisian uprising that the Dauphin's party and Joan were counting on to give support to their attack on the city. Joan was possibly hoping to exchange Franquet for him. See *Chronique d'Antonio Morosini*, ed. G. Lefèvre-Pontalis (Paris, 1902), 3:274–5. Even after the plot was unmasked, Joan still hoped that the Parisians would rise on her side.

3. Perrinet Gressart was an independent captain who had governed La Charité as his own since 1423 and gave full allegiance to no one in the civil war. La Trémoille had been captured by him and held to a magnificent ransom. Gressart was a characteristic self-made man of the day: his niece married the uncle of Pope Alexander

VI. Around the time of Joan's attempt to take La Charité, the *Chronique d'Antonio Morosini* denies a rumour that she is dead and affirms that she is still "capable of amazing the whole world" (3:230-2).

4. Huizinga, *The Waning of the Middle Ages* (London, 1972), pp. 176-8. The fifteenth century was a time of saints: in Italy alone, eighty-six saints, alive between 1400 and 1520, have been canonised (Denys Hay, *The Church in Italy in the Fifteenth Century* [Cambridge, 1977], pp. 80-1).

5. See Peter Brown, "A Dark-Age Crisis: Aspects of the Iconoclastic Controversy," *The English Historical Review* 346 (January 1973): 1-34; Arnold van Gennep, "A propos de Jeanne d'Arc," *Religions, Mœurs et Légendes, Essais d'Ethnographie et de Linguistique*, 2d ser. (1900), p. 123, on use of word saint for a living person.

6. Van Gennep, op. cit., pp. 99-100.

7. On Jean d'Aulon's evidence only, in Pernoud, *Retrial*, pp. 132-3.

8. On 9 November 1429, Joan wrote a letter to the citizens of Riom, also on the lower Loire, asking for contributions to her campaign to retake La Charité: "*Chers et bons amis, vous savez bien comment la ville de Saint Pierre le Moustier a esté prinse d'assault; et à l'aide de Dieu, ay entencion de fair vuider les autres places qui sont contraires au roy; mais pour ce que grant despense de pouldres, trait et autres habillmens de guerre a esté faicte devant ladicte ville. . . . je vous prie sur tant que vous aymez le bien et honneur du roy . . . que vueillez incontinant envoyer et aider pour ledit siège, de pouldres salpestre, souffre, trait, arbelestres fortes et d'autres habillemens de guerre.*" The letter is still extant in the Riom city archives (Q. 5:147-8).

9. 3 March, Tisset-Lanhers 2:99.

10. 10 March, ibid., p. 108.

11. 3 March, ibid., p. 100.

12. 3 March, ibid., pp. 99-100.

13. 10 March, ibid., pp. 107-8. Rebecca West, writing of Saint Teresa of Avila's visions, describes vividly the seer's need to share her experience—as in Teresa's case, with members of the Church: "In the Church was such a confirmation of her individual experience as amounted to its infinite multiplication: that the visit of Christ, the presentation of wisdom, are beneficences directed to the highly personal part of the individual, but in the collective experiences of all the other children of the Church, there is proof that the tide of the Godhead can rise higher and higher till it swamps not only a saint's cell but the life there is, that the universe is conquerable by delight, that delight is its destiny, that some day there will be place for pain, and that the part of the individual which partakes of continuity with the rest of the universe rejoices in the salvation of its substance"(*The Strange Necessity* [London, 1928], p. 55). Joan, when she wanted to see Catherine de la Rochelle's vision, wanted to feel her delight.

14. Q. 5:295; Tisset-Lanhers 2:99.

15. Bourgeois, p. 265.

16. Ibid., p. 230.

17. Tisset-Lanhers 3:90; Q. 1:99-100.

18. Marcellin Defourneaux, *La Vie quotidienne au temps de Jeanne d'Arc* (Paris, 1952), pp. 173-4.

19. Paul Johnson, *A History of Christianity* (London, 1976), p. 259.

20. NCE, "John of Capistrano"; Norman Cohn, *Europe's Inner Demons* (London, 1975), pp. 50-3.

21. A caution however: as George Holmes, *Europe: Hierarchy and Revolt, 1320–1450* (London, 1975), p. 156, writes: "The basic difficulty is the relationship between religious ideas and religious movements. . . . The concept of "heresy" which governs the evidence is a very unsatisfactory one for the historians. It is based on abstract criteria of belief and therefore encourages historians to treat religious movements as episodes in the history of thought, which is misleading in the same way as a history of socialism masquerading as a history of the modern working class." Preachers like Brother Richard, Ferrer and Capistrano plumbed emotional depths in their listeners that had nothing to do with the intellectual content of their sermons. In many ways, they could have preached the opposite—fleshly licence, all-loving ecumenism, and Satanism—and had the same effect.

22. Bourgeois, p. 265.

23. Rankin-Quintal, p. 120.

24. 3 March, Tisset-Lanhers 2:97.

25. NCE, "Nicolette Boylet"; Huizinga, op. cit., p. 182; Dominic Devas, *St. Colette*, Catholic Truth Society pamphlet no. B 344 (London, 1934).

26. See Siméon Luce, *Jeanne d'Arc à Domrémy* (Paris, 1886), pp. 254–87; W. S. Scott, *Jeanne d'Arc* (London, 1974), pp. 75–7, 223.

27. Huizinga, op. cit., p. 182; Devas, op. cit., pp. 19–20.

28. Holmes, op. cit., p. 169; and NCE, "Catherine of Siena" and "Bridget of Sweden."

29. See Giuseppe Fatini, ed., *I Fioretti di San Francesco e le lettere di Santa Caterina* (Rome, 1941), pp. 53–135; *The Revelations of Saint Birgitte*, ed. and trans. W. Patterson Cumming (London, 1929).

30. See Millard Meiss, *Painting in Florence and Siena after the Black Death* (New York, 1964), pp. 88–90; Holmes, op. cit., p. 160.

31. André Vauchez, "Jeanne d'Arc et le prophet non-féminin à la fin du XIVe et début du XVe siècle," lecture, Colloque d'Histoire Médiévale, Orleans, October 1979, and "Les Soeurs de Jeanne," *Le Monde*, 6 Jan. 1980; Yvonne Lanhers, "Jeanne d'Arc vue par ses contemporains," *Bulletin de la Société des Amis du Vieux Chinon*, vol. 8, no. 3 (1979), p. 277; R. Jacquin, "Un précurseur de Jeanne d'Arc," *Revue des Deux Mondes*, 15 May 1967.

32. Huizinga, op. cit., pp. 182–3; NCE, "Denis the Carthusian."

33. Philippe de Commynes, "Mémoires," in *Historiens et chroniqueurs du Moyen-Age*, ed. Albert Pauphilet and Edmond Pognon (Paris, 1952), p. 1267.

34. Huizinga, op. cit., pp. 177, 180; NCE, "Francis of Paola"; *Francis of Paola: Letters*, ed. F. Preste (Rome, 1665).

35. See France, op. cit., 1:xxxvi, 2: Appendices ii and iii, for a list of other prophets of Joan's day; Vauchez, op. cit.

36. Keith Thomas, *Religion and the Decline of Magic* (London, 1973), p. 163; see also Keith Thomas, "Women and the Civil War Sects," *Past and Present*, no. 13 (1958), pp. 317–40, for a treatment of the same theme at a later date. There is a most interesting link between prophecy and radical politics. See Christopher Hill, *The World Turned Upside Down* (New York, 1972), pp. 70–85, 223–24.

37. Bryan Wilson, *The Noble Savages: The Primitive Origins of Charisma and Its Contemporary Survival* (London, 1975), passim.

38. Lina Eckenstein, *Women under Monasticism* (Cambridge, 1896), pp. 256–85; NCE, "Hildegard of Bingen" and "Elisabeth of Schönau."

39. Eckenstein, op. cit., p. 256.

40. Ibid., pp. 270–5; J. P. Strachey, ed., *Poem on the Assumption* (Cambridge, 1924), pp. 15–26.

41. Margery Kempe, *Memories of a Medieval Woman,* trans. and ed. Louise Collis (New York, 1964).
42. Robert E. Lerner, *The Heresy of the Free Spirit in the Later Middle Ages* (Berkeley, 1972), pp. 156–74.
43. Ibid., pp. 71–7; Denys Hay, *The Church in Italy in the Fifteenth Century* (Cambridge, 1977), pp. 70–71.
44. H. C. Lea, *The History of the Inquisition of the Middle Ages* (London, 1888), 3:367.
45. Lerner, op. cit., pp. 190–2; Hadewijch d'Anvers, *Ecrits mystiques des Béguines,* ed. Fr. J.–B. P. (Paris, 1954), Intro., for discussion of Bloemardinne, Heylwig and other Beguines whose inspiration was committed to paper; G. G. Coulton, *Life in the Middle Ages* (Cambridge, 1928), 1:146–7, edits a contemporary description of the ecstasies of Christine von Stommeln, another Beguine.
46. Lerner, op. cit., p. 47; Johnson, op. cit., pp. 44, 49–50.
47. 23 February, Tisset-Lanhers 2:63. She said this after the most famous, eloquent reply, when asked if she were in a state of grace: *"Si je n'y suis pas, Dieu m'y mette, et si j'y suis, Dieu m'y maintienne,"* a beautiful paraphrase of a current prayer she is likely to have heard.
48. Article XXXIX, in Tisset-Lanhers 2:201; Article IX (Estivet), ibid., p. 250.
49. 17 March, ibid., 1:169: Letter to the English, Orleans, 29 April.
50. "Journal du siège," Q. 4:125, 128; "Chronique de la Pucelle," ibid., p. 208.
51. 3 March, Tisset-Lanhers 2:98.
52. 13 March, ibid., p. 123.
53. 3 March, ibid., p. 97 (the sense of the passage remains obscure, and it is not certain whether "butterflies" are intended literally); Article II, ibid., p. 161.
54. Article LII, ibid., p. 220.
55. Bibliothèque Nationale Ms. Fr. 7301; Henri Wallon, *Jeanne d'Arc* (Paris, 1876), p. 146.
56. Pernoud, *Retrial,* p. 112.
57. Tisset-Lanhers 2:98–9.
58. 3 March, ibid., pp. 95–7.
59. Pernoud, *Retrial,* p. 92.
60. 1 March, Tisset-Lanhers 2:83.
61. Ibid., p. 79.
62. 10 March, ibid., pp. 104–5.
63. 1 March, ibid., p. 81.
64. The Great Schism had been settled at the Council of Constance in 1417 with the election of Martin V. John XXIII, elected by the schismatic council of Pisa in 1409, was deposed and imprisoned; the pope in Rome, Gregory XII, abdicated to smooth the solution; but Benedict XIII, of the Avignon line, was beyond the council's reach in Spain and enjoying the support of the King of Aragon. He died in 1424; his successor, Clement VIII, resigned in July 1429. This news had not yet reached the count of Armagnac. In 1425, a third anti-pope had styled himself Benedict XIV. No one knew where he was hiding, but his existence was not forgotten. The count was asking Joan which of these three was the true pope (ibid. 3:115–17).
65. Ibid. 2:81.
66. Ibid., pp. 189–90.
67. Ibid., p. 113.
68. Pernoud, *Retrial,* pp. 138–46; Douglas Murray, pp. 281–90.
69. 22 February, Tisset-Lanhers 2:46–7; 9 May, ibid., p. 302.

70. Evidence of Gobertus Thibault, Q. 3:74.
71. Le Comte C. de Maleissye, *Les Lettres de Jeanne d'Arc, et la prétendue abjuration de St. Ouen* (Paris, 1911), pp. 12–13.
72. 22 February, Tisset-Lanhers 2:41.
73. 15 March, ibid., p. 133; 24 February, ibid., p. 63.
74. 1 March, ibid., p. 87; 14 March, ibid., p. 129.

CHAPTER 5 HARLOT OF THE ARMAGNACS

1. Tisset-Lanhers 2:6–7.
2. Ibid., p. 313.
3. Blasphemy, (False) Prophecy, Conjuration of Demons, Heresy, Magic Arts. The preamble to the promoter Jean d'Estivet's list of 70 charges, in which he invites the opinions of lawyers and doctors and theologians, does use the word *sorcière* (ibid., p. 159), but witchcraft never constituted a specific accusation. For invaluable background information, see Richard Kieckhefer, *European Witch Trials* (London, 1976) and Mary Douglas, ed., *Witchcraft: Confessions and Accusations* (London, 1970), pp. xiii–xxxviii. Cf. Douglas's introduction, p. xxv: "What happens when an accusation has been made depends on the state of community politics and on what pattern of relationships needs defining at the time. For witchcraft beliefs are essentially a means of clarifying and affirming social definitions." And Peter Brown's essay, "Sorcery, Demons and the Rise of Christianity," pp. 21–2: "This [occurrence of accusations of witchcraft] is when *two systems of power* are sensed to clash within the one society. On the one hand there is *articulate* power, power defined and agreed upon by every one (and especially by its holders!); authority rested in precise persons; admiration and success gained by recognised channels. Running counter to this there may be other forms of influence less easy to pin down: *inarticulate* power: the disturbing intangibles of social life; the imponderable advantages of certain groups; personal skills that succeed in a way that is unacceptable or difficult to understand. Where these two systems overlap, we may expect to find the sorcerer." Both these general principles apply smoothly to the situation of Joan of Arc, an individual endowed with personal qualities that brought her to "inarticulate" power through unofficial channels in a society that was deeply divided and searching restlessly for clear-cut definitions.
4. G. du Fresne de Beaucourt, *Histoire de Charles VII*, 6 vols. (Paris, 1881–91), 1:p. 171; E. Cosneau, *Le Connétable de Richemont* (Paris, 1886), p. 140; quoted in M. G. A. Vale, *Charles VII* (London, 1974), pp. 29, 39.
5. Georges Bataille, ed., *Le Procès de Gilles de Rais: Les Documents* (Paris, 1965), pp. 224 ff.
6. Vale, op. cit., pp. 155–62.
7. Shakespeare, *Henry VI, Part II*, Act I, Scene 4; Act II, Scenes 3 and 4. See Banquo:
      Thou hast it now: King, Cawdor, Glamis
      All as the weird women promis'd (Act II, Scene 4).
8. Symon des Phares, *Recueil des plus célèbres astrologues*, ed. E. Wickersheimer (Paris, 1929), p. 238.
9. Ibid., p. 239.
10. Hugh Trevor-Roper, "The European Witch-Craze of the Sixteenth and Seventeenth Centuries," in *Religion, the Reformation and Social Change* (London, 1967), pp. 103–4; Norman Cohn, *Europe's Inner Demons* (London, 1975), pp. 176–7.

11. Emile Mâle, *L'Art religieux du douzième siècle en France* (Paris, 1960), pp. 318–72, 410–16, fig. 235.
12. *Les Très Riches Heures du Duc de Berri*, ed. J. Longman and R. Cazelles, preface by Millard Meiss (London, 1969). The illumination of Lucifer's fall was one of the last paintings made by the Limbourgs for the book and was added later as an afterthought (fol. 64v, pl. 65).
13. Ibid., fol. 108v, pl. 91 (Hell), and fol. 166r, pl. 123 (The Exorcism).
14. Bourgeois, p. 236.
15. Ibid., p. 230.
16. *The Rohan Book of Hours*, ed. Marcel Thomas (New York, 1973), pp. 9–17, and "Office of the Dead—The Judgement," fol. 159, pl. 63.
17. Millard Meiss, *Painting in Florence and Siena after the Black Death* (New York, 1964), pp. 74–5; Marina Warner, *Alone of All Her Sex* (London, 1976), p. 326.
18. Mâle, op. cit., pp. 150 ff.
19. Ibid., p. 367.
20. Cohn, op. cit., p. 235; Mâle, op. cit., pp. 369–70.
21. George Every, *Christian Mythology* (London, 1970), pp. 34–5. There is a large Luca della Robbia ceramic of the Fall in the Walters Museum, Baltimore, in which the serpent has a woman's face and breasts. Michelangelo's Sistine Chapel Temptation is probably the most famous rendering. In Joan of Arc's time, the seducers of Saint Antony were painted as entrancing maidens, by Sassetta for instance, in a tempera panel now in the Yale University Art Gallery. The demonic nature of one of his temptresses is revealed by her golden bat's wings. In an anonymous Flemish illumination (British Museum Add. Ms. 381b.f.133b), a young woman dressed in the height of contemporary fashion offers Saint Antony a golden cup. Her lifted skirts reveal clawed feet underneath.
22. Malcolm Vale, "Jeanne d'Arc et ses adversaires: la victime d'une guerre civile?" lecture, Colloque d'Histoire Médiévale, Orleans, October 1979, makes a most carefully analysed case for considering Joan's trial in the context of heresy hunting, not only of the civil war.
23. G. A. Holmes, "Cardinal Beaufort and the Crusade against the Hussites," *English Historical Review* 349 (October 1973): 721–50.
24. Letter of the duke of Bedford of 9 March 1428; quoted in Vale, "Jeanne d'Arc," p. 6 of typescript kindly lent by the author; quoted also in Holmes, op. cit.
25. Vale, op. cit., pp. 9–10.
26. Fr. François-Marie Lethel, in his paper, "La soumission à l'Eglise Militante, un aspect théologique de la condamnation de Jeanne d'Arc," Colloque d'Histoire Médiévale, Orleans, October 1979, concluded that only a radical theology of individual sainthood could have spared Joan condemnation by the Inquisition after she had refused to submit to the church's authority: "*Mais, il faut le reconnaître, de telles perspectives sont vraiment très neuves dans l'Eglise; ce sont celles de Vatican II.*"
27. Geoffrey Bullough, ed., *Narrative and Dramatic Sources of Shakespeare* (London, 1960), 3:26, 56. Amusingly, Shakespeare noticed that the sources disagreed, and so Joan starts off as "*foule*" in his *Henry VI, Part I*, and is then miraculously transformed by her visions:
    And whereas I was black and swart before,
    With those clear rays which she infus'd on me,
    That beauty am I bless'd with which you see (Act I, Scene 2).
28. Pernoud, *Retrial*, p. 144.

29. Q. 4:382; Rankin-Quintal, p. 120.
30. Q. 4:406.
31. Ibid., pp. 361–2. The greatest disappointment caused by Monstrelet's low regard for Joan is that he records that she was captured, and that the duke of Burgundy visited her, but tells us *nothing* more: "*et parla a elle aulcunes parolles, dont je ne sui mie bien recors, jà soit che que je y estois present*" (Q. 4:402). Alas, his conveniently feeble memory!
32. Article VIII, in Tisset-Lanhers 2:166–7.
33. Natalie Zemon Davis, "City Women and Social Change," in *Society and Culture in Early Modern France* (London, 1975), p. 71.
34. Article IX, in Tisset-Lanhers 2:167. The records of the court case at Toul have never been recovered, so we cannot know much of the matter, not even the man's name. Natalie Zemon Davis, "Ghosts, Kin, and Progeny: Some Features of Family Life in Early Modern France," *Daedalus* (Spring, 1977), pp. 106–7, discusses the reform of marriage laws in the early sixteenth century, inspired because the Church authorities were "weary of breach-of-contract suits."
35. Article I, in Tisset-Lanhers 2:246.
36. Article IX, in Tisset-Lanhers 2:250.
37. Pernoud, *Retrial*, pp. 69–70, 71–2.
38. Ibid., p. 163.
39. Ibid., pp. 149–50. Régine Pernoud, *Jeanne devant les Cauchons* (Paris, 1970), describes the evening meal these Englishmen had, for she discovered the bills for it in the Compotus Roll of John Baysham, Receiver General for Richard Beauchamp, earl of Warwick, now in the archives of Warwick Castle, Ref. BL 373.
40. Evidence of Jean Massieu, Martin Ladvenu and Pierre Cusquel, in Pernoud, *Retrial*, pp. 182–3.
41. Q. 4:477; English historians continued to repeat the story of her pretended pregnancy. Thomas Heywood in *The Life of Merlin* (1651) writes: "Many battles were fought in divers parts of the kingdom, between the English and French, in which, the French for the most part prevailed, some said, by the help of a woman called Joan of Arc, whom they stiled, The maiden of God, who was victorious in many conflicts, and, at length, came to a town called Compeine [sic], with intention to remove the siege laid unto it by the duke of Burgoin [sic], and the English, but, by the valour of a Burgonian knight, called Sir John Luxemburgh, her company was distressed, and she too alive, and afterwards carried to Roan, and there kept a season, because she feigned herself with child, but the contrary being found, she was adjudged to death, and her body burnt to ashes." Q. 4:210.
42. Pierre Marot, "De la réhabilitation à la glorification de Jeanne d'Arc: *Mémorial du Vième centenaire de la réhabilitation* (Paris, 1956), pp. 94–5.
43. *Henry VI, Part I*, Act I, Scene 6; Act II, Scene 1. Shakespeare's sources were Edward Hall (1548) and Raphael Holinshed (1587), and he combined their differing viewpoints. He did not use Holinshed's living phrase: "her [Joan's] pranks so uncouth and suspicious." See Bullough, op. cit., pp. 23–31, 56–61, 75–7.
44. Article XI, in Tisset-Lanhers 2:171.
45. E. Bouteiller and G. de Braux, *Nouvelles recherches sur la famille de Jeanne d'Arc: Enquêtes inédites* (Paris, 1879). Tisset-Lanhers, 2:48, do not mention this ignominious end, but record Baudricourt's loyalty to Charles as his *bailli* at Chaumont from 1437 to his death.
46. See G. B. Shaw, *Saint Joan* (London, 1975), pp. 49–62; Jean Anouilh, *L'Alouette* (Paris, 1953), pp. 47–62.

47. Pernoud, *Retrial*, p. 111. But he was shown the prophecy after his capture at Jargeau, so it would not have influenced his command before.
48. Ayroles 5:20; Anne E. Curry, "L'Effet de la libération de la ville d'Orleans sur l'armée anglaise," lecture, Colloque d'Histoire Médiévale, Orleans, October 1979.
49. *Henry VI, Part I*, Act V, Scene 3.
50. See Keith Thomas, "The Relevance of Social Anthropology to the Historical Study of Witchcraft," in Douglas, op. cit., pp. 47–79.
51. *Henry VI, Part I*, Act I, Scene 5.
52. 27 February, Tisset-Lanhers 2:78; Rankin-Quintal on her wounds, p. 83; Jean Pasquerel's evidence in Pernoud, *Retrial*, p. 145.
53. Pernoud, *Retrial*, pp. 106–7.
54. Ibid., p. 144.
55. 27 February, Tisset-Lanhers 2:78–9. Imperviousness to pain is still used in horror films as a sign of preternatural forces at work, e.g., in *The Mummy* or *Rasputin*.
56. *Chronique d'Antonio Morosini*, ed. G. Lefèvre-Pontalis (Paris, 1902), 3:336–8. Morosini is a lively chronicler, full of colour and anecdote, but extremely unreliable. From the first, he is highly sympathetic, to the Pucelle and her exploits, and here he reports a hopeful rumour originating in Bruges that he heard in mid-December 1430. For other ransom attempts, see Tisset-Lanhers 2:299.
57. Rankin-Quintal, p. 68.
58. Evidence of Isambart de la Pierre and Martin Ladvenu, in Pernoud, *Retrial*, p. 178. Guillaume Erard later represented the English at the peace treaty of Arras in 1435, and he died in England, working for Louis of Luxembourg, in 1439 (Tisset-Lanhers 2:399–400).
59. Henry Chadwick, *Priscillian of Avila: The Occult and the Charismatic in the Early Church* (Oxford, 1976), p. 97.
60. Evidence of Catherine [le]Royer, in Douglas Murray, p. 227.
61. 3 March, Tisset-Lanhers 2:95.
62. Trevor-Roper, op. cit., pp. 92, 130; cf. Matthew 4:5, 8.
63. 3 March, Tisset-Lanhers 2:94; Article XVIII, ibid., p. 180.
64. 1 March, ibid., p. 87; Article VII, ibid., p. 166.
65. Rankin-Quintal, p. 42.
66. 24 February, Tisset-Lanhers 2:62.
67. 1 March, ibid., p. 86; Barrett, p. 80.
68. 3 March, Tisset-Lanhers 2:91.
69. 15 March, ibid., p. 133. Beaulieu-les-Fontaines, in Vermandois, was John of Luxembourg's castle near Compiègne. According to Perceval de Cagny, Joan was held there four months after her capture, and was transferred to John's stronghold of Beaurevoir, deeper in Burgundian territory, only after this attempt to break out (Q. 4:34).
70. Christine de Pisan, *The Book of Fayttes of Armes and of Chyvalrye*, trans. William Caxton [1489] and ed. A. T. P. Byles (Early English Society, 1932), p. 20.
71. 3 March, Tisset-Lanhers 2:101.
72. 14 March, ibid., pp. 126–27, 1:143–5.
73. 14 March, ibid. 2:131, 1:153. All that is left now of the castle of Beaurevoir is one round tower on an emplacement of earth in a field. The stone walls are constructed on a curve and the mortar has almost all gone, but the blocks still lie securely, so well-cut were the scantlings. The day I walked across the field to see the tower, an immense wind was blowing in the wide open countryside; standing inside, even though the crown of the tower has gone, I could almost hear the desperate babble

of the wind urging freedom. It is a wild, desolate place, not in the least like tame agricultural land.

74. Article LVI, 23 May, Tisset-Lanhers 2:223. Joan sprang back, saying she would not want the devil to take her, even from prison.

75. Article VIII, expounded to Joan by Maître Pierre Maurice, the most kindly of Joan's assessors, a canon of Rouen and representative of the University of Paris at her trial. Maurice was very sorry, the notary Boisguillaume reported, when Joan reassumed male dress and by so doing condemned herself to death (23 May, ibid., pp. 329, 417).

76. Bourgeois, p. 262.

77. Denys Hay, *The Church in Italy in the Fifteenth Century* (Cambridge, 1977), p. 76.

78. B. L. Manning, *The People's Faith in the Time of Wycliffe* (London, 1919), p. 42.

79. Pernoud, *Retrial*, p. 77.

80. Léopold Delisle, *Nouveau témoignage rélatif à la mission de Jeanne d'Arc* (Paris, 1885); L.A., no. 35, pp. 33-4.

81. Manning, op. cit., p. 92-3.

82. 22 February, Tisset-Lanhers 2:46.

83. Bourgeois, p. 262.

84. 25 March (Palm Sunday), Tisset-Lanhers 2:140, 18 April, ibid., p. 286: "It seems to me I am in great danger of death," said Joan, ill after eating Cauchon's carp. "And, if it be so, may God do what he will with me, I beg you to let me be confessed, to receive holy communion and be buried in sacred ground."

85. 7 June, Tisset-Lanhers 2:366; Pernoud, *Retrial*, pp. 185-7.

86. H. C. Lea, *The History of the Inquisition of the Middle Ages* (London, 1886), 1:546.

87. Pernoud, *Retrial*, p. 202.

88. Rankin-Quintal, pp. 54-64.

89. Ronald Knox and Shane Leslie, eds., *The Miracles of King Henry VI* (Cambridge, 1923), pp. 3-6.

CHAPTER 6 HERETIC

1. In *The Works of St. John of the Cross*, trans. E. Allison Peers (London, 1943), 1:102-4.

2. Adrien Harmand, *Jeanne d'Arc, ses costumes, son armure* (Paris, 1929), pp. 397-9, gives an illustration of Joan's mitre.

3. H. C. Lea, *The History of the Inquisition of the Middle Ages* (London, 1888), 1:399 ff., 443 ff.; see also Malise Ruthven, *Torture: The Grand Conspiracy* (London, 1978), pp. 43-71, on the Inquisition's methods.

4. See Tisset-Lanhers 2:383-425, for biographies and attendance records of the 131 assessors.

5. Le Graverent was busy with another trial, in Coutances, and was not present at Joan's. But he preached a vitriolic public sermon on a procession to St. Martin des Champs in Paris just over a month after Joan's execution. "He said that her parents were very poor people, that she had gone about dressed as a man when she was about fourteen years old, that after that her father and mother would have liked to kill her if they could have done so without guilt, and that she had therefore left them, in the devil's company, and had ever since been a murderer of Christian people, full of blood and fire, till at last she was burned" (Bourgeois, pp. 264-5; Tisset-Lanhers 2:402-3).

6. Jean le Maistre was a local Rouen preacher, but otherwise little is known about him. See Tisset-Lanhers 2:140.

7. Perceval de Boulainvilliers, Q. 5:117.

8. Pernoud, *Retrial*, p. 106.

9. Q. 5:342.

10. 27 February, Tisset-Lanhers 2:71; ibid., p. 72; 3 March, ibid., p. 91.

11. Ibid., pp. 46–9; Barrett, pp. 3–4.

12. Tisset-Lanhers 2:56.

13. 24 February, ibid., p. 60.

14. Barrett, p. 62; 24 February, Tisset-Lanhers 1:62: "*Respondit quod in nomine vocis venit claritas.*" But the French differs: "*Respond que au devant de la voix vient clarité*"—"in front of" or "before."

15. *The Life of Saint Teresa of Avila*, trans. J. M. Cohen (London, 1957), pp. 197–8.

16. 24 February, Tisset Lanhers 2:62–3; Barrett, p. 64.

17. 27 February, Tisset-Lanhers 2:71; Barrett, p. 68. Savonarola described candidly how he communicated his heavenly inspiration. His experience, toward the end of the century, may have been similar to Joan's. He said of his "voices": "These words were not from Holy Scriptures, as some thought, but newly come forth from heaven just at that time. And since a single vision contains many words of this kind sent from heaven I only disclosed as much as seemed necessary—and that clothed in a vision—to show by whose command had come the words I was proclaiming publicly, lest the unbelievers laugh" (Donald Weinstein, *Savonarola and Florence: Prophecy and Patriotism in the Renaissance* [Princeton, 1970], pp. 70–1).

18. 27 February, Tisset-Lanhers 2:72; Barrett, p. 69.

19. Tisset-Lanhers 2:72.

20. *Saint Teresa*, pp. 174–5.

21. 27 February, Tisset-Lanhers 2:72–9; Barrett, p. 69.

22. 1 March, Tisset-Lanhers 2:84–6; Barrett, pp. 78–82. G. B. Shaw, *Saint Joan* (London, 1975), p. 131:
    JOAN: Do you think God cannot afford clothes for him [Michael]?
    LADVENU: Well answered, Joan.

23. Julian of Norwich, *Revelations of Divine Love* [1373], trans. Clifton Wolfers (London, 1973): "At the same moment the Trinity filled me full of heartfelt joy, and I knew that all eternity was like this for those who attain heaven. For the Trinity is God, and God the Trinity; the Trinity is our Maker and keeper, our eternal lover, joy and bliss—all through our Lord Jesus Christ" (p. 66).
    Richard Rolle, *The Fire of Love* [1343], trans. Clifton Wolfers (London, 1972): "This is the love which lays hold of Christ, and brings him into our hearts; which sweetens our minds so that in our hearts we burst out singing our hymns of praise, rejoicing in spiritual music. I believe that there is no pleasure to compare with this" (p. 184).

24. 3 March, Tisset-Lanhers 2:91.

25. 12 March, ibid., p. 114.

26. 14 March, ibid., p. 128.

27. 13 March, ibid., pp. 122–3.

28. Norman Cohn, *Europe's Inner Demons* (London, 1975), pp. 196–7.

29. *Dives and Pauper* I, 1, 4, quoted in B. L. Manning, *The People's Faith in the Time of Wycliffe* (London, 1919), p. 13.

30. 13 March, Tisset-Lanhers 2:122; Barrett, p. 110.

31. *Saint Teresa*, p. 138.

32. 17 March, Tisset-Lanhers 2:138–42.
33. Ibid., pp. 209–10.
34. Ibid., pp. 214–15.
35. Ibid., Barrett, pp. 196–7.
36. Tisset-Lanhers 2:208; Barrett, p. 190.
37. Cohn, op. cit., pp. 100–2.
38. The Bourgeois, always perspicacious, makes this point clearly: Joan sinned because she claimed that her saints "appeared to her frequently and talked to her as one friend does to another; not by revelation as God has sometimes spoken to those he loves, but bodily, by mouth, as a friend speaks to a friend" (p. 261).
39. Ibid., pp. 253–4.
40. E. H. Gombrich, "Icones Symbolicae: Philosophies of Symbolism and Their Bearing on Art," in *Symbolic Images: Studies in the Art of the Renaissance* (London, 1972), p. 135.
41. Ibid., p. 177.
42. See Jean Baudrillard, "La Précession des simulacres," and Mario Perniola, "Icônes, visions, simulacres," in *Traverses* (10 February 1978), both illuminating analyses of the fundamental quarrel in Christianity about the nature of an image.
43. F. Sanchez-Ventura y Pascal, *The Apparitions of Garabandal* (Detroit, 1966), passim.
44. J. Huizinga, *The Waning of the Middle Ages* (London, 1972), p. 256.
45. Giovanni Battista Vico, *The New Science*, trans. T. G. Bergin and M. M. Fisch (Ithaca, 1948), para. 378; quoted in Gombrich, op. cit., p. 184.
46. J. Huizinga, "Mr. Shaw's Saint Joan," in *Men and Ideas: History, the Middle Ages, the Renaissance*, trans. James S. Holmes and Hans van Marche (London, 1960), p. 224.
47. Tisset-Lanhers 2:192.
48. 14 March, ibid., p. 127.
49. Pernoud, *Retrial*, p. 128.
50. Siméon Luce, *Jeanne d'Arc à Domrémy* (Paris, 1886), pp. xci ff.; Emile Mâle, *Religious Art* (New York, 1970), pp. 54–56; NCE, "Michael"; Edward Lucie-Smith, *Joan of Arc* (London, 1976), p. 18; Louis Réau, *Iconographie de l'Art Chrétien* (Paris, 1958), 2(2):44–51.
51. Réau, op. cit., 3(1):262–72; 3(2):877–82; Gervase Mathew, *The Court of Richard II* (London, 1968), p. 97; John Bugge, *Virginitas; An Essay in the History of the Medieval Ideal* (The Hague, 1975), pp. 3–4, 131; Jacopus de Voragine, *The Golden Legend*, trans. William Caxton, ed. F. S. Ellis (London, 1900), 4:66–72, 5:238–40. 7:1–30.
52. Vita Sackville-West, *Joan of Arc* (London, 1973), pp. 42–3.
53. The existence of Catherine, Joan's only sister, is mentioned only once by a contemporary, Jean Colin, at the rehabilitation when he says that she had been his wife. As she is not mentioned in the letters of ennoblement of 1429 beside other members of Joan's family, she must have already been dead (unless she was adopted). The probability of her death is corroborated by Catherine Robert's evidence of 1456. She said that Joan had asked her aunt, Aveline de Vouthon, the mother-in-law of Durand Laxart (who went with Joan to Vaucouleurs) to call her new baby Catherine in memory of her sister (E. Bouteiller and G. de Braux, *Nouvelles recherches sur la famille de Jeanne d'Arc: Enquêtes inédits* [Paris, 1879]).
54. Huizinga, op. cit., pp. 165–7.
55. Manning, op. cit., p. 2.
56. Keith Thomas. *Religion and the Decline of Magic* (London, 1973), p. 29.

57. NCE, "Fourteen Holy Helpers"; David Hugh Farmer, *Oxford Dictionary of Saints* (Oxford, 1978), p. 156.

58. The features of Catherine's story may have migrated from another Alexandrian woman's biography—that of the historical Hypatia, a renowned philosopher who was the head of the Plato Academy in the Greek city, the centre of Neoplatonism as propounded by Plotinus. Hypatia represented the highest learning flourishing in direct opposition to Christianity. She became the victim of the furious and cruel factionalism that tore apart the fourth- and fifth-century world and, in particular, of the quarrel between Cyril of Alexandria, a zealot, and Nestorius, the patriarch of Constantinople, who led the opposing parties in the dispute about Christ's dual nature, the god-man.

This is not the place to discuss the fine points about the doctrine of the Incarnation that so inflamed the Byzantines, from its leaders to the populace. Hypatia was only one of its many distinguished casualties. She was blamed for the continuing opposition to Christianity among the Neoplatonists. As she returned home one day in her carriage, she was dragged from it by a mob incited—perhaps even hired—by Peter the Reader, a bigot and a supporter of Cyril, and carried off to a church on the harbour where she was lynched. Her naked body was mutilated with the oyster shells that the fishermen piled on the quayside.

As Socrates wrote in his *Ecclesiastical History:* "After tearing her body in pieces, they took her mangled limbs to a place called Cinaron, and there burnt them. An act so inhuman could not fail to bring the greatest opprobrium, not only upon Cyril, but also upon the whole Alexandrian Church. And surely nothing can be further from the spirit of Christianity than the allowances of massacres, fights and transactions of that sort. This happened in the month of March, during Lent, in the fourth year of Cyril's episcopate, under the tenth consulate of Honorius, and the sixth of Theodosius" (anon. trans. [London, 1914], chap. 15, pp. 348–9).

Sylvester Houédard, scholar and poet, believes that the whirring blades on the Catherine wheel are the transmuted images of the oyster shells that killed Hypatia. If Hypatia is the model for Catherine of Alexandria, if the Christians made a saint of their own victim, as they adopted Mercury and Dionysius and other pagan deities and heroes, then it reveals a fascinating buried link between Joan and her patron Saint Catherine. Joan's literalism was forced upon her by the limitations of her sophistication and the expectations of her judges, as we have seen; she herself was Neoplatonist in inclination, seeing no incompatibility between the world of spirit and the visible creation. Her mind was peopled by beautiful images of beings on the higher rungs of the ladder of existence.

59. *Les Belles Heures du Duc de Berry*, intro. by James J. Rorimer, notes by Margaret B. Freeman (London, n.d.), pls. 12–13.

60. Natalie Zemon Davis, *Society and Culture in Early Modern France* (London, 1975), p. 75.

61. Henri Wallon, *Jeanne d'Arc* (Paris, 1876), p. 111.

62. Yann Grandeau, "La Pieté d'Ysabeau de Bavière," notes toward a lecture, Colloque d'Histoire Médiévale, Orleans, October 1979.

63. Ambrose, *Patrologia Latina*, ed. J. P. Migne, 16:241, 1093; John Chrysostom, *Patrologia Graeca*, ed. J. P. Migne, 50:579–85.

64. Bourgeois, p. 262.

65. Robert and Iona Opie, eds., *The Oxford Dictionary of Nursery Rhymes* (Oxford, 1977), pp. 108–9.

66. 24 February, Tisset-Lanhers 2:65–8.

67. Charles Péguy, *Les Tapisseries de Sainte Geneviève et Jeanne d'Arc* (Paris, 1957), pp. 72–3, © Editions Gallimard. Because Péguy's poetry is so musical, he is extremely hard to translate, and this is a literal version:

> *The weapons of Satan are false symbols,*
> *Stone of papier-mâché, marble painted like majolica.*
> *The stone of Jesus is pure pentelic marble*
> *The weapons of Satan are the bad doctor*
> *(Are there any good ones?), the bad actor*
> *Who plays against the sense and the bad reader*
> *Who reads against the text . . .*
> *The weapons of Satan are false culture*
> *That sows tares . . .*
> > *It's every opening*
> *That has not been opened and every closure*
> *That has not been closed and every square*
> *That has not been squared and every arch*
> *That has not been arched . . .*
> > *And all horticulture*
> *That is not for flowers, all tree-culture*
> *That is not for fruit, all vineyard-keeping*
> *That is not for wine, it's all agriculture*
> *That is not for wheat, it's all bee-keeping*
> *That is not for honey, it's all forestry*
> *That is not for forests . . .*
> > *It is the stitch*
> *When it is badly sewn . . .*
> *The weapons of Satan . . .*
> > *are every structure*
> *That is not organic . . .*

Writing of a scene in Balzac's short story *Sarrazine*, Roland Barthes describes the savage shock caused by the collision of two antithetical categories. In the Balzac case, an ancient eunuch is touched by a young girl; the ensuing crisis is exactly the same in kind as the crisis provoked by Joan of Arc's incorporation of antitheses when she lived as a boy but remained a girl: "*L'Antithèse, c'est le mur sans porte. Franchir ce mur est la transgression même. Soumis à l'antithèse du dedans et du dehors, du chaud et du froid, de la vie and le mort, le vieillard et la jeune femme sont en droit séparés par la plus inflexible des barres: celle du sens. Aussi tout ce qui rapproche ces deux côtés antipathiques est-il proprement scandaleux (du plus rude des scandales: celui de la forme). . . . Le mariage de la jeune femme et du castrat est deux fois catastrophique (ou si l'on préfère, il forme un système à deux entrées): symboliquement, il est affirmé que le corps double, le corps chimérique est inviable, voué à la dispersion de ses parties: lorsqu'un corps supplémentaire est produit, qui vient s'ajouter à la distribution déjà accomplie des contraires, ce supplément . . . est maudit: le trop éclate: le rassemblement se retourne en éparpillement; et structuralement, il est dit que la figure majeure issue de la sagesse rhétorique, à savoir l'Antithèse, ne peut se transgresser impunément: le sens (et son fondement classificatoire) est une question de vie ou de mort: de la même façon, en copiant la Femme, en prenant sa place par-dessus la barre des sexes, le castrat transgressera la morphologie, la grammaire, le discours, et de cette abolition du sens, Sarrasine mourra*" (*S/Z* [Paris, 1970], pp. 70–1).

CHAPTER 7 IDEAL ANDROGYNE

1. Père Fronton-du-Duc, *L'Histoire Tragique de la Pucelle d'Orléans* (Pont-à-Mousson, 1581; reprinted Pont-à-Mousson, 1859), Act I, Scene 1.
2. Pernoud, *Retrial*, pp. 177–82.
3. Sign of cross: 1 March, Tisset-Lanhers 2:82.
4. Guillaume de Désert's evidence, in Pernoud, *Retrial*, p. 181. Haimond de Macy's evidence, ibid., p. 150.
5. Jean Fave's evidence, ibid., p. 181.
6. Ibid., pp. 177–182.
7. Tisset-Lanhers 2:345–6.
8. Ibid., pp. 338–9.
9. Barrett, pp. 152–4.
10. 22 February, Tisset-Lanhers 2:52–4; Barrett, p. 57.
11. 28 May, Tisset-Lanhers 2:344–5; Barrett, pp. 318–19.
12. 24 February, Tisset-Lanhers 2:68; Barrett, pp. 65–6.
13. 27 February, Tisset-Lanhers 2:73–4; Barrett. p. 70.
14. 27 February, Barrett, p. 66; Tisset-Lanhers 2:74.
15. 3 March, Barrett, pp. 84–5; Tisset-Lanhers 2:92–3.
16. 12 March, Barrett, p. 103; Tisset-Lanhers 2:115.
17. Tisset-Lanhers 1:295–6, 2:171; Barrett, p. 152, Article XII.
18. 15 March, Barrett, p. 125; Tisset-Lanhers 2:133–4.
19. Barrett, pp. 227–8; Tisset-Lanhers 2:246.
20. Jean Gerson, *De Mirabili Victoria Cujusdam Puellae*, Q. 3:298 ff.
21. D. G. Wayman, "The Chancellor and Jeanne d'Arc," *Franciscan Studies* 17, nos. 2–3 (June-September, 1957): 273–305.
22. Ayroles, 1:46.
23. Henricus Gorkhum, *De Quadam Puella*, Q. 3:413 ff.; Ayroles, 1:35 ff.; Wayman, op. cit.
24. Bourgeois, pp. 263–4.
25. *Proverbes Français, antérieurs au XV siècle*, ed. Joseph Morawski (Paris, 1925), no. 737.
26. *Le Miroir aux Dames*, poème inédit du XVe siècle (Neuchâtel, 1908), ll. 505–10.
27. Quoted in Mary Daly, *The Church and the Second Sex* (New York, 1975), p. 85.
28. Ambrose, *Expos. Evang. Sec. Lucam*, Bk. X, no. 161; Daly, op. cit., p. 85.
　　　The most absurd yet logical development of this fundamental principle in Joan's transvestism appears in Pierre de Sermoize, *Joan of Arc and Her Secret Missions*, trans. Jennifer Taylor (London, 1973), p. 66, where the author asserts that Joan was "gynandromorphous," having secondary male characteristics, like joined labia majora, for instance(!).
29. See K. Hastrup, "The Sexual Boundary: Transvestism and Homosexuality," *Journal of the Anthropological Society of Oxford* 6, no. 1 (1975); and "The Sexual Boundary: Purity, Virginity and Heterosexuality," ibid. 5, no. 3 (1974). Later in this chapter, I mention some of the stories in which the motif of the transvestite girl appears. Natalie Zemon Davis's bibliography for "Women on Top," in *Society and Culture in Early Modern France* (London, 1975), and "Women's History, in Transition: The European Case," *Feminist Studies* 3 (Spring-Summer 1976): 83–103, lists many other examples with exciting comprehensiveness. They include Boccaccio's ninth story, for the second day, in *Decamerone*, ed. Ugo Foscolo (London, 1825) 1:200–16; Ben Jonson's play *Epicoene or The Silent Woman* (1609); and Thomas

Shadwell's play *The Woman-Captain* (1680). David Kunzle, *The Early Comic Strip: Narrative Strips and Picture Stories in the European Broadsheet from 1450–1825* (Berkeley, 1973), describes the heroine as she appears in this medium; see also Stith Thompson, *Motif Index of Folk Literature*, rev. ed. (Bloomington, Indiana, 1955–58).

30. Acts of Paul, in *The Apochryphal New Testament*, trans. M. R. James (Oxford, 1969), pp. 274–7.

31. *La Passion des Saintes Perpétué et Felicité*, translated and annotated by A. Levin-Duplouy (Paris, 1972), 32 pp.; Herbert Musurillo, S.J., *Symbolism and the Christian Imagination* (Baltimore and Dublin, 1962), pp. 47–8; Saint Jerome, Sermon 281, on their feast day, quoted in France Quéré-Jaulmes, *La Femme dans les grands textes des Pères de l'Eglise* (Paris, 1968), pp. 211–13.

32. The equation of moral worth with manliness is very ancient and has roots in pre-Christian philosophy. Virgil's *Fourth Eclogue*, for instance, contains the verse:

> *at simul heroum laudes et facta parentis*
> *iam legere et quae sit poteris cognoscere virtus.*

One translator at least seizes on the etymology of the word *virtus* to render it as "manliness":

> *as soon as thou canst read*
> *Of famous heroes, and of many a deed wrought by thy father,*
> *And canst fully know wherein consists true manliness*

Edward J. G. Scott, trans., *The Eclogues of Virgil* (London, 1884), p. 29.

A Neopythagorean manual for the education of young ladies instructs them: "We must deem the harmonious woman to be one who is well endowed with wisdom and self-restraint. For her soul must be very wise indeed when it comes to virtue so that she will be just and courageous." The last word, in the Greek, is literally "manly." Quoted in Sarah B. Pomeroy, *Goddesses, Whores, Wives, and Slaves* (New York, 1976), p. 134 (from Holger Thesleff, *The Pythagorean Texts of the Hellenistic Period*, trans. Flora B. Levin [Aabo, 1965], p. 142).

33. For the legend of this Saint Margaret, see Jacopus de Voragine, *The Golden Legend*, trans. William Caxton, ed. F. S. Ellis (London, 1900); Réau, *Iconographie de l'Art Chrétien* (Paris, 1958) 3(2):891.

34. John Anson, "The Female Transvestite in Early Monasticism: The Origin and Development of a Motif," *Viator* 5 (1974): 1–32; Vern L. Bullough, "Transvestites in the Middle Ages," *American Journal of Sociology* 79 (6): 1381–94; Marie Delcourt, *Hermaphrodite, Myths and Rites of the Bisexual Figure in Classical Antiquity* (London, 1950), pp. 84–102; letter to author from Dom Sylvester Houédard, 15 May 1977.

35. Anson, op. cit., p. 22; Saint Eugenia, showing her breasts to her fellow monks to prove her femaleness, is carved on a capital at Vézélay (I am most grateful for this information to Adey Horton); Réau, op. cit., 3(1):461–2; Synod of Ver (844), Canon 7; my thanks to Janet Nelson for drawing my attention to this.

36. 12 March, Tisset-Lanhers 2:113–14; Barrett, p. 101.

37. 12 March, Tisset-Lanhers 2:115; Barrett, pp. 102–3; Bourgeois, p. 264.

38. David Hugh Farmer, *Oxford Dictionary of Saints* (Oxford, 1978), "Wilgefortis," p. 404.

39. Vern Bullough, op. cit., pp. 1387–8; Réau, op. cit., 3(3):1342–5; *Acta Sanctorum*, July IV, p. 50; Delcourt, op. cit., p. 92.

40. Cf. Alison Lurie, "The Language of Fashion," *Observer Magazine*, 24 September 1978, who wrote: "The slacks and sweaters of the war period, and the jeans and

pants outfits of the Sixties and early Seventies were serious gestures towards sexual equality. . . . The Annie Hall style is more ambiguous. It announces that the wearer is a good sport, a pal . . . almost like one of the chaps. . . . But this style also conveys an antifeminist message. Because the men's clothes are usually several sizes too large, they imply, "I'm not big enough to wear a man's pants or do a man's job." It is a look of helpless cuteness, not one of authority."

41. Voragine, op. cit., 5:238–40, emphasis added.
42. 22 February, Tisset-Lanhers 2:45; Barrett, p. 54; for spinning's association with women in the classical tradition, see Pomeroy, op. cit., p. 199.
43. "La Fille d'un Roy," in *Miracles de Notre Dame par personnages*, ed. Gaston Paris and Ulysse Robert, 8 vols. (Paris, 1889–1900), vol. 7, pp. 3–117.
44. *Devant moy les feray en laisse*
    Mener comme chiens acouplez.
    P. 78, ll. 2153–4.
45. See Pierre Samuel, *Amazones, guerrières et gaillardes* (Grenoble, 1975), pp. 20, 218. In 1978, the Royal Shakespeare Company performed *The Women Pirates* by Steve Gooch an unsuccessful pantomime-like treatment of Mary Read's friendship with Anne Bonney; *The Singular Life of Albert Nobbs*, New End Theatre, Hampstead, 1978, was adapted by Simone Benmussa from George Moore's story in the collection *Celibate Lives*.
46. Diana Trilling, "The Liberated Heroine," *Times Literary Supplement*, 13 October 1978; cf. Jo with Enid Blyton's George in *The Famous Five* books, or Nancy Blackett in the Arthur Ransome books.
47. Catherine Clément, *Miroirs du sujet* (Paris, 1975), pp. 83–4.

CHAPTER 8 KNIGHT

1. Ed. T. Tyrwhitt (London, 1822), Prologue, "The Squire," 1:166.
2. *Le Jouvencel*, ed. L. Faure-Lecestre (Paris, 1887–89), vol. 2, chap. 19: "*Ceux qui ne sont pas nobles de lignée le sont par l'exercice du métier des armes qu'ils suivent, qui est noble par soi-même. Et vous dis que, depuis qu'un homme d'armes a une bassinet sur la tête, il est noble, et suffisant de combattre un roi. Les armes ennoblissent l'homme, quel qu'il soit.*"
3. John Barnie, *War in Medieval Society: Social Values and the Hundred Years War, 1337–99* (London, 1974), p. 72; Philippe Contamine, *Etât et société au fin du Moyen Age* (Paris, 1973), pp. 185 ff.
4. Perceval de Cagny, Q. 4:45.
5. Rankin-Quintal, p. 118. For the dating of her departure from Domremy and the enormous literature on the subject, see Tisset-Lanhers 2:49–50.
6. Douglas Murray, p. 217.
7. 22 February, Tisset-Lanhers 2:47–8; Barrett, p. 55.
8. Pernoud, *Retrial*, pp. 66–7. Durant Laxart was married to Jeanne, daughter of Joan's mother's sister Aveline, and lived at Burey, on the road from Domremy to Vaucouleurs. Joan told her parents she was going there to help with her cousin's lying-in. The new baby was called Catherine. Laxart, or Lassois, or Laxois was present at the coronation and gave evidence in 1456 (Tisset-Lanhers 2:48–9).
9. 22 February, Tisset-Lanhers 2:51–2.
10. Jean Morel's testimony, in Douglas Murray, p. 214.
11. René I le Bon (1409–80) was also king of Naples, but was unable to secure his throne

from Alphonse V of Aragon. His daughter Margaret of Anjou married Henry VI of England and became queen. (See Shakespeare's *Henry VI, Part II* and *Part III*.) He was a poet and a patron, notably of Nicolas Froment, and his portrait appears on one of the wings of Froment's masterpiece, *The Burning Bush*. See J. Huizinga, *The Waning of the Middle Ages* (London, 1972), p. 18.

12. 22 February, Tisset-Lanhers 2:52–3. The companions of Joan are known to us: Jean de Novelonpont, known as Jean de Metz; and Bertrand de Poulengy; and their two servants, Julien and Jean de Honnecourt. Colet de Vienne, accompanied by an archer called simply Richard, also left Vaucouleurs in Joan's party. Very little is known beyond their names. Jean de Metz and Bertrand de Poulengy both gave evidence at the rehabilitation, and the former was ennobled in 1448–49 for "services rendered during the war."

13. Pernoud, *Retrial*, pp. 73–5, 77–9; Douglas Murray, pp. 223–5, 229–31.

14. Douglas Murray, p. 274.

15. 10 March, Tisset-Lanhers 2:106.

16. 22 February, ibid., p. 52.

17. Douglas Murray, p. 273. This is one of Joan's remarks that lends itself to elaboration by the school of historians who believe that she was royal herself. They argue she is implying to D'Alençon, "I'm one of you."

18. L'Abbé J-J. Bourassé, *Les Miracles de Madame Sainte Kathérine de Fierbois* (Tours, 1858), trans. Andrew Lang (Chicago and London, 1897). See Henri Bas and Charles Pichon, *Sainte Catherine de Fierbois et l'épée libératrice* (Tours, 1926), pp. 21–60.

19. Vita Sackville-West, *Joan of Arc* (London, 1973), pp. 83–4.

20. Bourassé, op. cit. Soldiers in the company of Raoul de Gaucourt, the French commander who opposed Joan's proposals at Orleans, visited the shrine in 1414.

21. Huizinga, op. cit., p. 71.

22. 27 February, Tisset-Lanhers 2:75.

23. 27 February, ibid., pp. 75–6.

24. Huizinga, op. cit., p. 71.

25. Jean Chapelain, *La Pucelle ou la France Delivrée* (Paris, 1656); Bas and Pichon. op. cit., pp. 25, 76–7.

26. 27 February, Tisset-Lanhers 2:76–7. A sword that for a long time was believed to belong to Joan is still in the Musée de Dijon (W. S. Scott, *Jeanne d'Arc* [London, 1974], p. 148). It has "Vaucouleux, Charles Septieme 1491" engraved on the blade, but this may be of a later date than the hilt, which is "small enough for a woman's grasp."

27. 10 March, Tisset-Lanhers 2:106.

28. Bibliothèque Nationale Ms. F. Fr. 5524; Pernoud, *Retrial*, p. 135; Henri Wallon, *Jeanne d'Arc* (Paris, 1876), fig. 200.

29. See Chapter 9, pp. 185–6.

30. 27 February, Tisset-Lanhers 2:77.

31. Christine de Pisan, *The Book of Fayttes of Armes and of Chyvalrye*, trans. William Caxton [1489] and ed. A. T. P. Byles, p. 290.

32. 27 February. Tisset-Lanhers 2:78.

33. A. Cabassut, "La Dévotion au nom de Jésus dans l'église d'occident," *Vie Spirituelle* 86 (1952):46–69; NCE, 7:76–7.

34. 3 March, Tisset-Lanhers 2:97.

35. 18 March, Tisset-Lanhers 1:178–9.

36. P. S. Lewis, "Decayed and Non-Feudalism in Later Medieval France," *Bulletin of the Institute of Historical Research* 37 (1964): 175.

37. Bérault Stuart, *S'ensuit ung livret en traicte*, ed. Elie de Comminges (New York, 1971), p. vi; B. de Broussillon, *La Maison de Laval*, vol. 3 (Paris, 1900); "Les Mont-fort-Laval, 1412–1501," cartulaire no. 1218, reproduced pl. 127, facing p. 80. I am indebted to Michael Jones, of the University of Nottingham, for this information.

38. *The Bedford Book of Hours*, British Museum Add. Ms. 18850. f.288b.

39. E. Bouteiller and G. de Braux, *Nouvelles recherches sur la famille de Jeanne d'Arc: Enquêtes inédites* (Paris, 1879), between pp. xxxii and 3, quoting J. Quicherat, *Revue Historique*, July–August 1877.

40. W. S. Scott, *Jeanne d'Arc* (London, 1974), p. 149. This hat was kept until the French Revolution, when it was burnt ceremoniously in Orleans in 1792.

41. An account given by Q. 5:258 mentions Hauves Poulnoir, a painter, who received twenty-five *livres tournois* for providing material for one large and one small standard and painting them. The *Régistre des Déliberations de la Ville de Tours*, IV, fol. 250, records that 100 *livres* were given to the bride by the magistrates after Joan had asked them for a gift.

42. Q. 5:138–9.

43. Mark Twain, "Joan of Arc," in *The Complete Essays*, ed. Charles Neider (New York, 1963), p. 315.

44. Pisan, op. cit., pp. 22–4: "that he be not testyf hastyf hoot fell ne angrey But amesured and attemporat rightful in justice benynge in conuersation ofhye may-tnene & of lytyl wordes Sadde in countenaunce no grete dyseur of truffes very-table in worde and promesse hardy: sure: & dyligent: not covetous fiers to his enemyes pyetous to them that he vainquissed. . . ."

45. Q. 5:107–8.

46. Ibid., p. 108.

47. Article XIII of Jean d'Estivet's draft of the charges, in Tisset-Lanhers 2:173: "*la chose est notoire, puisqu'elle a été prise dans une huque dorée ouverte de tout côté.*"

48. Q. 5:112–13.

49. *Oxford Book of French Verse*, ed. St. John Lucas and C. Dionisotti (Oxford, 1952), p. 33:

> *Le temps a laissié son manteau*
> *De vent, de froidure et de pluye.*
> * Riviere, fontaine et ruisseau*
> *Portent, en livree jolie*
> *Gouttes d'argent d'orfaverie.*
> *Chacun s'abille de nouveau . . .*

50. Marcellin Defourneaux, *La Vie quotidienne au temps de Jeanne d'Arc* (Paris, 1952), pp. 109–10.

51. Mary Evans, *Costume Through the Ages* (London, 1930), pp. 40–2.

52. James Laver, *Costume* (London, 1903), pp. 32–8.

53. Alain Chartier, *Le Quadrilogue invectif*, ed. E. Droz (Paris, 1923), p. 62: "*Qui ne se veult esveiller au son doulx d'une chançon que fera il au bruit horrible d'une trompete? Se la robe trayne deux piez par terre et les manches sont larges a dextre ou a senestre et les poulaines de demy pie de long que prouffitera tout cecy pour fuyr vigoureusement ses ennemis?*"

54. Huizinga, op. cit., p. 258.

55. Pisan, op. cit., p. xix.

56. Laver, op. cit., p. 34.

57. Fernand Braudel, *Capitalism and Material Life, 1400–1800*, trans. Miriam Kochan

(London, 1973), pp. 123–4, 243. Gervase Mathew, *The Court of Richard II* (London, 1968), pp. 25–6.

58. Chartier, op. cit., pp. 36–7.
59. Rankin-Quintal, p. 55.
60. Q. 5:168–9.
61. Martin le Franc, *Le Champion des Dames*, in Q. 5:44–50. He describes her lavish clothes:

> *Se la Pucelle se vestoit*
> *De pourpoint et robe escourtee;*
> *Car elle en estoit redoubtee*
> *Trop plus, et aperte, et legiere,*
> *Et pour ung fier prince contee,*
> *Non pas pour simplette bergiere.*
> *Chappiau de faultre elle portait,*
> *Heuque frapee et robes courtes:*
> *Je l'accorde; aussi aultre estoit*
> *Son fait, que cil des femmes toutes.*
> *La longue cote (tu n'as doubtes)*
> *Es fais de guerre n'est pas boine . . .*
> *Armes propres habis requierent;*
> *Il n'est sy fol qu'il ne le sache . . .*
> *Quant a proie faulcon on lasche,*
> *Ses longues pendans on lui oste.*

62. 21 February, Tisset-Lanhers 2:37; 22 February, ibid., p. 44; 24 February, ibid., pp. 58–60; 27 February, ibid., pp. 69–70; 1 March, ibid., p. 81; 3 March, ibid., p. 81; 3 March, ibid., p. 90; 10 March, ibid., p. 104; 12 March, ibid., p. 112; 28 March, ibid., p. 157.
63. 13 March, ibid., pp. 120–4.
64. G. B. Shaw, *Saint Joan* (London, 1975). See pp. 94–6 for Cauchon's speech about Joan as a proto-Protestant, rather than a witch. "What will the world be like when The Church's accumulated wisdom and knowledge and experience, its councils of learned, venerable pious men, are thrust into the kennel by every ignorant labourer or dairymaid whom the devil can puff up with the monstrous self-conceit of being directly inspired from heaven? It will be world of blood, of fury, of devastation, of each man striving for his own hand." See J. Huizinga, "Bernard Shaw's Saint," in *Men and Ideas: History, the Middle Ages, the Renaissance*, trans. James S. Holmes and Hans van Marche (London, 1960), pp. 207–39.
65. 13 March, Tisset-Lanhers 2:120; Barrett, p. 107.
66. Her requests were never answered. See 17 March, Tisset-Lanhers 2:144; 2 May, ibid., p. 298; 24 May, ibid., p. 337. Isambart de la Pierre, in 1452, gave evidence that he had advised Joan to appeal to the Council of Basle for judgement. Cauchon, overhearing Joan agree with alacrity, flew into a rage and instructed the notaries not to make a record of her submission. No record of it does exist. See Pernoud, *Retrial*, pp. 210–11; Tisset-Lanhers, 3:31.
67. Pisan, op. cit., p. 195.
68. Steven Runciman, *The History of the Crusades* (London, 1971), 1:145–6, 292.
69. Jean Mollinet, quoted in Huizinga, *Men and Ideas*, p. 199.
70. Gentile da Fabriano's panel is in the Boston Museum of Fine Arts; for the other knightly saints, see Louis Réau, *Iconographie de l'Art Chrétien* (Paris, 1958), 3(3): 81, 507–8, 571–9.

71. Ibid., 3(3):900–17, 935–9. The painting of Saint Maurice by the Master of Moulins is in the Glasgow Museum.

72. *The Book of Saints*, ed. Benedictine Monks of St. Augustine's Abbey, Ramsgate (London, 1966), under "Gangulphus"; Réau, op. cit., 3(3):568–9. As Saint Gand, he is also the patron of glove-makers. To prove his wife's adultery publicly, he plunged her arm in a spring, which immediately boiled, so lifting off her skin like a glove.

73. Huizinga, op. cit., passim.

74. George Holmes, *Europe: Hierarchy and Revolt, 1320–1450* (London, 1975), pp. 223–24.

75. George Holmes, "Cardinal Beaufort and the Crusade against the Hussites," *English Historical Review* 349 (October 1973): 721–50.

76. Honoré Bonet, *L'Arbre des batailles* (1387), see Intro.; Pisan, op. cit., pp. xliv–vii; discussed in Barnie, op. cit., pp. 59–65.

77. D. G. Wayman, "The Chancellor and Jeanne d'Arc," *Franciscan Studies* 17, nos. 2–3 (June–September 1957):273.

78. M. G. A. Vale, *Charles VII* (London, 1974), pp. 169, 188.

79. Tisset-Lanhers 2:185–7.

80. 17 July 1429, Q. 5:126.

81. *Chronique d'Antonio Morosini*, ed. G. Lefèvre-Pontalis (Paris, 1902), 3:83–5.

82. 3 March 1430, Q. 5:156–9. The letter was originally composed in Latin and survives in a German version.

83. Q. 4:503; G. G. Coulton, *Life in the Middle Ages* (Cambridge, 1928), 1:210–3.

84. Barnie, op. cit., pp. 90–1; Defourneaux, op. cit., p. 124.

85. Pernoud, *Retrial*, p. 133.

86. Cf. C. P. Cavafy, "Expecting the Barbarians":

> *Because night is here but the barbarians have not come.*
> *Some people arrived from the frontiers*
> *And they said that there are no longer any barbarians.*
> *And now what shall become of us without any barbarians?*
> *Those people were a kind of solution.*

The Complete Poems, trans. Rae Dalven (London, 1961), pp. 18–19.

87. He fought at Montereau, leading the assault in October 1437. See Vale, op. cit., p. 74. It was good sense for a king not to fight: the capture of Jean le Bon and his imprisonment in England had been a catastrophe.

88. Pisan. op. cit., pp. 281–2. The Bourgeois clearly attributed the sudden death of the earl of Salisbury in 1428 to the attack he led on a holy day.

89. 24 February, Tisset-Lanhers 2:57.

90. 14 March, ibid., pp. 130–1.

91. 14 March, ibid. Article xxxix, ibid. 2:203; see ibid. 3:40 for how Thomas de Courcelles changed the text to the French verbatim version to inculpate Joan; Morosini, *Chronique*, 3:274–5.

92. Pisan, op. cit., pp. 64–5.

93. Q. 4:399–400: "*Et meysemenment ladicte Pucelle fist trenchier la teste a yceluy Franquet.*" In the illuminations, Joan is shown cutting off his head, though the French is ambiguous and could mean she merely ordered his death.

94. Pernoud, *Retrial*. pp. 137–8. Jean d'Aulon remembered that Joan had said "she never saw French blood without her hair standing on end" (ibid., p. 128).

95. 15 March, Tisset-Lanhers 1:163.

CHAPTER 9 THE VINDICATION

1. (Oxford, 1921), quoted in Bryan Wilson, *The Noble Savages: The Primitive Origins of Charisma and Its Contemporary Survival* (London, 1975), p. 1.

2. Q. 3:393; Tisset-Lanhers 2:299, suggest that La Hire's appointment as captain-general of Normandy may have inspired a tentative rescue operation on Joan's behalf. But there is no hard evidence of it.

3. See Chapter 8, p. 165, and note 9.

4. Q. 4:439, 447; 5:210.

5. Ibid., 4:439, 447; 5:210, 260, 321–36; see also Grosdidier des Mattons, *Le Mystère de Jeanne d'Arc* (Paris, 1935).

6. 27 February, Tisset-Lanhers 2:76–7.

7. 10 March, ibid., 2:107.

8. 10 March, ibid., p. 106.

9. 1 March, ibid., p. 85.

10. 17 March, ibid., p. 144.

11. See R. Fawtier and L. Canet, *La double expérience de Catherine Benincasa* (Paris, 1948), pp. 245–6, for the extreme hypothesis that Catherine's ring was a ring of flesh, the foreskin of the Christ Child.

12. Q. 5:321–36; Henri Guillemin, *The True History of Joan of Arc*, trans. William Oxferry (London, 1972), pp. 174–5.

13. See Paul Doncoeur and Yvonne Lanhers, *La Réhabilitation de Jeanne la Pucelle: L'Enquête ordonnée par Charles VII en 1450 et le codicile de Guillaume Bouillé* (Paris, 1956); *L'Enquête du Cardinal d'Estouteville en 1452* (Paris, 1958); *La Rédaction épiscopale du procès de 1455–6* (Paris, 1961).

14. Guillemin, op. cit., p. 178.

15. M. G. A. Vale, *Charles VII* (London, 1974), pp. 60–2.

16. P. Ourliac, "La Pragmatique sanction et la légation en France du Cardinal d'Estouteville (1451–3)" *Mélanges d'archéologie et d'histoire de l'école française de Rome* (1938), pp. 403–32; Vale, op. cit., pp. 62–5.

17. Doncoeur-Lanhers, op. cit., pp. 7–10; Douglas Murray, pp. 157–77. The witnesses were very unsatisfactory: Beaupère gave unsympathetic evidence; Jean Toutmouillé, who had not attended the trial but had seen Joan once on June 7, changed his story (see Tisset-Lanhers 2:424); Guillaume Duval went to one session of the trial only; none of these three witnesses were called later. Isambart de la Pierre (Le Maistre's assistant) and Martin Ladvenu, the two Dominican friars, and Jean Massieu and Guillaume Manchon, the two officials of the court, were more expansive as well as sympathetic and gave evidence again in 1456.

18. In 1455–56, Jean de Mailly was called before the tribunal. He could not remember being present at the trial (Douglas Murray, pp. 255–6). He attended once, on May 23. He did remember the abjuration and the burning, but only vaguely (Vale, op. cit., p. 60).

19. Guillemin, op. cit., pp. 181–2.

20. Pernoud, *Retrial*, p. 31.

21. Ibid., p. 117.

22. Vale, op. cit., p. 67.

23. Françoise Michaud Fréjaville, "Les Comptes de la forteresse de la ville d'Orléans au XVe siècle," lecture, Colloque d'Histoire Médiévale, Orleans, October 1979.

24. For the development of the procession at Orleans, commemorating the relief of the

siege, see L.A., nos. 1015–17, pp. 439–42, where Lanéry d'Arc gives a list of orators who delivered the panegyric about Joan of Arc from 1429 until 1852 (with several gaps when the feast was suspended).

25. Mgr. Pierre-Marie Brun, "Le Premier monument à Jeanne d'Arc sur l'ancien pont d'Orléans," in *Images de Jeanne d'Arc* (Paris, 1979), catalogue of exhibition at Hôtel de la Monnaie, Paris, June–September, 1976, pp. 27–9; see also l'Abbé Dubois, *Notice historique sur Jeanne d'Arc et les monuments érigés à Orleans à son honneur* (Orleans, 1824).

26. Davis Bitton, *The French Nobility in Crisis, 1560–1640* (Stanford, 1969), chap. 5; Natalie Zemon Davis, "Ghosts, Kin, and Progeny: Some Features of Family Life in Early Modern France," *Daedalus* (Spring, 1977), pp. 98–9.

27. Bitton, op. cit., p. 113.

28. A. Vallet de Viriville, *Nouvelles recherches sur la famille et sur le nom de Jeanne d'Arc, dite la Pucelle d'Orleans* (Paris, 1854), passim; for Louis XIII's grant of arms on 25 September 1612, see Q. 5:225–32.

29. Guillaume Cousinot de Monteuil, *Chronique de la Pucelle*, published in Denis Godefroy, *Histoire de Charles VII* (Paris, 1661), and with *La Chronique Normande de P. Cochon*, ed. A. Vallet de Viriville (Paris, 1859); Q. 4:203–53. *The Breviarum Historiale*, ed. Léopold Delisle (Paris, 1885), gave a contemporary's view of events, written in Rome; Quicherat edited, in 1879, another brief contemporary account: *Relation inédite sur Jeanne d'Arc extraite du livre noir de l'hôtel de ville de La Rochelle* (Orleans, 1879). Monstrelet and Wavrin record the events of Joan's life in the course of their histories, in the traditional manner of the chronicler, rather than writing her biography.

30. F. Guessard and E. de Certain, eds., *Le Mistère du siège d'Orléans* (Paris, 1862).

31. Jean Hordal, *Heroinae nobilissimae* etc. (Pont-à-Mousson, 1612).

32. Henri Wallon, *Jeanne d'Arc* (Paris, 1876), p. 31.

33. Ibid., genealogy of D'Arc family between pp. 418–19.

34. L.A., p. 356. This statue was a reproduction of the bridge monument at Orleans and was destroyed in 1793.

35. Michel de Sachy de Fourdrinoy, *Une Légence tenace: La noblesse des neveux de Jeanne d'Arc* (1973), pp. 219–25.

36. Wallon, op. cit., pp. 414–16, also reproduces the document, which declares: "*Jacobum Darc dicti loci de Dompremeyo, patrem; Isabellam ejus uxorem, matrem; Jacqueminum et Johannea Darc et Petrum Pierelo, fratres ipsius Puellae, et* totam suam parentelam et lignagium . . . *et* . . . *etiam et* eorum posteritatem masculinam et foemininam *in legitimo matrimonio natam et nascituram nobilitavimus, et per praesentes* . . . *nobilitamus et nobile facimus*" (emphasis added).

37. Fourdrinoy, op. cit., pp. 222–3; Siméon Luce, *Jeanne d'Arc à Domrémy* (Paris, 1886), pp. xxxiiii–xliv, reports some of the findings of Charles du Lis about Joan's family. Charles's own works include the *Discours sommaire, tant du nom et des armes, que de la naissance et parenté de la Pucelle d'Orléans, et de ses frères* (Paris, 1612). *The Grand Almanach du Monde Catholique* (Paris and other cities, 1912), p. 102, contains details about Claude du Lis.

38. Etienne Pasquier, *Oeuvres* (Amsterdam, 1723), 1:135, quoted in Bitton, op. cit., p. 116.

39. Etienne Pasquier, *Les Recherches de la France revues et augmentées de quatre livres* (Paris, 1596), Book VI, chaps. 4 and 5, quoted in L.A., no. 81, pp. 62–3.

40. Charles du Lis, *Recueil d'inscriptions et poésies en l'honneur de la Pucelle d'Orléans*, intro. by P. Le Verder (Rouen, 1910). Charles's research was thorough. In about 1625,

he managed to buy from Rheims two of Joan's original letters for his private collection, a purchase that reveals the general indifference at the time to her heroic status; for at a later date, it would have been quite impossible to buy privately any historical relics of Joan.

41. Charles du Lis, *De l'extraction de parenté de la Pucelle d'Orléans avec la généalogie de ceux qui se trouvent aujourd'huy descendu de ses frères, l'an 1616* (Paris, 1610).

42. Bitton, op. cit., p. 80.

CHAPTER 10 AMAZON

1. (London, 1938), p. 4.

2. 21 February, Tisset-Lanhers 1:40; see Paul Doncoeur, "Jeanne d'Arc, s'appelait-elle D'Arc?" *Nouvelles Littéraires*, no. 1198, (17 August 1950).

3. 24 March, Tisset-Lanhers 1:181; 2:148; Doncoeur, op. cit.

4. Paul Robert's *Dictionnaire de la langue française*, 6 vols. (Paris, 1967), gives *Arc* from Latin *arcus*, meaning "bow," first appearance in *Chanson de Roland* (1080); both Littré and Robert cite La Fontaine as a source for the same usage; *arc* also appears as an architectural term *arch* and a geometrical term *curve* or *bow* (as in "bow window"). The curve, as opposed to the straight line, appears to be associated with the female in male/female contrasting pairs of symbols. The vase, chalice, coastal bay, harbour, vessel, womb stand opposite to the "male" cross, mountain, knife, penis. The same symbolism can be read in the bow and arrow, with their erotic analogies, the vagina and the phallus, reinforced perhaps by the curious phenomenon that the orifice at the tip of the phallus is the shape of an arrowhead. For discussion of cup and lance symbolism, see Jessie L. Weston, *From Ritual to Romance* (Cambridge, 1920), pp. 71–6.

5. See Tisset-Lanhers 2:39, for the details of the orthography of Jacques d'Arc's name in contemporary documents. Charles du Lis, *Discours sommaire, tant du nom et des armes, que de la naissance et parenté de la Pucelle d'Orléans, et de ses frères* (Paris, 1612), writes: *"Ils l'ont appellée Day, pour se conformer à la prononciation du pays"* (p. 7).

6. Q. 5:150, "Anoblissement de Jeanne d'Arc et sa famille."

7. Doncoeur, op. cit.; Michel de Montaigne, *Journal d'un voyage en Italie* (1580), quoted in Q. 5:246; L.A., no. 748, p. 330.

8. Christine de Pisan, *The Book of Fayttes of Armes and of Chyvalrye*, trans. William Caxton [1489] and ed. A. T. P. Byles (Early English Text Society, no. 189, 1932), pp. 286–7.

9. By 1897, the association of Joan's name with the bow, emblem of the Amazon, was so firm that the Abbé Mourot, one of her most learned and fervent cultists in Lorraine, produced an interesting background reason: he remembered that one of Merlin's prophecies about the virgin from the *bois chesnu* who would rise and save France declared that she would be born under the sign of Sagittarius, the archer. This is an excellent example of justification with hindsight. Abbé V. Mourot, quoted in Michèle Lagny, "*Culte et images de Jeanne d'Arc, 1870–1921*," thesis for University of Nancy (1973), p. 245. The prophecy was reported by Mathieu Thomassin (Q. 4:305), see Chapter 1, n. 60. But, before Mourot, it was not suggested that this was a reason for Joan's taxophile name (or at least I have not come across such an explanation). For Jacques d'Arc, "the bowman," see Doncoeur, op. cit.

10. Charles du Lis, *Recueil d'inscriptions et poésies en l'honneur de la Pucelle d'Orleans,*

intro. by P. Le Verder (Rouen, 1910), p. 47. Latin epigram by J. Thaumas; French verses by Hannibal de Lorrigne.

11. Perceval de Boulainvilliers, Q. 5:115–21.

12. Footraces were held in honour of Hera by maidens at Elis; athletics were open to women, from the first century A.D. in Greece, we learn from inscriptions; e.g., at Delphi, three Trallian athletes are commemorated, including Hedea, who won prizes for singing and playing cithara in Athens, for running in footraces at Nemea, and for driving a war chariot at Isthmia. Sarah B. Pomeroy, *Goddesses, Whores, Wives, and Slaves* (New York, 1976), p. 137.

13. Virgil, *Aeneid*, ed. R. B. Mynors (Oxford, 1969), Book VII, p. 281, ll. 808–12:
> *illa vel intactae segetis per summa volaret*
> *gramina nec teneras cursu laesisset aristas,*
> *vel mare per medium fluctu suspensa tumenti*
> *ferret iter celeris nec tingeret aequore plantas.*

14. Boulainvilliers, Q. 5:116. He writes: *"tanta celeritate secundo et tertio incursa movebatur quod minime terram calcare credebant, adeo ut una puellarum exclamaret: 'Johanna . . . video te volantem juxta terram.' "*

15. Antoine Astesan, *La Vièrge Guerrière Jeanne de France*, fragment d'un poème, trans. and ed. Antoine de Latour (Orléans, 1874).

16. Q. 5:22–23.

17. Philip Forest of Bergamo, *De pluribus claris scelestisque mulieribus* (Valencia, 1497); L.A., no. 60, pp. 46–7; Q. 5:521–8.

18. L.A., no. 60, p. 46; Philip Forest of Bergamo, op. cit., vol. 144.

19. Homer, *The Iliad*, trans. E. V. Rieu (London, 1976), chap. 9, p. 175, l. 557.

20. Virgil, *The Aeneid*, trans. W. F. Jackson Knight (London, 1969); and Latin version ed. Mynors, op. cit.

21. Ovid, *The Metamorphoses*, trans. Mary M. Innes (London, 1973), Book III, pp. 78–80; Book II, p. 62; Book XI, pp. 254–5; Book VIII, pp. 186–90.

22. Sylvia Plath, "Edge," in *Ariel* (London, 1965), p. 85.

23. Ovid, op. cit., Book II, p. 61.

24. Ibid., Book I, p. 41.

25. Ibid., Book VIII, p. 187.

26. Virgil, op. cit., Book XII, p. 200.

27. Ibid., Book XI, p. 299.

28. Ibid.

29. See Robert Graves, *The Greek Myths*, 2 vols. (London, 1966), 1:352–5; 2:124–32, 239, 313, 319–20. See Mandy Merck, "The City's Achievements: The Patriotic Amazonamachy and Ancient Athens," in Susan Lipshitz, ed., *Tearing the Veil* (London, 1978), pp. 95–115. See also Pomeroy, op. cit., pp. 23–5; Pierre Samuel, *Amazones, guerrières et gaillardes* (Grenoble, 1975), pp. 43–57; Marina Warner, *Alone of All Her Sex* (London, 1976), pp. 279–80.

30. Virgil, op. cit., Book XI, pp. 296–7.

31. See Samuel, op. cit., pp. 43–57; Merck, op. cit., pp. 97–8, for the early sources.

32. Heinrich von Kleist, *Penthesilea*, trans. Robert Nye in *Fugue and Sisters* (London, 1976), p. 56; also trans. Julien Gracq (Paris, 1954). Peter Wollen and Laura Mulvey wrote and directed *Penthesilea* (1974), which filmed Kleist's play in emblematic and balletic style and then discussed in a rambling but interesting manner the implications of the Amazon myth for feminism.

33. The frescoes in the Sala della Manta, Saluzzo, parallel the Nine Male Worthies with

nine Amazons: Delphila, Sinope, Hippolyta, Semiramis, Ethiope, Lampheto, Tomyris, Teuca and Penthesilea. Another frequent selection of the Nine Female
Worthies consists of Lucretia, Veturia, Virginia; Saint Helena, Saint Brigid, Saint
Elizabeth; Jael, Esther, Judith. Another, German, engraved collection, printed in
1531, chose Julia, Portia, Hippolyta, Lucretia, Thisbe, Admete, Artemisia, Argeia,
and Hypsicratea. For the origins of the group, see Jacques Longuyon, *Les Voeux du
Paon* (1312), and Thomas III, marquis of Saluzzo, *Le Chevalier Errant;* see Paolo
d'Ancona, "Gli Affreschi del Castello di Manta nel Saluzzese," *L'Arte* 8 (1905):94-198.

34. Ditié, p. 46, ll. 285-7.
35. Ibid., p. 45, ll. 217-24.
36. See L.A., no. 35, pp. 33-5, for publication of Jean de Colonne's brief text, *Nouveau
    témoignage relatif à la mission de Jeanne d'Arc,* Léopold Delisle (Paris, 1885).
37. D'Ancona, op. cit. I am most grateful to Dr. Elizabeth McGrath of the Warburg
    Institute for the observation about the Worthies' plastic qualities.
38. Eustache Deschamps, *Oeuvres complètes* (Paris, 1891).
39. J. Huizinga, *The Waning of the Middle Ages* (London, 1972), pp. 69-70.
40. Deschamps, *Oeuvres,* 1:199-201, 3:192-4:

> Duc Godefroy de touz n'est pas le mendre
> Jherusalem conquist et le pais . . .

41. D'Ancona, op. cit., p. 19.
42. Bourgeois, pp. 269-70.
43. Homer, op. cit., Book XVIII, pp. 514-15; Pomeroy, op. cit., pp. 118, 187-8.
44. Herodotus, Book VIII, p. 93; Philip Slater, *The Glory of Hera* (Boston, 1968), p. 10.
45. Boccaccio, *De Claris Mulieribus,* trans. Donato di Casentino and ed. Luigi Tosti
    (Milan, 1841), p. 419.
46. Memoirs of Pius II, Q. 4:510: "*Dux foemina belli facta est. Allata sunt arma; adducti
    equi; Puella ferociorem ascendit, et ardens in armis, hastam vibrans, saltare, currere
    atque in gyrum se vertere haud aliter coegit equum, quam de Camilla fabulae
    tradunt.*"
47. Samuel, op. cit., pp. 22-35. Sir Walter Raleigh is one of the many explorers who
    sighted Amazons—in Guyana.
48. Jose Toribio Medina, *Descrubimento del Rio de las Amazonas sugun la relacion de
    Fr. Gaspar de Carvajal* [Seville, 1894], trans. American Geographical Society (New
    York, 1914), p. 204.
49. Ibid., p. 214.
50. L.A., no. 69, pp. 52-3.
51. Antoine Dufour, *La Vie des femmes célèbres* (Geneva, 1970); L.A., no. 64, p. 49.
52. Dufour, op. cit., pp. 33-4.
53. Ibid., p. 162.
54. L.A., no. 64. p. 49.
55. Valerandi Varanii, *De Gestis Joannae Virginis Francae Egregiae Bellatricis,* ed. E.
    Prarond (Paris, 1889); L.A., no. 1453, pp. 648-50.,
56. Léon Tripault. *Joanne Darciae obsidionis Aurelianae Liberatricis res gestae, imago
    et iudicium* (Orleans, 1583); L.A., no. 871-3, pp. 386-93.
57. André Thévet, *Les Vrais Portraits et vies des hommes illustres recueillis de leurs
    tableaux, livre* etc. (Paris, 1584); L.A., no. 91, pp. 70-1.
58. See engraving of 1621, L.A., p. 391.
59. See ibid., no. 101, pp. 78-9.
60. Boiardo, *Orlando Innamorato* (1483); Ludovico Ariosto, *Orlando Furioso* (1516);

Torquato Tasso, *Gerusalemme Liberata* (1570). Their heroines have predecessors in the fourteenth century, in France, England and Italy, including the Nut Brown Maid, who responds to the challenge:

> *Culte your here up by your ere*
> *Your kirtel by the knee*
> *With bone in hand for to withstande*
> *Your enmys if nede be.*

Quoted in Gervase Mathew, *The Court of Richard II* (London, 1968), p. 133. See also Samuel, op. cit., pp. 182–3.

61. Peter Burke, *Popular Culture in Early Modern Europe* (London, 1978), pp. 254–7.
62. Tasso, op. cit., ed. Lodovico Magugliana (Milan, 1950), Book III, verse 21, p. 66.
63. Jean Hordal, *Heroinae nobilissimae* etc. (Port-à-Mousson, 1612):

> *Ora, di quanto questa valorosa*
> *Fanciulla supera la favolosa*
> *Bradamante. Di quanto più buggia*
> *Grada sì, ma sbelletata è fallace,*
> *Cede a la venta, nuda che sia,*
> *Di tanto di cede Ariosto mendace.*

64. For Claude Deruet's career and work, see F. G. Pariset, "Claude Deruet," *Gazette des Beaux Arts* 52, no. 1, pp. 153–73; *Revue des Arts* 9 (1959): 275–82, 10 (1960): 261; "Le Mariage d'Henri de Lorraine et de Marguerite de Gonzague-Mantoue," in *Fêtes de la Renaissance*, ed. J. Jacquot (Paris, 1975), 1:153–89.
65. In the Musée Historique Lorraine, Nancy.
66. In the Musée des Beaux-Arts, Rouen.
67. Jean Chapelain, *La Pucelle ou la France delivrée* (Paris, 1656); L.A., no. 1719, pp. 755–9.
68. Dossier on Fovatier's statue in Centre Jeanne d'Arc, Orleans.
69. See Carol Schreier Rupprecht, "The Martial Maid and the Challenge of Androgyny (Notes on an Unbefriended Archetype)," *Spring* 1974: 269–93.
70. Paula Weideger, *Menstruation and Menopause: The Physiology, the Myth and the Reality* (New York, 1976), p. 16.
71. See Graves, op. cit., 1:35; Merck, op. cit., p. 110; Samuel, op. cit., pp. 22–76.
72. Ariosto, op. cit., ed. Piero Nardi (Mondadori, 1964), Canto XLV, pp. 693–9.
73. "Jeanne d'Arc ou la Pucelle d'Orléans," cited in L.A., no. 1795, pp. 187–8.
74. *Jeanne d'Arc* (Marseille, 1870); L.A., no. 1969, p. 894.
75. Thomas Keneally, *Blood Red, Sister Rose* (London, 1974), p. 187.
76. Joan has several degenerate descendants in other armed maidens, and they continue to exercise the fascination and the seductiveness of the classical Amazon. The Bionic Woman of the television serial of the seventies, though she wears ordinary dress most of the time, has the bisexual name of Jamie Summers. "She does not use a tin opener but her nail, and to make a cake, she uses her hand, double-quick, even faster than a mixer" (information from Lorraine Haigh, to whom I am most grateful). Wonder Woman, the American comic strip that first appeared after the war, features a series of armed maidens from an Amazon colony in outer space with names like Diana Prince (reminiscent of both the goddess and the maleness). Even the Playboy Bunny, the fetish of the Playboy Clubs, bastion of male sexism and sexual capitalism, wears the remnants of a transvestite dress: stiff collar, bow tie and cuffs with links. The whalebone corsage is the last vestige of the armour of her ancestors, and the sexual definition of Clorinda's flowing, golden hair is achieved by the cutaway of the Bunny's costume at the crotch.

CHAPTER II PERSONIFICATION OF VIRTUE

1. *Ariel* (London, 1965), p. 74.
2. Peter Burke, *Popular Culture in Early Modern Europe* (London, 1978), pp. 51–2.
3. Guillaume de Lorris and Jean de Meung, *Le Romaunt de la rose,* ed. Ronald Sutherland (Oxford, 1967); see C. S. Lewis, *The Allegory of Love* (Cambridge, 1936), chap. 3, passim.
4. Christine de Pisan, *Le Dit de la rose,* ed. Ferdinand Meuckenkamp (Malle, 1891); Charles Frederick Ward, *Epistles on the Romance of the Rose, and Other Documents in the Debate* (Chicago, 1911), passim.
5. Jean Gerson, *Tractatus Contra Romantium de Rosa;* Barbara Tuchman, *A Distant Mirror* (London, 1979), pp. 480–1.
6. *Ditié,* p. 46, ll. 265–70.
7. Rankin-Quintal, pp. 10–11.
8. Martin le Franc, *Le Champion des Dames,* ed. Arthur Piaget (Lausanne, 1968); L.A., no. 1472, pp. 659–61.
9. *Le Bien et le mal des dames* (Paris, c. 1530), in L. Petit de Julleville, *Répertoire du théâtre comique en France au Moyen-Age* (Paris, 1886), pp. 261–2.
10. *Le Mirouer des femmes vertueuses* (Lyon, 1546). It places her birth under the sign of Gemini, which also ruled during relief of Orleans: "*Ecce puella valens geminis vivat aurelianos.*" The anonymous author claims to have heard from an eyewitness that Joan prophesied her death in Compiègne, before she was captured. Gemini was again the ruling sign: "*Nunc cadit in geminis burgundo vincta puella.*" But the author's fatalism becomes more didactic in his concluding lines. The English were defeated, he says:

> La par experience chascun voit
> Ce que on dit communement
> Que Dieu (vray juge) quand que ce soit
> Rend a ung chascun son payement.

11. François de Billon, *Le Fort inexpugnable de l'honneur du sexe féminin,* intro. by M. A. Screech (New York and Mouton, 1970; Paris, 1955). See fol. 48 for Joan, L.A., no. 80, p. 62.
12. Guillaume Postel, *Les Très Merveilleuses Victoires etc.* (Paris, 1553; Rouen, c. 1750); Pierre Marot, "De la réhabilitation à la glorification de Jeanne d'Arc," *Mémorial du Vième centenaire de la réhabilitation* (Paris, 1956), p. 94.
13. Postel, op. cit., chaps. 6 and 8, pp. 23, 26; see also M. A. Screech, "The Illusion of Postel's Feminism," *Journal of the Warburg and Courtauld Institutes* 16 (1953): 162–70.
14. Erich Neumann, *The Great Mother: An Analysis of the Archetype,* trans. Ralph Manheim (New York, 1955), pp. 329–30.
15. See Etienne Catta, "Sedes Sapientiae," in Hubert du Manoir de Juaye, S.J., ed., *Maria: Etudes sur la Sainte Vièrge,* 8 vols. (Paris, 1949–71), vol. 6, for Christian interpretations of Seat of Wisdom as applying to the feminine, incarnate in Mary; see Gertrud Schiller, *Iconography of Christian Art,* trans. J. Seligman (London, 1971), 1:23–5, for visual personifications of Wisdom as female in Christian churches, e.g., on Chartres's west front, where the Virgin appears as Wisdom with Christ, the Logos, on her knees; in church of San Francesco, Pisa, where Wisdom appears surrounded by the Virtues, all female; in a thirteenth-century moralised Bible, now in the Bibliothèque Nationale, Paris, in which Solomon is accompanied by Lady Wisdom.

16. Robert McQueen Grant, *Gnosticism: A Sourcebook* (New York, 1961), pp. 143–208.

17. Robert E. Lerner, *The Heresy of the Free Spirit in the Later Middle Ages* (Berkeley, 1972), pp. 230–2.

18. Christopher Hill, *The World Turned Upside Down* (New York, 1972), p. 259.

19. Pierre Lemoyne, S.J., *La Gallerie des femmes fortes* (Paris, 1647); L.A., no. 111, p. 85.

20. Lemoyne, op. cit., pp. 358–9.

21. Henry Chadwick, *Priscillian of Avila: The Occult and the Charismatic in the Early Church* (Oxford, 1976). p. 72.

22. Marina Yaguello, *Les Mots et les femmes* (Paris, 1978), pp. 91–113.

23. Ibid., passim; Anne-Marie Houbédine, "Les Femmes et la langue," *Tel Quel* 74 (Winter 1977): 84–95; Robin Lakoff, *Language and Women's Place* (New York, 1974); Mary Ritchie Key, *Male/Female Language* (Englewood, N.J., 1975). The association of the male gender with qualities of courage, action, strength was recognised long ago, even by Sophocles in *Antigone*. His heroine uses the masculine pronoun of herself when she stands up to Creon in order to emphasise her forcefulness. He replies: "I am not a man, she is the man if she shall have this success without penalty" (ll. 484–85), quoted by Sarah B. Pomeroy, *Goddesses, Whores, Wives, and Slaves* (New York, 1975), p. 100. This is the same concept of manliness, as opposed to womanishness, as is contained in Lady Macbeth's famous speech, "Unsex me here" (Act I, Scene 5), and in Macbeth's lines to her (Act I, Scene 7):
    > *bring forth men children only,*
    > *For thy undaunted mettle should compose*
    > *Nothing but males.*

    The feminine gender is rarely applied in English to anything but female individuals. Anthony Powell gives a rare example, in *The Valley of Bones* (London, 1977), p. 72, when he uses *she* of the army company of one of his characters.

24. David Mitchell, *Queen Christabel* (London, 1977), p. 54.

25. Yaguello, op. cit., pp. 92, 101.

26. Arnold van Gennep, "Le Sexe des mots," in *Religions, Mœurs et Légendes: Essais d'Ethnographie et de Linguistique*, 1st ser. (1908), pp. 265–75. In case it might seem that a gender system based on male and female categories cannot escape a hierarchical use of them, it is worth noting that languages exist in which gender is used quite differently, with a corresponding difference in sexual definition and value themselves. The Californian Indian Yana language uses gender subjectively—not objectively as we do in English—as do also the Youagirs in northeast Siberia and the speakers of the Darkhat dialect in Mongolia. *My house* is feminine if the speaker is a woman, but masculine on the lips of a man. Other languages create altogether different classification systems, based on oppositions other than sexual: the Tully River Blacks distinguish animals, for instance, by their size, not their sex; the Dravido-munda languages of southern India and the Iroquois divide the natural world into animate and inanimate. Thus our use of masculine and feminine in language is not inbuilt and immovable; it can be changed.

27. See Roy C. Strong, *Portraits of Queen Elizabeth I* (Oxford, 1963), pp. 33–41; Frances Yates, *Astraea: The Imperial Theme in the Sixteenth Century* (London, 1975), pp. 59–69.

28. Eric Hobsbawm, "Man and Woman in Socialist Iconography," in *History Workshop 6* (Autumn, 1978): 121–4.

29. Cesare Ripa, *Iconologia overo Descrittione delle Imagini universali, cavate delle*

statue, e Medaglie antiche, e da buonissimi Auttori Greci, et Latini di Cesare Ripa Perugino (Milan, 1602).

30. Ibid., pp. 90–3.

31. Prudentius, *Oeuvres*, ed. A. Lavarenne, vol. 3, *Psychomachie: Contre Symmaque* (Paris, 1948).

32. See Adolf Katzenellenbogen, *Allegories of the Virtues and Vices in Medieval Art* (London, 1939), passim; Emile Mâle, *Religious Art from the Twelfth to the Eighteenth Century* (New York, 1970), pp. 71 ff., 138 ff., 192 ff.; Mâle, *L'Art religieux du treizième siècle en France* (Paris, 1925), pp. 100–6; Mâle, *L'Art religieux à la fin du Moyen-Age* (Paris, 1908), pp. 365–70. Battles of Virtues and Vices appear represented in Clermont-Ferrand, Tournai and Aulnay in different media; at Chartres, in the stained glass, the Virtues still carry their lances, inherited from the battle scene. See Petit de Julleville, op. cit., pp. 315, 324, for description of *Les Sept Vertus et Les Sept Pèches Mortels,* a morality play performed in Tours in 1390.

33. Lina Eckenstein, *Women under Monasticism* (Cambridge, 1896), pp. 238–55.

34. Mantegna's version is now in the Louvre, Paris; Dora Panofsky, *Pandora's Box: Changing Aspects of a Mythical Symbol* (London, 1956), discusses it, pp. 43–4; Jean Seznec, *La Survivance des dieux antiques* (London, 1940), discusses Perugino's and Mantegna's treatments of the *psychomachia theme,* pp. 99–100. The National Gallery, London, has an exquisite example, *The Battle of Love and Chastity,* fifteenth century, artist unknown. Chastity swings a ball and chain; Love's arrows are broken.

35. See Millard Meiss, *Painting in Florence and Siena after the Black Death* (New York, 1964), pp. 99–100, pl. 95 for Andrea de Firenze's allegory of Christian Learning in S. Maria Novella's Spanish Chapel in Florence; in a fifteenth-century Florentine miniature, attributed to Botticelli and now in the Musée Condé, Chantilly, the Seven Liberal Arts, again all maidens, are arranged on the Hill of Knowledge with their chief proponents, all male, sitting beside them; at Chartres, the Virgin is enthroned as Wisdom, with the Liberal Arts at her side; Francesco Pesellino (and studio) worked on the same theme in a painting now in the Birmingham Museum of Art, Alabama.

36. The medieval fondness for systematic classification never quite established the Celestial Beatitudes, and Hildegard's list is fairly idiosyncratic. The usual source is Matthew 5:3–10 (the Sermon on the Mount). The twelfth- to thirteenth-century mosaic in St. Mark's, Venice, for instance, follows this scheme: Poor in Spirit (Humility); Mourners (Contrition); Meek (Benignitas); Hunger and Thirst after Righteousness (Abstinence); Mercy (Misericordia); Pure at Heart (Castitas); Peacemakers (Patientia); Persecuted (Modestia): Constantia is usually added, to make Nine Beatitudes in all. At Chartres, on the north porch, in the archivolts of the left bay, fourteen Beatitudes are represented, all young women as well. For Hildegard's vision, see *Patrologia Latina,* ed. J. P. Migne, 197:383–738.

37. The other exponents are Grammar, Donatus; Arithmetic, Pythagoras; Logic, Zeno; Astronomy, Ptolemy; Rhetoric, Cicero. See, for instance, Niccolò de Bologna's illumination for *Novella in Libris Decretalium* by Giovanni d'Andrea, Ms. B. 42. Biblioteca Ambrosiana, Milan, in *Gothic Illuminated Manuscripts,* ed. Emma Pirani (London, 1970), pl. 7.

38. In the Scrovegni chapel, Padua, Giotto painted La Fortezza as a large-set, earthy woman carrying a mace and a shield with a lion rampant; the mosaics in San Marco, Venice, show Fortitudo dressed in Roman costume, holding open a lion's jaws with her bare hands; Botticelli also painted La Fortezza with her mace, a most

powerful and beautiful image, now in the Uffizi, Florence; in Rouen cathedral, La Force is depicted as a helmeted woman in armour throttling a dragon. It would be impossible to provide a full list of examples in which Fortitude is represented as an armed maiden; even the famous set of Italian playing cards, engraved c. 1475 and once attributed to Botticelli, show the Virtue in this guise.

39. Bourgeois, p. 201.

40. Glynne Wickham, "Les Fêtes du couronnement de Jacques ler," in *Fêtes de la Renaissance,* ed. J. Jacquot (Paris, 1975), 1:281.

41. E. H. Gombrich, *Symbolic Images: Studies in the Art of the Renaissance* (London, 1972), pp. 124–5.

42. 3 March, Tisset-Lanhers 2:95.

43. Bibliothèque Nationale 12476 f. Fr. miniature, engraved in L.A., no. 1472, p. 661.

44. Engraving by Léon Gaultier, L.A., p. 77.

45. This became a familiar theme in medieval didactic literature. The *Speculum Humanae Salvationis,* a popular illustrated handbook, presented Judith and the Virgin Mary side by side: Judith triumphant over Holofernes, Mary over Satan. See Fitzwilliam Museum, Cambridge, Ms. 43-1950, chap. 30.

46. Prudentius, op. cit., 2:107–8, ll. 40–41.

47. Pernoud, *Retrial,* p. 138.

48. Ibid., p. 123.

49. Q. 4:71.

50. Henri Wallon, *Jeanne d'Arc* (Paris, 1876), p. 140.

51. Ibid., reproduces the miniature, p. 141.

52. John Bugge, *Virginitas: An Essay in the History of the Medieval Ideal* (The Hague, 1975), p. 50.

53. I am grateful to Dr. Floridus Röhrig, of the Stiftlichen Museum, Klosterneuberg, Austria, for his helpful information about this painting, and to Elizabeth MacGrath and Sadika Tancred for their help in translating his letter for me.

54. Minerva was a living symbol in Joan's day. Christine de Pisan, in spite of her keen Christian loyalties, invokes her blessing and her inspiration alone in the prologue of her book about chivalry. "*O minerue, deesse darmes et de chevalerie, qui par vertu desleue entendement par sus les aultres femmes trouuas et institutas entres les autres nobles ars et sciences, qui de toy nasquirent lusage de forgier de fer et dacier. . . . Dame et haults deesse, ne te desplaise ce que moy, simple femmelette, sy comme neant enuers la grandeur de ton renomme scauoir, ose presentement emprendre a parler de sy magnifie office comme est celuy des armes.*" This cannot be said to be written without faith. Christine confirms her belief in Minerva's reality when she concludes her invocation with a claim to be Minerva's compatriot: "*et en tant te plaise moy estre fauourable que je puisse estre aucunement consonante en la naction dont tu fus nee, qui comme adonc feust nommee la grant grece le pais doult les alpes qui ores est dit puille et Calabre* [Apulia and Calabria] *en ytalie ou tu nasquis, et* je suis comme toy femme ytalienne" (*Fayttes of Armes and of Chyvalrye,* trans. William Caxton [1489] and ed. A. T. P. Byles [E.E.T.S., 1932]), pp. 7–8 (emphasis added).

CHAPTER 12   CHILD OF NATURE

1. Act II, Scene 1, in *Schiller's Historical Dramas,* trans. Anna Swanwick (London, 1847).

2. Jean François Six, "Jeanne d'Arc et Voltaire," *Le Monde*, 3 June 1978.
3. Michèle Lagny, "Culte et images de Jeanne d'Arc, 1870–1921," thesis for University of Nancy (1973), a graph of signatures in *Livre d'Or* of Domremy; see also Eugen Weber, *Peasants into Frenchmen: The Modernisation of Rural France, 1870–1914* (London, 1977), pp. 111–12.
4. *Livre d'Or*, Archives Départementales des Vosges, Epinal.
5. Ibid., September 1870.
6. Ibid., 1870:

> *Elle ne viendra pas; on ne voit plus chez nous,*
> *Depuis longtemps déjà les anges redescendre;*
> *Mais Dieu peut envoyer, s'il ne veut nous la rendre,*
> *Son génie à nos chefs et son âme à nous tous.*

7. Ibid., 1839:

> *Homage à la chaste Pucelle!*
> *Honte éternelle au célèbre écrivain*
> *Qui trempant dans la fange un pinceau tout divin*
> *Profana sans pudeur une gloire si belle!*

After seeing Schiller's drama in Berlin in 1821, Chateaubriand wrote to the duchess of Duras: "*C'est un mélodrame, mais un mélodrame superbe. La cérémonie du sacre est admirable. Quand j'ai vu la cathédrale de Reims et quand j'ai entendu le chant religieux au moment de la consécration de Charles VII, j'ai pleuré sans comprendre un mot de ce qu'on disait. . . . Quel peuple que ce peuple français. . . . Schiller chante Jeanne et Voltaire la déshonoré*" (10 April 1821, Correspondence 2:242–3, quoted in *Jeanne d'Arc et sa légende*, introduction by Catherine Legrand, catalogue for Tours exhibition, 1979, p. 12).
8. Voltaire, *La Pucelle d'Orleans*, in *Oeuvres complétes*, 66 vols. (Renonard, 1819–25), vol 9.
9. Ibid., p. 21:

> *Et le plus grands de ses rares travaux*
> *Fut de garder un an son pucelage.*

10. Ibid., p. 367:

> *A ce discours. peut-être téméraire*
> *Jeanne sentit une juste colère:*
> *Aimer un âne et lui donner sa fleur!*
> *Mais que cet âne, ô ciel! a de mérite!*

11. Jules Michelet, *Jeanne d'Arc*, in *Histoire de France*, vol. 5 (Paris, 1844; first published as separate edition, Paris, 1853).
12. Quicherat (see list of abbreviations).
13. Auguste Vallet de Viriville, *Procès de condamnation de Jeanne Darc dite la Pucelle d'Orléans traduit du latin et publie intégralement pour la première fois en français* . . . (Paris, 1867), was the first translation of the trial into the vernacular. Eugene O'Reilly, a lawyer of Rouen, translated the trial and the rehabilitation and related documents for the first time during the following year in two volumes. These works had an incalculable effect on Joan's prominence.
14. Denis Diderot and Le Rond d'Alembert, *Encyclopédie*, vol. 7 (Paris, 1782), pp. 443–4.
15. See *Jeanne au théâtre*, catalogue of exhibition held at Maison de Jeanne d'Arc, Orleans, November 1975–February 1976, p. 13.
16. Joseph Calmette, *Jeanne d'Arc* (Paris, 1946), p. 132. This could be a painting by the German Raymond de Baux, a specialist in battle scenes, exhibited at Tours in 1979 in *Jeanne d'Arc et sa légende*. Baux's works are, however, dated later than Schiller's

play in most cases, so the playwright's immediate inspiration might be another equestrian portrait, in the collection of the museum in Orleans, that was lost in the bombing during World War II.

17. Schiller, op. cit., Act IV, Scene 1; Act V, Scene 14.

18. *Jeanne au théâtre*, pp. 13–18, gives an interesting and full list of the melodramas inspired by Schiller's play. See also L.A., nos. 1789–1802, for French verse dramas, often influenced by Schiller, written between 1809–46; also nos. 1831–1910 for editions of Schiller and versions or translations in other languages of this popular play.

19. Alexandre Soumet, *Jeanne d'Arc* (Paris, 1825). Ten years after the defeat of Napoleon at Waterloo, the interpreters of Joan recited in the final scene:

> *Terre de Saint-Louis,*
> *De ces tyrans des mers cesse d'être sujette.*
> *Anglais, disparaissez, la France vous rejette . . .*

L.A., no. 1794, p. 816. The diarist Crabb Robinson saw one of these by-products of Schiller, T. J. Serle's *Joan of Arc*, in December 1837 at Covent Garden. He reported Serle's ingenious plot: "The melodrama of Joan of Arc also a very efficient spectacle. Miss Hoddart produced an impression though she was not equal to the character—she has a fine figure (a little plump for the heroine, though). The visions by which she is called to her great work are finely conceived, and the *catastrophe is satisfactory*—Her life is offered by the She-Wolf of France to Lionel, if he will degrade himself by marrying her, which however she refuses, because by doing [so], she will save France. The pile is lighted, Lionel gives her a dagger with which she stabs herself. The French then burst in, the English fly and she receives the dying homage of the King. Her crime consisted in wilfully saving Lionel's life by forcing the King to allow him the protection of the altar at his Coronation. The love part is better than Schiller's expedient" (from *The London Theatre, 1811–66*, selections from the diary of Henry Crabb Robinson, ed. Eluned Brown [London, 1966]).

20. Giuseppe Verdi, *Giovanna d'Arco*, libretto by Temistocle Solera, performed in translation by Rodney Blumer, by the Oxford University Opera Club, Oxford Playhouse, 15–19 February 1977. Conductor: Denis Arnold; Jeanne: Helen Walker.

21. Piotr Tchaikovsky, *The Maid of Orleans*, libretto by the composer, after Schiller, performed by the University College London Opera, Collegiate Theatre, February 1978. Conductor: Guy Woolfenden; Johanna: Dianne Stafford. Other operas about Joan were written and composed during the century, but they are for the most part forgotten. L.A., nos. 1957–73, gives the inventory from the 1793 production of a lost opera by Andreozzi in Venice until the end of the century. Michael Balfe (1808–70), the Irish composer and singer and a favourite with English audiences in the 1830s, presented his *Joan of Arc* in 1837 at Drury Lane.

22. Jules Barbier, *Jeanne d'Arc* (Paris, 1869). I read it in Henri Darbélit's version edited for performance by children (Paris, 1894). Gounod also wrote a new Mass for Joan of Arc, which was performed in July 1887, on the 458th anniversary of the coronation of Charles VII. Joan, though the inspiration of the Mass, was not yet a saint. *The Graphic* of 30 July commented that the work was an "avowed imitation of Palestrina." Sarah Bernhardt played Joan, again, in 1909, when she was *sixty-five*. Emile Moreau wrote *Le Procès de Jeanne d'Arc* for her; it was a huge success.

23. Queen Victoria, *Darling Child*, ed. Roger Fulford (London, 1976): "Lohengrin is our great favourite but I delight in Gounod too," wrote the queen. "His Faust, Romeo and Juliet, and Mireille and Joan of Arc are so lovely" (p. 223).

24. *Jeanne au théâtre*, p. 12. This pantomime is not extant; but another French one of

the same period is and perhaps reveals a similar spirit of masque-like adventure. *Dorothée, pantomime en 3 actes, ornée d'un prologue terminé par le triomphe de La Pucelle* (Paris, 1782), tells the story of the chaste Dorothée, who is assaulted, insulted, threatened and finally sentenced by a wicked official. But just as she is about to be burned, Dunois appears, issues challenges on her behalf, prevails against all comers and is finally joined by La Pucelle—Joan—for the triumphant deliverance of Dorothée into her husband's hands.

25. Robert Southey, *Joan of Arc: In Poems, Ballads and Lyrics* (London, 1863), pp. 1–137. It was an innovation for an English writer to treat Joan. Walter Savage Landor, "Dialogues of Famous Women," in *Imaginary Conversations* (London, 1829), was one of the few who followed Southey's example, with a dramatic poem about Agnes Sorel and Joan.

26. Southey, op. cit., p. 3.

27. Ibid., p. 14.

28. Ibid., pp. 6–7.

29. Ibid., p. 119.

30. Ibid., p. xiii.

31. Byron's "Vision of Judgement" is a swinging attack on Southey for his monarchist "Wat Tyler" poem, and it sets out to redress the "stupidity . . . gross flattery, the dull impudence, the renegade intolerance and impious cant" with a burlesque of George III's arrival in heaven and of Southey's own rude reception there:

    > He first sank to the bottom—like his works,
    > But soon rose to the surface—like himself;
    > For all corrupted things are buoy'd like corks . . .

    Works of Lord Byron (London, 1832), 12:243–96. Raymond Williams, *Culture and Society, 1780–1950* (London, 1963), discusses Southey's relationship to Owen, pp. 39–43.

32. Southey, op. cit., p. 135.

33. Thomas de Quincey, *Works*, vol. 3, *The Last Days of Immanuel Kant and Other Writings* (Edinburgh, 1863), pp. 206–45.

34. Michelet, op. cit., p. 180: "*Le Sauveur de la France devait être une femme. La France était femme elle-même. Elle en avait la mobilité, mais aussi l'aimable douceur, la pitié facile et charmante, l'excellence au moins du premier mouvement. Lors même qu'elle se complaisait aux vaines élégances et raffinements extérieurs, elle restait au fond plus près de la nature.*"

35. De Quincey, op. cit., p. 209.

36. Ibid., p. 206.

37. Ibid., p. 244.

38. Ibid., p. 245.

39. Ibid., p. 218.

40. Ibid., p. 219.

41. Alphonse de Lamartine, "Jeanne d'Arc," *Le Civilisateur, Journal Historique* (April–May 1852).

42. Ibid., p. 52: "*Et puis nos péres le savaient: La femme, inférieure par ses sens, est supérieure par son âme. Les Gaulois lui attribuaient un sens de plus, le sens divin. Ils avaient raison.*"

43. Ibid., pp. 61–62: "*Cette noblesse de cœur et de front qu'on retrouve dans ceux qui cultivent la terre paternelle plus que dans ceux qui travaillent dans l'atelier d'autrui.*"

44. Ibid., p. 69: "*Faut-il s'étonner qu'une telle concentration de pensée dans une pauvre jeune fille ignorante et simple ait produit enfin une véritable transportation de sens*

en elle, et qu'elle ait entendu à ses oreilles les voix intérieures qui parlaient sans cesse à son âme?"

45. Ibid., p. 74: "*L'idée d'une jeune fille conduisant les armées aux combats, couronnant son jeune roi et délivrant son pays, était née de la Bible et du fabliau à la fois. C'était la poésie des veillées de village. Jeanne d'Arc en fit la religion de la patrie.*"

46. Casimir Delavigne, "La Vie de Jeanne d'Arc" and "La Mort de Jeanne d'Arc," in *Les Messéniennes* (Paris, 1819), pp. 115–22. The title refers to the resistance of the women of Messenia against Sparta.

47. Alexandre Dumas, *Jeanne d'Arc (1429–1431)* (Paris, 1842). His son also wrote a novel about Joan, called *La Restauration de Charles VII*, or *Tristan le Roux* (Paris, 1866).

48. 24 February, Tisset-Lanhers 2:65–8; Scott, p. 75: "and she had heard it said that persons suffering from fever drank of it; and she has seen them going to it to be cured."

49. Tisset-Lanhers 2:65–68; Scott, pp. 75–6.

50. 1 March, Tisset-Lanhers 2:87; Scott, p. 88.

51. Pernoud, *Retrial*, p. 62; Douglas Murray, pp. 219–20.

52. Pernoud, *Retrial*, p. 65.

53. Ibid., pp. 65–6. Douglas Murray, p. 221.

54. Edmond Richer, *Histoire de la Pucelle d'Orleans*, Bibliothèque Nationale, Fonds Français Ms. No. 10448, 5 vols., vol. 1 (1911), p. 67; quoted in Tisset-Lanhers 2:65. Richer was a former theologian of the University of Paris, and he wrote his work in answer to the slurs of Du Haillan. He drew fully on manuscripts of the trial, one of which du Lis lent him (see Chapter 10 for du Lis's involvement in the growth of Joan's historiography) and the other was consulted in the Bibliothèque Nationale. His study of Joan was not published for two hundred years, although it was plagiarized and summarised (without acknowledgement) by the Abbé Lenglet-Dufresnoy, in *Histoire de Jeanne d'Arc*, 3 vols. (Paris, 1753–54).

55. The most subtle and discriminating discussion of innocence and its rights can be found in Michael Walzer, *Just and Unjust Wars* (London, 1978), an extraordinary work that prompts much close questioning of presumptions about peace and war.

56. George Boas, *The Cult of Childhood* (Leiden, 1966), pp. 22 ff, discusses the development of the idea of primordial innocence, as opposed to original sin, in the work of such philosophers as Agrippa von Nettesheim, a feminist *avant la lettre*, and in the interpretations of the *loci classici* of the rise of the Child: Matthew 18:1–6 ("Except ye be converted, and become as little children, ye shall not enter the kingdom of heaven"), and Mark 10:14 ("Suffer the little children to come unto me . . ."). Trenchantly, Boas surveys the eclipse of many anti-child texts in the New Testament (e.g., Paul's famous "When I was a child, I thought as a child . . .) by the passages that exalt child wisdom.

57. Perceval de Boulainvilliers, in Q. 5:116: "*agnorum custodiae a parentibus deputatur, in qua nec ovicula noscitur deperiisse, nec quicquam a fera exstitit devoratum.*"

58. *Chronique d'Antonio Morosini*, ed. G. Lefèvre-Pontalis (Paris, 1902), 3:41–3, reports how people laughed at the news of Joan's coming: "*en faisaient les plus belles moqueries du monde, surtout d'une pucelle gardeuse de moutons.*"

59. Bourgeois, pp. 233–4: "When she was very small and looked after the sheep, birds would come from the woods and fields when she called them and eat bread in her lap as if they were tame."

60. Bourgeois, p. 269.

61. Jacques Audiberti, "Pucelle," in *Théâtre*, vol. 2 (Paris, 1952). This is one of the

more interesting modern dramas about Joan, but it has been rarely revived since its first production in Paris in 1950.

62. Ibid., p. 145.

63. Boas, op. cit., p. 46, discusses the relationship of ideas about angels to ideas about children, as embodied in the appearance of cherubim in Renaissance art as winged babies, for the first time in the Western iconographical tradition, which had hitherto preferred Ezekiel's bodiless heads and flaming wings covered with eyes. The most famous cherubim in the new style of *putti* stand at the foot of the Madonna's throne in Raphael's *Madonna detta del Baldacchino*, in the Pitti Gallery, Florence.

64. Booklet of 18 April 1909, on occasion of the declaration of Joan of Arc's beatification. Now rare. Collection of Centre Jeanne d'Arc, Orleans.

65. The stained glass windows were endowed by private subscription, raised through the efforts of Mgr. Dupanloup, bishop of Orleans and one of Joan's most fervent venerators. He founded an action committee in May 1878 to raise a statue and install windows in honour of the heroine, as it was a disgrace, he considered, that Joan of Arc should be without honour in her own cathedral. He declared that he would personally give the first window, on the subject of "Domremy." The following year, he launched a national subscription. When Dupanloup died in 1878, a substantial sum had been raised—102,965 *francs*. The three princes of Orleans had taken over the commission of the "Domremy" glass, the duke of Aumale had assumed one for Les Tourelles and Dupanloup himself had changed to the coronation.

    Fourteen candidates entered for the competition to design the windows; Gibelin and Jac-Galland won it, and their cycle was unveiled on 7 May 1897, with the new bishop, Mgr. Touchet, an equally fervent admirer of Joan of Arc, in the *cathedra*. Both Dupanloup and Touchet have magnificent funerary monuments in the cathedral of Orleans. By exalting the servants of the saint, the monuments provide an accurate image of late nineteenth century triumphalism. *"Mgr. P. M. Brun, Mgr. Dupanloup et Jeanne d'Arc,"* Association des Amis du Centre Jeanne d'Arc, bulletin no. 2 (January 1979): 4–9.

66. André Laurent, *La Basilique du bois chesnu* (Colmar, 1974). Royer's cycle consists of eight large tableaux, painted between 1910 and 1913. The first communion at Domremy is juxtaposed to the last communion in prison.

67. Maurice Boutet de Monvel (1850–1913), *Jeanne d'Arc* (Paris, 1973). The large-scale versions of the book illustrations in oil and gold leaf are in the Corcoran Museum, Washington, D.C.

68. For Saint Geneviève, see David Hugh Farmer, *Oxford Dictionary of Saints* (Oxford, 1978), pp. 164–5; for Saint Margaret, ibid., pp. 260–1. The miniature in the *Heures d'Etienne Chevalier*, now in the Louvre, by Jean Fouquet, Joan's contemporary, shows Margaret as a shepherdess and resembles closely the miniature of Joan in the fields at Domremy in the *Vigilles of Charles VII* by Martial d'Auvergne (Bibliothèque Nationale F.f. 9677), painted a few years later.

69. Michelet, op. cit., p. 180.

70. Mark Twain, *Personal Recollections of Joan of Arc, by the Sieur Louis de Conte* (Her Page and Secretary). Freely translated out of the ancient French into Modern English from the Original Unpublished Manuscript in the National Archives of France by Jean François Alden (New York, 1896; London, 1922).

71. William Searle, *The Saint and the Sceptics: Joan of Arc in the Works of Mark Twain, Anatole France, and Bernard Shaw* (Detroit, 1976), pp. 15–55, discusses illuminatingly Twain's attitude to Joan of Arc.

72. Ibid., p. 34.

73. Mark Twain, "Joan of Arc," in *The Complete Essays*, ed. Charles Neider (New York, 1963), pp. 320-1.
74. Searle, op. cit., pp. 59–96, analyses Anatole France's contradictory view of Joan.
75. Marie-Edmée Pau, *Histoire de notre petite sœur, Jeanne d'Arc*, with foreword by the bishop of Saint Dié (Paris, 1879). Lagny, op. cit., also discusses Pau's life and work.
76. Pau, op. cit., p. 114.
77. 21 February, Tisset-Lanhers 2:41: "*Elle dit en outre que sa mère lui apprit le Pater Noster, l'Ave, le Credo; et elle n'apprit sa croyance de personne que de sadite mère.*"
78. 22 February, ibid., p. 45: spinning and sewing, and also "*pendant qu'elle était dans la maison de son père, vaquait aux besognes familiales de la maison . . .*"
79. It is made of plaster, painted to look like bronze. The poke bonnet worn by Isabelle is an inexplicable anachronism, neither of Joan's date nor of the period of the sculptor. The full inscription reads: "*L'Abbé Lucien Vivenot promoteur de ce monument à voulu rendre hommage à la mère de Jeanne d'Arc, enfant de Vouthon, jeune fille de Vouthon, femme de Domremy, glorieuse maman de France et mettre en evidence le rôle detérminant de la mère dans la formation des enfants.* Derrière les saints cherchez leur mère. *Ce groupe statuaire a été inauguré le dimanche 7 septembre 1961 au Nom des Mamans par Mme Hahn Docteur en Médecine et Maman de Sept Enfants. SCIENCE DEVOUEMENT VIE CHRETIENNE et Bénit par son Excellence Mgr. Petit, Evêque de Verdun*" in the presence of three other bishops and several deputies from Lorraine.

CHAPTER 13   SAINT OR PATRIOT?

1. "Le sommet de la vie de Jeanne d'Arc, c'est sa mort, c'est le bûcher de Rouen," *Théâtre* (Paris, 1965), vol. 2, preface to 1948 edition, p. 1514.
2. Owen Chadwick, *The Secularisation of the European Mind in the Nineteenth Century* (Cambridge, 1975), pp. 111-12, discusses nineteenth-century anticlericalism brilliantly.
3. Charles Wayland Lightbody, *The Judgements of Joan* (London, 1961), p. 158.
4. This statue was moved from the Place du Martroi in Orleans to a less prestigious position near the site of the battle of Les Tourelles (where it now stands) when the Foyatier equestrian statue of Joan was raised in 1858.
5. Douglas Johnson, *France and the Dreyfus Affair* (London, 1966), gives a clear account of the period. J.-B. Duroselle, "L'Antisémitisme en France de 1886 à 1914," is a masterly survey of the intellectual background to the Dreyfus affair, in *Cahiers de Paul Claudel*, vol. 7, *La Figure d'Israël* (Paris, 1968), pp. 49–70. Jean-Paul Sartre, *Réflexions sur la question juive* (Paris, 1954), addresses the issue with memorable judgement and clarity.
6. Barrington Moore, Jr., *The Social Origins of Dictatorship and Democracy* (London, 1977), p. 491. Joan has been an inspiration for political adherents of all colours, with the most surprising contrasts. There is a statue of her, for instance, in the Lenin Museum, Moscow, which was presented to Lenin by workers from a factory in the Urals (catalogue, Musée Jeanne d'Arc, Chinon [Tours, 1973]). Lightbody, op. cit., pp. 164–5, gives an amusing list of the variety of groups who have identified with Joan: from the corn-pone backwoods feeling of the Jerome Kern song "You can't keep a good girl down" to the more serious Jewish and anti-Semitic treatments of the subject. Leaders are often stirred to deep involvement with Joan

of Arc. Indira Gandhi has related the "call to service" she received as a young girl to Joan's experience: "Rather morbid it sounds now, but I didn't think of it in those terms. It was the sacrifice of Joan of Arc that attracted me, the girl who gave up her life for her country" (Bruce Chatwin, "Indira Gandhi," *Sunday Times Magazine*, 27 August 1978). Lucien Millevoye (1850–1918), writer and homme politique, tried to persuade Maud Gonne to make love in front of a statue of Joan of Arc in a Paris church whose sacristan he had bribed, in order that she might "conceive an Irish patriot hero." F. Stuart, *Black List Section H.* (London, 1975), p. 26.

7. Margaret Murray, *The Witch Cult in Western Europe* (1921; reprinted Oxford, 1962), pp. 24, 238–9, 271, 161. Norman Cohn, *Europe's Inner Demons* (London, 1975), pp. 107–15, demolishes Murray's arguments.

8. Michèle Lagny, "Culte et images de Jeanne d'Arc, 1870–1921," thesis for University of Nancy (1973); Tisset-Lanhers 2:65.

9. Régine Pernoud (preface) and Frédérique Duran (photographs), *Dans les pas de Jeanne d'Arc* (Paris, 1956), pp. 11–12; *Jeanne au théâtre*, catalogue of exhibition held at Maison de Jeanne d'Arc, Orleans, November 1975–February 1976, p. 19, gives a description of this spate of dramas.

10. In 1888, the decision to take the administration of the Maison de Jeanne d'Arc away from the Church and give it into the care of secular authorities provoked a row, Catholics protesting, in the words of one woman, *"Jeanne est aux femmes, aux femmes seules, et à Dieu"* (Lagny, op. cit., p. 120).

11. *Livre d'Or*, Archives Départementales des Vosges, Epinal, September 1853:

> *Enfants du léopard, vous dont les lois cruelles*
> *Ont du sang innocent inondé le bûcher,*
> *Anathème à jamais sur vos mains criminelles,*
> *La honte est le chemin où vous devez marcher!*

12. Lagny, op. cit., pp. 113–30.

13. Ibid., pp. 98–9.

14. Joseph Fabre, *Jeanne d'Arc: Libératrice de la France* (Paris, 1882); Joseph Fabre, *Jeanne d'Arc, drame historique en cinq actes* (Paris, 1890), performed at the Châtelet with Mme. Segond Weber in January 1891; Fabre also wrote a mystery play in sixteen tableaux, *La Délivrance d'Orléans*, for the feast of the relief of Orleans, performed in May 1891.

15. Charles Péguy wrote about Joan of Arc as a young man in 1897, before his conversion to intense religious faith in 1910, and again after it. Because of the cyclical character of all his work, it is difficult to discern a progression, though Péguy incorporated into *Le Mystère de la charité de Jeanne d'Arc* (1910), some lines from this earlier three-act drama, *Jeanne d'Arc*. He planned fifteen or twenty poems of the full length of the 1910 *mystère* to climax with Joan's death, but never completed this enormous project. He did, however, write the marvellous *Tapisseries de Sainte Geneviève et Jeanne d'Arc* (Paris, 1957) in 1912, and Joan appears in *Châteaux de Loire* (1912), *Eve* (1913), *M. Fernand Laudet*, and *La Note conjointe sur M. Descartes et la philosophie cartésienne*. Sister Jean-Théophane Jung OK TJO, "La Figure de Jeanne d'Arc dans l'Oeuvre de Péguy de 1910–1914," thesis for Sorbonne University (1979).

16. Anatole France, *Vie de Jeanne d'Arc* (Paris, 1908), 2 vols.

17. An Austrian newspaper published a cartoon of Joan of Arc, played by the actress Yvette Guilbert, a reactionary, carrying a banner aloft with the slogan "Wieder Milden Juden" at the head of the forces of reaction, including Esterhazy (the real culprit) and Drumont, the author of the 1,200-page *La France juive* (Paris, 1886),

the most anti-Semitic tract of the period (*Der Floh* [Vienna], January 1898, reprinted in Jean Grand-Carteret, *L'Affaire Dreyfus et l'image* [Paris, 1898], p. 192).

18. The definitive work is Eugen Weber, *L'Action Française, royalism and reaction in twentieth-century France* (Stanford, 1962); see also Zeev Sternhell, *La Droite révolutionnaire, 1885–1914: Les Origines françaises du fascisme* (Paris, 1978).

19. Weber, op. cit., p. 17; Dominique Pado, *Maurras, Béraud, Brassilach* (Monaco, 1945), quotes Maurras's last words winding up his long defence at his trial for treason in 1945: "*Venez faux trémoins! Venez faux instructeurs! Je vous attends! Je vous attends depuis quatre mois dans ma prison, sous le symbole de Jeanne d'Arc et d'Andre Chénier*" [Chénier was executed in 1794 during the Revolution] (p. 88); see also Eric Vatre, *Charles Maurras: Un Itinéraire spirituel* (Paris, 1978).

20. Weber, op. cit., p. 22.

21. Charles Maurras, *Jeanne d'Arc, Louis XIV, Napoléon* (Paris, 1937), p. 30:
> Le Patrimoine maintenu
> Et la Patrie sauvée
> Par la royauté rétablie.

22. Ibid., p. 28.

23. Ibid., p. 69.

24. Weber, op. cit., pp. 235, 219–39.

25. François Coppée, "Moisson d'épées," in *Les Récits et les élégies* (Paris, 1878):
> Or monsieur Saint Michel exauça la prière
> Que murmurait tout bas la naïve guerrière,
> Et quand elle arriva dans le lieu du repos,
> Les croix que l'on avait, pour ses nombreux tombeaux,
> Faites hativement de deux branches coupées
> Par miracle et soudain devinrent des épées . . .

26. Weber, op. cit., pp. 42, 53–4.

27. Ibid., p. 55; Pierre Marot, *De la Réhabilitation à la Glorification de Jeanne d'Arc* (Paris, 1956), p. 155.

28. Jean-Marie Dunoyer, "La Race des véhéments," *Le Monde*, 30 September 1978.

29. Maurice Barrès, in *Unpublished Notes* (London, 1920), wrote: "This daughter of the people was a foundling of democracy, of the people breaking into speech," and "Democracy, when it came into power, recognised itself in this Maid" (pp. 117–18). Barrès's politics are complex, and he never gave his open support to the Action Française. See J. M. Domenach, *Maurice Barrès par lui-même* (Paris, 1969).

30. Léon Bloy, *Jeanne d'Arc et l'Allemagne* (Paris, 1915). Bloy denounces Germany, "*C'est le chef d'oeuvre de Luther, cent ans après que la Fleur du Moyen-Age avait été suffoquée dans les flammes horribles d'un bûcher, d'avoir substitué à la douce Croix de bois qui avait consolé les peuples et fortifié les Martyrs, cette Croix de fer implacable dont le monde est épouvanté*" (p. 259).

31. Quoted in Sternhell, op. cit., p. 74.

32. Robert Brassilach, *Domremy*, a play that was printed in a private edition, as recently as 1961. Thierry Maulnier, *Jeanne et ses juges* (1949), a play performed in 1951 in Paris, 1953 in Orleans. Maulnier (b. 1909) wrote for the Action Française newspaper from 1930, but broke with them after the Occupation in France. Maulnier thought Joan "a masterpiece of helmeted sanctity" (Guillemin, *Jeanne, dite Jeanne d'Arc—The True History of Joan of Arc*, trans. William Oxferry [London, 1972], p. 201).

33. Sarah Moore Grimké, *Joan of Arc: A Biography* (Boston, 1876), cited in Lightbody, op. cit., p. 165.

34. David Mitchell. *Queen Christabel* (London, 1977), pp. 254-5, 263; Richard J. Evans, *The Feminists* (London, 1978), is a concise and illuminating account of the suffragette movement's different political affiliations. The association of Joan with feminism has been maintained by St. Joan's International Alliance, which was founded in 1911 as the Catholic Women's Suffrage Society, became international in 1931 and is dedicated to struggling for the equality of the sexes, in all such areas as labour, marriage and property. It has consultative status with the United Nations and the International Labour Organisation.

35. Mgr. Pierre-Marie Brun, "Le Premier Monument à Jeanne d'Arc sur l'ancien pont d'Orléans," in *Images de Jeanne d'Arc* (Paris, 1979), pp. 5-7; Joseph Calmette, *Jeanne d'Arc* (Paris, 1946), p. 134.

36. Rev. Francis M. Wyndham, *The Maid of Orleans: Her Life and Mission* (London and Orleans, 1894), reprints in English the decree for the introduction of the cause of canonisation, pp. 76-87; Anthony West, "Pawn to King 7," *Books and Bookmen*, July 1975, pp. 32-3, is a brilliant and cynical analysis of its political rationale; Guillemin, op. cit., also shows a cynical eye, pp. 198-201. William Searle, *The Saint and the Sceptics: Joan of Arc in the Works of Mark Twain, Anatole France, and Bernard Shaw* (Detroit, 1976), pp. 139-44, gives a very interesting account. The first hearings held before the Sacred Congregation in Rome, in 1888, and the second, in 1893, are reported in *Aurelianem Beatificationis et Canonizationis Servae Dei Ioannae de Arc Puellae Aurelianensis Nuncupataei; Positio Super Introductione Causae* (Rome, 1893). Saint Thérèse of Lisieux and the curé D'Ars were both canonised five years after Joan. As saints who had lived within the memories of many people still alive, they provided proof of the continuing health of the faith in beleaguered times. The Russian poet Anna Akhmatova was in Paris soon after the beatification. In a letter containing a memoir of Modigliani, she commented that she had seen "the little statuettes of the new saint. They were in exceedingly doubtful taste and began to appear in shops that sold religious objects" (Amanda Haight, *Anna Akhmatova: A Poetic Pilgrimage* [Oxford, 1976], p. 16). It forms a fascinating reminder that the sainthood of Joan and Thérèse was occurring at the same time as the paintings of someone as "modern" as Modigliani.

37. Wyndham, op. cit., pp. 80, 82.

38. Mgr. Pierre-Marie Brun, *Jeanne d'Arc entre l'Elysée et le Vatican*, Bulletin de la Société Archéologique et Historique de l'Orléannais, no. hors série (1977), pp. 9-10.

39. Giscard said: "*La jeunesse n'a pas de haine, mais elle a faim de justice. Elle est prête à crier sa vérité jusqu'au sacrifice. Elle a besoin d'une voie qui aimante sa vie. Quand elle l'a trouvée, il n'y a pas pour elle de plus grave péché que la patience. La jeunesse alors est irrésistible.*" With eight percent unemployment in Haute-Normandie at the time and massive lay-offs of staff in steelworks in Lorraine, the PSU (Parti Socialiste) declared that Joan of Arc was just the thing to solve contemporary problems: 53 million statues of her in steel, and the industry would be saved (*Le Monde*, 29 May 1979).

40. O. Chadwick, op. cit., pp. 127 ff.

41. Georges Bernanos, *Sanctity Will Out*, trans. R. Batchelor (London, 1947), p. 21.

42. Hugh Honour, *Romanticism* (London, 1979), p. 311. The quotation continues: "We were nature like them and our culture must, by way of reason and liberty, lead us back to nature" (from *Uber naive und sentimentalische Dichtung* [1795-96]). Wordsworth's famous phrase "shades of the prison house begin to close" in *Ode on Intimations of Immortality* reflects the same idea.

43. 21 February, Tisset-Lanhers 2:41.

44. Charles VII had been granted the Dauphiné at the age of fourteen; his son Louis's main grievance against him later was that, at the age of seventeen, he had still not been granted it. He was, however, allowed to be present with his father at the battle of Montereau (one of the few in which Charles took part) in 1437 when he was fourteen. For the different attitudes to age, see Natalie Zemon Davis, *Society and Culture in Early Modern France* (London, 1975), pp. 105–8, 113; William A. Christian, Jr., *Person and God in a Spanish Valley* (New York and London, 1972), pp. 21–4, describes fascinatingly the period of *la mocedad* or "youth" in mountain districts in Spain today. See also Philippe Ariès, *L'Enfant et la vie familiale sous l'ancien régime* (Paris, 1960).

45. *Thérèse de l'Enfant Jesus: Histoire d'une âme* (Bar-le-Duc, n.d.), *Autobiography of a Saint*, trans. Ronald Knox (London, 1958), p. 171.

46. See *Thérèse*, pp. 447–62, for the Little Flower's love of Joan d'Arc; the Archive de Lisieux has the photographs, two of which were exhibited at the Monnaie de Paris, June-September 1979.

47. Alexandre Dumas, *Jeanne d'Arc (1429–1431)* (Paris, 1842), p. vi.

48. Sarah B. Pomeroy, *Goddesses, Whores, Wives, and Slaves* (New York, 1975), pp. 109–11.

49. Alphonse de Lamartine, "Jeanne d'Arc," *Le Civilisateur, Journal Historique* (April-May 1852), p. 111.

50. Thomas de Quincey, *Works*, vol. 3, *The Last Days of Immanuel Kant and Other Writings* (Edinburgh, 1863), p. 234.

51. For an extended and illuminating analysis of the development of medieval drama out of the Easter liturgy, see O. B. Hardison, Jr., *Christian Rite and Christian Drama in the Middle Ages* (Baltimore, 1969), pp. 35–79.

52. *Joan the Woman* (1916) was De Mille's reply to the conspicuous extravagance and titanic scale of D. W. Griffiths's *Intolerance*. It began with a shot of an Allied soldier in the trenches in France and dissolved into the battlefields of the fifteenth century. De Mille deployed two thousand cowboys as cavalry and soldiers in the ferocious sequence about the battle of Orleans. Much of the fighting takes place with vivid realism in a moat, with waterlogged soldiers in plate armour floundering about and drowning. Geraldine Farrar is far too mature-looking and far too stout to make a convincing Joan of Arc for us now, but the choice shows that the image of Joan as a cropped youth had not yet become universal. De Mille was free to choose an actress who seems to us now out of character simply because she was big box-office.

    De Mille's film was among the first in what has become a rich tradition of the cinema. Georges Méliès, in 1900, made a fifteen-minute sequence (very long at that time) of twelve tableaux of Joan's life. These are now lost. In the same year as De Mille, Marco de Gastyne made *La Marveilleuse Vie de Jeanne d'Arc*, with Simone Genevois as Joan. She is magnetic and appealing, suggesting both the force and the frailty of the heroine. The battle sequences are superb: Gastyne was allowed to use units of the French army and cavalry. But as he was required to go to their billets, the settings are not very faithful to the facts. The principal battle—of Orleans—was, for instance, filmed in the marshes around Aigues Mortes and shows wonderful, long cavalry charges that, of course. never took place. But the siege tower Gastyne had built, the scene of its burning and the cuts to shots of Genevois on horseback, brandishing her standard, are thrilling. The coronation sequence is also magnificent. Gastyne was allowed to take down the statue of Joan in the parvis in front of Rheims cathedral. As his entire crew numbered four people. and he had only one costumier, it took him all day to dress the crowd of extras.

I cannot provide a full filmography of Joan of Arc, but the following films have evoked her, in differing ways:

Sheltered Daughters (1921), with Justine Johnson in the role of a girl who imagines herself to be Joan of Arc; Carl Théodor Dreyer's masterpiece, *La Passion de Jeanne d'Arc* (1927-28) [see also note 64, Chapter 1]; *Das Madchen Johanna* (1935), with Angela Salloker as Joan, made in Germany, by Gustav Ulcicky, a director who worked throughout the Nazi reign in Germany. Consequently, this version is nationalistic, militaristic and ferociously anti-English. In 1942, Diana Barrymore, daughter of John Barrymore and the actress and writer Michael Strange, played another actress in the role of Joan, one who is only wooed successfully when her paramour puts on disguise (*Between Us Girls*, director Henry Koster). In 1948, Victor Fleming directed *Joan of Arc*, made in Hollywood for the huge budget of 4.6 million dollars, in technicolor, with Ingrid Bergman. Bergman became identified—not very appropriately, perhaps—with the heroine and also played her in the poor Maxwell Anderson play, *Joan of Lorraine*, on which the Fleming film was based. The same year, perhaps influenced by Bergman, *The Miracle of the Bells* was directed by I. Pichel. In this story, Alida Valli plays an actress who is discovered and given the role of Joan of Arc. A trilogy about Joan, Elizabeth I and Lysistrata, called variously *Fémina*, *Destinées* or *Love, Soldiers and Women*, with Michèle Morgan as Joan, was directed by Jean Dellanoy in 1952. The three women are figures of Faith, Hope and Chastity. (Bergman was again cast as Joan in the filmmaker Roberto Rossellini's production, on stage, of Honegger's oratorio, *Jeanne au Bûcher*, made in 1954 [see note 54 below].) Another Hollywood beauty, Hedy Lamarr, also played Joan, in Irwin Allen's *The Story of Mankind* (1958), an earnest overview with Harpo Marx as Isaac Newton (!). Otto Preminger cast the most famous Joan of all, the one who most corresponds to our contemporary feeling about her, in 1957 in *Saint Joan*. Jean Seberg headed an all-star cast: John Gielgud as Warwick, Richard Widmark as the Dauphin, Richard Todd as Dunois and Anton Walbrook as Cauchon. In 1962, Robert Bresson tried to rescue Joan from the romantic gloss of the epics with *Le Procès de Jeanne d'Arc*, in which he cast—as he usually prefers—an amateur, Florence Carrez, in the principal role. In 1971, the recurring theme of a young woman chosen to play Joan, this time a peasant, was again attempted in the Russian film *The Début*, directed by Panfilov. The most recent film about Joan I have come across is Steven Rumbelow's *St Joan*, made on a shoestring (four thousand pounds) in England in 1977. In this version, Monica Buferd in the title role puts on a Hitler moustache and cap to stress the director's vision of Joan as a protofascist.

There have been, of course, many television treatments of Joan's life and personality, but they are beyond the scope of these notes.

53. Claudel, *Théâtre*, ed. J. Madaule (Paris, 1964-5), pp. 1217-42, © Editions Gallimard. A beautiful recording, with the Czech Philharmonic Chorus and Orchestra, under Serge Baudo, with Nelly Bourgeaud as Joan, was made in 1974. Honegger said of this work that it was enough for him to hear Claudel read and reread the text to hear the music: "*Il le fait avec une telle force plastique, si je puis dire, que tout le relief musical s'en dégage, clair et précis, pour quiconque possède un peu d'imagination musicale*" (Marcel Landowski, *Honegger* [Paris, 1957], p. 110). Another twentieth-century composer to have been inspired by the subject of Joan is Olivier Messiaen (b. 1908), who collaborated with another experimental composer, Pierre Schaeffer (b. 1910), on a musical *mystère* in 1941 by Pierre Barbier, *Portique pour une fille de France*. The part called *Les Sept Paroles de Jeanne d'Arc*, constructed like the

seven dicta of Christ on the cross and organised like the *improperia*, the reproaches of the Easter liturgy, was composed by Messiaen. Others who took part were Yves Baudrier and Léo Préger, and it was performed at Lyon and Marseilles in May 1941. I have not been able to hear this work, only to read the text.

54. The oratorio was performed at the opera in Paris in 1945, in solemn celebration of the end of the war and of the Occupation.

55. Claudel, op. cit., p. 1520: "*Ce que Jeanne n'a pu faire avec les armes, elle va le consommer avec son sang. Ce qu'elle a commencé avec cet insigne vexillaire à son poing de paysanne qui porte les noms de Jésus et de Marie, c'est l'oriflamme rouge du bûcher, jaillissant sous ses pieds comme un tourbillon d'ailes irresistibles, qui va lui donner éfficacité. C'est cette bouffée triomphale qui porte jusques aux pieds du Crucifié l'âme d'une victime innocente, c'est le souffle du feu purifiant et unificateur qui va rétablir et dégager les communications, qui va réapprendre à la France à respirer et à faire de cette vaste disponibilité de volontés et d'intelligences une seule conscience et un seul désir.*" © Editions Gallimard.

56. Pico della Mirandola, *Oration on the Dignity of Man*, quoted in Robert E. Lerner, *The Heresy of the Free Spirit in the Later Middle Ages* (Berkeley, 1972), pp. 241–2.

57. Claudel, op. cit., p. 1526: "*Elle embrasse l'holocauste. Cette flamme dont on la menaçait, elle s'y jette volontairement. Ce n'est pas assez dire qu'elle accepte, elle l'épouse: Frère le Feu, cette grande flamme joyeuse et irrésistible dont, jadis, saint François d'Assise a fait l'éloge. C'est le véhicule dont elle avait besoin, non plus le gros cheval de labour sur le lequel, jadis, elle s'acheminait vers Vaucouleurs, mais la grande paire d'ailes, aigle et colombe, au cri de "Jésus" qui va l'emporter jusqu'aux portes du Paradis: cette flamme, cette aspiration lumineuse, triomphante de la chair et de la fumée.*"

58. Martha Graham, *Seraphic Dialogue*, first performed in 1955, music by Norman dello Joio. I saw it at Covent Garden in July 1976, with Yuriko Kimura as Joan and Peter Sparling as Saint Michael.

59. See above, note 52.

60. *Thérèse*, pp. 233–4.

61. E. Bouteiller and G. de Braux, *Nouvelles recherches sur la famille de Jeanne d'Arc: Enquêtes inédites* (Paris, 1879), p. xxx; and Guillemin, op. cit., pp. 174–5, describes this episode. The Bourgeois's first-hand account is telling: "A lot was heard nowadays," he wrote in 1440, "about the Maid. . . . Many people were deceived by her and firmly believed that by her holiness she had escaped the fire, some other woman being burned instead of her. But she was really burned, and all the ashes certainly thrown into the river for fear the enchantments that they might have been used for. . . . When she [the imposter, Claude des Armoises] was near Paris, this great mistake of believing her to be the Maid sprang up again so that the University and the Parlement had her brought to Paris whether she liked it or not and shown to the people at the Palais on the marble slab in the great courtyard. . . . She admitted she had 'dressed as a man and fought as a hired soldier in the Holy Father Eugenius' wars and twice committed homicide in this war. She turned soldier again in Paris and formed part of the garrison; then she went away" (pp. 337–8).

The desire for the return of a lost leader is deeply felt and gives rise to the myth of his or her survival at frequent intervals in history. There were sightings of both the murdered kings Edward II and Richard II after their deaths; Edward VI was also believed not to have died, and many claimed to be his living self. See Keith Thomas, *Religion and the Decline of Magic* (London, 1973), pp. 496–9. Even pop idols today attract the same legend: Elvis Presley has been "seen" since his death.

62. The definitive account of the original thinking behind Joan's royal descent is given by Pierre Marot, "La Génèsē d'un roman: Jean Caze, l'inventeur de la 'bâtardise' de Jeanne d'Arc," lecture, Colloque d'Histoire Médiévale, October 1979. For the literature on the theory of her survival, see Guillemin, op. cit.. p. 26.

63. For Gastyne's film, see note 52 above.

64. Roland Barthes, in the notes to the exhibition "Ma–Espace-Temps du Japon," defines *Utsuroi* in a revealing sequence of other ideas relating to space and time in Japanese thought: *"Utsuroi: la pointe la plus subtile de la variation: moment fugitif où l'eau se ride d'un contre-jour, vertige de ce qui tremble sous la lumière, bois, métal, verre. C'est pas la fleur du cérisier qui est belle, c'est le temps bref où elle va faner. L'ombre en mouvement défait la constance figée des objets: intervalle de vide: l'âme a déjà quitté quelque chose, elle n'en a pas encore rejoint une autre"* (Musée des Arts Décoratifs, Paris, February 1979).

65. Maurice Maeterlinck, *Jeanne d'Arc, pièce en douze tableaux* (Monaco, 1948). His cycle includes the conventional peaks—Chinon, Orleans, Rheims—but then unfolds one *mystère* at Beaurevoir, during which her voices forbid her to try and kill herself by jumping off the tower, and she disobeys. Maeterlinck also dramatises her abjuration, a rare scene in plays about her. The only other place I have seen the leap from Beaurevoir represented was on a nineteenth-century plate, one of a series of ten, inscribed firmly "Tentative d'Evasion" and showing Joan floating down from the tower, as if winged, her hands folded over her breast in prayer.

Index

Index

A NOTE ABOUT THE AUTHOR

Marina Warner read French and Italian at Oxford University. She lives in London, where she reviews books and theatre regularly. She is at present working on a novel.

A NOTE ON THE TYPE

This book was set on the Linotype in Janson, a recutting made directly from type cast from matrices long thought to have been made by the Dutchman Anton Janson, who was a practicing type founder in Leipzig during the years 1668–87. However, it has been conclusively demonstrated that these types are actually the work of Nicholas Kis (1650–1702), a Hungarian, who most probably learned his trade from the master Dutch type founder Dirk Voskens. The type is an excellent example of the influential and sturdy Dutch types that prevailed in England up to the time William Caslon developed his own incomparable designs from them.

Composed, printed and bound by American Book–Stratford Press Saddle Brook, New Jersey

Typography and binding design by Dorothy Schmiderer